Air Navigation

With the Jeppesen CR-3

Flight Computer

Phil Croucher

TABLE OF CONTENTS

MATHS

1

I n many countries (especially Europe), the navigation exam is more to do with maths, using navigation as a background because, to navigate successfully, you need to know how to shuffle numbers and angles around.

Aviation, in common with many other disciplines, uses a precise language so that communication can take place with the minimum of effort. So do maths and science, in the shape of graphs and algebraic symbols. You may also come across circuit diagrams with the electronics involved with radio navigation.

NUMBERS

Factors & Rounding

Underneath the heading of arithmetic, numbers can be added, subtracted, multiplied or divided (it is assumed that you know how to do them all).

A **prime number** is a natural number (greater than 1) that can only be divided by 1 and itself. A number greater than 1 that is not a prime number is a composite number.

When you divide one number into another, it is a *factor* if the division takes place without leaving a remainder. For example, 4 divides into 20 5 times exactly. If you tried to divide 3 into 20, you would be left with a *remainder* of 2.

Often, if a remainder leaves you some way between two numbers, you must round up or down to get an exact number. If the number is less than halfway, it is the custom to round down, or truncate. If it is halfway and above, you round up.

The Decimal System

The following numbers are used in the decimal system:

    0 1 2 3 4 5 6 7 8 9

Their position determines value. For example, the number 6 has a different meaning in each of the following:

    146
    164
    614

In the above examples, it occupies the position of a *unit*, a *ten* or a *hundred*, respectively. A fourth place would be a *thousand*.

Thus, the smallest numbers (the units) are always on the right hand side.

Zero (0) is often used as a placeholder when a unit is missing:

    620
    602

The Sexagesimal System

Time, angles and geographic co-ordinates use a base of 60, as originated by the Sumerians, and handed down to us through the Babylonians and other peoples.

The number 60 has twelve factors, namely 1, 2, 3, 4, 5, 6, 10, 12, 15, 20, 30, 60, of which 2, 3, and 5 are prime numbers. With so many factors, many fractions involving sexagesimal numbers are simplified. For example, you can divide one hour evenly into sections of 30, 20, 15, 12, 10, 6, 5, 4, 3, 2, and 1 minute(s). 60 is the smallest number that is divisible by every number from 1 to 6; that is, it is the lowest common multiple of 1, 2, 3, 4, 5, and 6.

Positive & Negative Numbers

A number is considered to be positive if it is greater than zero. There is usually nothing in front of positive numbers, but if you mean to make a distinction between positive and negative numbers, you can put a plus sign (+) in front - such as +20°C.

Negative numbers have a minus sign (-) in front of them. You might see this on thermometers when the temperature is colder than freezing (-20°C). However, they are also used in algebra, discussed later.

Fractions

A fraction is a number that is not a whole number, described as *vulgar*, *simple* or *common* fractions. Decimal fractions are discussed below.

Just to confuse matters, a fraction such as ½ is also called a *proper fraction*, because the numerator (the small number) is above the larger one (denominator). In other words, the fraction has a value of less than 1.

capt.gs

An improper fraction has a value of more than one, such as $^{22}/_7$, which will become significant as the value of π (pi) which we will come across in *Geometry*, below.

If you multiply or divide the numerator and denominator by the same number, you get a fraction with the same value as the original one. Reducing a fraction by division is called *cancelling*. When you can't cancel any more, the fraction is said to be in its lowest terms.

However, you can only add or subtract fractions that have the same denominator. If you have two with different denominators, you have to find the lowest common denominator, or a number into which they both divide as whole numbers. The lowest common denominator for 3 and 2, for example, is 6. For 4 and 8, it is 8.

For example, with 4 resistances in parallel, of 1, 3, 8 and 15 ohms, to find the unknown total resistance R:

$$\frac{1}{R} = \frac{1}{1} + \frac{1}{3} + \frac{1}{8} + \frac{1}{15}$$

The least common denominator is 120, so....

$$\frac{1}{R} = \frac{120 + 40 + 15 + 8}{120}$$

which becomes:

$$\frac{1}{R} = \frac{183}{120}$$

The non-reciprocal of which is:

$$\frac{R}{1} = \frac{120}{183}$$

As the denominator is greater than the numerator, the answer will be less than 1.

DECIMAL FRACTIONS

Decimal fractions work the same way as the numbers do in the decimal system (above), except that the values go from right to left and they are separated from the main number by dot called a decimal point. The figure to the right of the dot represents tenths, the second one hundredths, and so on. For example, 1.5 (one and five tenths) is the same as 1½. 0.01 kilovolts is 10 volts (to multiply a decimal number, simply move the decimal point to the right by the same number of zeros). A recurring decimal (with the same last number multiple times) sometimes has a dot above the last digit, which tells you that it never really divides properly. Although π carries on forever, it is not a recurring decimal but a transcendental number. It's probably the only one.

Percentages

Whereas decimals deal with tens, percentages deal with hundreds, so anything that is a percentage is a part of a hundred. 25% is a fourth part of a hundred, or a quarter.

Averages

The word *Mean* (as used in the term *Local Mean Time*) simply means *average*. Centre of Gravity calculations are averages, where you take a series of numbers, add them up, and divide them by the number of numbers involved. Technically, this gives you an arithmetic mean. The *median* of a set of values is the middle one. The *mode* is the most common value.

Measurements

There are two main systems of measurement in general use, metric or Imperial. The metric (or SI) system works in tens, and the Imperial tends to use somewhat arbitrary values (feet, yards, etc.) laid down in the time of Elizabeth I. These include *firkins*, which are counted in units of two, such as two firkin big, or two firkin heavy, etc.

The *International System of Units* (SI) is now recommended for scientific purposes instead of CGS (*centimetre*, *gram*, and *second*) and Imperial. This table shows the primary units:

Item	*SI*	*Anglo-American*
Mass	Kilogram (kg)	0.0685 Slug
Weight (Force)	Newton (N) (kgm/s^2)	0.2248 lb
Length	Metre (m)	3.281 Feet 39.4 inches
Time	Second (s)	Second
Temperature	Kelvin (K)	Celsius (C)

These are derived units:

Item	*SI*	*Anglo-American*
Weight	Kg (9.807 N)	2.2046 lb
Density	Kg/m^3	$lbs//ft^3$
Pressure	Pascal (N/m^2)	Millibar
Velocity	m/sec	3.281 ft/sec
Acceleration	m/s^2	3.281 ft/sec^2
G	$9.807 m/s^2$	32.2 ft/sec^2
Power	Watt (Nm/s)	.7376 ft.lb/sec Horsepower
Metric Horsepower	75 Kgm/s	.9863 HP
English Horsepower	76.04 Kgm/s	550 ft.lb/sec
Energy	Joule	

Unfortunately, many manufacturers use the old systems!

LENGTH

The basic unit of measurement in the metric system is the metre, as multiplied or divided into kilometres, centimetres, millimetres, etc.

The Imperial system uses inches, feet, yards and miles in that order.

In navigation, a typical length can be expressed as:

- A **kilometre**, which is 1000 metres, and was originally 1/10,000 of the average distance between the Equator and either Pole on a meridian passing through Paris (thanks to Napoleon, although the Sumerians were there first). It is equivalent to 3280 feet, and 8 km equals 5 statute miles. As a rate, it is expressed in km/hour.

- 1 **nautical mile** (nm) is an angular distance taken as an average of 6080 feet, or 1852 m (as a reminder, check out your calculator - see right). However, 6046 feet is used in the USA, so be careful with their calculators (a *geographic mile* is the distance subtended by one minute at the Equator)

  | 8 |
  | 5 |
  | 2 |

  A **knot** is 1 **nautical mile** per hour. It was originally measured by allowing a rope with a log on the end to stretch out behind a ship. The rope had coloured rags tied in knots at regular intervals, which were counted over time. For aircraft, we need *airspeed*, *groundspeed* and *relative speed*, discussed later.

- A **statute mile**, which is 5280 feet and is an Imperial measurement, introduced as an arbitrary figure by Queen Elizabeth I. In aviation, it is used only in visibility reports in some countries. 1 nautical mile is equal to 1.15 statute miles.

MASS & VOLUME (CAPACITY)

Units of volume in general use are Imperial Gallons, US Gallons and Litres. Units of mass (weight) are pounds (lbs) and kilograms (kg). To convert from volume to weight and *vice versa*), you need to know the *specific gravity* of the liquid concerned, based on that of water, which is taken as 1, since 1 Imperial Gallon of it weighs 10 lbs (1 litre weighs 1 kg). As fuel is less dense than water, a typical SG value (found in most flight manuals) for jet fuel is 0.79, or the equivalent of 7.9 lbs.

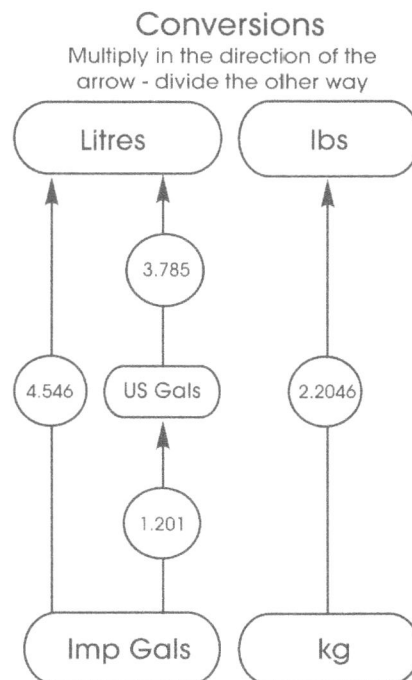

Conversions

Multiply in the direction of the arrow - divide the other way

ALGEBRA

This is a system of using letters instead of numbers when you are more concerned about the ratio or relationship between them rather than their values, although algebra can be used to find an unknown value when you know several others.

If you fly 90 miles in 3 hours, your average speed would be 30 knots. This is the result of dividing 90 by 3:

```
90 ÷ 3 = 30
```

The figures would be different for another journey, so to save us writing down different numbers every time, we need a procedure, such as "To find an average speed in knots, divide the number of miles travelled by the number of hours in the air."

Or, even shorter: "To get an average speed, divide the distance by the time."

As we are now using more general units, you can use minutes or seconds instead of just hours.

Mathematically, the above could be made even shorter:

```
Average speed = Distance ÷ Time
```

But even that can be tedious, so try:

```
S = D ÷ T
```

or, using the ordinary rules of arithmetic:

$$S = \frac{D}{T}$$

Obviously, you can't divide letters - they are there to show you what to do with the numbers when you get them. In other words, to use the formula, you *substitute* the letters for the correct figures.

For example, using x to represent almost anything unknown:

$$x + 6 = 8$$

You know that some number plus 6 equals 8. Of course, this is 2. You found that out by subtracting 6 from 8, which is the reverse of addition.

S, D and T were chosen above because they suit the problem, but you could have used A, B or C or X, Y and Z, if you remembered their basic meaning.

Other letters can be used when you want to mix different things. You can't add 3 helicopters and two aeroplanes together, but you can express their relationship like this:

$$2h + 3a$$

Things can also get more complex. If you had two aeroplanes, and you knew the wingspan of one of them, you can find the wingspan of the other without going out in the rain and measuring it (if you had a tape measure long enough) by using a simultaneous equation.

Otherwise, some letters are already reserved, such as *s* for distance (when Galileo started all this off, he used the word *scale* from his own language). Similarly, Ampere was concerned with the *intensity* of electric current, so he used *I* to represent it.

Symbols & Signs

Because of the limited number of letters in the alphabet, there are also various ways of distinguishing them. For example, if you were faced with several resistors in an electrical circuit, you could label them R_1, R_2, R_3, etc.

However, you should not put the numbers above, like this: 5^2, 5^3.... because a number in that position already has a special meaning, such as squaring or cubing, respectively (squaring means multiplying a number by itself, and cubing means doing it three times, and so on).

The number above is an *index*, and it has some curious properties. When you apply an index to the number 10, it is called a power, such as "10 to the power of 2" when you mean 10^2.

Such powers indicate the number of places the decimal point must be away from 1. It is a convenient way of expressing large (or small) numbers. 10^6 is also 1 000 000, or 1 with 6 zeros after it. 10^{-6} means 0.0000001.

10^{28} expresses how many electrons there are in a coulomb, a unit which is used in electricity.

Powers have another property that is made use of in the slide rule part of the flight computer. You can add them together to get the same effect as multiplication - $10^3 + 10^3$ is the same as 10^6, and you have just multiplied 1 000 by 1 000 to get 1 000 000. When you operate the slide rule, you are not adding numbers, but indices.

Other useful symbols include:

Symbol	Meaning
$\geq$	Greater than or equal to
$\leq$	Less than or equal to
$\approx$	Approximately equal
$\sqrt{}$	Square root
$\propto$	Proportionality

Hooke's Law can use the proportionality sign. For example, the tension in a spring is directly proportional to its extension:

$$T \propto extn$$

With any such relationship, if one variable is increased by a given factor, such as 2, the other is increased by the same factor, so if you double the tension, you also double the spring's extension.

Equations

An equation is a statement that shows the relationship between quantities, and how they change when one is increased or decreased. You can recognise it by the equals sign (=), and the expressions either side must balance.

To use the Lift Formula as an example, when one of the quantities on the right side is varied, Lift on the left side will follow.

$$\text{Lift} = C_L \left(\tfrac{1}{2}\, \rho\, V^2\right) S$$

Coefficient Of Lift — C_L; Air Density (rho) (same as mass) — ρ; Surface Area Of Aerofoil — S; Average — $\tfrac{1}{2}$; True Airspeed — V

Some letters, when used as symbols, have been allocated meanings by international agreement, or they may change according to the context in which they are used. For example, the Greek symbol ρ (rho) represents air density in Meteorology and resistivity in electronics. Even within disciplines it can change - μ (mu) can mean amplification factor or permeability, depending on the (electronic) context. When making your own formulae, its best to state the meaning you use to help the person who reads it later.

Say you now knew the average speed and the distance, but needed to find the time. You can just move the figures around in the formula. What we need to do is get T by itself on one side of the equal sign.

Remembering that the figures either side must balance each other, you can multiply both sides of the equation by the same figure, in this case T. The short cut is just to move T from one side of the equation to the other, and reverse its function:

        ST = D

Notice that T is now a mutliplier, where it was previously a divisor.

Note also that ST is a shorthand way of saying S x T (the period, or full stop, may be used in algebra instead of the multiplication sign - S.T).

If you divided the equation by S you would now get:

$$\frac{D}{S} = T$$

Which now isolates the time on one side of the equation.

SIMULTANEOUS EQUATIONS

These are used when you have two or more unknown quantities. You need an equation for each one. For example:

        a + b = 8
        a - b = 4

The simple way is to cancel the *b*s out. You end up with:

        2a = 12

        a = 6

QUADRATIC EQUATIONS

These involve a square value, of which a positive number will have two - one with a minus value and one with a plus value. A negative number has no roots.

To solve a quadratic equation, turn both sides of it into a square.

As simultaneous and quadratic equations are not often used in aviation, we will proceed to ignore them.......

GRAPHS

Pilots use graphs a lot, especially when calculating performance. A graph is a visual representation of the relationship between several numbers, on the basis that it is easier to look at pictures.

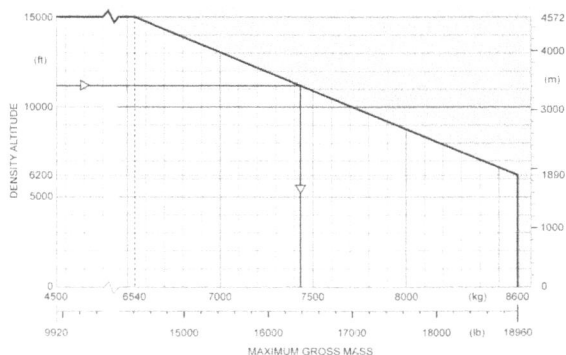

The same principle is used when dealing with vectors.

Say you have a fuel tank that reduces its contents over time, and as the level goes down, you make a mark on the side of the tank. This doesn't tell you very much, unless you added the time taken. Now place the fuel tank on a conveyer belt and stick a pencil to the level float inside the tank (a bit of poetic licence needed here). As the belt moves, marks would be made on the wall as the level reduced and you would have a graphical representation of your fuel usage over time. Both sides of the graph would need some sort of scale to keep them in proportion to each other.

The value of zero on whatever scale is called the *origin*. It comes in useful when drawing tangents from it to the curve of the graph (as used in power graphs).

Slopes

Sometimes you can get information from a graph without looking at any numbers. If the slope of a graph is steep, for example, there is rapid movement. If it is shallow, movement is slow. This is often what happens with temperature readings from the atmosphere, as used in meteorology.

The value of a straight line graph (where the rise in y is equal to the run of x) can be easily calculated with a formula, ending up with dy/dx, where *d* represents a change. However, when the graph is curved, the change in y as compared to x varies, and you need to find some way of calculating the value without drawing the graph. To do this you need to use an infinitesimally small change in order to find the slope of a tangent drawn to that point.

To use another aviation metaphor, if your speed is constant, you can find the distance travelled with a simple calculation (speed x time). However, if your speed is constantly varying, you need something more powerful.

You essentially need to calculate the area underneath a sine wave, meaning a rectangle with one side that is curved. This kind of calculation (differential calculus) is at the heart of Inertial Navigation/Reference systems.

EXAMPLE

In the graph below, you can find information about the profitability of a company.

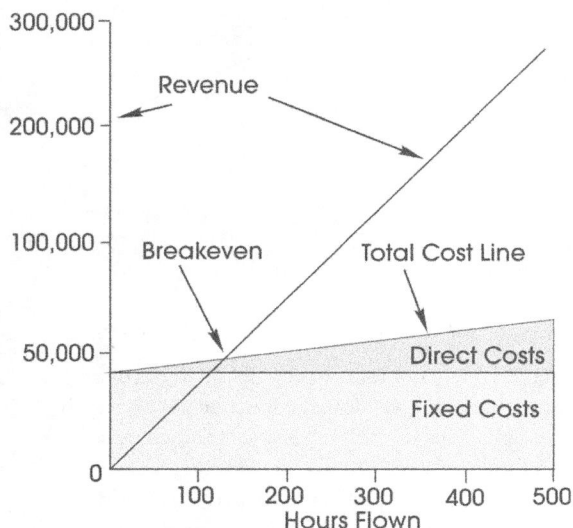

The fixed costs are a straight line, and those that mount up when you start flying are the sloped line (the more you fly, the more it costs). The slope from the origin is the money you take in (revenue).

GEOMETRY

Geometry concerns the relationships between lines and angles.

- The **perimeter** is the total length of all the sides of a two dimensional object. The perimeter of a circle is its circumference.

- The **area** is the space inside the perimeter, found by multiplying the length by the breadth or, in the case of a circle, the square of the radius (half the diameter) multiplied by π.

- **Volume** is found by multiplying the area by the height.

Circles

These are what makes geometry so interesting. They use the value of π, which represents the ratio of the circumference of a circle to its diameter, being 22 divided by 7. It is commonly taken to have a decimal value of 1.3412, but it actually goes on forever.

The *diameter* of a circle is the length of a straight line across it, through the middle. The *radius* goes from the centre to the circumference, or half the diameter.

TRIGONOMETRY

Angles & Arcs

Angles are measured in degrees and radians. A radian is an angle of 57.29° which subtends an arc of the same length as the radius of a circle (it is popular with scientists).

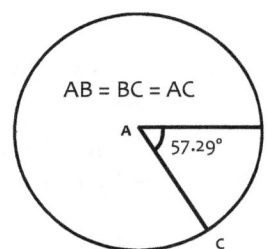

$360° = 2\pi$ radians. As the radius of a circle is equal to $2\pi r$, its circumference can be written as the angle in radians round the circle multiplied by the radius (r).

Note: Make sure you use the right mode with your electronic calculator!

Triangles

There are three types of triangle:

- An **equilateral** triangle has three sides the same length.

- An **isosceles** triangle has two sides of equal length, and two angles of equal value. The third side is 1.4 times the length of a short side, or the short sides are 70% the length of the long side. As soon as you see a bearing change of 45°, you can bet you are dealing with an isosceles triangle.

- A **scalene** triangle has three sides of different lengths.

All the internal angles of a triangle should add up to 180°. An angle of 90° is called a right angle. One less than that is an **acute angle**. Angles in between are **obtuse** angles.

A right angled triangle has two others that add up to 90°. Pythagoras stated that the square of the hypoteneuse (the long side) is equal to the sum of the squares on the other two sides (although this refers to areas, Pythagoras is usually used to find the length of a side).

When whole numbers are involved, such as 3 – 4 – 5, we have a *Pythagorean Triple*, commonly used in exam questions. For example, in the picture below, the Inertial Navigation System (INS) shows an error on landing – it thinks the aeroplane is in a different place than it actually is, due to certain inbuilt errors, discussed elsewhere.

You can see the proportions involved.

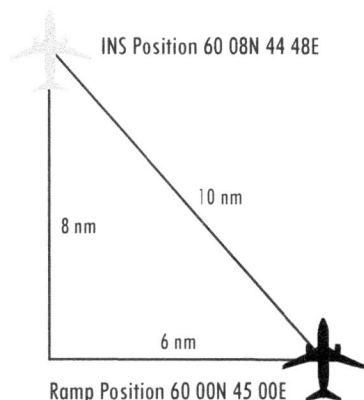

INS Position 60 08N 44 48E

10 nm

8 nm

6 nm

Ramp Position 60 00N 45 00E

Once you realise that the sides are multiples of 3, 4 & 5, the need for doing any calculations is much reduced!

The value of one of the other angles in a right angled triangle depends on the relationship between two sides of it. In the case of angle A in the picture below, if you divide the height of the helicopter (opposite side) by the distance it has travelled through the air (the hypoteneuse), you have the sine of angle A.

Hypoteneuse

B
Opposite
A
C

Adjacent

Two angles that add up to 90° are called *co-angles,* so angle B is called a cosine (C is already 90°). Its value again depends on dividing the height of the helicopter by distance it has travelled through the air, but the helicopter's height is now *adjacent* (i.e. next to) to B, rather than being opposite A.

If you divide the helicopter's height (opposite) by the distance it has travelled over the ground (adjacent), you have the *tangent* of angle A.

To find the length of any side, you need to remember these letters:

    SOH CAH TOA

The initial letters of each group refer to Sine, Cosine and Tangent, respectively, and the others refer to one side of the triangle, namely Hypoteneuse, Adjacent and Opposite (there is an easy way to remember them below).

    Some Old Hens

    Can Always Have

    Turnips Or Apples

To find Angle A in the previous example, you would therefore use this formula:

    Sine =   Opposite
             Hypoteneuse

To find out which formula you need, take the above letters and cross out the items you know, then use the one where both are crossed out together:

    S̶O̶H̶ CA̶H̶ T̶O̶A

Once you have done the division, use your calculator to find the angle corresponding to the result.

These relationships remain the same regardless of the size of the triangles.

EXAMPLE

Performance rules require you to clear a building by 35 feet as you get out of a landing site.

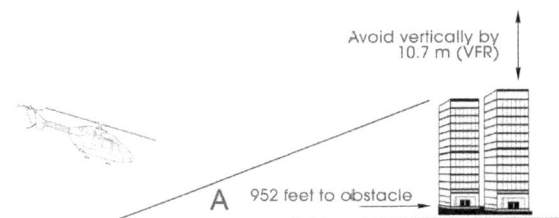

Avoid vertically by 10.7 m (VFR)

A   952 feet to obstacle

You first need to find the angle between the surface and the top of the obstacle. Angle A is 40°.

The tangent of angle A multiplied by the distance to the base of the obstacle gives you the height required, 952 x 0.84 = 800 feet. Then add the 35 feet clearance required (you do it this way because it is easier to line up on the top of the building than try to estimate the height above it).

VECTORS

A vector is a quantity that has size and direction, such as force or velocity (non-directional scalar quantities like mass have size only, and can be combined by simple addition or subtraction). The length of a vector is proportional to the quantity involved. For example, to represent a speed of 60 knots, you might draw a line 6 inches long, with each inch standing for 10 knots (all the other lines in the drawing must have the same scale).

Now you can work out problems with diagrams rather than complex formulae, because vectors can be combined to produce a resultant such as Total Reaction shown on the right (the single force which is exactly equivalent to two, or more, forces is called their *resultant*). When two forces are applied to or

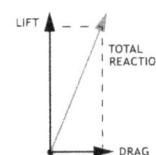

LIFT

TOTAL REACTION

DRAG

from a point, their resultant is the diagonal of a parallelogram based on that point. The resolution of a vector is the process of finding its effect in two mutually perpendicular directions.

Simple trigonometry (especially Pythagoras) can be used to find the unknown value.

A Vector Diagram is a picture of a vector with an arrow showing the direction the force is acting in. Such a diagram when used in navigation is called the *Triangle Of Velocities*.

Velocity is the rate of change of position in a given direction, equal to distance divided by time. Unfortunately, this is often used synonymously with the word *speed*, as the units used are the same, but speed is only concerned with the time taken over a distance travelled, not the direction.

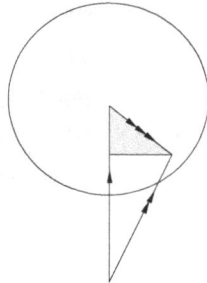

THE 1 IN 60 RULE

This is a rule of thumb that can solve many problems in aviation without getting the calculator out (as such, it shouldn't really be used in exams). The sine or tangent of a small angle is more or less the same as the number of degrees in the angle divided by 60.

Although it is only accurate to within 5% up to about 40° for sines and 10° for tangents, it is a very useful tool (used in Navigation) for quickly working out by how much your track is in error if you have been drifting off.

In other words, it is accurate enough to be a very good rule of thumb, as the angles involved are very small.

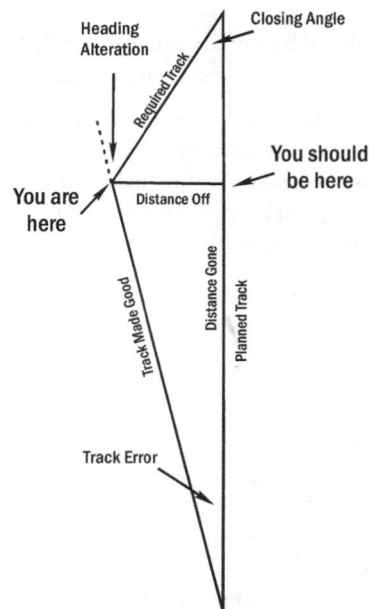

For example, after flying for 180 miles, you are 9 miles away from your planned track. 9 in 180 is the same as 3 in 60, so you are 3° off (it's a tangential relationship if you want to work it out properly).

The formula starts off like this:

$$\frac{\text{Error}}{60} = \frac{\text{Distance Off}}{\text{Distance Gone}}$$

It ends up like this:

$$\text{Error} = \frac{\text{Distance Off} \times 60}{\text{Distance Gone}}$$

Of course, when you are off track, there is the potential for getting lost, so the first thing to do is parallel the original track. Now, at least, you shouldn't get any further off track while you work out how to get to the destination.

- To **parallel your original track**, alter course by the track error in the appropriate direction

- To **get back on the original track** (provided you haven't gone more than halfway), alter course by double the track error. Then apply the correction as a single figure to keep you there

- To **track directly to the original destination**, you would need an extra bit, called a *closing angle*, which you can find by altering the formula above:

$$CA = \frac{Distance\ Off\ x\ 60}{Distance\ To\ Go}$$

Add the combination of closing angle and track error to the heading the appropriate way.

Notes: The time to regain track may be more than that used to create the error in the first place. Also, these rules are approximate, because altering heading changes the relationship of the wind to your machine. 1 in 60 is used for convenience - if the exact figures for π are used it should be 1 in 57. The Tan may be used up to 25°, and the Sine is accurate up to 40° (within 10% up to 70°).

Tip: If you have travelled ¼ of the way along your track, the heading alteration is 4 times the closing angle.

You can use the 1 in 60 rule to see if you are still inside an airway. If the centreline was 045°, and you were on the 040° radial, you would be off track by 5°. If the DME says you are 45 nm away, it's a simple calculation:

$$Dist\ Off = \frac{TE\ x\ Dist\ Gone}{60}$$

The answer is 3.75 nm, so you are OK.

The 1 in 60 Rule works for glideslopes, too.......

Gradients, Etc

You need to know how high you should be at particular distances from the runway as a gross error check. For example, you should be at the Outer Marker at about 1400 feet. This ensures that you haven't hit a false glideslope (if you join the glideslope from below, you should be OK).

RATE OF DESCENT

Radar will give you a distance to touchdown so you can calculate a smooth rate of descent. You don't want to be making sudden drops at the last minute to make the glideslope and risk spilling the coffee.

Glidepath gradient calculations are variations on the 1 in 60 rule - the standard 3° glidepath is an ROD of 300 ft per nm, or 100 feet per degree. 3° slopes can be calculated by multiplying your groundspeed by 5, as derived from:

$$ROD = \frac{GS\ x\ 10}{2}$$

Note: At 60 kts, the ROC/ROD equals the gradient.

If the speed changes on the approach, a strong headwind causes a *decrease* in groundspeed and rate of descent, and a tailwind does the opposite. Every 10 kts decrease in groundspeed on a 3° glideslope means a decrease in ROD of 50 fpm, and *vice versa*.

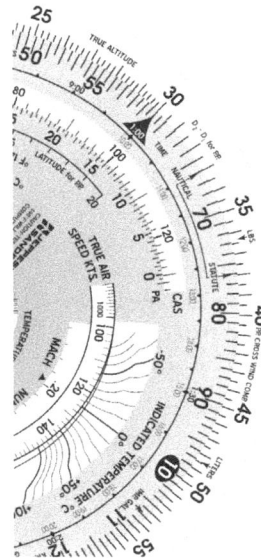

You can use the slide rule on the flight computer to solve these as a proportion problem. If you put the 60 kt index on the slide rule against 30 (3°) on the outer scale, you can read 450 fpm against 90 kts, and so on ....

For a 2.5° glideslope, just put the index against 25, or 35 for a 3.5° glideslope. The rate of descent required to maintain a 3.25° glide slope at a groundspeed of 140 kts is around 800 ft/min.

HEIGHT ON THE GLIDESLOPE

Use the formula:

$$Height = \frac{GP\ Angle\ x\ dist\ to\ go\ in\ ft}{60}$$

Note: The formula refers to the touchdown point. If the distance is quoted from the threshold (like with DME) add 50 feet because you will be at the screen height.

If the glideslope is published as a percentage, place the 10 index on the inner scale of the flight computer and against the percentage value on the outer scale, reading the degree value on the outer scale against the 60 index on the inner scale. In the picture below, the gradient is 5%.

EXAMPLES

1. If an ILS has a glideslope of 2.5°, what height should you be at 6 nm from the touchdown point?

At 60 nm, you would be 2.5 nm high, which is 15,200 feet. 6 nm is a tenth of that, so you should be at 1520 feet (1500 in the exam).

2. The outer marker of an ILS with a 3° glide slope is 4.6 nm from the threshold. Assuming a glideslope height of 50 ft above the threshold, what is the approximate height of an aircraft passing the outer marker?

$$\frac{Range\ (ft)\ x\ GP\ Angle}{60} = Ht\ (ft)$$

Substituting:

$$\frac{27968}{60} \times 3 = 1398.4$$

Add the 50 ft above the threshold to get 1450 ft, in round figures. Another formula is:

```
Height = GS Angle x 100 x distance
```

where *distance* is in nautical miles.

3. With a minimum climb gradient of 200 ft/nm, at what altitude should you be 5 nm after departure to comply with the procedure?

This is simply a ratio, so:

$$\frac{200}{1} = \frac{?}{5}$$

You should be at 1000 feet. How far will you be away from the departure point when you get to 2000 feet? 10 nm. If you set this up on the flight computer, you don't even have to move the wheel for the second answer.

4. If your groundspeed is 120 kts and your vertical speed is 500 fpm, what is your gradient? Again, a proportion problem. the answer is 2.5°.

INSTRUMENTS

Aircraft instruments base their readings on the measurement and comparison of the different temperatures and pressures found inside and outside the aircraft. They will cover four areas of aircraft operation - *Control*, *Performance*, *Navigation*, and *Miscellaneous*, which includes voltmeters, gear position indicators, etc.

Instruments must be able to be read easily, in terms of position, lighting and clarity. They can have up to four sub-systems, not all of which will be in the same case:

- Detection (e.g. temperature probe).
- Measurement (aneroid capsule).
- Coupling (suitable linkage between measurement and indication).
- Indication (pointer, or digital display).

At the point of measurement, a measuring body absorbs some energy and converts it to a quantity that has a functional relationship with the quantity measured. As some energy is absorbed, that quantity will never be the same as the true value. Corrections are usually included with amplification signals because the sample is small.

Displays can be *circular*, as shown on the right, or *straight* (like a tape) or *digital*, or even a combination, as with this display from an AW 139):

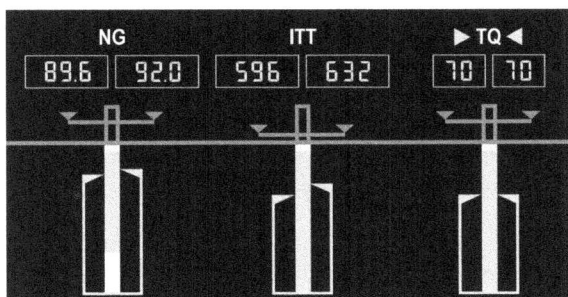

Instruments can also be classified into four groups, after the variations in properties of certain materials against variations in temperature:

- **Expansion**
- **Vapour-pressure**
- **Electrical**, based on:
  - *Resistance*, or
  - *Increase in electromotive force*
- **Radiation**

Most will be electrical.

Right: Circular Instrument

Lighting

White lighting is usually combined with grey cockpit interiors because

- you have unrestricted use of colour
- warning indicators become more prominent
- black instrument cases against a grey background will emphasize their size and shape

Individual instruments may be lit by:

- integral lighting, which is built into the instrument
- ring, eyebrow, or post lighting, all of which are fitted to the outside of the instrument case
- floodlighting

PRESSURE   022 01 02/02 02

In many systems, the pressure of a liquid or gas must be measured and indicated, either directly, where the source of pressure is connected to the instrument (mostly Bourdon tubes), or remotely, where it can be some distance away, with electrical signals being sent instead. Such systems would have a transmitter at the pressure source and an indicator on a panel. This means you won't have yucky fluids in the cockpit, and you don't have to carry a lot of plumbing. Indicators can be based on *synchronous receivers*, *DC* or *AC ratiometers* or *servos*.

Pressure is the *force per unit area*, or the force exerted on an area divided by the size of that area:

$$P = \frac{F}{A}$$

where F is Force (N) and A is the Area in m^2. The result:

$$\frac{N}{m^2}$$

is equal to 1 *pascal* (Pa), which is the standard unit of pressure under the SI system (see *Principles of Flight*).

There are several types of pressure, including:

- **Absolute pressure**, or the difference between the pressure of a fluid and absolute zero (a vacuum). It is usually measured in inches of mercury, as on a Manifold Air Pressure gauge. It would be the sum of gauge pressure (next) and atmospheric pressure, and is what forces the fuel and air charge into the cylinders of a piston engine.

- **Gauge pressure**, on the other hand, is measured against ambient air pressure, so it is absolute pressure minus atmospheric pressure. In other words, any variance from atmospheric pressure is called gauge pressure. For example, fuel and oil pressure instruments indicate the amount that the pump has raised the pressure of the fluid above that of the atmosphere, positive or negative. If the absolute pressure stays constant, gauge pressure varies with atmospheric pressure.

- **Differential pressure** is just the difference in pressure between two points, as represented by the airspeed indicator. Two inlet ports may be used, with each connected to one of the sealed volumes whose pressure is to be monitored.

Pressure Sensing

Pressure is measured against a reference, such as a column of mercury, or by acting over a known area and measuring the force produced. Aneroid gauges use metallic pressure sensing elements that flex under pressure.

Aneroid means *without fluid*, or *not wet* (depends on which book you read), to distinguish between aneroid and hydrostatic gauges, which do use fluid, although aneroid gauges can be used to measure liquid pressure. The pressure sensing element may be a Bourdon tube, a diaphragm, a capsule, or bellows, all of which will change their shape in response to the pressure. The deflection is transmitted by a suitable linkage that will rotate a pointer around a graduated dial, or activate a secondary transducer that might control a digital display, the most common of which measure changes in capacitance that follow the mechanical deflection.

In order of sensitivity, you have:

DIAPHRAGMS

Diaphragms are simply circular metal discs that are corrugated to give them strength, to provide larger deflections. They are used to detect low pressures. One side of the disc is exposed to the pressure to be measured, and the other is linked to the indicating mechanism.

ANEROID CAPSULES

In gauges used for small measurements, or for absolute pressure, the gear train and needle may be driven by an enclosed and sealed chamber, called an *aneroid*, as used in aneroid barometers, altimeters, altitude recording barographs, and the altitude telemetry instruments in weather balloon radiosondes. The sealed chamber is used as a reference pressure and the needles are driven by the external pressure.

A capsule consists of two diaphragms placed face to face and joined at their edges to form a chamber that may be completely sealed or left open to a source of (absolute) pressure. They are also used for low(ish) pressures, but are more sensitive than diaphragms.

SPRING

BELLOWS

Bellows are an extension of the capsule (think of them as several unsealed capsules joined together), but operate like a helical compression spring - indeed, there may even be a spring inside to increase the *spring rate* and to help the bellows return to its normal length once the source of pressure is removed. They are used for higher pressures and commonly used, for example, to measure the output of a low pressure booster pump. Two would be used in a manifold pressure gauge, one open to the induction manifold and the other evacuated and sealed,

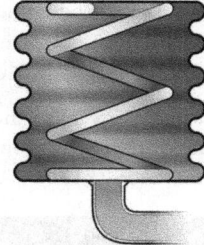

THE BOURDON TUBE

The most commonly used pressure sensor was invented by French watchmaker Eugene Bourdon in 1849, in which a C-shaped elliptical hollow spring tube is sealed at one end, with the other end connected to a source of pressure. The pressure differential from the inside to the outside causes the tube to change from an elliptical to a more circular shape, and to straighten out, rather like an uncoiling hose. Which way it moves is determined by the curvature of the tubing, as the inside radius is slightly shorter than that on the outside, and the ratio between the major and minor axes depends on what sensitivity you need - the larger the ratio, the greater it is.

The pressure range is governed by the *tubing wall thickness* and the *radius of the curvature*.

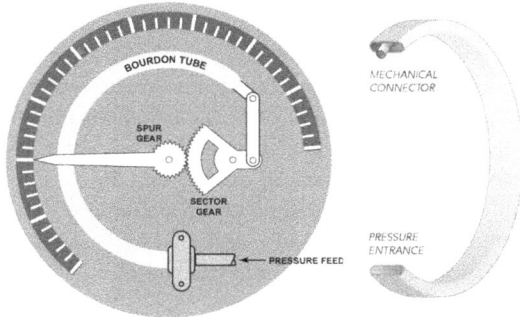

The end result is that a specific pressure causes movement for a specific distance. When the pressure is removed, the tube returns to its original shape. To do this, the material used requires a form of heat treatment (*spring tempering*) to make it retain its original shape closely while allowing some elasticity under a load. Beryllium copper, phosphor bronze, and various alloys of steel and stainless steel are good for this purpose, but steel has a limited service life due to corrosion. Most gauges use phosphor bronze.

In summary, a Bourdon-based gauge uses a coiled tube which causes the rotation of an indicator arm connected to it, as it expands from pressure increase.

MANOMETER

The term *manometer* is often used to refer specifically to liquid column hydrostatic instruments. These consist of a vertical column of liquid in a tube whose ends are exposed to different pressures, with the difference in fluid height being proportional to the difference in pressure.

The simplest design is a closed-end U-shape, with one side connected to the region of interest. A force equal to the applied pressure multiplied by the area of the bore will force the liquid downwards until, eventually, the two levels will stand the same distance above and below the original level. If you take into account the area of the tube bore and the density of the liquid, you can calculate pressure from the difference in the levels. Any fluid can be used, but mercury is preferred for its high density and low vapour pressure, so the tube can be shorter.

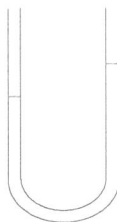

Manometers are used for calibration purposes.

TEMPERATURE

Knowledge of the air temperature is needed for performance calculations, anti-ice control and calculation of true airspeed (TAS), amongst other things.

The white arc on a temperature gauge represents a special operating range. A yellow arc is an exceptional range.

Total Air Temperature (TAT)

In the same way that we must deal with two types of pressure (static and dynamic), there are two types of temperature (static and total). On large jets, TAT is used to determine maximum N_1 or EPR. It is displayed with a calculated OAT in the cockpit.

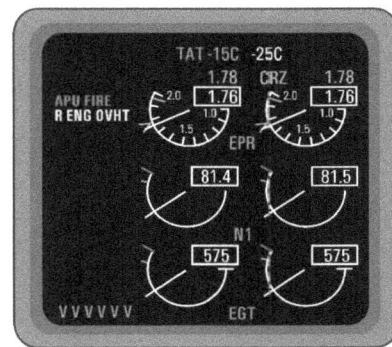

As SAT is calculated, it may also be called the *Corrected* or *True Outside Air Temperature* (COAT).

Whatever detects the temperature must necessarily be in the airstream. At higher speeds, the boundary layer can be slowed down or stopped (relatively speaking) and be affected by adiabatic compression (and friction) that raises the temperature, so whatever temperature is indicated will be higher than the Static (Outside) Air Temperature (SAT) by an amount that is proportional to TAS, so the errors get larger as speed increases (although RAM rise is negligible up to about Mach 0.3).

TAT is the temperature that would be recorded if you could stop dead during flight (i.e. with nothing frictionally induced - on the ground, TAT/RAT = SAT). It is technically the maximum rise possible (SAT + 100% of RAM Rise), and can be thought of as the *indicated* air temperature, or what the aircraft feels, which is the same as the OAT plus adiabatic heating. In modern aircraft, TAT & SAT come from the ADC, because the information is needed for the Flight Management System. If your system cannot measure TAT correctly, you must use a Recovery Factor (see below).

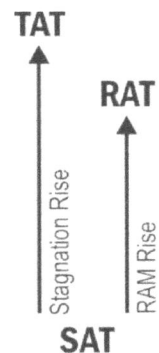

TAT is higher than or equal to SAT, depending on the Mach number and the SAT.

Static Air Temperature (SAT)

Where the air has only partially been brought to rest (as it would be if you used a more basic thermometer than the Rosemount, mentioned overleaf), you don't get so much of a temperature rise. The difference is called *RAM rise*, and the indicated temperature is *RAM Air Temperature*, which is equal to SAT + a percentage of RAM Rise.

The formula used is:

$$\text{SAT} = \frac{\text{TAT}}{(1 + 0.2 \text{ KM}^2)}$$

Where K = recovery factor (below) and M = Mach no.

The ADC does this as a function of Mach number. If you don't have one, you can obtain TAS as a function of Calibrated Airspeed and local air density (or static air temperature and pressure altitude which determine density) on the flight computer.

Recovery Factor

The difference between TAT and SAT is the *stagnation rise*, and the proportion of stagnation temperature that can actually be sensed by the aircraft instruments is the *recovery factor* or *K value*, which is governed by the thermometer. Thus, the recovery factor expresses the sensitivity of a temperature sensor as a percentage. It is determined by flight testing and will be found in the flight manual.

With a recovery factor of 1, a thermometer is measuring TAT, which is SAT + 100% of stagnation rise. If a more basic thermometer has a recovery factor of 0.8, it is only measuring SAT + 80% of the RAM rise, or the temperature of air that has been brought only partially to rest, so the measured temperature is called the Ram Air Temperature (RAT), and the difference between it and the Static Air Temperature is called the ram rise. If the recovery factor is zero, only SAT is measured. For example, what is the Ram Air Temperature if the SAT is -20°C, the stagnation rise is 10°C and recovery factor 80%?

$$-20 + 8 = -12°C$$

If a temperature sensor with a recovery factor of 0.75 indicates 30° and the SAT is 25°, what is the RAM rise? 6.7°. The trick is to remember that the 5° is 0.75.

RAT would only equal TAT when the ram rise is equal to the full stagnation rise (using a thermometer with a K factor of 1). This is assumed with the Rosemount probe, hence its other name of *Total Air Temperature Probe*.

Recovery is factored in for Mach number compressibility.

The recovery factor of a flush bulb temperature sensor varies between 0.75 - 0.9.

Thermometers

REMOTE BULB THERMOMETER

This consists of a bulb and a Bourdon tube filled with liquid or vapour, so the Bourdon tube could also loosely be regarded as measuring temperature, but it is still really measuring pressure. Expansion of the liquid causes the tube to lengthen, which moves the indicator, using the usual suitable linkage, as described above. With the vapour system, only the bulb has liquid in, which alters the pressure in the tube as it expands, with the same results, but you will get indicator errors with changes in atmospheric pressure.

RESISTIVE COIL THERMOMETER

The small, but stable, resistance of a nickel or platinum coil changes with absolute temperature. The coil is in a circuit with a fixed voltage, changes in which (from resistance) are measured with a meter calibrated in °C.

BIMETALLIC STRIP THERMOMETER

Below about 150 kts, a thermometer like that shown below is good enough for getting the OAT.

The probe sticks out into the airstream, and the dial is inside the cockpit. The works consist of a helical (coil-shaped) bimetallic strip that twists as the temperature changes, and moves the pointer.

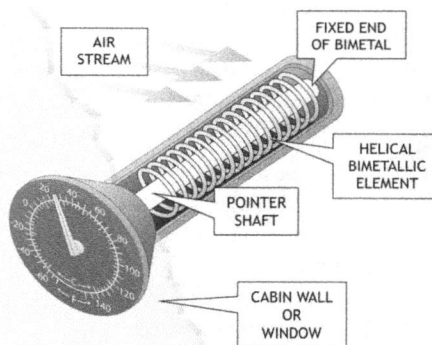

The probe cannot be shrouded from the Sun, and it is necessarily next to the fuselage skin, so its readings can be affected by kinetic heating, even at low speeds - at 150 kts, the rise can be around 3°. Being crude instruments, they are also subject to other errors, so a professional rule of thumb is to assume an error of about 2-3°.

THERMISTOR

The change in resistance with these is greater than with a resistive coil, and therefore easier to detect, but you don't get the same results from one instrument to another, thus consistency is a disadvantage. The information, however, is extracted in the same way as the coil, above.

RATIOMETER

This device measures an unknown electrical resistance by balancing two legs of a (Wheatstone) bridge circuit, one of which includes the unknown component. They are commonly used in Air Data Computers that use solid state capsules. As the bridge becomes unbalanced, the varying voltage across the middle can be measured.

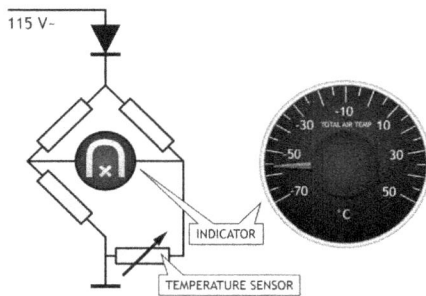

For temperature measurement purposes, you can replace the voltmeter with a wiper arm that is positioned by a servo loop, and how far the arm moves is a measure of the temperature change. It will centre at 15°C.

The main advantage of this device is that it works independently of the supply voltage.

THE ROSEMOUNT PROBE

Otherwise known as the *Total Air Temperature Probe*, this has a small (i.e. quick reacting) platinum* based resistance coil inside concentric cylinders, mounted on a streamlined strut around 50 mm or so from the fuselage skin, which therefore has little influence on it (skin temperature can be increased by kinetic energy).

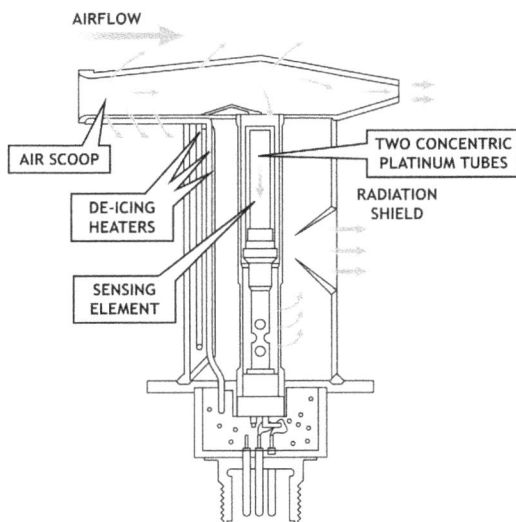

*An uncompensated instrument has one platinum sensor. A fully compensated one has two.

The probe is open at the front with a smaller hole at the back to allow air to flow through, but it is forced through 90° to encourage water and dust particles to separate as it speeds up, so the aircraft must be moving for the probe to work (although the airflow through the probe is quite slow because of the restrictions within it).

A heating element prevents icing (the detector works on vibration), and is self-compensating, in that, as temperature rises, so does resistance in the element, which reduces the heater current. Although the heater affects the temperature sensed, the error is small, around 1°C at Mach 0.1 and 0.15°C at Mach 1.0, so light aircraft that use the probe aren't affected anyway.

Aside from skin temperature, direct sunlight will give an artificially high reading and, when flying from cloud to clear air, readings will be low for however long it takes for moisture to evaporate from the element in the probe.

Errors

Instrument error comes from the usual imperfections in manufacturing and can be sorted out by fine calibration. *Environmental error* is caused by solar heating or icing, for which the Rosemount probe has a heater. Probes are usually mounted to keep them in shadow, but the residual effects of environmental error can only be minimised, and not corrected for. Some heating is caused by compression as air is brought to rest*, which is the difference between SAT and TAT, so it is only a problem when you need to find SAT. There is also frictional heating in the boundary layer, but both heating errors can be fully compensated for, either automatically or by calculation.

*Compressibility error in the ASI is normally corrected with use of the flight computer.

Flat plate sensors, with their sensing element flush with the aircraft skin, are susceptible to environmental errors because of their relative lack of shielding. They are affected by frictional heating in the boundary layer (not compressibility), and instrument error.

TEMPERATURE COMPENSATION

Various methods can be used to make an instrument over- or under-read according to which way the temperature is going. For example, a thermal junction can get hot by itself, which will vary the emf it produces and give you false readings. In mechanical terms, a bimetal strip made of invar and brass or steel can be attached to a capsule to make it expand or contract slightly, or you could arrange to vary the resistance of an electrical current.

FLIGHT INSTRUMENTS

The artificial horizon or attitude indicator (AI*) is in the centre, because it is a primary instrument (it tells you which way is up), the heading indicator is below, No 1 altimeter at the top right, the vertical speed indicator below that, and the airspeed indicator at the top left with turn coordinator underneath.

The idea is to have the most important instruments as close together as possible to reduce the scanning distance.

*An ADI is an *Attitude Director Indicator*. It contains Flight Director bars.

The idea is to have the most important instruments as close together as possible to reduce the scanning distance.

As mentioned, instruments cover four areas of aircraft operation:

- **Control**, such as the artificial horizon and engine instruments

- **Performance**, that show you what the aircraft is doing (ASI, VSI, altimeter, compass)

- **Navigation** (VOR, ADF, DME)

- **Miscellaneous** (Warning flags, gear position indicators, pressure and temperature, etc)

A *primary instrument* is one which gives instant and constant readouts (also called *direct*), and is the one whose indications you want to keep steady. A *secondary instrument* is one that you have to deduce things from, such as the altimeter increasing, telling you that the pitch must have changed* (you might also say that the altimeter gives you an indirect indication of pitch attitude). The ASI and VSI also give indirect indications of pitch, and the HI and TC indicate bank. A primary instrument will tell you at what rate things are changing, but a secondary one will only indicate that a change is taking place.

*The needle, ball and airspeed method of instrument flying refers to the Sperry turn indicator - as long as the needle and ball were centred, you were flying in a straight line. In a turn, keeping the ball centred meant you were

not slipping or skidding, and holding the correct airspeed meant you were either flying straight and level or climbing or descending at a constant rate. In this case, the primary instruments were the ASI, turn and bank indicator and the VSI. However, using such slow, indirect indications is mentally tiring, as attitudes have to be continually deduced, which led to the development of the artificial horizon and DGI, that gave more instantaneous readings (once gyros became more reliable!)

Instruments are further grouped under the headings of *pitch*, *bank* and *power*.

Pitch

- **Artificial Horizon** (Attitude Indicator). The most important pitch instrument, because it gives direct, instantaneous readings.

- **Altimeter**. Although it indicates pitch indirectly, it is a primary pitch instrument.

- **Airspeed Indicator.** Secondary pitch instrument, although its value becomes less at higher airspeeds, as changes are more pronounced and the range indicated by the needle is less and more difficult to read. Any given power setting has only one pitch attitude where altitude and airspeed are constant.

- **Vertical Speed Indicator** (VSI). A secondary pitch instrument, to be used with the altimeter. Don't forget that it will give a brief reverse indication if you jerk the controls.

Bank

- **Artificial Horizon** (Attitude Indicator). Also the most important bank instrument, for similar reasons under *Pitch*, above.

- **Heading Indicator.** An indirect instrument, because if you change heading, bank must be involved somewhere.

- **Turn Coordinator**. Shows a rate of turn (3°/sec for rate 1), so it is an indirect indication of bank.

Power   022 01 03

Power instruments are not strictly in the traditional T, but you have to check them anyway. In this respect, **the ASI is a primary power instrument**, as it changes in relation to power application.

Engine and temperature instruments have already been covered elsewhere.

PITOT-STATIC SYSTEM   022 02 01

This consists of a series of pipes around the cockpit through which air flows to feed three common instruments: the altimeter, the ASI and the VSI.

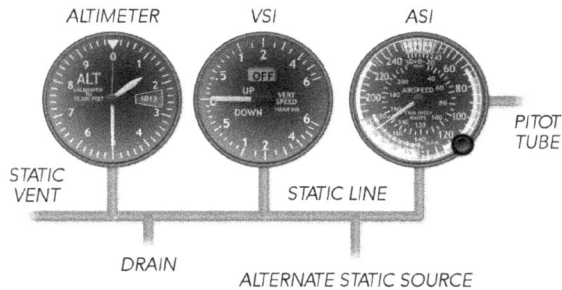

An aircraft is acted on from all directions by *static pressure*, which is fed into the system through static lines that are connected to static ports or static vents on *both sides* of the machine, to ensure that they balance out when it yaws, or performs strange manoeuvres (static balancing). They may or may not be heated (generally not on smaller machines). Warning lights associated with pitot/static heating systems usually come on when the heating element or the power relay has failed, so one light can have two meanings.

The static pressure is so called because it stays pretty much the same, except when there is disturbed airflow around the static ports. It's the normal barometric pressure that decreases with height, so any changes are relatively slow. Information from the static ports may also be fed to non-flight systems, such as autopilots or flight directors.

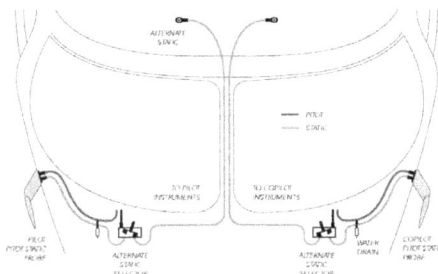

An *alternate static source* takes its feed from inside the aircraft in case the main one starts leaking or gets blocked, either through ice, a bird strike, or whatever. When it is used, some error will be introduced into the instrument readings because the cabin air pressure is affected by the airflow over the cabin (there are also different pressure errors), so indicated airspeeds and altitudes will read slightly *higher* than normal (that is, the altimeter and ASI will over-read). The VSI will show a momentary reverse as the alternate source is selected, then it will stabilise and produce normal readings. In a pressurised cabin, the pointer of the VSI will indicate a climb, then settle down and read incorrectly.

If the alternate gets blocked, or you don't have one, smashing the VSI glass (preferably not the ASI or altimeter) will have the same effect.

Otherwise known as the *Total Pressure Probe*, the *pitot tube* (pronounced pee-toe) is used to detect *total pressure* (as mentioned by Bernoulli). It is connected to the ASI and sticks out beyond the boundary layer. Total pressure (sometimes called *stagnation pressure*) is the pressure obtained when a moving gas is brought to a stop through an adiabatic process - in this case, it includes the static pressure that affects the aircraft from all sides, and an extra element that comes from forward movement, since the pitot tube is pointed towards the direction of flight (within 5°). If the fluid (air) is an ideal one (meaning not viscous), total pressure is equal to the sum of potential energy, kinetic energy and pressure energy, but the first is ignored in a pitot tube, and the kinetic energy is converted to pressure energy anyway.

This creates an equal volume above the level of the flow, which is *dynamic pressure*, and a measure of airspeed. In simple terms, dynamic pressure of the air against the front surfaces of an aircraft (as detected by the pitot tube) is greater than the pressure of the undisturbed air sensed through the static ports. The difference is proportional to the square of the speed, so instruments can be calibrated in units of speed, such as knots.

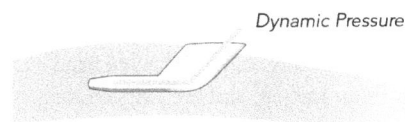

The formula for *dynamic pressure* is:

$$\text{Dynamic Pressure} = \tfrac{1}{2}\rho V^2$$

Where ρ (the Greek letter "rho") is air density and V the true velocity. As you can see, its strength depends on the speed of the relative airflow, and its density.

You cannot measure dynamic pressure by itself, as static pressure is always present, so you should really write:

$$q = (q + ps) - ps$$

The pitot tube may be heated to stop it icing up, so watch your hands (tell the passengers). If the pitot is not at the front, it will be in another relatively undisturbed place, parallel to the relative airflow for best effect. Sometimes, a static source will be incorporated in a pitot head, as a small hole or series of holes around the side of the base.

A pitot tube failure will affect the ASI. A static system failure affects the ASI, VSI and altimeter.

If the static system fails:

- The ASI will over-read in the descent and under-read in the climb
- The altimeter will read the same in the climb or descent
- The VSI will read zero

If the pitot system fails:

- The ASI will under-read in the descent and over-read in the climb

Pitot-static systems are checked during regular maintenance, usually something like every 2 years for IFR machines. Preflight checks will be simpler, usually just making sure that nothing is blocking the holes (take the red covers off!) and that the heating works. Do not blow into the holes, at least, not with instruments connected (or with the pitot heat on!)

Errors

Errors in measurement will affect displayed speed, height and vertical speed. Accuracy depends on the shape of the probe and where it is placed. The total *pressure error* comes in two categories, *position* or *configuration error* (inherent from the design), and *manoeuvre error*, from the way you handle the machine, which mostly affects the VSI. Position error is defined as the *amount by which the local static pressure differs from that in the free stream airflow*, so it will vary substantially with the Mach number. 95% of it is caused by turbulent flow around the pressure head.

The ASI and altimeter can develop positive or negative position errors. Configuration errors will have been established during flight testing, and are displayed on calibration cards or programmed out by electronics, if you have them. Standby instruments, however, will have uncorrected errors given on a calibration card. When accelerating, the static system is less sensitive, so the ASI & altimeter will over-read and the VSI will show a climb.

The greatest pitot-static errors occur when manoeuvring. If the left port gets blocked, for example, the altimeter over-reads when sideslipping to the left but is otherwise OK in symmetrical flight although, in theory, with static ports in pairs on opposite sides of the fuselage (at right angles to the relative wind so they are not affected by speed), any errors due to sideslip should be eliminated.

Parallax error is due to the angle from which you read the instrument.

If the pitot probe is blocked but the pitot drain and static ports are free, in straight and level (cruising) flight the IAS will tend to reduce, eventually indicating zero.

If the pitot probe and drain are blocked but the static port is free, the IAS will increase during a steady climb and decrease during a steady descent.

If the pitot probe, drain, and static ports are all blocked, the IAS will remain constant despite changes in airspeed.

In addition to airspeed indicators, systems that rely on information directly or indirectly (via Air Data Computers) from the pitot-static system are also unreliable if the pitot static system is blocked.

If only the static vent is blocked, the altimeter will freeze on the altitude that the blockage occurred, the VSI will show zero climb or descent, and the IAS will over-read in the descent or under-read in the climb.

Here is a summary of the errors involved:

Situation	ASI	Altimeter	VSI
Blocked Pitot	Zero	Works.	Works.
Blocked pitot & drain + open static.	High in climb, low in descent.	Works.	Works.
Blocked static + open pitot.	Low in climb, high in descent.	Frozen.	Frozen.
Alternate static.	Reads high.	Reads high.	Momentary climb.
Broken VSI glass.	Reads high.	Reads high.	Reverses.

Air Data Computer

Aircraft operating at high speeds and altitudes can get significant instrument errors if they use the probes found on smaller aircraft. As well, the traditional pitot-static system uses a lot of pipes from the air data instruments (altimeter, ASI and VSI). The ADC was developed in an attempt to reduce the plumbing and improve reliability and accuracy, by allowing the instruments to be operated electrically from remote places.

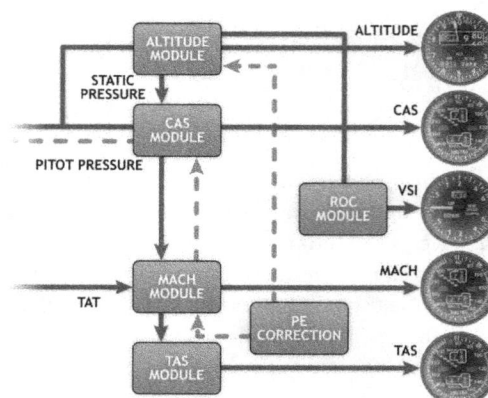

The ADC is a "black box" that sits between the usual sensors (static and dynamic pressures, but also TAT) and the instruments, translating them into electrical equivalents for transmission to the relevant indicators, which have no pressure sensing elements, so they can be simpler (and cheaper) to make.

The TAT value is needed to correct for the compressibility errors found at high speeds, and the TAT probe uses the standard formula mentioned above to calculate SAT, which value is also needed to correct for non-standard temperatures.

Each module is a servomechanism whose output signals are fed through a *transducer* (such as the E & I bar used in a servo altimeter) before being transmitted to their associated indicators.

The data can also be fed to the autopilot and Flight Director, Flight Management System, GPWS, area navigation aids, instrument comparison systems, and the EFIS symbol generators to be converted for electronic display. Standby instruments use the pitot-static plumbing.

There are two ADCs in most modern air transport aircraft to provide redundancy.

The most significant advantages of an air data computer are position error correction* (so the ADC puts out CAS, not IAS), and remote data transmission capability. It works on TAT, and static and total pressures.

*A *Static Source Error Correction* (SSEC) can be programmed in to compensate for position error. SSEC is typically a function of Mach number, AoA and flap position.

THE ALTIMETER

Static pressure is inversely proportional to altitude, so if you know the static pressure, you can figure out how high you are (in the standard atmosphere).

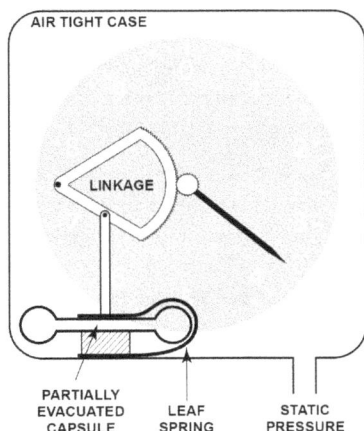

AIR TIGHT CASE
LINKAGE
PARTIALLY EVACUATED CAPSULE
LEAF SPRING
STATIC PRESSURE

The altimeter is a barometer with the scale marked in feet rather than hectopascals. It does not measure the true height, as a radio altimeter does, but the weight of the air above the aircraft, which compresses the capsule inside.

As you go up, pressure is less, so the altimeter translates air pressure into an *estimate* of altitude, although it will be better sealed than a barometer, so that air pressure in the cockpit doesn't affect it - the only pressure that should be there is static pressure from the pitot-static system. The readings could be inaccurate due to temperature and pressure variations from standard.

Inside a *sensitive* altimeter are *two* aneroid capsules (vacuums), which are corrugated for strength and kept open with a large leaf spring (a *simple* altimeter is a little more basic, with only one capsule - they are commonly used as cabin altimeters on pressurised aeroplanes since, at high altitudes, the capsule's movements are difficult to detect). The capsules' movements as you go up and down are magnified through the spring by a "suitable linkage" that connects directly to the pointer, using jewelled bearings. If the capsules expand, as they would when you go up, the pointer increases the reading. There is also a temperature compensation system to correct any spring and linkage tensions. Outside, there is a small knob, linked to a subscale which is visible through a small window. Rotating the knob causes the subscale to move and adjust the instrument to an *altimeter setting* (see *Meteorology*).

Caution: The three-needle display (on the right, below) can be easily misread:

The dials work like a clock. The long, thin pointer indicates hundreds of feet and the short, wide one, thousands. A very thin one, maybe with an inverted triangle at the end, as above, shows feet in ten thousands.

Only in standard ISA conditions will the true altitude be indicated directly. When it is extremely cold (below about -16°C), it will be a lot lower than shown, so corrections must be applied (altitudes given with radar vectors from ATC are corrected already). If this is something you need to take note of, you could perhaps mark the corrections directly on to the approach chart, next to the heights they refer to (you must recalculate *every* significant height).

Servo Altimeter

The servo-assisted altimeter typically uses a digital readout and is connected to the ADC. It is more accurate than the simple pressure altimeter due to its use of an induction pick-off device.

In this instrument, the aneroid capsules are connected to one end of a pivoting magnet (an I-bar) which influences an E-bar that has windings on each of its arms. At sea level, on a typical servo altimeter, the tolerance in feet from the indicated altitude must not exceed ±60 ft. In fact, the quoted accuracy is 1 hPa at mean sea level (±27 ft, and ±50 ft at 10 000 ft).

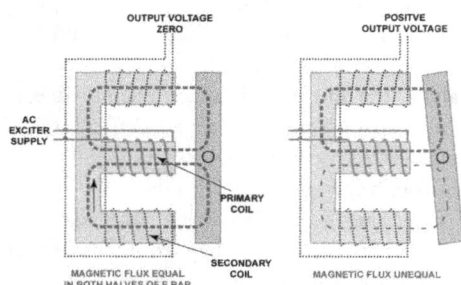

An AC current is fed to the primary winding on the centre arm, and as long as the gaps between the E and the I bars are equidistant, no voltage is induced in the coils on the other arms. The E-bars are wired in opposite directions and are connected in series to an amplifier unit - one example of the use of transformers.

Once the capsules increase or decrease in size, however, the gaps vary in size to create different magnetic fluxes and an output voltage that will be in or out of phase with the voltage in the primary coil, according to the direction of the displacement. Its magnitude will vary with the amount of the deflection.

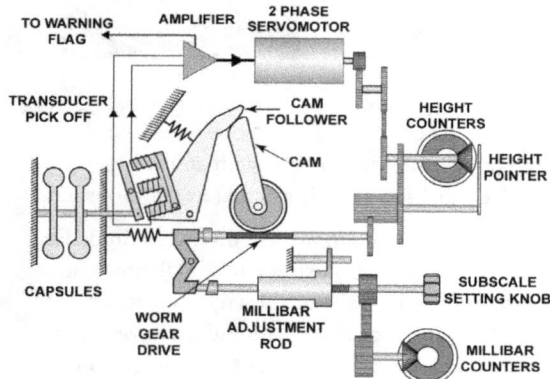

The signal goes to the amplifier, then to the servomotor control winding so that the pointer and height counters are driven in the relevant directions (for more about servos, see *Remote Sensing & Indication*). At the same time, the servomotor gear train spins a worm gear that rotates

the cam and cam follower to try and balance the magnetic fluxes at the I-bars, reaching the null point when the aircraft is levelled off and no more voltages are produced.

Turning the altimeter setting knob on the front drives the worm gear directly. All this complexity allows increased sensitivity at higher altitudes, as the aneroid capsules only have to drive the I-bar and not the whole instrument. The rest is done by the servo motor, which removes lag and pressure errors, and can drive more robust displays.

If servo altimeters are used, a standby pneumatic one must be in close proximity and easily visible.

Encoding Altimeter

An *encoding altimeter* is used with Mode C from a transponder so your altitude can be shown on ATC ground radar displays.

The encoding assembly is mechanically activated by the aneroid capsule. Older versions consist of a light source, various lenses and an encoder disc with a special pattern on it (in eleven concentric circles) that works like a bar code when the light is reflected from it to produce binary inputs that correspond to 100-ft increments in altitude. One turn of the disc covers the complete range of the altimeter. Naturally, there are now digital versions of the same thing that can also be fitted externally.

STOP The adjustment knob on the altimeter does not affect what ATC see on their radar screens! All encoding systems transmit your altitude corrected to 29.92 inches, or 1013.25 hPa which is the pressure altitude. The ground equipment makes any regional corrections directly.

Errors

Altimeters suffer from:

- **Mechanical errors**, which include:

  - *Scale error.* The difference between the indicated altitude and the basic altitude at which the measurement is taken.

  - *Friction error.* Causes irregular or jerky movement of the needle when the inner workings are sticking together. It is fixed by gentle tapping or vibration.

  - *Position error* can arise from unusual attitudes or the behaviour of the airflow due to the shape of the surrounding fuselage as opposed to the smooth free stream. It is sometimes confused with "installation error", and is generally greater at low airspeeds as the angle of attack is abnormal, but manoeuvring doesn't help. On an aircraft with 2 altimeters, and only one compensated for position error, in straight symmetrical flight, the higher the speed, the greater the error will be between them, but an ADC should compensate (a non-compensated altimeter, however, will indicate a higher altitude). If the static source on the right gets blocked, in a sideslip to the right, the altimeter will over-read.

- **Temperature error**, caused by linkages in the instrument shrinking or expanding, but this includes the temperature of the atmosphere, particularly when cold (see the *Meteorology* section). If the temperature is lower than ISA, *you* are lower! A correction is required whenever temperatures are significantly below standard. For temperatures down to -15°C, the calculation is 4% for every 10°C of deviation from ISA, and the same deviation is assumed to apply for all heights. At a constant indicated altitude over a warm air mass, the altimeter reading will be less than true altitude. Going into a colder air mass, it will over-read. This error is zero at sea level and increases with altitude.

- **Elastic error**, which includes:

  - *Hysteresis,* an irregular response to pressure changes (technically where changes lag behind the force that produces them) because a capsule under stress provides an imperfect response. This varies a lot with time passed at an altitude and is measured by the difference in two readings, when increasing and decreasing. Essentially, the altimeter gets used to a certain position and takes time to catch up if you move from it. The effects are negligible in slow climbs or descents, but a rapid descent will cause a delay, which is fixed with a vibrator, whose purpose is also to make the linkages work more smoothly. Indicated readings will lag behind true altitude, and the aircraft will be lower than indicated.

  - *Drift.* A slow increase in readings without an increase in altitude after levelling off from a climb - after descending the readings should return to normal. Drift should not be more than around 0.2% for every 15,000 ft change in altitude for flights over an hour long.

  - *Secular error.* The slow change over time of the entire scale error curve, mainly from internal stresses in the metal. Fixed by resetting zero.

- **Time lag** from the distance a pressure change has to travel in the pipes, at its worst during rapid altitude changes. Due to lag, the altimeter will under-read in a climb, and over-read in a descent.

- **Reversal error**, a momentary display in the wrong direction after an abrupt attitude change.

Between areas with different pressures, you could be at a different height than expected.

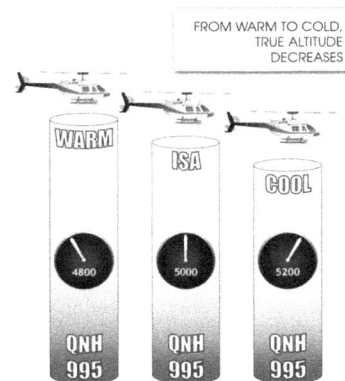

FROM WARM TO COLD, TRUE ALTITUDE DECREASES

For example, flying from high to low pressure, your altimeter would over-read (from HIGH to LOW, your instrument is HIGH), so you would be lower than planned and liable for a nasty surprise, especially in the lee of a mountain wave. Conversely, going from low into high pressure, without the altimeter setting being adjusted, the altimeter will indicate lower than the actual altitude above sea level. The same goes when you move between areas with different temperatures.

The standard atmosphere has a temperature element that also affects the altimeter. Remembering that air density decreases as it gets warmer, a point in your imaginary column of air above a station would be higher on a warm day than otherwise. If, therefore, as is typical near the Rockies in Winter, the air is *very much* colder than standard (actually below about -16°C), you will be lower than you should be (the phrase above is still valid, in that going from HIGH *temperature* to LOW, your instruments will be HIGH). A *cold low* will lower True Altitude to a point where it is dangerous to fly in mountains. This is serious because, in low temperatures, combined with other effects from the movement of wind over ridges, you could be *as much as 3,000 feet below your projected altitude* (although, with some navaids, you rely more on a radio signal than the altimeter). You could have a 150-foot difference on a published minimum of 500 feet and be too close to the ground. Normally, as mentioned, down to -15°C, you would apply a 4% increase for every 10°C below standard*. When the surface temperature is below -15°C, correct your altitudes by the values in this table:

Surface Temp (ISA)	Correction
-16°C to -30°C	+10%
-31°C to -50°C	+20%
-51°C or below	+25%

*Most people do so when it is 0°C or colder.

capt.gs

Pilots are responsible for altimeter corrections for pressure, temperature and, where appropriate, wind and terrain effects, except when being radar vectored.

Radar vectoring altitudes given by ATC are compensated and require no correction.

You can refuse IFR assigned altitudes if temperature error reduces obstacle clearance limits to an unacceptable level, but once the assigned altitude has been accepted, you cannot adjust it for altimeter temperature error. When the aerodrome temperature is -30°C or colder, add 1,000 feet to the MSA to ensure obstacle clearance. The difference between True and Indicated altitude is called the D value.

A static blockage causes the altimeter to stay at the height at which the blockage occurred. A partial blockage would cause a significant time delay.

Another factor is creating a wind from a temperature difference. A cooler column has a lower pressure at a given altitude, and the warmer one has a higher pressure, causing air to move from left to right in this case so, after Buys Ballot's law, low temperature is to the left in the Northern hemisphere with your back to the wind. The vertical distance between two pressure levels is less in cold air. Pressure in the upper levels depends on the mean temperature of the column of air beneath.

Altimetry

Altimetry is the science of measuring vertical distances in the atmosphere. The decrease of pressure with altitude depends on gravity and air density (the *hydrostatic balance*).

```
pressure = g x density x height diff
```

As vertical pressure variation follows the general gas laws, if you know the pressure on the ground and that at your height, you can work out your distance from the surface. 1 hPa is equal to 27 feet in the lower atmosphere.

STOP The word *height* refers to the vertical distance from a particular datum, usually the surface of an airfield (QFE, as used in Europe, is the airfield datum pressure, which makes the altimeter read your height above the airfield).

Altitude means vertical distance above *sea level*, so the aircraft in the picture below has a *height* of 1,000 feet (above the aerodrome, or QFE) and an *altitude* of 1,500 feet (above the sea, or QNH). The difference is the *elevation* of the aerodrome.

Elevation is the vertical distance of a point on the Earth's surface from mean sea level. *Indicated altitude* is what is shown on the dial at the current altimeter setting. *Calibrated altitude* is the indicated altitude corrected for instrument and position error. *True Altitude* is the actual one above mean sea level, and is discussed later.

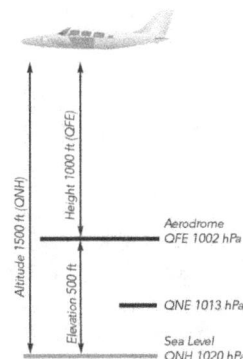

CRUISING LEVELS

Cruising levels are expressed in terms of:

- **Flight Levels** - the altimeter reading with two digits knocked off the end. FL 30 means 3,000 feet when set to 1013.25 hPa. Usually, the *lowest usable FL* corresponds to, or is immediately above, the minimum flight altitude. Flight levels must be used above the transition altitude (below).

- **Altitudes**, below the lowest usable flight level, or at or below the transition altitude, based on QNH.

- **Heights** - used within the traffic pattern and based on QFE, if used, taken from the airfield elevation, but the threshold elevation is used for instrument runways if there is more than a 2 m difference, and precision approach runways.

TRANSITION ALTITUDE

A transition altitude is normally specified for an aerodrome **by the State in which it is located**. It is as low as possible, but normally at least 3,000 feet in Europe, rounded up to the nearest 1,000. In the USA and Canada, and other countries, it is 17,999 ft. Below the Transition Altitude, vertical position is controlled by reference to altitude. Above it, Flight Levels are used, for which the altimeter must be set to 1013.

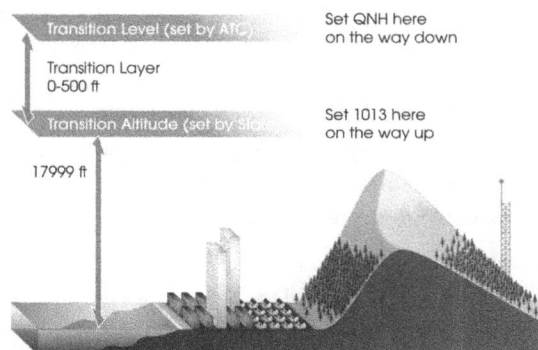

The *Transition Level* is the lowest available flight level (see below) above the Transition Altitude when the altimeter is set to 1013.2 hPa, so it would normally be FL 30 in UK, including when the QNH is more than standard. However, if the QNH is less than standard, the transition level will be higher than that. The Transition Level is determined **by the ATS unit concerned**, since it varies with pressure from day to day, and it is always *higher* than the Transition Altitude. The difference between transition altitude and transition level is the *Transition Layer*, which will be *more than zero and less than 500 feet.*

The change in reference between flight levels and altitudes is made, when climbing, at the Transition Altitude, and, when descending, at the Transition Level. In other words, when passing through the transition layer, report flight levels when going up and altitudes when going down. When descending to go below Transition Level, if you are cleared to a Flight Level, you must keep 1013 set on your altimeter. If you are cleared to an altitude, and no more FL reports are needed, set the QNH as soon as you start descending and report altitudes. Flight level zero is at the atmospheric pressure level of 1013.25 hPa. Consecutive Flight Levels are separated by intervals of at least 500 feet.

EXAMPLE

If the QNH is 985 hPa and the transition altitude is 3,000 ft, how deep is the transition layer (1 hPa=30 ft)?

For this, you need to work out the pressure altitude at 3,000 ft.

```
1013 - 985 = 28 hPa difference

28 x 30 = 840

3000 + 840 = 3840 ft PA
```

The next flight level is FL 40 which is at 4,000 ft PA. The transition layer is:

```
4000 - 3840 = 160 ft thick
```

ALTIMETER SETTINGS

Three altimeter settings are used throughout a flight:

- **QFE** (Field Elevation) is used near an airfield, particularly in the circuit, showing the approximate height above the aerodrome reference point. At the field elevation (FE), the altimeter will therefore read zero feet, and the QFE will be shown in the subscale. *Airfield QFE* is measured at the highest point of the airfield surface, and *Touchdown QFE* at the touchdown point.

- **QNH** (*Nautical Height*) is used for general transit elsewhere, below the transition altitude, showing the approximate altitude above sea level (at the aerodrome reference point, it shows the field elevation). It is forecast for 1 or 2 (or even 3 in Australia) hours ahead over large areas, so don't expect accuracy. It is QFE reduced to MSL **under ISA conditions** and should not differ from Local

QNH by more than about 5 hPa although, in places like New Guinea, there could be a 10 hPa difference between the highlands and the coast.

- **QNE** (*Nautical Elevation*) is the altimeter reading at the runway threshold with 1013.25 on the subscale, used when the subscale does not go low enough to set QFE. It is a height, not a setting or a flight level.

Trivia: The Q stands for *Query*.

QFF is similar to QNH, but is the QFE reduced to MSL using long term mean conditions at the surface, including temperature and water vapour content (the temperature between there and sea level is assumed to be constant). QFF allows accurate surface charts to be drawn, as it is the basis for isobars. When above MSL and warmer than ISA, it will be less than QNH, and more when the temperature is colder than ISA (the opposite below MSL). For meteorologists only!

Tip: If QFE, QNH and QFF have the same value, the 1013.25 hPa level must be at MSL, in ISA conditions.

The barometric pressure is constantly changing and varies from one place to another. What would happen if you departed the spot in the diagram above and returned several hours later to find the 1020 QNH above had reduced to 995 hPa? The altimeter would be over-reading by 675 feet and you would only be 325 feet off the ground (1020 - 995 x 27 = 675, 1500 - 675 = 825 AMSL = 325 AGL). The altimeter needs constant updating as you fly.

Although altimeters are calibrated to ISA, the actual sea level pressure varies from hour to hour, and place to place. You would be very lucky to hit the standard atmosphere more than, say, 25% of the time, so you need a means of adjusting any instruments based on it to cope with the differences. To allow you to set the zero reference correctly, an altimeter has a *setting window* (also called the Kollsman window) in which you can adjust the figures of a *subscale* for the correct pressure on the ground by turning a knob on the front.

This is actually part of an important preflight check, where you make sure that if you turn the knob to the right, the height readings increase, and *vice versa*. If the subscale is set wrongly, the zero reference will be displaced by an amount proportional to 1 inch per 1,000 feet, so your relative height to obstacles, like mountains, will not be maintained.

For example, if the proper altimeter setting is 29.92 inches, but you have 30.92 inches set in the subscale, the altimeter will be over-reading by 1,000 feet. When flying from high to low pressure, your altimeter will also over-read (from HIGH to LOW, it is HIGH), so you would be lower than planned and liable for a nasty surprise. It's therefore much safer to be going the other way (that is, from LOW to HIGH, where your instrument is LOW).

To convert from inches to hectopascals, start at 29.92 and find the difference between it and the current pressure. Divide the difference by 0.03 inches and apply the result to 1013. In other words, 1 hPa is about equal to 0.03". For example, if the current pressure is 30.02, that is, 0.1" above 29.92" (or 3 x 0.03), add 3 hPa and set 1016.

A more formal way is to use this formula:

$$\frac{hectopascals}{1013.25} = \frac{ins}{29.92}$$

Better yet, below is a table:

hPa	Inches (of Mercury)									
(Mb)	0	1	2	3	4	5	6	7	8	9
970	28.64	28.67	28.70	28.73	28.76	28.79	28.82	28.85	28.88	28.91
980	28.94	28.97	29.00	29.03	29.05	29.08	29.11	29.14	29.17	29.20
990	29.23	29.26	29.29	29.32	29.35	29.38	29.41	29.44	29.47	29.50
1000	29.53	29.56	29.59	29.62	29.65	29.68	29.71	29.74	29.77	29.80
1010	29.83	29.86	29.89	29.92	29.95	29.97	30.00	30.03	30.06	30.09
1020	30.12	30.15	30.18	30.21	30.24	30.27	30.30	30.33	30.36	30.39
1030	30.42	30.45	30.47	30.50	30.53	30.56	30.59	30.62	30.65	30.68
1040	30.71	30.74	30.77	30.80	30.83	30.86	30.89	30.92	30.95	30.98

TRUE ALTITUDE

This is your (geometric) elevation above mean sea level, being the distance you could normally find with a tape measure, but it is impractical to throw one out of the window, so we use instruments such as the altimeter instead, to show an indicated altitude.

The only time an altimeter will indicate true altitude is in ISA conditions. As such conditions are rare, indications are almost always in error due to temperature.

The difference between true and standard (ISA) altitude is 4 feet per thousand feet per degree of deviation from ISA. That is, true altitude changes by 4% for every 10°C deviation from ISA conditions, or 2% for every 5.5°C*.

*4% is correct for the stratosphere, but it's more like 3.5% for lower altitudes. 4% for every 11°C is more accurate.

One source of error can occur when the temperature at a level might be close to ISA, when the lapse rate is not.

All calculations should be rounded to the nearest lower hPa. The barometric lapse rate near mean sea level is 27 ft (8m) per hPa. Also, the airport elevation must be taken into account - that is, *only use the layer between the ground and the position of the aircraft.* In practice, true altitude is obtained from knowing the OAT at the level you are flying at, and using a flight computer. This will be reasonably accurate when the actual lapse rate is, or is near, that of ISA, i.e., 2°C per 1,000 feet, but if it's very hot, or very cold, you need further adjustments.

INDICATED ALTITUDE

Indicated and Pressure Altitudes are the same in ISA conditions.

CALIBRATED ALTITUDE

The Indicated Altitude corrected for airspeed, altitude, imperfect pressure lines, etc.becomes Calibrated Altitude.

ABSOLUTE ALTITUDE

The geometric height above terrain - what would be measured by a radar altimeter.

PRESSURE ALTITUDE

Pressure altitude is the height in the standard atmosphere that you may find a given pressure, usually 29.92" or 1013 Mb, but actually whatever you set on the altimeter - if you set 1013 on the subscale and the needles read 6,000 feet, the PA *for that setting* is 6,000 feet. So what is indicated is the height of the pressure selected. PA is a starting point for any calculations for performance, TAS, etc., and is the altimeter setting used above the transition altitude, where all altimeters must be set to 1013 hPa so that everybody is using the same standard (every country has a different transition altitude). Below the transition altitude, local altimeter settings are used.

If an altimeter is set to 1013, it is measuring Pressure Altitude with respect to Mean Sea Level. In ISA conditions, Pressure Altitude is the same as True Altitude.

If the sea level pressure is different from 1013, obstacle clearance heights and airfield elevations, etc. must be converted before using them. To do this, get the local altimeter setting, find the difference between it and 29.92 (or 1013), convert it to feet (1"=1,000 or 1 hPa=27 feet at sea level), then apply it the *opposite* side of 29.92. You could also get PA from the altimeter, by placing 29.92 or 1013 in the setting window, and reading the figures directly. The significance of this concerns performance - if the pressure on the surface is less than standard, you are effectively at a higher altitude, and your machine will not fly so well. You often need to calculate the pressure altitude of a location so you know your performance.

For example, for a strip on the side of a mountain at 400 feet above sea level, with an altimeter setting of 29.72, your PA at that location would actually be 600 feet, since the difference between 29.92 and 29.72 is 0.2, or 200 feet *added*, and where you would enter your performance charts, since they are set for the standard atmosphere (the altimeter setting is *below* the standard pressure, so your answer should be *above*). Again, you are *adding* because the sea is *lower*, and the figures ought to be higher (see the examples below).

Pressure levels with altitude are:

Height	Pressure Level
Surface	1013
10,000	700
18,000	500
24,000	400
30,000	300
34,000	250
38,000	200

CALCULATIONS

Tip: *Always* draw a diagram and place the numbers in order, with the large ones at the bottom. When on a local QNH for an airport, errors from variations in ISA only apply to height above the airfield elevation - local QNH (which is calculated under ISA) applies up till then.

Q: What minimum flight level* will clear high ground rising to 1800 m AMSL by at least 1500 ft on a track of 225°(M), if the Regional QNH is 990 hPa? How much is the clearance at that level? (1 hPa=27 feet).

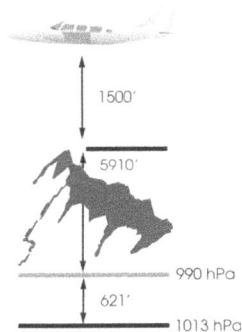

A: 1800 m is equal to 5910 ft. The difference between the QNH and QNE (1013 - 990) is 23 hPa, or 621 feet. Your minimum height is 621 + 5910 + 1500, or 8031 feet. The next applicable even flight level is FL 100, and the high ground is cleared by 3469 feet (10000 - 621 - 5910).

*For IFR flights outside controlled airspace, the determination of the lowest usable flight level is the responsibility of the PIC.

Q: An aeroplane is flying at 2500 feet AGL near an airfield which is 350 ft AMSL. The QFE is 982 hPa. If another aircraft flies over at FL 40, what is the approximate vertical separation between them? (1 hPa = 27 feet)

A: 664 feet. 350 feet divided by 27 is 13 hPa, so the QNH is 995 (982 + 13). The difference between the QNH and QNE is 18 hPa, so sea level is 485 above the standard pressure level. Add 2500 feet to 485 and 350 to get 3336 and subtract that from 4,000.

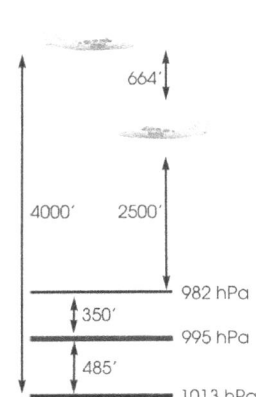

Q. A westbound aircraft is VFR at 8,500 feet. The OAT is -18°C and the altimeter is set to the nearest airport (30.22 - field elevation 2,000 ft). By how much will the aircraft clear a 7,500 ft ridge in the flight path?

A. This involves a temperature correction, with the complication that the QNH is measured at 2,000 ft AMSL. ISA at 8 230 ft (the pressure altitude at 8,500 ft AMSL on the QNH of 30.22" Hg) is -1° to the nearest degree, so the deviation is -17°C. Correction is made for the difference between the elevation and aircraft altitude, i.e:

```
8,500 - 2000 = 6500
```

Adjust by 4 ft per 1000 ft per °10C:

```
4 x 6.5 x 17 = 44.2
```

The conditions are below ISA, so the true altitude is less than indicated. The aircraft is at 8 456 feet, which will be 956 feet above the ridge.

DENSITY ALTITUDE

This is the altitude in the Standard Atmosphere at which the prevailing density occurs, meaning your real altitude from the effects of height, temperature and humidity, and is used to establish performance, as it is a figure that expresses where your machine thinks it is, as opposed to where it actually is - see *Performance*. For now, it is *pressure altitude corrected for non-standard temperature* (ignoring humidity), or the true air temperature at a given level. Thus, density altitude has the same value as pressure altitude at standard temperature.

To find DA on the flight computer, set the aerodrome elevation or Pressure Altitude against the temperature in the *airspeed* window.

In the picture, the temperature is -21°C at 10 100 feet. The indicated airspeed is 350 kts, and the TAS is 396. The Density Altitude is 8100 feet - quite a difference!

If you want a formula:

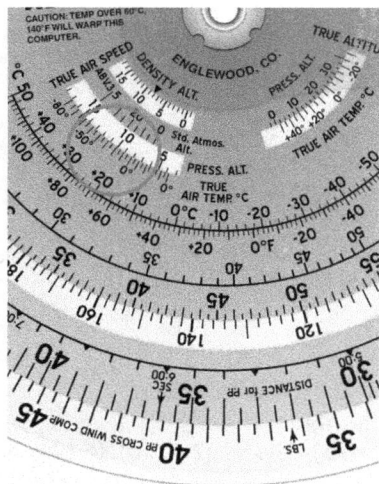

```
PA ± (118.8 x ISA Dev)
```

(Multiplying the ISA Dev by 120 is usually good enough, and should be used in the exams).

Altimeter Checks

Rotating the knob through ±10 hPa must produce a corresponding height difference of about ±300 ft in the relevant directions. At a known elevation on the aerodrome, vibrate the instrument by tapping, unless mechanical vibration is available:

- Set the scale to the current QNH. The altimeter should indicate the elevation, plus the height of the altimeter above it, within ± 20 m or 60 ft for altimeters with a test range of 0-9,000 m (0-30,000 ft) and ± 25 m or 80 ft for altimeters with a test range of 0-15,000 m (0-50,000 ft)

- Set the current QFE. The altimeter should indicate the height of the altimeter in relation to the QFE reference point, with the same tolerances

- Both should be set to the aerodrome QFE and should indicate within ±80' of zero, within 60 or 80' of each other. Thus, they can misread by up to 120 or 160 feet and still be "serviceable"

- With No 1 on QFE and No 2 on aerodrome QNH, the difference should equal the aerodrome elevation AMSL, to within 80 feet

- With both on aerodrome QNH, indications should be within ±80 feet of aerodrome elevation, and 80 feet of each other

STOP No 1 is the handling pilot's primary instrument and No 2 the secondary.

According to CS 25 the tolerance for an altimeter at MSL is ±30' per 100 kts CAS.

AIRSPEED INDICATOR 022 02 06

To find airspeed, you need to compare the general pressure outside the aircraft (the static pressure) with the pressure created from its movement through the air, so this instrument is connected to both the static and pitot pressure systems.

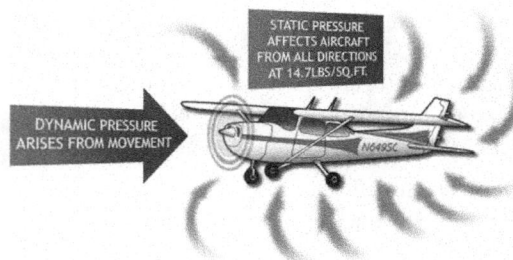

The ASI is similar to the altimeter inside, except that the capsule is fed directly with pitot (total) pressure, and its size will vary as a function of the dynamic pressure. The static port's job is to cancel out the effects of the air surrounding the aircraft. As the capsule expands under the pressure of the ram air, static air in the case can escape through the static port. If it were otherwise, the capsule would not be able to expand.

The ASI is a pressure gauge with its dial marked in knots or mph instead of PSI. It captures **total pressure** then subtracts static pressure to get dynamic pressure, which is proportional to forward speed, so it measures **differential pressure**. The needle is connected to the capsule through the usual suitable linkage.

Dynamic pressure varies with the square of the airspeed.

The combination of static and dynamic pressure is the *stagnation pressure*, because airflow is being brought to rest inside the pitot tube, or stagnating.

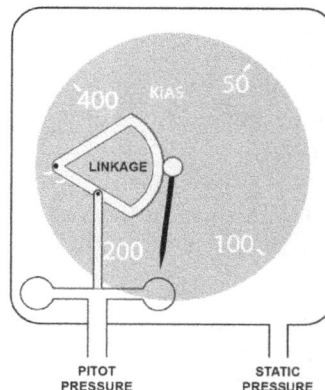

Because the atmosphere gets less dense as you climb, the IAS must be corrected. The rate is 1.75% per 1,000 feet.

There are several variations on the airspeed theme:

- **Indicated airspeed** (IAS) is the direct reading, corrected only for instrument error - turbulent flow around the pressure head accounts for 95%. Modern instruments have little error, so the direct reading is effectively IAS. A given IAS can result from flying through high density air at a low speed, or low density at a greater TAS (below), as you might get at high altitudes. The ASI cannot compensate for changes in density, but can only indicate the combination of density and velocity of the air.

- **Calibrated airspeed** (CAS) is the IAS corrected for pressure (system) errors, which are highest at low speeds and high angles of attack (IAS and CAS are about the same at speeds above the cruise). It was once known as the *Rectified Air Speed* (RAS), and is a measure of the dynamic pressure at *low speeds*. Instrument and position errors can be corrected out by the Air Data Computer in modern aircraft. *An aircraft at the same weight always takes off at the same CAS.*

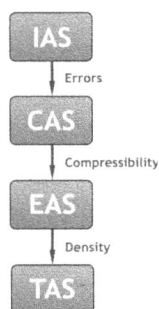

- **Equivalent Airspeed** (EAS) is CAS compensated for compressibility, or factors arising from high speeds. It is the speed that gives the same dynamic pressure that would come from TAS at sea level. It does not consider density error, and is effectively IAS/CAS where such errors are small (below 200 kts and 20,000 feet, around 1-2 kts). It's hardly worth working out because, at the speeds and altitudes where it is significant, a constant Mach number is used anyway (see below). EAS is always lower than or equal to CAS because, as the air is compressed inside the pitot tube, the dynamic pressure is greater than it should be, and the correction is a **negative** value, so it could be seen as a form of error. The bridge between EAS and TAS is Density Altitude.

- **True Air Speed** (TAS) is the CAS corrected for altitude and temperature, or density (its original calibration is based on the standard atmosphere). *It is the only speed* and the only figure used for navigation - the others are pressures and are to do with aircraft behaviour! On average, the TAS increases by 2% over the IAS for every 1,000 feet.

  If air density remains constant, the relationship between IAS and TAS will remain constant so, if we double the IAS (in conditions of constant density) we will double the TAS. Dynamic pressure is proportional to the square of the TAS so, if we

multiply the TAS by 2 the dynamic pressure increases by 4. With 4 times as much dynamic pressure and the same wing area, we need ¼ of the initial C_L to generate the same amount of lift.

You can find TAS from the CAS and Air Density, which can be derived from Pressure Altitude and temperature and which may involve a conversion from Fahrenheit to Centigrade (and from miles per hour to knots). Thus, in ISA conditions at sea level, CAS = TAS. However, as an example, given an altimeter setting of 30.40", an indicated altitude of 3450', an OAT of 41°F and an IAS of 138 mph, let's find the TAS in knots.

138 mph converts to 120 kts. 41°F also converts to 5°C. The PA is found in the usual way, where 1" equals 1,000'. The difference between 29.92" and 30.40" is 0.48, or 480 feet, which gives 2970' when subtracted from 3450' (29.92 is the "higher" figure in terms of distance above ground).

The TAS is 125 kts, and the Density Altitude (out of interest) is 2500'. If the TAS were over 300 kts, you have to apply a compressibility correction, which will bring TAS and CAS closer together.

If you maintain a constant CAS in level unaccelerated flight, from warm to cold air, TAS will *decrease* as air density *increases*, and *vice versa*. Thus, in ISA conditions, when descending at constant CAS, TAS decreases.

If you climb at constant IAS, you will be climbing at a constant dynamic pressure, but air density decreases, so you need more V^2 to produce the same dynamic pressure.

At 40,000 ft, ρ is about ¼ of its sea level value, so V^2 must be 4 times its own sea level value to keep dynamic pressure constant. In fact, TAS is twice the IAS, a point to be remembered when landing on high runways as the ground run will be longer.

To find out what happens to various speeds in the climb or descent, remember this picture:

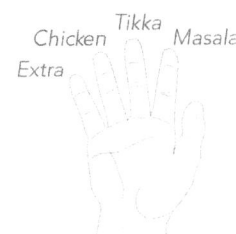

Chicken *Tikka* *Masala* *Extra*

The initial letters stand for *Equivalent, Calibrated* and *True* airspeeds, and *Mach number*. In the climb, select which one remains constant, and the speeds to the right will be increasing, with the ones to the left decreasing. The reverse for the descent.

Above the tropopause (i.e. in an isothermal atmosphere) the Mach number and TAS will react in the same way at the same time.

Colour Coding 022 02 05

Various colours are specified for ASIs.

The limits are:

- **Green scale**: The normal operating range. Starting at the flaps up, gear up, power-off stall speed, or V_{S1}, and ending at the maximum structural cruising speed, V_{NO}/V_{MO}, (expressed as CAS), where no damage will occur in moderate vertical gusts.

- **White scale**: The flap operating range. The lower limit is the power-off stall speed with the recommended landing flaps at gross weight with the gear extended and the cowl flaps closed (V_{S0}). The upper limit is the maximum (full) flap operating speed, or V_{FE}.

- **Yellow scale**: Starting at the maximum structural cruising speed, i.e. V_{NO}/V_{MO}, and ending at the never-exceed speed, or V_{NE} (the red line). Strong vertical gusts could cause structural damage if you fly in this range.

Modern jets have a red and white striped barber pole indicator for M_{MO} (the maximum safe Mach number against altitude), which is a limit speed pointer that moves according to conditions, unlike the red V_{NE} line described above, which is fixed (Mach numbers depend on temperature).

Such an instrument is often called a CSI, or *Combined Speed Pointer* or even a MASI, if it is combined with an ASI (but see also *The Machmeter*, later), because it also contains an altitude capsule that is connected to the limit speed pointer with the usual suitable linkage. The capsule expands or contracts according to altitude. In the picture, the Mach number is 0.814, and the TAS is 264 knots.

On the flight computer, if you set the *Mach Index* opposite the temperature, you can read the speed of sound directly against the inner scale 1.0. In the picture, the Index (a double-headed arrow) is in a window at the bottom. TAS 280 corresponds to a Mach No of 0.424.

At low levels, limiting speeds will be expressed as IAS, which is used for the takeoff and initial climb, during which the TAS increases while the speed of sound decreases with the temperature. At higher levels, a Mach number is used, with the changeover point somewhere around 25,000 feet. A speed of M 0.9 at low level could be 550 kts, as opposed to 350 kts at 35,000 feet, which may be too high for the airframe. For example, an aircraft with a V_{MO} (maximum safe IAS, based on EAS) of 350 kts and an M_{MO} of 0.84 is climbing to FL 360 in standard conditions at 330 kts IAS until M 0.83 is reached.

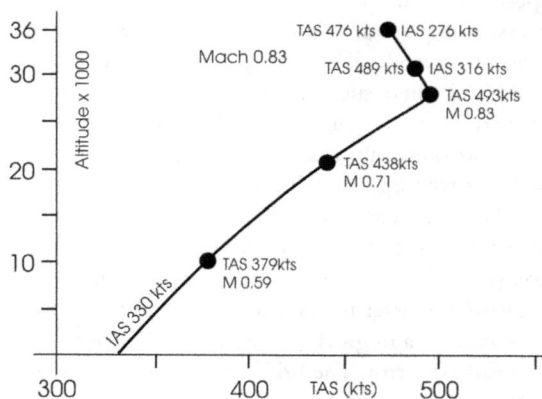

As it passes 10,000 ft, the IAS pointer will show 330 kts with a Mach number of 0.59 (see picture above). As it passes 20,000 ft, the IAS will still read 330 kts, but the Mach value will be 0.71. At 28,000 ft the Mach number will be 0.83, which is now used as a constant value so, on passing 30,000 ft, the IAS pointer will show 316 kts. At 36,000 ft it will show 277 kts.

In real life, a standard climb profile for the A 320 family of aircraft is 250 kts up to 10,000 feet (for ATC reasons), then a level acceleration up to 300 kts until reaching M0.78, which is maintained to avoid high speed buffeting.

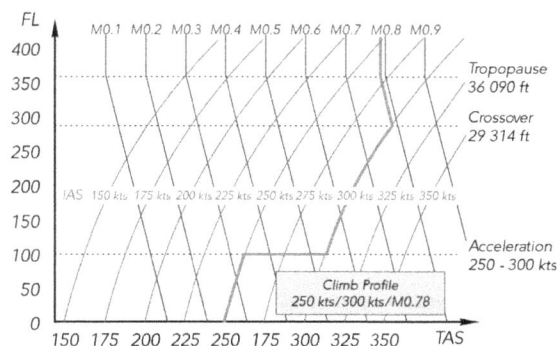

As you climb higher, the difference in pressure between the pitot tube and the static port reduces, leading to a decrease in dynamic pressure and IAS (or an increase in TAS, if you like) to the point of reaching the stalling speed. The point where the V_{MO} and M_{MO} meet is called the Mach transition, usually between FLs 290 & 310, depending on density altitude and the weight of the aircraft. VNAV mode (on the FMS) will switch automatically but, with FLC, you have to switch manually (all is explained in *Flight Management Systems*, later).

In ISA conditions, at the crossover altitude of 29 200 ft, you would expect the rate of climb to increase as the constant IAS climb is replaced by a constant Mach climb. At 29,500, the rate of climb would start to decrease, because TAS is decreasing.

In a descent from a high flight level, the maximum ground speed will be limited initially by the M_{MO}, then the V_{MO}.

A constant CAS and flight level produces a Mach number that is independent of temperature - i.e. it will not change.

A command bug is normally set to indicate the target speed or used as a datum for the autothrottle in automatic flight. Other bugs may be on the bezel (outside the glass), which can be used to define, for example, V speeds, mentioned below.

Errors

The ASI suffers from position and attitude errors*, plus those from the instrument itself, and lag. It is very susceptible to position error, which can be up to 10 or 20 kts at low speeds (check the flight manual), because the instrument will be calibrated for greatest accuracy in a particular flight condition (i.e. straight & level), otherwise the stagnation point will move to a different position.

*It will indicate wrongly in a sideslip.

If dynamic pressure is captured by the static port, the ASI will under-read, but the static pressure is lower along the fuselage anyway in flight, and the ASI will then over-read. calibration error will be greatest at the extremes of the operating envelope, that is, at very high and very low IAS, especially in larger aircraft.

However, density error is also important, since changes in air density affect the dynamic pressure, and make the ASI under-read at altitude (the ASI only reads TAS when density is standard, so to find it you have to apply a correction to CAS). The effect of temperature extending and contracting the linkages is fixed by a bimetallic strip that distorts to correct the expansion.

At high speeds (over 300 kts TAS, or 200 kts IAS) a further correction is made for air being compressed as it is brought to rest in the pitot tube. In the capsule, it will end up more dense than usual, and will vary the capsule's proportionality of expansion with dynamic pressure. At high altitudes with thinner air, the air flowing into the capsule is more easily compressed and will make the instrument over-read.

If the pitot tube and its drain get blocked, the ASI will behave like an altimeter because it has only static information - its readings (i.e. your airspeed) will increase (read high) as you climb, read low in the descent and not change at all when airspeed varies. This is a typical icing situation so, as you get higher, there is a danger that you will try to bring the speed back until you stall (without knowing why) which is what happened when the crew of one large jet missed the checklist item for the pitot heat. This would create an "airspeed disagree" message on a Primary Flight Display, when the Captain's and First Officer's ASIs differ by 5 knots or more. See below.

Tip: Use the readings from the GPS or INS.

As static pressure *increases*, the ASI reading will *decrease*, and *vice versa*. If the drain hole remains open, however, IAS will read zero, as there is no differential between static and dynamic pressures, due to the drain hole allowing pressure in the lines to drop to atmospheric.

A leak in the pitot total pressure line of a non-pressurised aircraft would cause an ASI to under-read.

If the static port gets blocked, the pressure inside the instrument (but outside the capsule) remains the same. The ASI will still read correctly in the cruise as long as the OAT doesn't change but, in the descent, it will over-read because the static element of pitot pressure increases inside the capsule - you will be closer to the stall than you think. In the climb, the static element of pitot pressure decreases, which causes a partial collapse of the capsule, so the instrument will under-read.

UNRELIABLE AIRSPEEDS

As mentioned above, these occur when the Captain's and First Officer's ASIs differ by 5 knots or more. Ways to prevent such situations include:

- Inspect all pitot heads and static ports during the pre-flight inspection

- Use pitot/static heat

- Understand the relationship between the ADC, the autopilot and flight director. Disconnect the latter two, plus the autothrust

- Monitor primary flight path parameters (pitch attitude, thrust setting and IAS) during periods of potential icing

- Be aware of normal attitudes and power/thrust settings for the various phases of flight

- Keep away from the low- and high-speed ends of the flight envelope

- Revert to safe default parameters for pitch attitudes and thrust settings

- Remain in VMC if possible

In summary, fly the approximate pitch and power normally expected for that stage of flight until it is discovered which (if any) system is indicating correctly or the problem is resolved. If in doubt, or until more accurate information is available, maintain a slight nose up attitude and maintain climb power.

STOP Some aircraft systems are configured, as a safety measure, to disable stick shakers and pushers if there is disagreement between systems so, if the aircraft approaches and/or enters a stall, they might not activate. If they do, in the absence of clear contrary indications, believe them!

SQUARE LAW COMPENSATION

In addition being calibrated according to the St Venant formula (for compressibility), ASIs work on a differential pressure that varies with the square of the airspeed, and if you plotted the results linearly, the graph would look something like this:

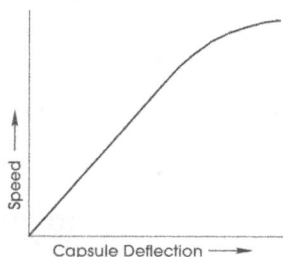

If you translated that to the instrument, you would have a logarithmic scale that would be difficult to read at low speeds, and the whole speed range would be too big to fit in the display. To create a linear display, the capsule or the linkage must be adjusted to produce the correct results or, rather, where the indication moves at the same rate as the

airspeed. Usually, the length or the point of leverage of a lever is adjusted to produce increased pointer movements for small deflections and decreased ones for large deflections - the *principle of variable magnification*.

V-Speeds

More in *Performance*!

Speed	Explanation
V_{LE}	Max gear extended
V_{LO}	Max gear operating
V_{NE}	Never Exceed speed.
V_{NO}	Normal Operations. 10% less than V_{NE}.
V_{MCG}	Minimum control speed on the ground
V_{MCA}	Minimum control speed in the air Now just referred to as V_{MC}
V_1	Decision speed - must be greater than V_{MCG} because you need to control the aircraft
V_R	Rotation speed - must be greater than V_{MCA} because you need to control the aircraft
V_{LOF}	Lift off speed

Increasing the flap angle has no effect on V_{MCG} or V_{MCA}, but it lowers the minimum value of V_1 because it decreases V_{LOF}. However, the maximum value of V_1 is increased because drag is increased.

THE MACHMETER

Here, we are interested in the *Free-Stream Mach Number*, which is assumed to be far enough away to be unaffected by the aircraft.

In the Type A Machmeter, shown here, dynamic pressure is measured by an airspeed capsule, while the static pressure is measured by an aneroid capsule at right angles to it. A complex linkage detects their movement ratios. In other words, an ASI and an altimeter (in the same casing) feed their movements to a *main shaft*, which is connected to a *ratio arm*, then a *ranging arm*, to the *indicator* (rat ran in). When altitude decreases, the ratio arm slides to the end of the ranging arm, which reduces the ASI's involvement in the whole affair. As you go higher, it slides to the root, giving it more influence. Thus, the Mach number is found by dividing the dynamic pressure by the static pressure - *there are no temperature sensors.*

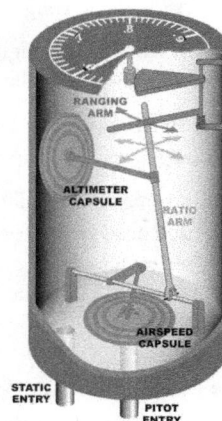

Type B Machmeters use the Air Data Computer, which does have a temperature sensor and is therefore able to correct properly for temperature rise and can display more accurate figures, usually to three decimal places.

Errors

As the instrument contains an ASI and an altimeter, it suffers the errors of both (position pressure error), with those from the ASI being numerically predominant. As they are very small, the indicated Mach number is taken as the true Mach number.

The Machmeter does not suffer from compressibility error, though, as compressibility is a function of D-S* divided by S*, and it is this ratio which is use to calculate the Mach number.

*The static element of pitot pressure.

The Machmeter does not suffer from density error either, because it cancels out on both sides of the equation.

Machmeter readings are subject to *position pressure error, due to* incorrect pressure sensing from disturbed airflow around the pitot tube and/or static ports. If the pitot becomes blocked, the Machmeter shows the same errors as an ASI. The Mach number will stay unchanged until static pressure changes in a climb or a descent.

Blocked static sources mean that excess static pressure is trapped in the *case* and will cause the instrument to under-read below the altitude at which the blockage occurred (in a descent it will over-read above that altitude). If the static line fractures inside the pressure hull, static pressure will be too high and it will under-read. Likewise, if the pitot line leaks, the instrument will under read. At high speeds, temperature become artificially increased at speeds above about 300 kts, because of compressibility (this is already accounted for in the CR flight computer, so don't add any figures again from charts or tables).

The static pressure (S) on the top line of the equation above is the static element of pitot pressure. It should be cancelled out by the static pressure surrounding the capsule (S) on the bottom line, but this is artificially low due to the blockage. The airspeed capsule is expanded.

The static pressure (S) on the bottom line is also affecting the altitude capsule. It should increase during the descent, but the blockage stops this, so the altitude capsule remains in its expanded state. Because both capsules are expanded, the instrument is will over-read.

VERTICAL SPEED INDICATOR

There is a capsule inside this, too, but it is connected only to the static system. However, there is a *restrictor*, or *calibrated leak* between the inside and outside of the capsule that makes the pressure outside it lag behind, so the VSI measures the *rate of change* of *static pressure* with height, based on pressure difference between the inside of the capsule and the inside of the casing.

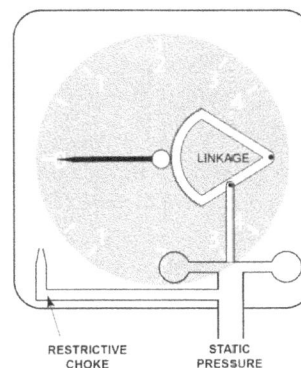

In other words, the difference between the instantaneous static pressure and that shortly beforehand is measured, with one chamber (the capsule) being inside the other (the case). Static pressure is fed in directly to the capsule so that any changes are due to movement of the aircraft. The flow through the restrictive choke, however, is constant, so the pressure inside the case is always lagging behind that in the capsule, and we are dealing with the rate of change in static pressure, as determined by vertical speed.

During level flight there is no pressure differential across the metering unit, but in a descent (for example), static pressure increases and flows into the capsule and case. The capsule will expand as normal, but the restrictor will keep the pressure inside the case relatively low and create a differential that distorts the capsule. A suitable linkage transfers the capsule's movements to the dial.

The VSI is a trend *and* a rate instrument, showing the direction of movement (up or down), and how fast you're going, in hundreds of feet per minute on a logarithmic scale, with zero at the 9 o'clock position, so it is horizontal during straight and level flight. Any movement up or down is shown in the relevant direction.

The advantage of a logarithmic scale is that, at low rates of climb or descent, the pointer movement is much larger and easier to read.

About 10% of the indicated vertical speed should be used to determine the number of feet to lead by when levelling off from a climb or descent.

Between +50°C and -20°C, the VSI is accurate within limits of ±200 feet per minute.

Errors

A complex choke system self-compensates for temperature, density and air viscosity, using two capillary tubes to give a laminar flow and two sharp-edged orifices for a turbulent flow. Errors that result from the two types are of opposite sign and cancel each other out.

Aside from the usual position error, the VSI suffers from lag, which may last up to 6-8 seconds before the air inside and outside the capsule stabilizes. This means that, for example, once you level off and the altimeter is stable, the VSI will take a few more seconds to settle to neutral. There is also *reversal error*, which occurs when abrupt changes cause movement briefly in the opposite direction.

If the static source becomes blocked, pressure differentials disappear and the instrument reads zero. If the restrictor gets blocked, there is a greater difference in the rate of pressure change so the VSI will over-read. A leak in the case will make the instrument over-indicate in the climb and under-indicate in the descent.

Diaphragm overload stops prevent damage if the rate of climb or descent exceeds the maximum design values of the instrument, so an aircraft descending at 6,000 ft per minute might only indicate 4,000 ft per minute.

STOP When breaking the glass of the VSI if the static source gets blocked, remember that the flow of air will be through the capillary tube, which is designed to create a lag. This means that the ASI and altimeter will lag as well! The rate of climb will indicate in reverse. Breaking the glass of the other two would have a similar effect to using alternate static.

IVSI

An *instantaneous (or Inertial Lead) VSI* uses two accelerometers in the static line, or a static input to an acceleration pump, to reduce lag errors, which introduces turning errors.

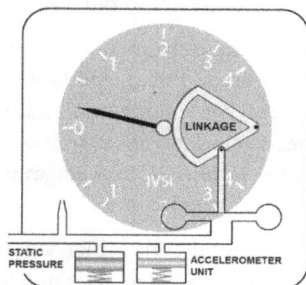

The accelerometers are small cylinders with weights inside (they act like pistons), held in balance by springs and their own mass. The weights are centralised when stabilised in the climb or descent, but, when levelling, they act in opposing directions to sharply reduce instrument indications by puffing air into the appropriate places

(inertia causes an immediate differential pressure). When returning to level flight from large angles of bank, the IVSI will initially show a climb. If the turn is maintained it will stabilise to zero, then indicate a descent on rollout. Thus, IVSIs should not be relied upon while initiating or ending turns at bank angles of more than about 40°.

THE COMPASS　　　022 03/061 02

The Earth has its own magnetic field, with lines of force that are more or less parallel with the curvature of the Earth, but increasing their angle towards the Poles until they move vertically downwards in a circle surrounding the true pole.

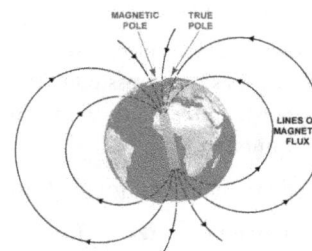

Although the origin of the Earth's magnetic field is not known, its blue pole was near the North pole (it is now heading from Canada down the 0° meridian, according to the European Space Agency's SWARM satellites) where the direction of the magnetic force points straight down to the Earth's surface. In fact, the geographic North Pole is magnetically a South Pole, and *vice versa*, which is why the North end of a compass needle points to it.

A Direct Reading Magnetic Compass (DRMC) has a pivoted magnet that is free to align itself with the horizontal component of the Earth's magnetic field.

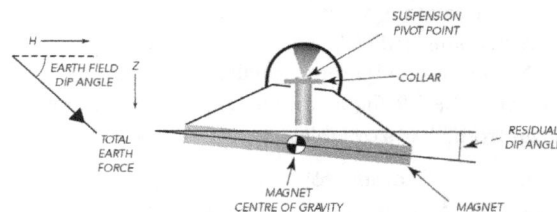

It must have certain properties to do this, namely:

- **Horizontality**. The needle must dip as little as possible, so the centre of gravity is made to lie below the pivot point, with pendulous magnets, that oppose the vertical component of the Earth's magnetic force (Z). Although there is still some dip, if it is less than 3° at mid-latitudes, it is OK.

- **Sensitivity**. This can be improved by increasing the length and/or the pole strength of the magnet. However, multiple magnets will do just as well, and they can also be employed as the weights under the pivot point mentioned above. Pole strength can be increased by using special alloys. In addition, you could use a jewelled pivot to reduce friction, and a

capt.gs

suspension fluid which both lubricates it and reduces the effective weight of the whole assembly. Modern compasses are sensitive, down to 0.01 gauss, but even that gives excessive hunting (in fact, you need gyro assistance when the magnetic field is below about 0.06 gauss).

- **Aperiodicity**. The ability to settle quickly after a disturbance, without overshooting or oscillating, which is helped by the (transparent) suspension liquid and a wire spider assembly. The two magnets above are also useful here, as they keep the mass of the assembly near the pivot, reducing inertia. Light alloys reduce inertia even more.

Being magnetic, the compass will be affected by all the fields generated by the aircraft itself, causing a phenomenon called *Deviation*, which is discussed under *The Compass Swing*, below. To try and eliminate errors, particularly magnetic dip, a remote indicating gyrocompass may be used, which is slaved to a DGI (discussed later). The master unit is mounted near the rear of the aircraft, so it is removed from as much influence as possible (hence the term *remote*). It contains a gyroscope under the influence of a magnetic element.

The usage limits of a magnetic compass lie between 73°N and 60°S, so the **North reference for an EFIS system** would be magnetic North between 73°N and 65°S and True North above these latitudes. A magnetic compass is most effective about midway between the Poles.

E2B

A typical E2B direct indicating *standby* compass, as used in most aircraft today, consists of a floating inverted bowl suspended on a pedestal in silicone fluid, for damping (the transparent liquid also increases sensitivity and aperiodicity). Silicon is used because it doesn't interfere with the Diakon used to make the bowl, and temperature/viscosity changes are small. The bearings are marked on the outside of the bowl, and there are two parallel magnetised needles inside, for correcting coefficients B and C only, suspended under the pivot point. Here is what the insides look like:

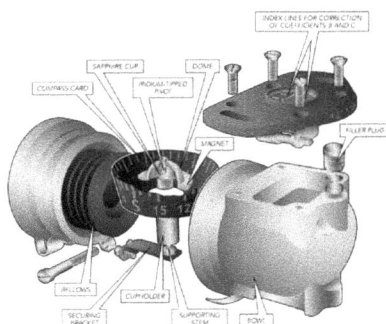

Dip

As the compass needle tries to follow the Earth's lines of force, it dips near the Poles, to where it is vertical (and unreadable), due to the vertical component of the Earth's magnetic force, which is called Z (in UK, the dip angle is around 67°). The bit we are interested in is H, the directive component, which is zero at the poles. At the Equator, there is no dip, so H is maximum, but as soon as you move away, the compass's Centre of Gravity becomes misaligned with its pivot point, and will move towards the Equator, or away from the nearer Pole.

H is about the same at magnetic latitudes 50°N and S, but the formula used to calculate the dip angle is:

$$\text{Dip} = \text{Cos}^{-1} \frac{H}{T}$$

Dip should obviously be minimised as much as possible, and is the reason why true tracks and headings are flown in Polar areas - the North and South magnetic Poles are the only places on the Earth where a freely suspended magnetic compass will stand vertical. On Northern routes, the dip effect causes a compass to turn much slower than you are used to in lower latitudes.

Magnetic dip is the angle between the horizontal and vertical forces acting on a compass needle toward the nearer pole.

An *aclinic line* is a line representing points of zero magnetic dip. An *isoclinal line* connects points of equal dip.

As the magnetic pole and lines of force do not coincide with either the true poles or lines of longitude, there is a way of accounting for any magnetic variation, discussed below. Unfortunately, although the C of G's position below the suspension point assists with minimising Z (and dip), it also gives rise to errors. Before you start relying on the compass (either to navigate or align your DGI), make sure you are in steady, level flight. Also, make turns gently, because the swirling fluid will keep the compass moving afterwards.

ACCELERATION ERRORS

These are caused by inertia on East-West headings. Because the C of G of the compass is under the pivot point, accelerating makes the bulk of the compass lag behind the machine. If you were just going N-S, all you would get is extra dip but, because you are going East or West, the displaced C of G, not being vertically in line with the pivot point, creates a couple that makes the compass turn in the direction of the acceleration (clockwise when heading East) to read less than 90° during the turn. A deceleration has the opposite effect.

Acceleration errors are maximum on East/West headings and near the magnetic Poles, and nil on North/South headings, and at the Equator. The term here is ANDS - *Accelerate North, Decelerate South*, or SAND in the Southern

Hemisphere. In the Northern Hemisphere flying East, if you accelerate, the needle deflects to the nearest Pole (North, for an easterly deviation) and South when you decelerate so, if you take off on runway 45 in the Northern hemisphere, the compass will read below 045°.

- During deceleration after landing on runway 18 (a Southerly direction), a compass in the Northern hemisphere would indicate no apparent turn.

- During deceleration after a landing in an Easterly direction, a magnetic compass in the Northern hemisphere indicates an apparent turn South.

- During deceleration after a landing in a Westerly direction, a magnetic compass in the Southern hemisphere indicates an apparent turn North.

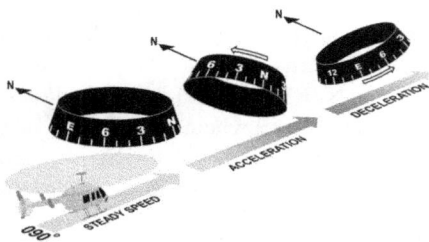

TURNING ERRORS

These are the main cause of error in a DRMC.

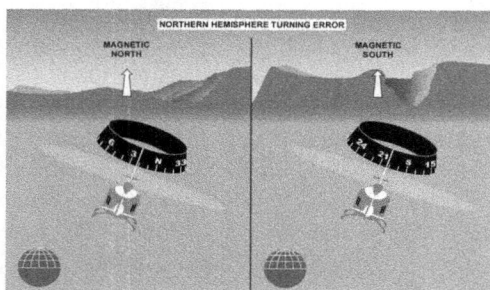

A Mr Keith Lucas discovered that a simple compass under-estimates turns on Northerly headings, and over-estimates them on Southerly ones in the Northern hemisphere (UNOS, and ONUS in the South). This happens because you are banking and the compass tries to follow the lines of dip, with a little help from liquid swirl. To put it another way, to eliminate the hemispheres from the equation, during turns through the *nearest* Pole (within 35°), the compass is sluggish, so you need to roll out early. During turns through the *furthest* Pole, it will be lively, so roll out late. The errors are maximum (30°) at the Poles and decrease by 10° towards East and West, where they are nil, so the lead/lag required is approximately equal to the latitude. Turning errors can have two elements, both of which work in the same sense:

- **Magnetic**, which depends on the angle of bank. In a turn from North to East, for example, the North-seeking end will move down towards Earth, so its readings will decrease and a turn in the opposite direction will be indicated. The more the bank, the more the error, so it is more apparent with a fast aircraft for the same rate of turn.

Turning error actually depends on the tangent of the angle of dip multiplied by the cosine of the heading and the angle of bank. It is nil on E-W headings because the cosine is nil. For a 5° angle of bank, the error will be in the order of 30°.

As an example, when flying South, you decide to make a right turn and fly due North. As soon as you start the turn, the compass will indicate a turn of around 30°, even though the nose has hardly moved - an extra fast turn is shown in the direction of the bank. It will then slow down so that the reading is approximately correct on passing through West, then it will lag as you approach North, so you roll out early, anticipating by the number of degrees of your latitude, plus an allowance for the rollout.

- **Dynamic**, which depends on speed and the rate of turn. In a flat turn, the dip makes the C of G of the compass move toward the Equator and it moves to the outside of the turn, producing a clockwise movement as above.

A rough calculation as to how much to overshoot or anticipate by when turning to the North or South comes from this formula:

$$\frac{Bank\ Angle\ +\ Latitude}{2}$$

So, to turn right on to a southerly heading with 20° bank at 20°N, you stop on an approximate heading of 200°.

In practice, just overshoot or undershoot by an amount equal to the latitude, regardless of the bank angle.

In real life, you would simply do a timed turn at 3° per second - such calculations would have a low priority on a dark rainy night.

Direction

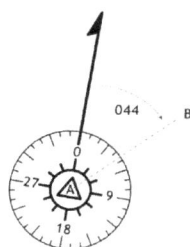

Direction (for us) is the position of one point relative to another, regardless of distance between them, measured in an angular fashion from the observer's meridian with reference to True, Magnetic or Grid North, using up to 360 numerical degrees*.

*The complete circle of direction (or *compass rose*) is split into 360 *degrees*, which are split into 60 *minutes* and 60 *seconds*, so the complete expression of an angle is in degrees, minutes and seconds - 30° 45' 53". North is 0°, so, going round the clock, East is 90°, South is 180° and West is 270° (the *cardinal* directions. NE, SE, SW & NW are intercardinal).

A *bearing* is a direction obtained by observation. It is the horizontal clockwise angle from a North baseline, or the angle between whichever North you use and any line between two points, such as that between A and B in the diagram above. The bearing is 044°, and the opposite is the *reciprocal*, found by adding or subtracting 180°, or 224°. Because you go clockwise, and the largest number is 360°, 355° is less than 010°.

STOP This is not the same as the *relative bearing* from your aircraft, which is measured from the longitudinal axis!

- **True North** is a line from any point on the Earth's surface to the North Pole (i.e. up, towards the top of the Earth), along the local meridian. Modern navigation systems such as INS/IRS output True North and their readings are changed to magnetic according to a lookup table.

- **Magnetic North** is the direction to the North *magnetic* pole, as shown by the North-seeking needle of a magnetic compass. Its usual symbol is a line ending with half an arrowhead. It was discovered by Soviet explorers to be the rim of a magnetic circle 1,000 miles in circumference, around 600 miles from the True Pole, approximately in Northern Canada. It moves by 1° every 5 years.

- **Grid North** is a line established with vertical grid lines drawn on a map, explained later. It may be symbolised with the letters *GN* or *y*

All meridians run North to South.

MAGNETIC BEARINGS

The North *Magnetic* Pole was discovered by Soviet explorers to be the rim of a magnetic circle 1,000 miles in circumference, around 600 miles from the True Pole. Both magnetic Poles move slowly around their respective True Poles, over a period of around 960 years. The North magnetic pole and various lines of force described below change their positions to the West.

That there is a True and a Magnetic North indicates that a compass will not point towards True North, since it relies on magnetism for its operation, and the two Norths (or Souths) do not coincide at their respective Poles. This is because the Earth generates its own magnetism, which may be varied by local deposits of metals under the ground, for example, which bend the magnetic flux lines. The way to Magnetic North will therefore vary across the ground from place to place, and a freely suspended compass will turn to the direction of the *local* magnetic field (the *Horizontal Component* is toward Magnetic North). As well, the lines of force will be vertical near the poles.

VARIATION

To find the direction of the geographical Pole, or True North, you have to apply a correction called variation, which is the angle between the magnetic and true meridians (that is, variation is the correction that must be applied to magnetic headings or courses (at the same place) to make them true. It is technically called *declination*. If the magnetic meridian is to the right of the true one, variation is Easterly and has a plus (+) sign (think of what it makes the compass rose do). If it is left, it is Westerly and has a minus (-) sign So, -8 is really 8W. The **Magnetic Track Angle** (MTA) is the direction of the path of an aircraft across the Earth's surface against *Magnetic North*. The phrase to remember is *Variation East, Magnetic Least, Variation West, Magnetic Best so*, if the variation on your map is, say, 21° West, the final result should be 21° *more* than the true track found when you drew your line.

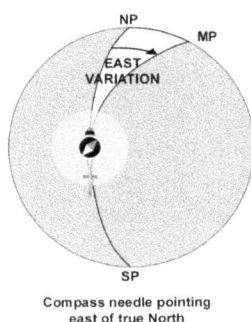

Compass needle pointing east of true North

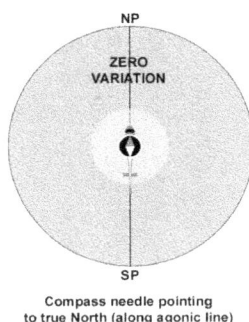

Compass needle pointing to true North (along agonic line)

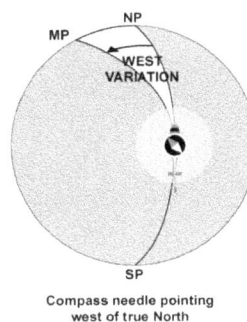

Compass needle pointing west of true North

- If you travel over many variations, use an average about every 200 miles.

- Variation on a VOR bearing is applied *at the station*, and on an ADF *at the aircraft*.

STOP Magnetic information in a Flight Management System is stored in *each IRS memory* - it is applied to the true calculated heading.

Variation can change temporarily from sunspot activity or magnetic storms. This is more of a problem in the Arctic or Antarctic areas, where the change can be ±5° for an hour or more. On a map, or chart, which would be drawn initially for True North, there is a dotted line called an *isogonal* that represents the local magnetic variation to be applied to any direction you wish to plan a flight on.

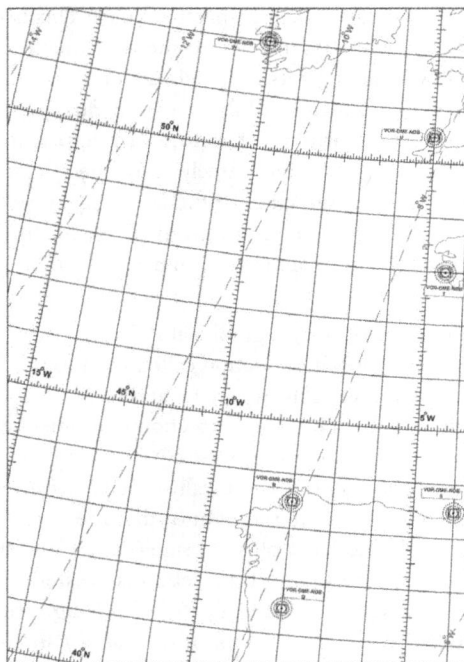

The charted values of magnetic variation normally change annually due to magnetic pole movement, causing values at all locations to increase or decrease. When plotted, isogonals are accurate worldwide to ±2°. They converge on both poles, geographic and magnetic.

An *agonic line* exists where magnetic variation is zero, or where the True and Magnetic meridians are parallel. There's one near Frankfurt, running North/South.

The compass cannot be corrected for variation.

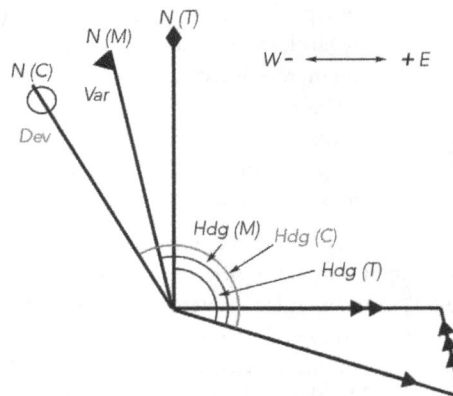

DEVIATION

Errors in the compass, plus an aircraft's own magnetism, from large amounts of metal and electrical currents, and any residual magnetism from hammering, etc. during manufacture, make the compass deflect from Magnetic North. This is deviation, which is unique to an aircraft, or even a compass position. It is applied to the compass heading to get the magnetic heading, and *vice versa.*

The net result of an aircraft's magnetic forces is represented by a dot somewhere behind the wings or rotor head. On Northerly headings, the dot lies behind the South part of the needle and merely concentrates the magnetic force. On Easterly headings, however, the dot is West of the South part of the needle and causes an Easterly deviation, and *vice versa.* It is proportional to Z and inversely proportional to H.

Deviation is the difference between a heading measured from the magnetic meridian and the same heading measured by a compass, at the same place. It is defined by the number of degrees which must be added (algebraically) to the observed reading to get the magnetic reading. Two aircraft flying in formation would have slightly different headings due to their deviations.

When deviation is West, compass North is to the West of magnetic North. When deviation is East, compass North is to the East of magnetic North. The phrase here is *Deviation West, Compass Best, Deviation East, Compass Least,* similar to Variation. This means that if the compass is reading 005° when it should be reading 360°, the deviation is 5° West, or -5°, as it must be "added" to the observed reading to get the proper one. If it is reading 346°, the deviation is 14° East, or +14°.

Thus, positive deviations deflect the compass needle to the right, and will have a plus sign even though the heading reads less. Negative deviations deflect the needle to the left and have a minus sign, although the heading increases. The key is to realise that they are based on what the deviation does to the heading on the compass rose.

When an aircraft is moved to a lower magnetic latitude, the value of deviation will decrease because the horizontal component of the terrestrial field is stronger.

Deviation varies with the heading and its values are displayed on a correction card next to the compass (they should not exceed 1° after correction). The values are obtained after a *compass swing*, a complex procedure normally done by an engineer, described soon.

For	Steer
000	001
045	043
090	089
135	133
180	184
225	223
270	269
315	316

Allowing for deviation is called *compensation*. So:

```
HDG(T) ± VAR ± DEV = HDG (C)
```

EXAMPLES

1. With a compass heading of 030°, deviation of 3°W and variation of 8°E, what is the true heading?

C	D	M	V	T
030	3W	027	8E	035

The Compass Swing

The magnetic compass is incompatible with aircraft, if only because it needs to be placed where it can be seen, which is typically in the middle of any stray magnetism.

The magnetic compass is incompatible with aircraft, if only because it needs to be placed where it can be seen, which is typically in the middle of any stray magnetism.

A compass swing allows you to find out by how much a compass reads differently from the proper figures on any heading, then make corrections that cancel out as many deviations as possible. In other words, the idea is to measure the angle between Magnetic and Compass North.

Airfields have clear areas in which this can be done. The aircraft is taxied there and everything electrical that would be used in flight turned on. Then the aircraft compass is compared against a landing compass on several headings by an engineer standing out in the rain (you need to find the errors on the cardinal and quadrantal points, so the aircraft is placed on each one in turn). The deviations are reduced by adjusting the magnets inside the compass and a calibration swing is done to see what deviations or residuals are left. Those figures are written on the deviation card. A compass swing should be done:

- on installation of the compass in the first place.

- as per maintenance schedules.

- whenever there is any doubt about accuracy.

- after a shock to the airframe or a lightning strike.

- if the aircraft has been left standing on the same heading for some time or has been moved to a significantly different latitude.

- when major components or electrical installations change.

Aircraft have built-in magnetism, whose influence on a compass can be classified broadly into 3 components, *hard iron*, *soft iron* and *electrical*. You can sum the individual effects and replace them with a single equivalent source.

HARD IRON

This is a more or less permanent effect that arises because the aircraft will have been on a particular heading* at a particular latitude for some time (more then three weeks or so) when it was being made, and will have absorbed some of the Earth's magnetism at that point. As such, it is the controlling factor in deviation. The effect is increased by hammering, and it will weaken when the machine starts flying, but some permanent magnetism will always remain. It is therefore unlikely to change.

There are vertical and horizontal effects, which are corrected with magnets. The field caused by such permanent magnetism is visualised as three components at the compass position:

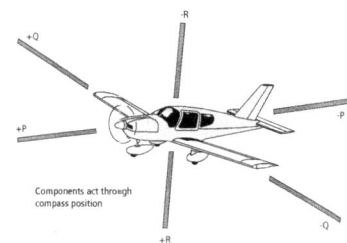

Components act through compass position

- **P** - fore and aft. It is minus if it pulls the red end of the compass needle to the rear (blue at the back), and plus if it pulls it to the front (blue at the front).

- **Q** - left to right (athwartships). Plus if it pulls the red end to starboard (blue starboard), minus if it pulls to port (blue to port).

- **R** - Up and down. Plus if it pulls the red end down (blue to the bottom), and minus if it pulls upwards (blue to the top). In level flight, it has no effect on the compass. Once it comes out of the vertical, however, the horizontal vector affects P and Q. When nose-up, for example, R will be acting forward, acting like P, so its maxima will be E-W (like Q when banking). The amount of the deviation depends on the value of R, and the angle between the longitudinal and horizontal axes. In practice, it is small enough to be ignored.

*P and Q only. If you built an aircraft at the magnetic Equator, where the Earth's lines of force are horizontal, you would get a fair amount of P and Q, and no R. If you built it facing SE in the Northern Hemisphere, you would get +PQR. R is always positive if the machine is built in the Northern Hemisphere, and negative otherwise.

The capital letters represent hard iron effects. Small letters are used for soft iron effects, described below.

P is zero when facing North, but will remain attracted to North as a 360° turn is started and cause a deviation that depends on the component's polarity. It will be maximum when facing East, zero again at South, maximum again at West (in the opposite direction) and zero at North, so it is a sine relationship with the aircraft's heading. The maximum deviation from P is called *Coefficient B*, which is expressed as an angle. Coefficients are discussed overleaf. Component Q's maxima are on North and South, and vary as the cosine of the aircraft heading. The maximum deviation is resolved with Coefficient C.

In summary, hard iron magnetism is permanent, and does not change with latitude, but the deviation caused by it increases with latitude because the H force is weaker, and the compass magnets are more easily deflected.

SOFT IRON

This is a temporary influence that only appears when the metal in the aircraft is affected by the Earth's magnetic field and, to a lesser extent, electrical systems (i.e. induced magnetism). That is, induced magnetism is from ferrous metals that are not permanently magnetised. The effect of soft iron depends on the heading and attitude of the aircraft, and its geographical position. As your heading changes, so does the soft iron magnetism.

As your heading changes, so does the soft iron magnetism.

Soft iron has a vertical element that is stronger in high latitudes because H is reduced. The horizontal element is also split further into X and Y to match the longitudinal and lateral axes of the aircraft.

Soft iron magnetism is visualised as coming from 9 soft iron rods near the compass that are affected by the Earth's magnetic field. The rods have length, but no thickness, and are *imaginary* - that is, they are simply a mathematical device that explains certain effects. You cannot use "bar magnets" as with hard iron magnetism, because of confusion as to which way the fields go in turns.

The rods are labelled with small letters (*a* - *k*) and are related to the XYZ components mentioned above like this: aX, bY, cZ, dX, eY, fZ, gX, hY and kZ.

The important ones are:

- cZ - fore and aft
- fZ - athwartships
- kZ - Vertical axes

cZ and fZ act like P and Q because they do not change polarity with heading. As Z acts vertically, it does not affect directional properties, and its sign will only change if the aircraft moved to the other magnetic hemisphere.

ELECTRICAL

Current flowing through a conductor produces a magnetic field that can deflect a compass needle. There can also be effects from lightning strikes.

COEFFICIENTS

Deviations from the components of hard and soft iron can be resolved into:

- **Coefficient A**, which is constant on all headings, and is found by dividing the sum of the deviations on the cardinal and intercardinal points by 8, so it is an average. It is caused by asymmetric soft iron around the compass, and is similar to a deviation caused by the lubber line being out of alignment. As the two are hard to tell apart, it is simplest just to move the compass.

  Apparent A (as opposed to Real A from soft iron) may be caused by an error in the magnetic bearing of an object used for swinging. Both are allowed for by rotating the compass by the result.

Aircraft	L/C	Result
000	352	+8
045	040	+5
090	094	-4
135	130	+5
180	172	+8
225	226	-1
270	273	-3
315	316	-1

  For example, the sum of the numbers in the right hand column is 17. Divided by 8, this gives a correction of 2° to be applied to all headings (if the aircraft is headed North and the compass reads 5°, the error deviation is classed as -5°, meaning that the aircraft compass is under-reading and 5° must be subtracted to make it correct).

- **Coefficient B** is like a **fore-and-aft** magnet and is used to resolve deviations from P + cZ. It produces maximum values on East and West (zero on N-S), varying as the **sine** of the heading. It is the result of dividing E - W by 2.

- **Coefficient C** is like an **athwartships** magnet, with maximum values on North and South, varying as the **cosine** of the heading. It is used to resolve deviations from Q + cZ and is the result of dividing N - S by 2.

- **Coefficient D** is for soft iron on quadrantals*.

- **Coefficient E** is for soft iron on cardinal points*.

capt.gs

*D & E are not particularly important. Put another way, dealing with A, B and C is enough trouble so we leave them alone. D is not compensated for anyway as it is in the vertical plane.

- Residuals should not exceed 1° for a gyromagnetic compass and 3° for a direct reader.

- Combined changes (say from multiple electrical items) should not exceed 2°

- Deviations in level flight should not exceed 10°

- The maximum limits are ±3° for a gyromagnetic compass and ±15° for a direct reader.

Errors from B and C are corrected before those from Coefficient A (in fact, C is done first), and are minimised by equal and opposite effects to those from the aircraft.

The E2B uses *scissor magnets*, and electromagnets are used in gyro compasses.

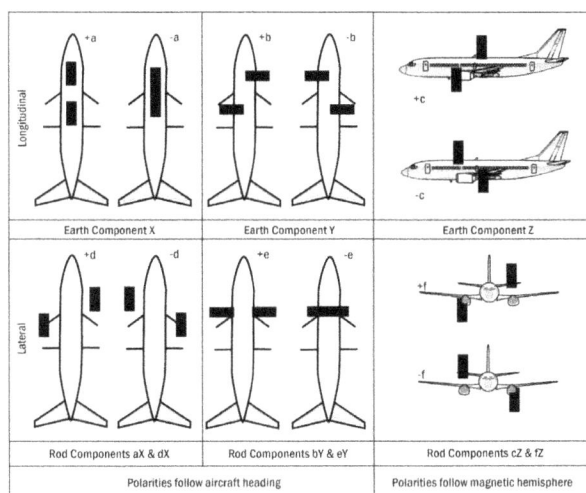

GYROSCOPES

Gyros are used in aircraft to establish three reference planes, namely Pitch, Roll and Yaw but, as they only have two reference rings (or gimbals - see *Types Of Gyroscope*, below), we need more than one to get the information we need. In fact, three instruments are usually run by gyroscopes, the *Attitude Indicator* (artificial horizon), *Directional Gyroscopic Indicator* (DGI) and *Turn Indicator or Coordinator*. The first two are typically suction-powered and the last by electricity, but many are now all electric.

Gyros (and accelerometers) are also called *inertial sensors* because they use resistance to changes in momentum to sense angular (gyro) and linear motion (accelerometer).

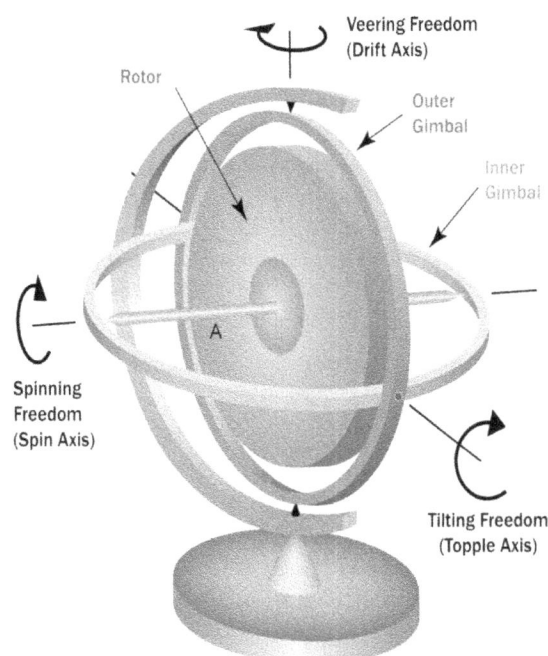

The Earth itself is a gyroscope. Around the Equator it spins at around 1,000 knots, as opposed to the more typical 250 knots for man-made gyroscopes. As such, it is able to maintain its present position in space to within 1° of the North Star. The problem for us is that we need the gyros to maintain a position with reference to the Earth, hence the various correction mechanisms, described later.

A gyroscope is a heavy rotating mass on a vertical or horizontal axis*, suspended in inner and outer *gimbals* which are in *frames*. Its operation depends on the resistance to deflection of a spinning wheel or disc, and only its Centre of Gravity remains fixed in space. The gyro is free to turn in any direction around it.

*A gyroscope's axis of rotation defines its orientation. A vertical gyro has its axis in *Earth Vertical* (as opposed to aircraft vertical) and a horizontal gyro is in *Earth Horizontal*, but more properly aligned with North.

You need a gimbal for each axis to be measured, so an artificial horizon has 2, because it measures pitch and roll.

Tip: During startup checks, pull and hold any erection or caging knobs *before* turning the power on, as the parts inside can clash against each other as they spin up (just one of those little things a pilot can do to save long-term maintenance costs).

Also, don't move the aircraft after flight until all the gyros have stopped running (takes about 15 minutes), otherwise they will go unserviceable more often. This particularly applies to autopilot equipped machines.

Rigidity

The spinning allows the gyro to maintain its own position in space, regardless of whatever it is attached to is doing. In other words, it resists attempts to alter its position. If you attached one to a camera in an aircraft, it could be bumping around all over the place due to wind or pilot input, and the camera would not move from where the operator put it. The same applies with the instruments mentioned above, as we shall see shortly. In fact, the gyro does not move, but the Earth moving around the gyro gives you that impression. The magnitude of this apparent movement depends on your latitude or, rather, the sine (drift) or cosine (topple) of your latitude.

Rigidity can be increased with:

- faster spin speeds
- increasing the gyro's peripheral mass
- increasing the gyro's radius

The greater the rigidity, the more force will be required to move the spinning gyro, which is an example of the *Law of Conservation of Angular Momentum*.

Precession & Wander

Any movement of the gyro's spin axis from its initial alignment is called *precession*. A force applied to a gyroscope's spinning mass is felt 90° away from where it is applied, in the direction of rotation. Put another way, pressure applied to the vertical axis is felt around the horizontal axis, and vice versa.

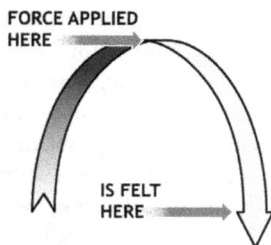

A mundane example comes from riding a bicycle - when you apply a force to turn one way or another, it is done at the top of the wheels, but the turning movement appears 90° later, hence the turn. More technically, precession is the *angular change in the plane of rotation under the influence of an applied force*. It is not wanted in some instruments, such as directional gyros.

The rate of precession depends on:

- the strength and direction of the applied force
- the rotor's moment of inertia (degree of rigidity)
- the rotor's angular velocity

WANDER

When a gyro moves from a preset position because of precession, it is said to wander.

The gyro is *drifting* when the axis wanders *horizontally*, and *toppling* when it wanders *vertically* (the term *topple* also refers to the tumbling that occurs when a gyro reaches a limit stop and a rapid precession occurs around a misaligned axis). Thus, a gyro with only a vertical axis cannot drift. Both are affected by real and apparent wander.

This is covered under *DGI*, where it is most relevant.

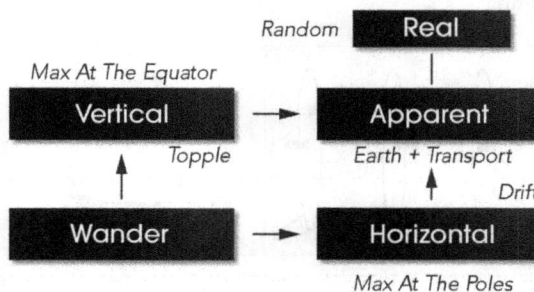

Drift occurs at 15° per hour multiplied by the *sine* of the latitude. Topple occurs at 15° per hour multiplied by the *cosine* of the latitude.

Types Of Gyroscope

The conventional gyro uses the principle of stored mechanical energy (inertia).

3 PLANES OF FREEDOM

Gyros with 3 planes of freedom have 2 gimbals and total freedom of movement around 3 axes. There are 3 types:

- **Space Gyro**. Free to move in all directions with reference to space because it has **3 gimbal rings with 3 planes of freedom**. Theoretical.
- **Tied Gyro**. As above, with the spin axis tied down in one local plane. 2 *degrees* of freedom (see below). An example is the DGI, where the spin axis is tied to the yawing plane.
- **Earth Gyro**. As above, but the spin axis is tied to *Earth vertical* by gravity, e.g. the artificial horizon.

2 PLANES OF FREEDOM

These show a rate of movement rather than a position:

- **Rate Gyro**. One gimbal, free to move around 2 axes (including the spin axis). Designed to show the rate of movement about the axis at right angles to the two free axes, as used in the turn and slip indicator, or the turn coordinator.

- **Rate Integrating Gyro**. These are used in Inertial Navigation Systems, and their gimbals are restrained by the viscosity of a fluid, as opposed to the springs that are used by rate gyros. The fluid's viscosity is affected by temperature, so a warm-up period is required. It is so dense that the weight of the rotor and can is effectively zero. As the aircraft turns about the sensitive axis, the precession is used to generate an error signal, the magnitude of which signifies the rate at which the aircraft is turning about the axis.

DEGREES OF FREEDOM (GIMBALS)

A French method of classifying gyroscopes uses the numbers of axes *not* including the spin axis, so a gyro with 3 *planes* of freedom has 2 *degrees* of freedom. A degree of freedom is the ability to move around an axis, so we count the number of gimbals. The spin axis cannot precess, but each gimbal allows it to do so in one other direction.

An airborne instrument, with a gyro that has 2 degrees of freedom and a horizontal spin axis could be a DGI.

- *Spinning* freedom is about an axis perpendicular through the centre

- *Tilting* freedom is about a horizontal axis at right angles to the spin axis

- *Veering* freedom is about a vertical axis perpendicular to the spin and tilt axes

Degs	Gyro	Purpose
1°	Rate Rate Integrating	Turn Indicator Inertial Navigation
2°	Earth Tied	A/H DGI
3°	Space	Theoretical

Attitude gyros use rigidity in space for their operation, while rate gyros use precession.

Gimbal Lock

In a 3-gimbal system, two gimbals can end up in line, effectively removing one from the equation. A fourth gimbal (used with Inertial Navigation Systems) can keep the 2nd and 3rd gimbals at right angles to each other to prevent gimbal lock.

Power

As mentioned, air-driven gyroscopic instruments are made to spin through suction or pressure (heading and attitude indicator) or electricity (turn instruments) although many are now all electric (even then, there should be separate and independent power supplies. If there is only one, you need suction, too).

SUCTION

With suction, air is usually *sucked out* of the casing, to create a vacuum that will be indicated on a gauge in the cockpit. It is part of the checklist before flight to ensure you have enough for the instruments to work properly, typically 4-5 inches of mercury.

If it is reading low, the filters are blocked or equipment is worn, and the gyros will run too slowly. If the reading is too high, the gyros will run too fast (the rotation speed of an air driven gyro is usually between 9,000 - 12,000 RPM).

Vanes (small bucket-shapes) on the gyro mass catch the air movement and force it to go round at several thousand RPM. The rest of the vacuum system has a pump driven by the engine, a relief valve*, an air filter, and enough tubing for the connections. Older aircraft may have a venturi tube on the side to create the initial vacuum.

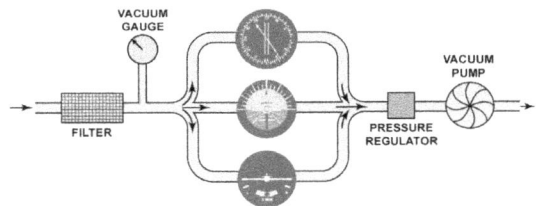

*Air-driven gyro rotors are prevented from spinning too fast by the vacuum relief valve, which is kept closed with a spring that is pre-adjusted for the required vacuum so that air pressure acting on the outside of the valve is balanced against spring tension. If the adjusted value is exceeded, the outside air pressure overcomes the spring, opening the valve to allow outside air to flow into the system until balance is restored.

A pressure-operated system is similar, but the inlet and outlet connections are reversed on each instrument

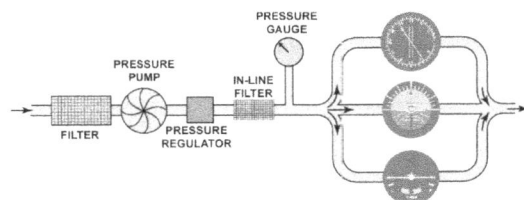

ELECTRICITY

At high altitudes, suction-driven gyros can lose rigidity because they cannot produce so much vacuum. They also require large amounts of plumbing. These can be resolved with electrical gyros, whose advantages include:

- Faster spin speed, therefore greater rigidity

- Spin speed is easier to initiate and maintain, as aircraft power is regulated, and you don't need other systems running first

- The container can be sealed to keep dirt out - suction driven instruments necessarily have a hole in them to let air in

- More stable operating temperature

- The ability to work at higher altitudes

- Acceleration errors are minimised because there is no heavy mass underneath the gyro (i.e. it is non-pendulous). Any there will be due to the mercury sloshing around.

The motor is usually a squirrel cage, using a power supply of 115v 400 Hz 3-phase AC in large aircraft, while smaller ones can have an inverter built in to produce 26 V (AC motors tend to be used in artificial horizons, while DC is used in turn and bank indicators). There must be some form of failure indication to show loss of power.

Fast erection involves giving the motors a higher error signal, which can be done in unaccelerated flight.

Ring Laser Gyros

These are used in inertial reference systems and use a partially silvered mirror (prismatic sensor) and 2 contra-rotating laser beams that go the opposite direction to each other in a precisely drilled tunnel round a triangular block of a vitro ceramic material* that does not expand or contract with temperature (it is very hard) - any change in length would produce the equivalent to real wander in a mechanical gyro (the mirror position or the discharge current can be altered to compensate). Noise from imperfections in mirrors is the same as random wander.

*The material used does not distort with age, which can degrade the accuracy and destroy the gas tight seal necessary to contain the helium and neon gases used in creating the laser. Two anodes and a common cathode create electrical discharges within the gases which cause the channels to act as gain tubes, producing the beams.

Put more precisely, the sustained oscillation is initially caused by the gas or plasma being ionised by the voltage, causing helium atoms to collide with, and transfer energy to, the neon atoms.

The servo mirror can move. The collecting mirror allows a small amount of light through so one beam can be flipped around by the prism and meet with the other one that is aimed directly at the detector, which determines any fringe pattern generated by interference when the beams are out of phase. They are in phase (coherent) when there is no acceleration. The counter-propagating waves normally beat together to set up a standing wave pattern inside the cavity. The optical path must be kept th a length that is a multiple of the lasing wavelength, that is, an exact number of wavelengths at the frequency for peak power.

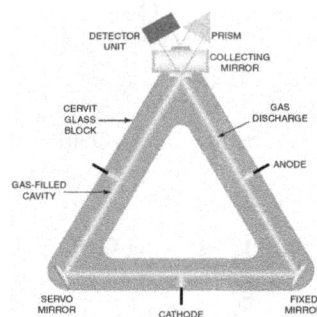

The resonant structure (the triangular block), is designed such that each beam will only resonate at one spot frequency. If the ring is stationary, the resonant frequency for both directions will be identical, as the path lengths are identical. When the beams combine at the detector they interfere with each other to form a fringe pattern of light bars at the photoelectric cells of the detector.

If the path length of the waves is altered artificially by movement, their frequencies change and so do their transit times. The light beam travelling in the same direction as the rotation must travel a slightly longer path while the opposite beam will travel over a shorter one.

There will be a change in the interference pattern, causing the light bars to move in a direction that depends on the direction of rotation of the RLG and the distance moved will depend on the rate of rotation. This output is converted to pulse signals that are representative of the rate and direction of rotation of the RLG.

Compared to conventional gyros, laser gyros are more accurate, and have a longer life cycle, as there are no moving parts (apart from the *dither motor* below) and therefore no friction. They are also very quick to align, smaller, use less power and do not suffer from precession.

LOCK IN

Picture: Ring laser gyros as used in an Inertial Unit:

At low input rates, the frequency differences become very near zero due to back scatter from one beam affecting the other. This makes them both synchronise.

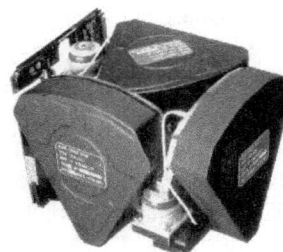

Dithering is the name of the technique, using a piezo-electric motor, that is used to counteract it. The entire apparatus is rotated clockwise and anti-clockwise about its axis at a rate convenient to the mechanical resonance of the system, ensuring that the angular velocity of the system is usually far from the lock-in threshold. Typical rates are 400 Hz, with a peak dither velocity of 1 arc-second per second.

ARTIFICIAL HORIZON

Otherwise known as the *attitude indicator*, or an *attitude and director indicator* (ADI) if it incorporates a flight director, this instrument represents the natural horizon and indicates the pitch and bank attitudes, that is, whether the nose is up or down, or the wings are level or not.

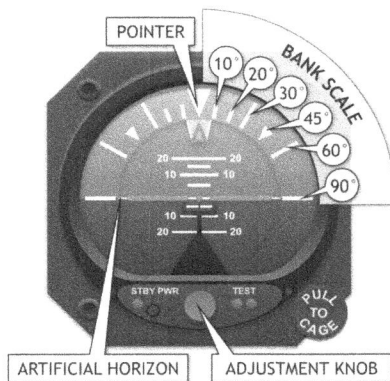

It does not necessarily show climb, descent, or turns.

Given that a gyro tries to keep its position in space, as you move around, it needs to be kept in line with the local vertical, so there is an erection mechanism, described below. The spin axis is *vertically mounted* (in line with Earth Vertical) so the instrument suffers from topple, in a cosine relationship. The housing (and aircraft) can rotate around it. The whole assembly is inside an *outer gimbal*, which is Earth Horizontal, with two degrees of freedom.

The instrument's C of G is below the suspension point, so it is nearly vertical when it is switched on, which reduces the erection time. In the suction-driven version, four *pendulous vanes* cover holes through which air tries to pass, but is blocked by the vanes as long as the instrument is vertical. When it is not vertical, the vanes, which are suspended from a pivot and kept vertical by gravity, open the hole by differing amounts to let more or less air through as required, to provide the correcting force.

In other words, the pendulous vane stays vertical*, but more of the hole is exposed as the instrument moves.

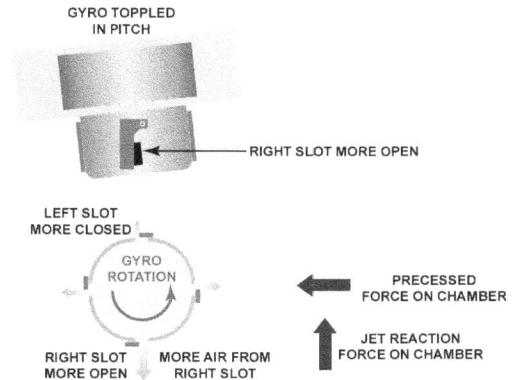

*To be picky, it is affected by centrifugal force, and will not be properly effective (see *Errors* below). This can be minimised with an offset for the vanes for a particular rate of bank (compensation tilt).

As it has a slow erection speed, and is relatively slow to operate, this system is not perfect in accelerated flight. Electrical systems are more responsive.

The aircraft symbol is attached to the casing and therefore the aircraft. The *horizon bar* (which stays in line with the Earth) is connected to the rear of the frame and to the housing with a *guide pin*, so when the nose pitches up, the outer gimbal comes off the horizontal. The movement is amplified by the beam bar and the guide pin is driven down - in a descent it goes up. Rolling rotates the instrument case.

Aircraft Pitched Nose Up

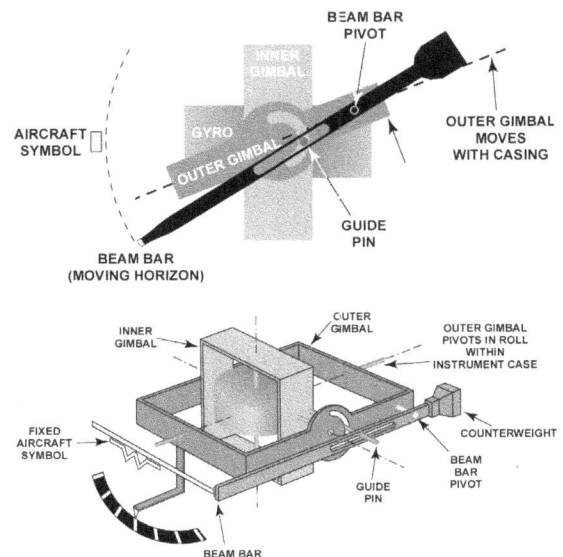

A standby artificial horizon must have its own power supply and its own gyro.

Errors

With all the rotating parts, there is bound to be friction, which will cause some errors in the readings. Others include *acceleration error*, during forward movement (as in a takeoff) which gives a false climb to the *right** - this is because of the pendulous mounting - the heavy bottom of the (suction) gyro suffers from inertia and creates an imbalance between misplaced centres of gravity (roll error) and closing one of the suction ports (pitch error) - the effect is similar to the compass. The resulting forces precess 90° away for false readings. Deceleration shows a false descent and roll to port.

When an aircraft has turned through 360° with a constant attitude and bank, both will be correct on a classic instrument. Having turned only 90°, you will observe too much nose-up and too little bank. At 180°, the nose will still be too high, but with a correct amount of bank. At 270°, too nose high, but with the bank too high. Centrifugal force created during a turn will also displace the mass of the instrument's heavy bottom, but modern designs minimise turning errors at low rates of turn.

*Electrical artificial horizons will show a climbing turn to the *left*, because they normally spin the opposite way.

Thus, an instrument showing a climb to either direction indicates *pitch* and *roll* errors. The pitch error is due to acceleration on the pendulous vanes, and the roll error comes from the inertia of the bottom-heavy housing.

Electrical Version

In an electrical artificial horizon, two *torque motors* are used, one parallel to the lateral axis, and one to the longitudinal axis. The laterally mounted one detects movement in roll, and a correction from the torque motor is applied to the pitch axis. Displacement in pitch is detected by the longitudinal switch which corrects around the roll axis.

The mercury switches that sense topple of the spin axis in the fore and aft plane and athwartships are on the inner gimbal. The torque motor associated with the fore and aft one is attached to the outer gimbal. It applies a torque about the roll axis, which is then precessed to act about the pitch axis. The torque motor associated with the athwartships mercury switch applies a force about the pitch axis, which is precessed to act about the roll axis.

The torque motors are squirrel-cage type laminated iron rotors mounted concentrically round a stator, with two windings - one provides a constant field and is called the *reference winding*, and the other is in two parts so it can be reversible, called the *control winding*.

Levelling switches are sealed glass tubes containing 3 electrodes (one at each end and one in the middle) and a small blob of mercury. An inert gas is also present to stop any arcing as the mercury comes into contact with the

electrodes. The glass tubes are set at right angles to each other on a switch block behind the gyro housing.

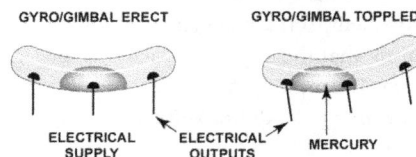

In the normal operating position, the mercury is in contact with the centre electrode, which is connected to the reference winding. If a displacement happens, the mercury makes contact with one of the side electrodes which completes a circuit to the relevant part of the control winding to apply the necessary torque correction.

In fact, the voltage to the reference winding is fed via a capacitor and, as we know, this will make the current lead the voltage by 90°. As there is no capacitance in the control winding, it lags the reference winding by 90°. The resulting magnetic field rotates the stator in the required direction, at the same time cutting the conductor in the squirrel-cage winding and inducing a further magnetic field that makes the rotor follow the stator field. This is immediately opposed because the rotor is fixed to the case, so a reactive torque is set up to cause the required amount of precession to correct the instrument.

In summary, an electrically driven artificial horizon has a greatly reduced amount of errors on takeoff because the gyro has greater rigidity, is less bottom heavy and it has a linear accelerometer cut-out switch.

Remote Vertical Gyro

As older artificial horizons must be small to fit into most instrument panels, there are practical limits to the size of the gyros inside them. A remote vertical gyro (actually three for redundancy) can be placed somewhere on the airframe that can take the size of the gyros and the information is fed to the cockpit over electrical cables.

The remote vertical gyro is electrically driven, spinning about a vertical axis. It has full freedom in roll and ±85° of freedom in pitch, within 1° of the vertical even during manoeuvres or severe turbulence.

Electrical pick-offs on the gimbals, measure the displacement of the aircraft around the rotor and supply their outputs to synchros within the attitude indicator . Reduction of turning and acceleration errors is made possible through rate switching gyros and longitudinal accelerometers which interrupt erection currents when the aircraft is subject to false gravity vectors.

The erection system is similar to that in the basic electrically driven artificial horizon, with two torque motors and two levels (similar to spirit levels), one for pitch and one for roll, which contain a special electrolytic fluid. When the gyro axis is vertical, the bubbles in the levels are centred and the electrolytic resistance at each end of the tubes is equal, so no current will flow to the torque motors. Should the axis of the rotor stray from the vertical, the bubble in one or both of the levels will be displaced, to cause an unequal electrolytic resistance within one or both of the levels. As a result, currents will flow to one or both of the torque motors, according to the displacement of the gyro spin axis. The mechanical output of the torque motor is applied to the relevant gimbal, and the resultant precession will erect the gyro, centralise the bubble and stop the flow of current.

The erection circuits provide fast erection for the first few minutes after power is applied, then at a slower rate to correct for small amounts of drift from friction or rotation of the Earth.

HEADING INDICATOR (DGI)

This is used to give a stable heading reference free from compass errors, although it has some of its own. It works in a similar way to the artificial horizon, except that the spin axis is *aircraft horizontal* in the *yawing plane*. That is, the spin axis is parallel to the surface of the Earth, so it can only turn in the horizontal plane and it will only be affected by drift.

The casing turns round a **horizontally tied gyro**, which has a compass card mounted on it, so the aircraft rotates around the compass card:

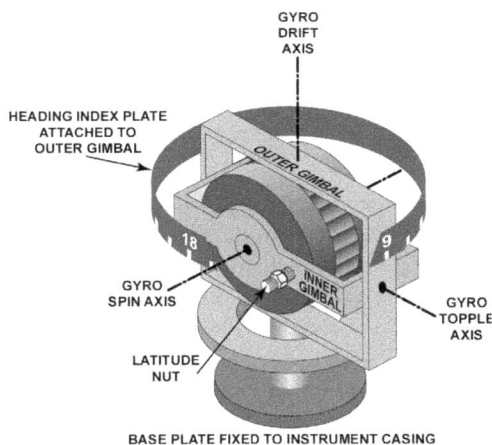

The instrument has **two degrees of freedom** with typical limits of 55° in pitch and roll. To help with re-erection after toppling, the mass of the gyro is spun at 10,000-12,000 RPM, with air jets from twin sources, very close to each other. When the gyro does not lie in the yawing plane, one jet (the drive component) will be pushing the gyro round, but the other (erection component) will strike the rim and cause a precession force at the top. This is

correcting for fine topple. The caging knob deals with gross topple.

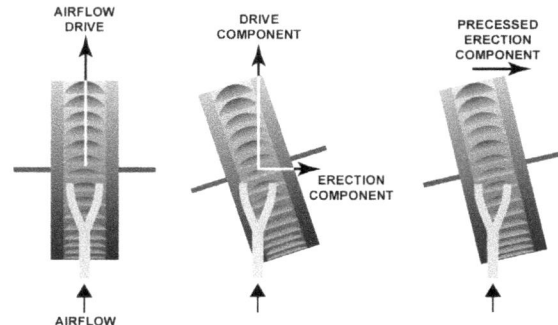

DGI indications are only valid for limited periods due to:

- rotation of the Earth.

- aircraft movement over the surface of the Earth.

- mechanical imperfections, plus low rotor speeds.

- gimbal system geometry, i.e. gimballing errors, which are small and transient inaccuracies that occur whenever the inner and outer gimbals are not at right angles to each other. This is particularly relevant when the spin axis is primarily horizontal, as with the DGI. Taking a descending turn as an example, the outer gimbal will be forced to rotate by a small amount about its own axis in order to maintain the spin axis horizontal. The amount of this rotation will be translated into a heading error for the duration of the manoeuvre. Gimballing error disappears after a turn is completed.

To make life easy, these are the reasons why the DGI is aligned with the compass every 15 minutes or so remembering, of course, to do it in level, unaccelerated flight, to avoid errors.

Wander

If you just sat in your aircraft (at the North Pole) and watched the DGI, you would see it change from its original setting at a rate of 15° per hour, all by itself, if you applied no compensation. This is because the gyro is trying to maintain its own position in space, and the Earth is moving. There are two main types of wander:

- **Real**, or mechanical (the main cause), which comes from friction in the bearings, power fluctuations and other imperfections, although this is less than 1° per hour in modern systems and may be considered negligible. However, it is unpredictable and can be measured only by checking your heading. This is sometimes called random wander as the effect is supposed to be random. A perfect gyro (in a question) has no

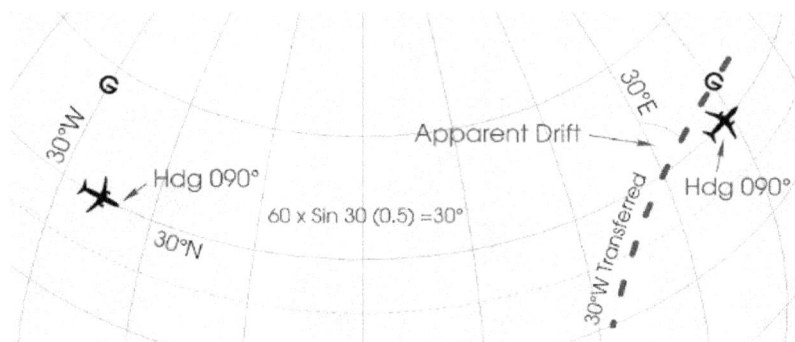

Apparent Drift

60 x Sin 30 (0.5) =30°

Hdg 090°   Hdg 090°

30°W   30°N   30°E   30°W Transferred

imperfections, and no random wander, so you need not account for it.

- **Apparent**, where the spin axis remains aligned to a point in space as the plane of reference changes, making the gyro *appear* to precess. It consists of:

  - **Earth Rate** (N-S), from the Earth's rotation. Although there is a vertical component, the horizontal component is meant when talking about this (assuming you are stationary). So, at the Poles, the gyro will appear to move at 15.04° per hour (in the horizontal plane) because that is the rate at which the Earth is spinning and orbiting round the Sun. The only time this won't happen is at the Equator (if the gyro's axis is aligned with a meridian and is parallel to the Earth's axis). Thus, it varies with the sine of the latitude, to the right in the Northern hemisphere and the left in the Southern hemisphere. The sign is negative in the Northern Hemisphere because the gyro under-reads as the Earth rotates. In the picture above, an aircraft that has its DGI aligned to True North at 30°W heads off in an Easterly direction. By the time it reaches 30°E, the spin axis of the DGI is to the right of True North, making it under-read. The reverse is true in the Southern hemisphere. You can see from the formula in the middle of the picture that the amount of drift can be calculated.

  At 60°N, the apparent drift rate of a free gyro is 13° per hour to the right, or anticlockwise (the sine of 15° is 0.87). At 45°N, it would be 10.5° and, at 15°N, 4° per hour.

  STOP Drift is multiplied by the sine of the latitude, and topple by the cosine of the latitude.

  Apparent drift is corrected with a latitude nut (below).

  - **Transport Wander** (E-W). Here, the spin axis appears to move because you are crossing meridians and convergency is added to the

mix, similar to the above. Here, flight to the West causes over-reading, and Eastward flight causes under-reading* (in the Northern hemisphere) so, if you held a steady heading of 090°, because the gyro is under-reading, you will be turning away to the *right* of Earth track and your *true heading* is *increasing*. This is not normally corrected for in light aircraft, but is minimised by resetting the gyro every 15 minutes or so.

*Eastward flight increases apparent drift because the gyro is rotating faster than the speed of the Earth, and Westward flight reduces it, so errors will be more than 15° per hour, and less, respectively. N/S travel will only be a problem as far as the latitude in the formula changes, so mean latitudes are used. A minor variation (**grid transport**) occurs when the great circle track curves away from a straight line track, and is proportional to the difference between convergence of the meridians as portrayed on the chart against how they should be on the Earth, and the rate at which you cross them.

LATITUDE NUT

The latitude nut (on the inner gimbal) introduces an equal and opposite precession force around the vertical axis to counteract apparent drift - usually for 45° of latitude when the device comes out of the box. In other words, a real wander is introduced to correct for fine drift. When wound outwards, the latitude nut exerts a greater force against the balance weight on the other side of the inner gimbal, where it is mounted. Assuming no other influence, going North of the preset latitude makes the DGI under-read and vice versa.

Watch out for aircraft flying in one hemisphere with their latitude nuts set for the *other* hemisphere. Use mean latitude for ER and TW where there is a North or South track component (**Note:** do not take mean latitude for a latitude nut - it only has one set value). Use the E or W component of groundspeed for TW calculations, taken from TAS and W/V.

TOTAL GYRO DRIFT

This is the sum of the Earth Rate + Transport Wander + Latitude Nut + Random (Real) Wander.

- The **Earth Rate** is:

    15° x sine latitude/hr

- **Transport Wander** is:

    ch long* x sine latitude/hr

    or:

    $$\frac{GS \times tan\ lat}{60}$$

- The **Latitude Nut** is:

    15° x sine of latitude setting

*change of longitude

The resulting *drift budget* is the drift rate, in degrees per hour. Multiply it by the time period. The signs for the Northern hemisphere are:

- *Earth Rate* (-)
- *Latitude Nut* (+)
- *Transport Wander* East (-) West (+)

Reverse them for the Southern Hemisphere. So, for a DI with a Latitude Nut set for 40°N at 240 kts groundspeed on a Westerly heading at 50°N, you would add +9.64, -11.49 and +4.77 together to get +2.92° per hour.

R	E(A)	L	T
0	-11.49	9.64	4.77

If you move to 30°S with a latitude nut set for 45°N, the rate would be 18.1° per hour, from:

    +15 x 0.5 = 7.5/hr

    +15 x 0.7 = 10.6

You may be given Real Drift (perfect gyros have no random wander). On the DGI, *gross topple* is corrected with the *caging knob*, which grabs the gimbals and holds the gyro in one position. You can also turn the knob to move the gyro about the yaw axis, which turns the compass card so you can realign the instrument with the compass.

EXAMPLE

1. What is the hourly wander rate at 49°N?

    -15 x 0.7547 = 11.32/hr

The minus sign before the 15 indicates the Northern hemisphere. If this were corrected by a latitude nut, the observed drift would be zero.

2. Flying from 60°N 010°E to 60°N 020°E over 1.5 hours in nil wind conditions, a perfect gyro compass with no latitude nut is aligned with the true North. What constant gyro heading should be followed on departure?

- (a) 66
- (b) 80
- (c) 76
- (d) 85

Only Apparent and Transport Wander need be calculated here. The former is -19.54 (NH) and the latter -8.66 (heading East). The total is -28.2 which, halved (as you are maintaining a constant gyro heading), is - 14 which, subtracted from 90 gives the answer 76.

The Gyromagnetic Compass

A direct-reading compass's indications get weaker near the Poles, are subject to short term inaccuracies in the shape of turning and acceleration errors, and can only be read in one position in the aircraft. Neither can it drive or send information to other instruments. The gyromagnetic compass tries to resolve these problems by stabilising (gyroscopically) a magnetic compass and providing electrical outputs to the instruments that need to be read by the crew, or systems like IRS or INS. It is continually sampled for errors and short- and long term corrections are sent to the compass and gyro. So a gyrocompass is a DGI that aligns itself. In an area with a weak magnetic flux, like the Poles, you have to disable the automatic slaving and use the instrument as a DGI.

The main components are:

- The **Gyroscope**, which provides short-term stability for azimuth reference. It will have 2 degrees of freedom and the input axis will be vertical (so the spin axis is horizontal).

- An **erection mechanism** to keep the axis horizontal.

- The **flux valve**, which is the detecting element for the Earth's magnetic field. It will be as far away from external magnetic influences as possible, say, in a tailboom or the rear of the fuselage and, if it ceases to provide reliable information, may generate a red HDG message on the HSI. It will provide a torque on the sensitive axis. Its output is fed to the stator in the slaved gyro control.....

- A slaving **torque motor** to make the gyro precess in azimuth at about 2° per minute in order to align the gyro with the Earth's magnetic field. A dot shows in a small window on the display when the gyro is being precessed in one direction and a cross shows when it is being precessed in the other. In normal operations, they should alternate quickly. There is a manual rapid precession system.

- The **Transmission and Display System** is simply the mechanism by which information is sent to the crew stations and instruments that need it. There is a feedback system to keep everything synchronised.

The most significant errors are:

- *Apparent & Real Wander*
- *Gimballing*
- *Mechanical Defects*
- *Low Rotor Speed*

A red flag labelled HDG indicates that the flux valve is not supplying reliable information.

THE FLUX VALVE

You cannot directly measure the Earth's magnetic flux, because its H component is steady, but you can produce your own flux that changes with H, then measure and interpret the voltage. This is done with a device that has three transformers at 120° to each other, with a curved horn on the end of each one to maximise reception.

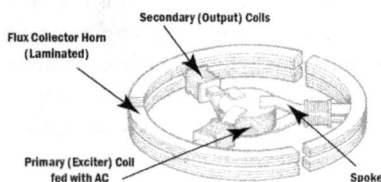

It is pendulously mounted, and free to swing up to 25° in pitch and roll, but is fixed to the aircraft in azimuth so it rotates with. As it dangles from a *Hooke's Joint* (the technical term is *pendulous*) it will swing within limits of around ±25°, to allow the aircraft to bank a little before it becomes inaccurate (it can switch itself off in a steep turn to avoid turning errors). The chamber that encloses the

Hooke's joint also contains a viscous fluid to dampen any unwanted movement. This is to capture as much of the Earth's H force as possible, rather than the Z force which will produce turning and acceleration errors (as the DGI part uses slow acting torquers, acceleration errors are barely noticeable). As the system *senses* rather than *seeks*, it is more sensitive.

Using three spokes ensures that we know which way is North (or South). They are made of two identical parallel permalloy* strips on top of each other, with insulation between them and the transformer windings around them in series, in opposite directions.

*Permalloy loses its magnetic influence once the power is gone or, rather, it has a low hysteresis factor. It also magnetises very quickly.

The two poles of the resulting electromagnet cancel each other out and, without other magnetic sources (i.e. from the Earth), the total flux in another winding that is wound round the whole assembly is zero, as would be found when that spoke is at 90° to the Earth's magnetic field and both strips are detecting the same constant component of H. The maximum influence is obtained when the spoke is in line with the Earth's magnetic field, and any in between vary as the cosine of the magnetic heading.

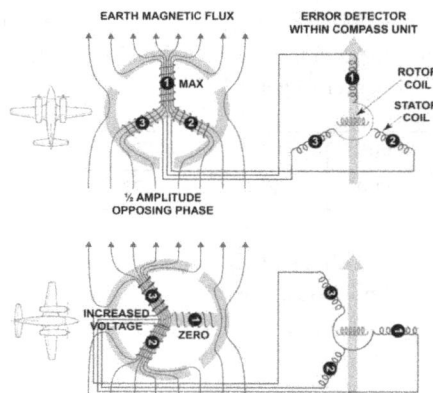

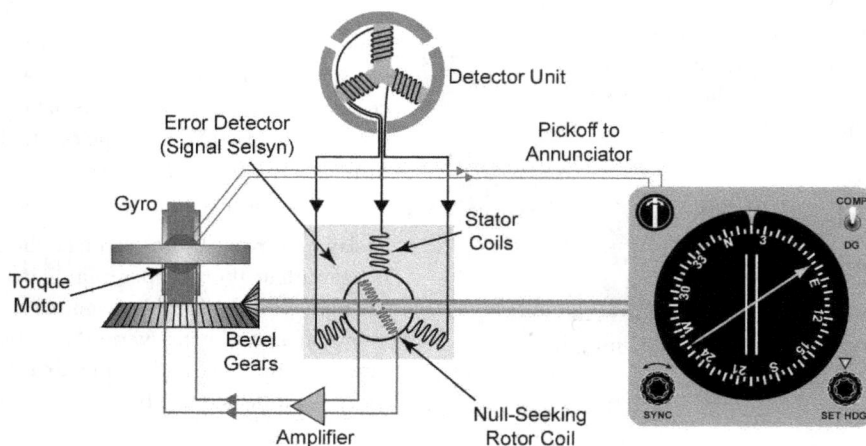

In the picture above, a different value of H is present in each spoke, due to the angle between it and Magnetic North. The size of the field in each spoke now needs to be measured and transmitted to the rest of the equipment.

An exciter coil is placed in the centre, at 90° to the spokes, and fed with 400 Hz single phase AC so that a reversing magnetic field is created through the primary coil round each spoke. As the pickoff coils are star connected to the stator winding of the signal Selsyn, the vector produced in the stator has a vector directly related to the direction of the Earth's magnetic field. When the AC reaches its peak, so much magnetism is produced that the spokes cannot deal with any from the Earth. In other words, ignoring any external magnetic influences, the cores would just saturate at the 90° and 270° phase points of the primary winding alternating current flow.

However, as the current reverses, the spokes become demagnetised, so current can be induced as the Earth's flux lines cut across them. As long as the aircraft is on a fixed heading, the field remains constant. When it turns, the field changes and a current is induced in the secondary coil. This varies the induction in each leg and the secondary pickoff coils produce a complex phased signal, part of which is more prone to saturation because the H element is working in the same sense. Where it is in the opposite sense, the magnetic peaks are simply reduced and can be measured.

More technically, adding magnetism from the Earth saturates a spoke before one of its AC peaks, and it won't die away for a similar period afterwards. The two fields no longer cancel each other out, and there is a blip of AC in the pickoff coil that varies with the Earth's magnetism. That is, when AC is pumped through a flux valve it produces a ripple at twice the frequency of the original current, so a sinusoidal voltage with a frequency of 800 Hz is obtained, with its amplitude directly in proportion with the Earth's magnetic field and the cosine of the magnetic heading. Thus, induction from the H component is greater in one permalloy strip than the other, over an extended AC angle, the fields will no longer cancel out, and H will attain twice its original value. The secondary coil has converted pulses of saturated magnetism to voltage.

Comparing the graphs below should provide some idea of what is happening.

In the centre picture, no external magnetic influence is evident at the flux valve, so both cores only just achieve saturation twice during each 360° cycle of the AC fed to the primary coil.

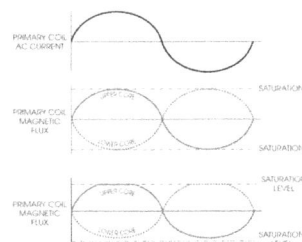

In the bottom picture, the Earth's own magnetic field applies a magnetic bias to the system, so one core will become totally saturated at 90° and the other at 270°. The different magnetic field strengths produce a current in the secondary winding.

The flux valve assembly rotates with the aircraft. It also dangles from a *Hooke's Joint* (the technical term is *pendulous*) so it will swing within limits of around ±25°, to allow the aircraft to bank a little before it becomes inaccurate (it can switch itself off in a steep turn to avoid turning errors). The chamber that encloses the Hooke's joint also contains a viscous fluid to dampen any unwanted movement. This is to capture as much of the Earth's H force as possible, rather than the Z force which will produce turning and acceleration errors (as the DGI part uses slow acting torquers, acceleration errors are barely noticeable).

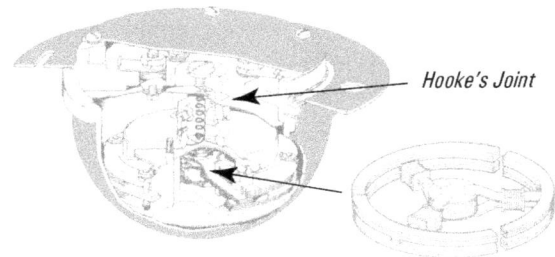

Hooke's Joint

Heading information from the flux valve is compared to whatever the display is indicating and the results sent to an *error detector* or *selsyn unit* (self-synchroniser).

The signals then go through an amplifier to the torque motor, which precesses the directional gyro in the horizontal plane at 2° per minute. On its way, the current also flows through the *annunciator*, which is a small dial with a dot or a cross, depending on the current direction, whose purpose is to tell you that synchronisation is taking place correctly. The *synchronisation knob* is there for manual correction of gross topple in level flight. That is, it has the same function as the caging knob.

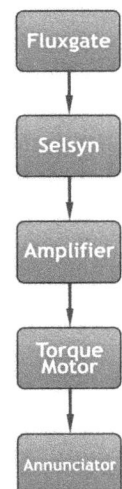

ERRORS

Gimballing errors arise from banking, and will disappear once a turn is complete.

Horizontal accelerations (Coriolis, turning) that make the flux valve tilt can cause heading errors. They will not be seen immediately and the rate of any heading error introduction depends on the limiting precession rate and the response time of the system (time constant).

- **Turning Error**. Although a high rate of turn in a fast aircraft would show the greatest heading error, the time spent in the turn is minimal - slow prolonged turns at high speeds generate the greatest errors. They decay after level flight is resumed. Errors from tilting can be limited by switching to an unslaved directional gyro mode whenever turns are sensed by suitable devices.

- **Coriolis Error**. An aircraft flies a curved path in space, so there will be a central force acting to displace the valve. The error is calculable, depending on groundspeed, latitude, dip and track, and can be compensated for automatically.

- **Vehicle Movement Error**. Whenever flying a true or magnetic rhumb line the aircraft must turn to maintain a constant track with reference to converging meridians. As with Coriolis error, the acceleration displaces the detector from the local horizontal plane. A correction can be applied in a similar manner to the Coriolis error.

- **Vibration**. This results in a heading oscillation, whose mean is not the actual mean heading. As the gyro slaving loop tends to average flux valve headings over time, the gyro would eventually precess to the erroneous flux valve mean heading. This can be limited to small values by careful design of the pendulous detector damping mechanism and through the detector's location in the aircraft.

As deviation is corrected electromagnetically, deviation cards are not needed.

TURN COORDINATOR

This is actually a combination of two instruments, one power driven, and the other not. The idea is to measure the *yaw* rate for low *bank* rates, and since yaw and bank have to be measured, the instrument is made sensitive to both by having its axis (i.e. the gimbal ring) *tilted upwards* by about 30-35°, though it is less sensitive to roll.

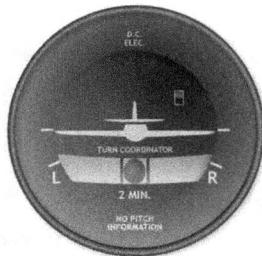

The roll is sensed first, and the rate increases when the correct angle of bank is set. This is what the instrument is sensing. Displacement remains constant for a given bank, regardless of airspeed. A small aircraft tilts to indicate whether you are banking, so it is a useful backup to the artificial horizon, especially as the gyro is electrically

operated and not affected if the suction system fails (although it gives you a rudimentary indication of bank, turns without the other instruments are done with timing). It becomes very useful when you are not able to use the full panel, as the amount that the wings of the aircraft move also indicates the rate of turn.

When the wings in the little aircraft hit one of the lower marks you are in a Rate 1 turn, which takes two minutes to go through 360°, making 3° per second.

Underneath the indicator is a steel ball (or similar) in a clear tube containing fluid, for damping purposes, called an *inclinometer*, which indicates the quality of the turn (it doesn't affect the rate of turn). When a turn is balanced*, centrifugal force offsets the pull of gravity and keeps the ball in the centre of the tube. In a slip (below, left), where the rate of turn is not enough for the angle of bank, the centrifugal force will be weak and the ball will fall to the inside of the turn.

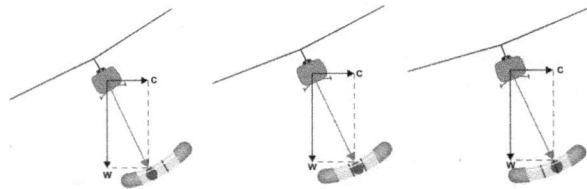

In a *skid*, the turn is too fast, so the extra centrifugal force causes the ball to be displaced more, to the outside of the turn (right, above).

*A turn is balanced if more than one half of the ball is inside the indicator marks.

Turn And Bank (Slip) Indicator

This instrument has a vertical needle instead of the horizontal small aircraft in the artificial horizon. As such it will only give you the *rate* of turn, since it is only sensitive to yaw, which is what is measured for **low bank angles**. It has the spin axis across the aircraft, so it spins up and away from you, with one end of the spindle held in place with a spring, so it has **one degree of freedom**. The spin rate is 10,000 RPM, and there are mechanical stops to keep it from going more than 45° either side of the centre.

The (rate) gyro is aircraft horizontal with 2 **planes of freedom**. During normal operation, the spring keeps the spin axis horizontal so the turn pointer is at zero, and the gyro's rigidity will tend to keep it there. The yaw induced when you turn is precessed to the top and bottom of the gyro. As the springs stretch to cope with gyro movement around the longitudinal axis, they apply a force that produces a *secondary precession* equal to and in the same direction as the rate of turn. In other words, a turn makes the gyro move, to create a primary precession that stretches a spring that creates another in the same direction as the original force.

Without the spring, you would still see a turn indication, but would have no idea of its magnitude, so the spring controls the angular deflection of the gimbal ring and introduces its own precessing force. As the precession is equal to the rate of turn multiplied by the angular momentum, the force is a measure of the rate of turn. In

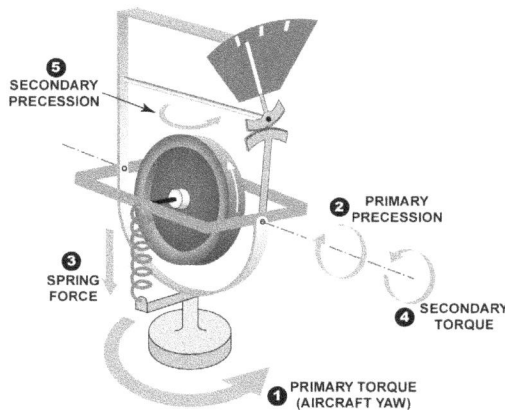

the picture above the aircraft is turning left and the yawing moment is the primary applied force **1**. This is precessed through 90°, producing the primary precessed force **2**, which makes the gyro topple. The amount of tilt determines the rate of turn indicated on the instrument.

As the gyro topples the spring stretches, giving the secondary applied force **3**. This is again precessed through 90°, providing the secondary precessed force **5**.

When the secondary precessed force is equal to the primary applied force, the secondary precession caused by the spring is proportional to the actual rate of turn. The gyro ceases to topple, and the angle between the spin axis and the yawing plane is proportional to the rate of turn.

ERRORS

All errors cause the instrument to under-read, except when the rate of turn is less than rate 1, when rotor speed is faster than normal, and the springs are slack. The ball is sensitive to gravity and centrifugal force.

If the TAS is within 100 knots of the calibrated TAS, the error in the indicated rate of turn should not be more than ±5% of the actual rate of turn.

During low rate turns there is little or no change of pitch required to maintain level flight. During steeper turns, however, the nose must be raised to maintain height. Any pitching moment while the spin axis is displaced from the yawing plane create additional precession, causing the instrument to over-indicate the rate of turn. As it is not normally used to monitor steep turns, this error does not seriously restrict its effectiveness.

If the rotor speed is low, the instrument will under-read the actual rate of turn because the gyro is less rigid and

will precess more quickly. The amount of secondary torque required to produce the secondary precession that matches the aircraft's rate of turn is therefore less than it should be, is achieved with less spring stretch and less tilt of the spin axis. Less tilt means that a lower rate of turn is indicated. In fact, the rotational speed of the gyro in a rate of turn indicator is lower than that in the direction indicator to reduce rigidity.

Conversely, with the gyro overspeeding, the balance of forces is only achieved when the spring is stretched by more than the correct amount, because the gyro is too rigid, so the indicated rate of turn is greater than it should be. A weak spring (due to age) needs to be stretched further, which gives a greater tilt of the spin axis, causing the instrument to over- indicate the rate of turn.

A weak spring (due to age) needs to be stretched further. This will result in a greater tilt of the spin axis, causing the instrument to over- indicate the rate of turn.

STOP This instrument gets less accurate as the bank increases. In a level turn with a 90° bank angle, the needle would centre itself, because you would be performing a loop in the horizontal plane. When taxying, the ball moves freely opposite the turn, and the needle deflects in the direction of the turn.

FLIGHT MANAGEMENT SYSTEMS

Understanding the FMS for your aircraft is vital for modern operations*. Luckily, they are similar between types, so that, if you understand the inner workings of the one on the Boeing 777, you can bluff your way through on the 737, 747, 757 and 767 (but not the 787). Indeed, the FMS chosen for the EASA exams is based on the 737**. As the idea is to reduce pilot workload (and to make sure they don't make mistakes!), the autopilot should usually be left alone to do the job.

*Air France 447 is one of the best known examples of why. On June 1st 2009, it was flying from Rio de Janeiro to Paris when it disappeared from radar over the middle of the Atlantic Ocean. It had flown through a thunderstorm, and there was no distress signal. The pitot tubes had frozen over in the storm, which made the autopilot disengage, and the pilots could not maintain enough airspeed to stay in the air due to the incorrect airspeed readings in the cockpit, hence the new training.

**The Smith version. Larger Boeings tend to use the Honeywell, as used in the Airbus and others, which comes in two flavours, one biased to Europe and one to the US.

The software used for the FMS is certified at a level equal to or lower than that for Fly By Wire. It can provide guidance for RNAV and non-precision approaches.

Please note that the procedures given here are generic and geared towards the exams. Your company's procedures will likely be very different.

Basic procedures include passing everything you enter through a logic check, with independent verification of entries when inputting the initial position through lat & long on the keyboard (from separate source documents). This is to avoid elementary mistakes such as transposing N and S or E and W. It is safer to use the database!

Although the idea is to enter your route before you start, you can get airborne with just the first waypoints and put the rest in later when you have the time (although including the destination ICAO code at least gives it a start for calculating the fuel). Whichever way you work, *one person should always fly the aeroplane.*

You should always understand the difference between where the FMS thinks you are and where you actually are. One tip is to use machine messages as a trigger to check your position, even if it is only a quick check.

A Flight Management System is a **mode-selectable colour flight display** that can be defined as a *Global 3D Flight Management System*, whose function is to provide automatic navigation along planned routes (LNAV) and optimum flight profiles (VNAV), plus performance management for *managed guidance** by the crew. The system can manage altitude, speed, direction, multiple navigation sources and engine power, and can estimate waypoint ETAs and fuel remaining, amongst other things.

Managed guidance exists when the FMS controls the autopilot. *Selected guidance* occurs when the pilots do the flying and parameters such as speed, attitude and heading are set by them.

Typical inputs would include GPS, IRS, DME, VOR, LOC, plus RWY THR (runway threshold).

If the autopilot is not available, the FMS can at least drive the Flight Director so you can fly manually. The concept was born in the 1970s, when latitude and longitude information was entered for every waypoint, often in

flight, and errors from mistyping were common, aside from increasing the workload. Hubert Naimer came up with the idea of a "best computed position" based on mathematically filtered information from several sources, and a database of navigational information that required no crew input. The first system was the UNS-1, in 1982.

FMS calculations are based on the FMS position which, depending on the system, may be calculated from a single source of the most accurate data available at a given time, or multiple sources from which a position will be derived.

> 🛑 Losing the GPS input to the FMS position will affect the integrity monitoring for RNP/PBN approaches.

A true FMS normally consists of 2 Flight Management Computers (FMCs) and 2 (M)CDUs, one each for the Captain and First Officer.

A dual configuration means that the system can be used as a sole means of navigation, although backup traditional systems are usually present. With 2 systems, you have *redundancy* and *integrity*, as they can check each other.

You can also use P/RNAV airways, down to 2 nm wide, and perform FMS approaches in non-radar environments.

The data must be presented on different displays, so there is a 3-position switch that can be set to NORMAL, BOTH ON L or BOTH ON R (from that, you will deduce that there are Left and Right systems).

With the switch on L or R, the system behaves like one FMC. The primary (Master) provides the guidance commands and maps the display, and the secondary (Slave) is synchronised with it. In NORMAL mode, the tasks are shared, each system effectively handling its own side of the aircraft, with separate inputs (and information synchronised through a common bus), except that your position and velocity (and guidance) come from a weighted average. The *composite navigation solution* is a second aircraft state calculated in each FMC from both error estimates. When the FMC switch is set to the ALTN position, the related CDU and EFIS displays will be connected to the other computer.

Single mode exists where only one FMS is operational. *Backup mode* exists when the FMC has failed in certain areas but still works a bit. You might have to *downmode* to Single FMC if there is a miscompare between databases on the start-up check, for example. An FMC can be *brickwalled* if there is too much of a discrepancy.

Data is combined from many sources, such as navigation systems, the Air Data Computer (airspeed, etc.), route information and operating requirements, to provide a centralised source of information and control for navigation and performance, if only to help manage fuel costs by calculating optimum levels, etc.

A dual system has an Inter System Bus (ISB) for communication between them. The twisted pair cable in the middle is the ARINC 429/629 data bus (the twist cancels out certain types of electrical interference).

Some components are hardwired directly to the FMS, but most just wait for their data to come round.

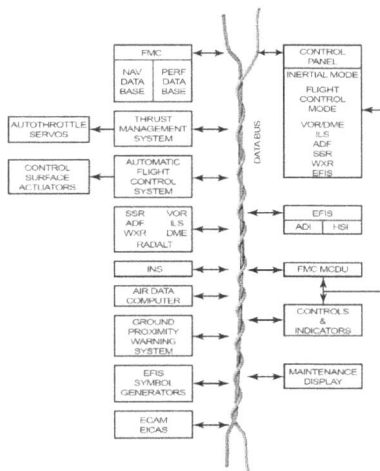

The twisted pair cabling eliminates certain types of electrical interference.

Aside from the Mode Control Panel:

the main interface between the crew and the FMS is the Control Display Unit, or CDU:

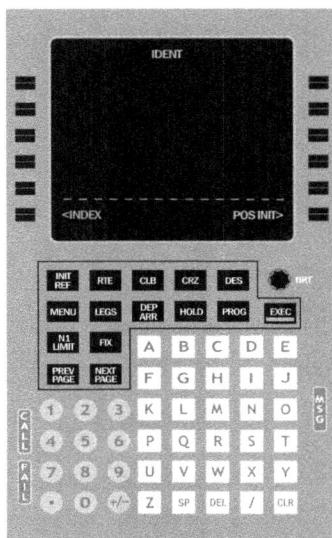

It is used before flight to manually input dispatch information to the IRSs and the FMC.

The alphanumeric keys represent the same characters as they would on any keyboard, except that the **SP** button is the space bar. The delete key clears a selected line, while the clear key deletes single characters.

The 15 function keys are short cuts that provide access to major functions, including:

- **MENU**. Provides access to the FMC and other subsystems.

- **INIT REF**. Provides access to these pages:

  - IDENT. Aircraft ID and navigation database verification.

  - POS. Position initialisation (on the ground) and position reference in flight.

  - PERF. Performance initialisation (gross weight, cost index).

  - THRUST LIM

  - TAKEOFF. Parameter reference and initialisation.

  - APPROACH. Parameter reference and initialisation.

  - NAVDATA. Information and saved flight plans.

  The most relevant page for the phase of flight will automatically be displayed. IDENT or POS, for example will show during the preflight phase.

- **RTE**. The ROUTE page displays the waypoint fixes and how the system proposes to get to them.

- **CLB**. Climb thrust and altitude control.

- **CRZ**. For managing the cruise in terms of altitude, fuel and speed.

- **DES**. Descent speed, fuel and planning.

- **LEGS**. Similar to the ROUTE page, but showing every fix to be overflown, as opposed to only the major ones. It is used often to manage altitude and speed, and to enter waypoints into the flight plan.

- **DEP/ARR**. Used to select published SIDs and STARs.

- **HOLD**. Allows you to add holding procedures to the active flight plan (which can be changed any time before takeoff and throughout the flight.

- **PROG**. Monitors the progress of the flight in terms of time, distance and fuel consumption.

- **EXEC**. This only works when the light bar on it is showing. It is used to confirm changes to the plan. When it is active, you will see an <ERASE prompt so you can erase a proposed action quickly.

- **N1 LIM**. Selects and controls engine performance limits during takeoff, climb, cruise and descent.

- **FIX**. Allows you to place waypoints on to the display in relation to known points within the navigation database. They do not have to be part of the active flight plan and are shown as green.

- **NEXT PAGE/PREV PAGE**. If the display has more than one page, these cycle round them.

Amongst other things, the Flight Management Computers (FMCs) can perform the following functions:

- **Flight Planning**. The basis of the flight profile is the route (or the *lateral flight profile*) you will fly from the departure point to the destination. The items making up the route are known as the *flight plan* (not to be confused with the ATC form).

  The information will come initially from the navigation database, and might consist of a departure airport (and runway) a SID, enroute waypoints (see overleaf) and airways, a STAR, and an approach procedure to a specific runway, although the latter two are often not selected until ATC at the destination is contacted. Once you're happy with all that, the details are assembled into a buffer where they are used for computing the lateral and vertical profiles. The information can also be transmitted from the ground via DataLink.

- **Navigation Computation** and Display, automatically tuning navigation aids and interfacing with the IRS to provide a great circle track to any point. The FMC knows where it is from data supplied by the usual sources, plus IRS. The Best Position is generated every 5 seconds, based on the IRS, as adjusted for the Radio Position, as the FMS assumes that radio is more accurate. The new Best Position updates the System Position, which is used for LNAV (Lateral Navigation).

Operation of the FMC is based around the track to a fix and the groundspeed to get there. However, LNAV can also factor in the TAS to work out the angle of bank to fly a holding pattern (for example) and construct the dimensions of the hold each time it passes over the fix. LNAV (see *Radio Navigation*) can fly the pattern drawn on the approach charts, based on the information entered into the Hold page and the TAS (this is a lot better than the guesstimates from steam driven instruments). Normal deviation from the flight path should not exceed 0.1 nm, but if it is working DME/DME only, this would be 0.3 nm.

- **Issue commands** in pitch, roll and thrust. Vertical Navigation, for example, is controlled by speed or rates of climb or descent. With speed control, the autothrottle is given a target thrust setting and the elevator will be used to control the speed and provide a variable rate of climb. When vertical speed is controlled, the elevator is controlled directly and the autothrottle will be adjusted to provide a fixed ROC/ROD and a variable speed.

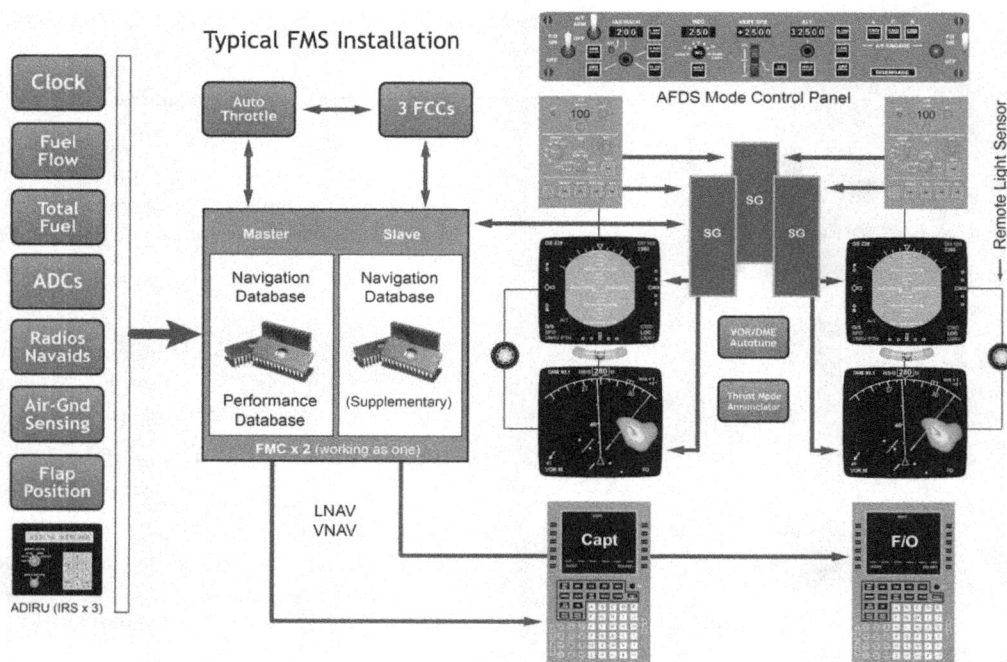

Typical FMS Installation

- Manage fuel

- Compute weight and balance

- Manage performance. For this, the gross weight, cost index target altitude and the route need to be fed into the system - you won't get a vertical navigation profile until the performance initialisation page has been completed. A least cost performance model is used, and the default setting is for ECON.

Output can be sent to the EFIS displays, flight director, mode control panel, autothrottle and engine controls.

Due to the accuracy and sensitivity of modern air pressure sensors (less lag, for one thing), air data, which is very accurate long term, can supplement the IRS (discussed later), which is very accurate in the short term.

An **Air Data Inertial Reference Unit** (ADIRU) is a combination of the two systems that supplies the following information to the EFIS displays as well as other systems, such as the engines, autopilot, etc.:

- **Air Data Reference** (airspeed, angle of attack and altitude). The ADR is a small computer that corrects pitot-static information (airspeed, altitude, vertical speed) for high altitude operations.

- **Inertial Reference** (position & attitude). The IRU senses and computes linear accelerations and angular rates about each axis. This is used for pitch and roll displays and navigation calculations.

AD and IR functions are combined because some of their functions overlap - the IRU knows how fast you are moving, and in what direction, and the ADR knows the TAS, so you get a single, fault tolerant source of navigational data for both pilots. The term means any integrated ADC/IRS unit, and may be complemented by a *Secondary Attitude Air Reference Unit* (SAARU), as with the Boeing 777. The ADIRU shows air data from the left pitot/static on the captain's side and the SAARU shows that from the right pitot/static on the FO's side.

The ADIRU can operate with 115 v AC or 28 v DC. The power supply feeds the ADR, the IR, the ISDU and the Air Data Modules (ADMs).

An **ADIRS** contains up to three fault tolerant ADIRUs, an associated control and display unit (CDU) in the cockpit and remotely mounted air data modules (ADMs). No 3 is a redundant unit that can supply data to the P1 or P2 display if the other two fail. As No 3 is the only alternate source of air and inertial reference data, there is no cross-channel redundancy between 1 and 2.

An inertial reference fault in 1 or 2 will cause a loss of attitude and navigation information on their associated PFD and ND screens. An ADR fault will cause the loss of airspeed and altitude information on the affected display.

Either way, the information can only be restored by selecting No. 3.

To do its job properly, the system needs information, such as clock time, aircraft weights, fuel loaded, winds, ISA deviations, etc., particularly *databases* of waypoints, navaids, airways, procedures, airports, and other data. Most of the information for a flight is in the FMC. Items such as navigation facilities, reporting points and airway designators can be input using up to 5 alphanumerics.

While searching for it, ensure that someone is flying the aircraft!

LNAV/VNAV

Lateral Navigation, and VNAV (*Vertical Navigation*) are used with custom routes stored in the navigation database, and were first fully integrated on the 757/767. Because the original use of the FMS was simply to take over routine tasks and improve fuel efficiency, not all installations can perform LNAV/VNAV. Luckily, most modern ones do, and the FMS is now the primary tool for Performance Based Navigation, discussed in *Radio Navigation*.

LNAV

LNAV provides guidance (steering) along the lateral path of the flight plan (it follows the route in the FMC for you), so it uses the autopilot roll channel.

VNAV

VNAV allows the vertical path of an aircraft to be better controlled and managed, so optimal profiles can be used, as opposed to FLC (Flight Level Change), which has no profile guidance and will simply maintain the selected climb speed until you reach the target altitude (vertical speed mode should not be used in the climb for safety reasons - if you select a rate that is higher than the aircraft can maintain, the speed will bleed off and you could end up stalling).

VNAV also allows more sophisticated guidance along a SID or a STAR, directing the autopilot along a three-dimensional tube in space to not only fly over the relevant waypoints, but also to arrive at each one at the desired altitude, as per any clearances or restrictions. On charts:

- An **AT** altitude is double lined: $\underline{\overline{4600}}$

- An **AT or Above** altitude is underlined: $\underline{4600}$

- An **AT or Below** altitude is overlined: $\overline{4600}$

- A Window is mixed:

   $\overline{6000}$
   $\underline{5000}$

VNAV should provide steering and thrust commands along the vertical path, usually based on the baro altitude* input from the ADC, although some systems do not have autothrottle capability. In other words, VNAV provides the vertical component of the flight plan along the chosen vertical path, taking into account altitude and speed restrictions and the limits of the airframe. **It is not intended to be used when not on the lateral flight path or purposely deviating from it.**

*There is a temperature compensation facility for ISA differences along the vertical profile.

- **Takeoff** uses a speed based climb (i.e. safety speed until acceleration height or flap retraction).

- **Climb** is speed based, using the most economical (ECON) or pilot selected speed (SEL SPD).

- **Cruise** is a 3D path based level segments determined by economics or pilot selection, including cruise-climb or cruise-descent.

- **Descent** is path-based, using an idle or near idle profile in terms of performance. A geometric path is shallower, and typically non-idle, used where restrictions have a higher priority. Although it is constructed upstream, i.e. from the lowest waypoint, the descent starts at the TOD, proceeding through the approach to the beginning of the missed approach. Put another way, the end of descent waypoint is the anchor position. The path can be made shallower by the system) as a protection for potential overspeeds to cope with adverse or unforecast winds and temperatures.

- **Approach** is a path-based descent determined by the approach procedure's vertical angle. It is a separate phase within the descent phase. LNAV minima indicate non-precision approaches, using the usual minimum step-down altitude below which you may not descend. That is, without vertical guidance, you must remain **at or above** the MDA without the required visual reference, or you need to conduct a missed approach at the missed approach waypoint (MAWP). LNAV/VNAV and LPV minima refer to APV approaches (RNAV approaches with vertical guidance).

- **Missed Approach** is similar to the climb phase - speed-based to a pre-determined altitude and waypoint.

Databases

There are two loadable databases that support the core flight management functions. These are:

- a **Navigation** database, for information relating to airports, navaids, airways, terminal procedures, and the like, along with RNP values for the associated airspace. In short, an airway manual in a chip. It does two jobs, relating to *navigation* and *flight planning*. It must be updated every 28 days (the RAC cycle) - the information, which may come from many commercial sources, is valid to the next expiry date, plus the next revisions. There is a permanent database and a supplementary one, which can be switched over at the right time (you might be halfway across the Atlantic when the main one expires). The data is checked at each phase of the process, from reception to loading. Pilots can insert extra (temporary) navigation data between updates but they cannot modify the original data.

- a **Performance** database, which is only updated when performance parameters change. It contains an average model of the aircraft and its engines, including flight envelopes and operating limits, to correct for the various conditions of flight. You can fine tune it and load defaults through the CDU, with alterations kept in NVRAM.

The system uses EPROMS for permanent storage, which means that the information they contain cannot be changed by pilots (but it can by engineers on the ground). NVRAM (*Non-Volatile RAM*) is Random Access Memory that keeps its contents when the power is switched off because it either uses a backup battery or is flash memory ("normal" RAM, which does lose information when the power is off is called *volatile*). This allows you to update navigation data between updates. Navigation and Performance also have their own processors, and there is a third to handle I/O (Input and Output) and the Built In Test (BIT). The information needed by them all is kept in (volatile) main memory.

In Use

Central control means that you will select radio and navaid frequencies through the FMS control panel, or CDU - you should not see separate boxes in the cockpit. That is, the CDU is the principal pilot interface to the FMS and any other systems that interact with it. You enter data with the *alphanumeric keyboard* and *line select* keys, and you *must* get used to the menu system!

Waypoint names, navaid identifiers, runway numbers, airport ICAO identifiers can all be stored as 5-letter waypoint identifiers.

The display screen shows 14 lines which can display 24 characters across in large or small fonts. There are three basic areas - the top line carries the title of the page you are on, plus its status, whether ACTive, or MODified, etc.

capt.gs

Text, or data lines (1-6) are in the middle area, aligned left and right and are adjusted by the Line Select Keys on either side of the display.

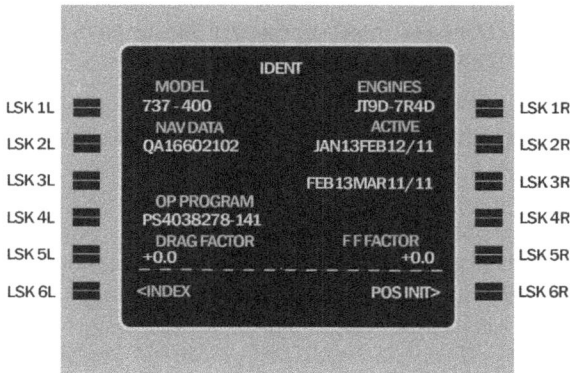

Text, or data lines (1-6) are in the middle area, aligned left and right and are adjusted by the Line Select Keys on either side of the display. The first three pages of the FMC/CDU that normally appear on initial start-up of the B737-400 Electronic Flight Instrument System are IDENT - POS INIT - RTE. To display the initial great circle track, you need DSRTK\STS.

Each data line has an information line above it describing what the text line is for (predictably called the title line). Data lines may also include prompts for input from the crew. When you see boxes, typically with gross weight figures, it means that the system requires information. If you see a < or > symbol next to a Line Select Key, you can get to another menu by pressing that key - for example **<INDEX**, as shown above.

Dashed lines allow you to enter data that is specific to a flight, such as the departure and destination airports.

If there is not enough space on the display, you may see an indication on the top right of the page number you are on out of how many, as in 1/2, meaning page 1 of 2 available. The previous and next page buttons above the number pad on the CDU will cycle you through them.

The alphanumeric keys on the MCDU are used to make entries to the *scratchpad*, which is actually the bottom line of the display that behaves rather like a one-line wordprocessor, in that the contents of the line can be edited in the normal way (it's also where you might get messages from the computer):

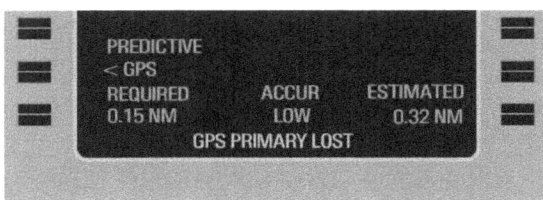

It is a working area where you can enter and/or verify data before it goes into the system. For example, if you wanted to go direct to a waypoint called ANKAR you would type:

    DIR TO ANKAR

Waypoints can be entered as Place Bearing/Distance, Place Bearing/Place Bearing, Along-Track Displacement, Latitude and Longitude. Otherwise, enter information on the scratchpad then press the relevant LSK to get that information into the system. The levels of message are *Alerting* and *Advisory*, in that order of priority.

Tip: Lat & Long figures are typically shortened in the main display. Pushing the button next to them brings them into the scratchpad (down-selection) so you can see the full readout. Up-selection is transferring data into the system by pressing the relevant LSK having entered it into the scratchpad.

Information in the scratchpad does not affect the FMS until it is moved to another line on the display. Data remains in the scratchpad over mode and page changes.

The FMS starts its power up sequence after you switch it on. The data on the **IDENT** page does not change regularly but still needs to be checked.

It will change according to the machine, but typical entries are shown.

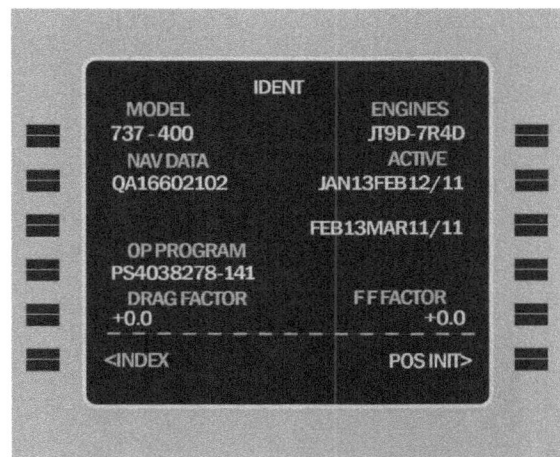

You then have to tell it where you are. When the initial position is put into an FMS, the system rejects initial latitude or longitude error.

Press LSK 6R next to where it says POS INIT.

You might then get a selection of positions, such as the last known one, etc. (at the top right).

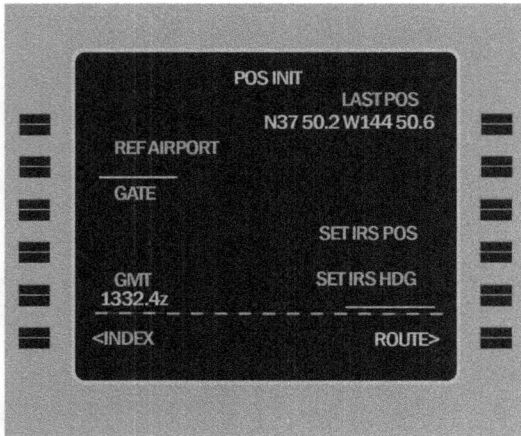

```
                    POS INIT
                         LAST POS
                         N37 50.2 W144 50.6
       REF AIRPORT

       GATE

                         SET IRS POS

       GMT               SET IRS HDG
       1332.4z
       <INDEX                  ROUTE>
```

LAST POS refers to the last recorded position when the aircraft was powered down, or when the brakes were last set. If you want to accept it, push LSK 1R to downselect the information into the scratchpad, then press 4R to set the IRS position (IRS positions are updated on the ground during the alignment procedure).

You can also use the Lat & Long of an airfield as a reference position, which is what the **REF AIRPORT** selection is for. Enter the ICAO code into the scratchpad, press LSK 2L, the 4R. You can also use the **GATE** position in the same way.

To enter a flight plan, the machine needs to know the destination, the route you propose to take, the alternate, the departure and the expected arrival procedure (all this should be in the database). The **ROUTE** page is the primary page for route construction, and you get there by pressing the LSK right next to where you see **ROUTE>**.

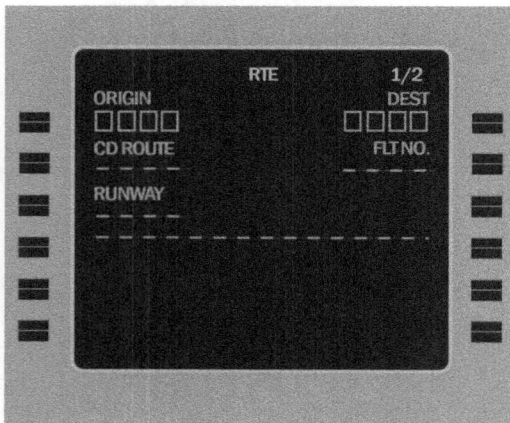

```
                    RTE         1/2
       ORIGIN              DEST
       □□□□               □□□□
       CD ROUTE           FLT NO.
       ----               ----
       RUNWAY

       ---------------------------
```

LSK 1L will have some empty boxes to the side. Enter the ICAO code into the scratchpad and push LSK (1L) to fill the boxes (empty boxes indicate required entries).

Do the same for the Destination with LSK 1R.

CD ROUTE refers to a previously saved flight plan. If there is a flight plan for the route in the database, it will be presented for your approval. Just press LSK 6L next to <**ACTIVATE** when it appears. This will also make the light on the **EXEC** key come on. This should be pressed to confirm your actions.

Another button that appears occasionally is **REVERSE**, which is a quick way of entering a return flight. If there is no flight plan, you can enter your own route. Generally, you follow established airways until you reach a specific waypoint where you can leave the system. More often than not, this is the first waypoint associated with an approach procedure (you join the system in the first place at the last waypoint associated with a departure procedure). With just that information, the system will deal with intermediate waypoints automatically.

Once all the information required on page 1 has been entered, the page indicator at the top right will show that there are now 2 pages available. You can get to page 2 with the **NEXT PAGE** key on the CDU. The left hand side is essentially one column labelled **VIA**, and the right hand side is another labelled **TO**, which is where individual fixes are entered. The **VIA** column indicates how to get to them. Thus, you type the fix information into the scratchpad, then upselect it with LSK 1R. The information will be checked, and if the fix name is not unique, you can choose from a selection. the closest one to your present position will be first on the list. Press the LSK next to your choice.

The FMS will assume a direct routing, so the word **DIRECT** will appear next to LSK 1L. If you want to choose a particular airway, enter its name into the scratchpad, then press the relevant LSK on the left side to change the **DIRECT** indication. If it is a long route it will not be unusual to go through several pages.

If you want to save the route and not have to type it all in again, go back to page 1 and push the LSK next to the <**SAVE** prompt.

Eventually, you will reach the **PERF INIT** (*Performance Initialisation*) page. Performance data is used for many purposes, such as vertical navigation (VNAV), setting target speeds, fuel calculations, etc. Although we know the route, until the aircraft's weight is known, climb or descent profiles cannot be constructed. Neither can the optimum cruise altitude or any speeds be calculated, which is quite important on a machine like the 777 that can calculate those required for any manoeuvres in real time, which helps greatly with fuel consumption, because the flaps can be deployed at the most appropriate times.

STOP   The data entered into the PERF INIT page must be correct and crosschecked!

Tip: On Boeings, you can enter the transition altitude. As you pass it, the altimeter setting on the PFD turns yellow as a reminder to set 1013.

The gross weight of the aircraft is entered using LSK 1L. 2L shows the calculated fuel (from the Fuel Quantity Indication System) in thousands of pounds and 3L shows the ZFW (normally you get this information from the loadsheet that comes from the dispatch office, but these days it comes over a datalink). 2L and 3L together make up the gross weight of the aircraft, and the sum of their values must match that in 1L.

Also on the left hand side will be the entry for the fuel reserves and the Cost Index - operating costs depend not only on how much fuel you burn, but also time - it might cost a lot less if you fly slower, for example. The cost index is a measure of how time affects costs - that is, *direct* operating costs (insurance, etc. are fixed costs) divided by fuel costs, which are expressed in cents per pound. If you fly slower or faster than the speed indicated by the index for that leg, costs will increase. The 777 (and probably others) has a sliding scale of 0-9999. The higher the number entered, the higher the speed will be and the more fuel will be used - you will get maximum range by using 0! It is very rare to find an entry into an FMS of more than around 500, on the 777, at least. This is because higher speeds will be very close to some structural limits. A good average starting value might be in the 250 range. It is possible, of course, to override the set speed for timing on approaches, etc

On the right hand side of the **PERF INIT** page you can enter the **CRZ ALT** (cruise altitude) and the **TRANS ALT** (transition altitude).

In flight, you will use the **FPL** or **PROG** page while the FMS continuously computes your position from the IRS, VOR, DME and ILS as required. The priority for the most accurate fix is a DME/DME crosscut, then DME/VOR, then VOR/VOR, and IRS last. It will tune DME frequencies in sequence according to route information in the navigation database (if it cannot decode the Morse identifier, it shows the frequency instead). Despite that, you should still monitor your position.

The **FLIGHT PLAN** or **LEG** page displays distance, true track, time prediction, plus waypoint elevation and distance relative to flight plan legs or waypoints. When two waypoints are entered here, the track between them is computed and displayed on the ND as a great circle arc.

There is a lateral offset function which allows you to fly along a leg with a constant offset distance to the right or left. The amount is manually entered on the CDU.

The FMS cross track (XTK), shown on the navigation display, is the abeam distance error (to the left or right) from the desired track to the position of the aircraft, or the distance between the actual position and the great circle track between active waypoints.

The Flight Director

Usually found on the EADI, the Flight Director's job is to reduce your workload by indicating the manoeuvres to execute, achieve or maintain a flight condition in pitch and roll, particularly when things are happening quickly, as they do when close to Decision Height on the ILS (assuming you are not using the autopilot). It uses a **computer** and **command bars** to presents data as control commands to show you the **optimal way to achieve your flight path**, using bank angles of 25° for intercepting desired tracks (it will intercept a track at 20°). In other words, the flight director gives you directions regarding *how to position the controls* in terms of position and intensity - you get no information about the flight path, for which you need a separate display.

A two-cue system might use command bars. In fact, the original FD was Sperry's Zero Reader, which was a cross-pointed indicator like the modern ILS display:

The horizontal bar is for the pitch channel, and the vertical bar for roll, in terms of information about the direction and amplitude of the corrections to be applied to the controls. They will centralise once the inputs required are enough, so the bars can be centred even when you are not straight and level. Command bars may be displayed when flying manually or when the autopilot is engaged. So, the essential components of a flight director are a *computer* and *command bars*. You engage the *heading select* mode (HDG SEL), once a heading is selected, after which the vertical bar will be centred if the bank angle is the same as the computed angle. In a helicopter, there may be a third (vertical) cue, for the collective pitch position.

Thus, if the F/D is in G/S mode on approach, the horizontal bar will indicate the pitch corrections needed to join and follow the glide slope. If it is deviating upward, you are not necessarily below the glideslope, but must increase the pitch attitude. The vertical bar informs you about the direction and amplitude of the corrections to be applied on banking the aircraft (in LOC mode, simply the correction to join and follow the localiser axis.

Command bars may be displayed when flying manually or with the autopilot engaged. The FD will be in a display mode that is a combination of the artificial horizon, localiser & glideslope, radio altimeter for your Decision Height and warning flags for instrument failure, so it also tells you which way up you are.

The visual guidance can come in the shape of a V-bar:

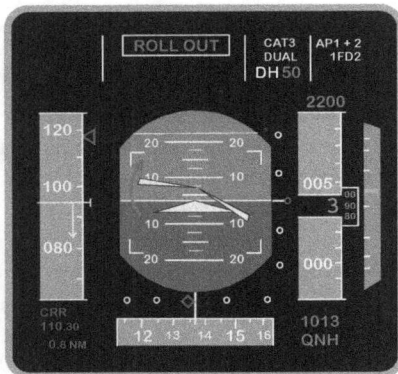

EFIS

Conventional instruments can go wrong, and tend to spread themselves around the cockpit, so you need three pairs of eyes in a big machine to keep track of them all. They also have to be continually monitored. The *Electronic Flight Instrument System* replaces the traditional ones with CRT or LCD displays, or at least flat computer panels, hence the occasional reference to the *Glass Cockpit*. These have no moving parts, and can be switched to show different instruments, or duplicate information, which is helpful if one fails. In emergencies, you can isolate some instruments for closer scrutiny.

With the glass cockpit, a lot of information can be concentrated into a small space, and the associated computers can take on some monitoring tasks, so you only need to pay some of them any attention when something actually goes wrong (see *Warning & Recording*, later).

The heart of the EFIS is the symbol generator, of which there are 3 in a standard system, which receives input from the sensors around the aircraft. A third (centre) SG may be involved if the left or right unit fails. If two are used and one fails, the remaining one can supply both sides, but the information would be the same. Switching is pilot controlled. Once brightness is selected, it is automatically controlled by light sensors. Other information that can be displayed includes graphics of the aircraft systems, checklists, maps from the GPS, etc.

The technology involves small computers using solid-state (i.e. no moving parts) 3-axis gyros and accelerometers to derive altitude, magnetometers to find heading, and pressure transducers to find air data (airspeed & altitude), all displayed on flat screens, through suitable software. Because of the potential problems with software, any EFIS system will be backed up by a selection of traditional instruments, or another, separate, EFIS system.

The benefits of using EFIS include:

- Increased reliability
- The output of many instruments can be combined into one, improving situational awareness
- You can put other information on, such as checklists and weather
- Colour

EADI/PFD

The *Electronic Attitude Direction Indicator* (EADI) or *Primary Flight Display* (PFD) can combine a lot of information in one small space.

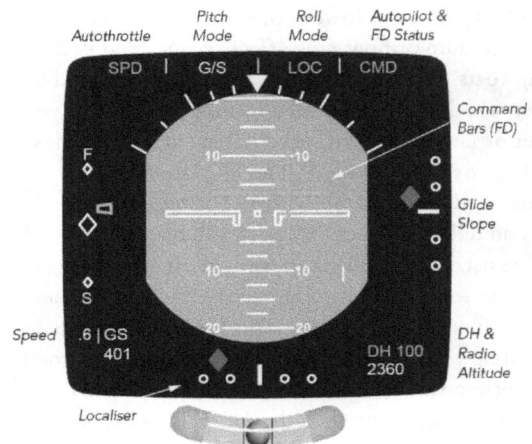

The above is the basic display. In the improved version, the Fast/Slow bar on the left is replaced by a speed tape.

On the left below is a typical takeoff display, in the middle is one for the cruise, and landing is shown on the right.

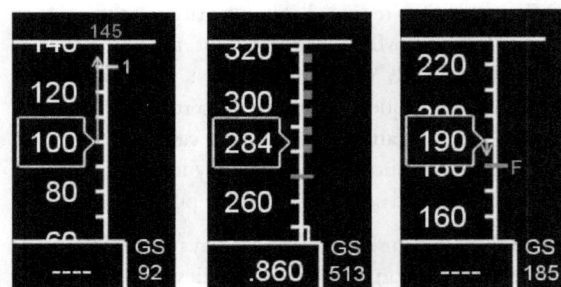

The attitude information could come from the IRS, if there is one, or more traditional gyroscopic sources (sideslip information will come from the inertial system). When the right equipment is switched in, you could also get ILS localiser/glideslope information, groundspeed, flight director commands, radio altitude, etc.

Between 1,000-2,500 ft AGL, radio altitude is shown digitally in white, with the Decision Height in green.

Below 1,000 ft, it changes to an analogue presentation, namely a white circular scale in 100-ft increments which unwinds as you descend and erases above the present height. The DH is a magenta marker on the circular scale, and is set through the EFIS control panel. Radio altitude is shown digitally in the middle. At DH, the scale and marker change to amber and flash for a few seconds. There is a reset button to fix that.

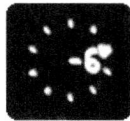

If you go beyond localiser and glideslope limits during an approach, and when below,500 ft agl, the deviation pointers turn from white to amber and start to flash.

The **Flight Path Vector** (FPV) materialises the instantaneous flight path angle (FPA) and track (TRK) flown by the aircraft. It may be used by itself or in association with the flight path director (FPD).

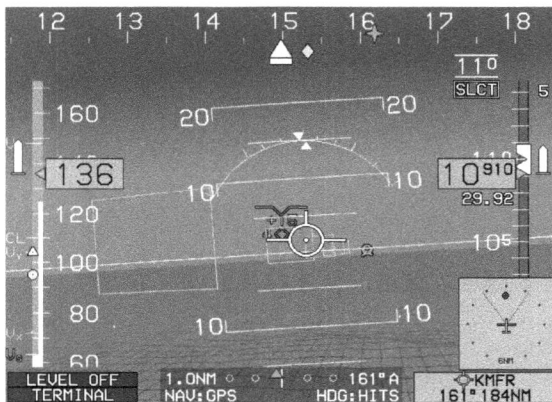

Picture: Courtesy, Chelton Systems, Inc.

It is a circular symbol that is superimposed on the AI part of the PFD when the FPV button is pressed. The symbol represents the aircraft's axis in relation to the vertical and lateral movement referenced to the Earth's surface. On the ground, the circle would be on the horizon line and centred in the display. In the picture, it is just below and to the right of the miniature aeroplane, indicating that the flight path is down and to the right.

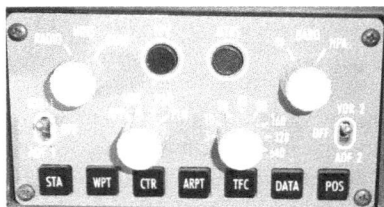

The FPV provides an almost instantaneous display of flight path angle and drift. For example, if you took off in a 15 kt crosswind the Flight Director would register the pitch while the FPV would be above the horizon and to one side. The lateral deviation provides a visual indication

of the drift from the crosswind, while the vertical deviation shows the attitude or pitch.

EHSI/ND

The *Electronic Horizontal Situation Indicator* (EHSI) or *Navigational Display* (ND) tells you where you are in one of three modes that have different capabilities.

If the signal from a VOR is lost, the deviation bar and pointer is removed from the display.

MAP

MAP mode is used for general bread-and-butter enroute navigation. It shows your position as a relationship between the current heading, navaids and actual track.

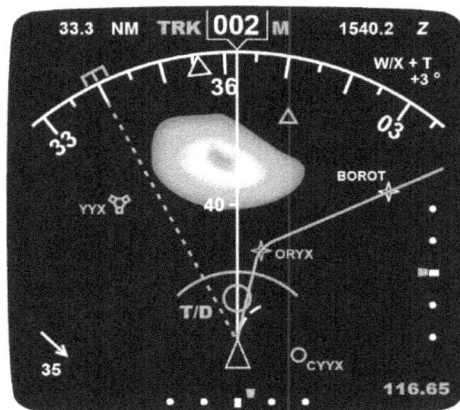

MAP Mode (Expanded)

It is oriented to the aircraft heading or track, which can be shown in True or Magnetic (True is automatically selected above 73°N and below 65°S). In expanded (ARC) mode, the arc can cover between 30-60° either side of the track. Heading information comes from the IRS.

Your (FMC) position is at the apex of the white triangle (the aircraft) at the bottom of the screen and the track is a white line extending vertically away from it (see the Expanded version). Range markings are selected through the control panel. It normally points to 12 o'clock, except in heading mode where it will only do so in nil wind conditions. Weather radar may be displayed in MAP, expanded VOR/ILS and expanded NAV modes.

In the picture above:

- The selected Course is 010°.

- The track is 002°.

- The heading is 356°, and the selected heading is outside the visible rose (dotted line).

- The aircraft is to the left of track and on the vertical profile.

- The W/V is 330/35 knots. Wind speed and relative direction are in the bottom left hand corner, shown according to the compass rose. It can be found on Map, Expanded ILS, Full ILS and Full VOR modes. When the track line coincides with the desired track, wind influence is compensated for.

- The ETA 15:40 and the distance to go is 33.3 nm.

The green circle ahead of your position is the Top of Descent (or Climb, as in T/C). The green arc behind it (the range-to-altitude ring, or banana bar) is where the selected altitude will be reached at the current vertical speed. The white arc extending away from the triangle is a trend vector with each dash representing 30 seconds ahead. The scales on the bottom and right that look like a localiser and glideslope show you deviations from LNAV and the VNAV descent path. A magenta line represents the active route, and the *active waypoint* is the one the system is currently navigating to. If you want a different heading than that chosen by the FMS, you must use the magenta heading select marker. When the track line coincides with the desired track, the influence of the wind is compensated for.

Fix information is a dashed green line. A dashed blue circle is a clean energy management circle. A dashed white one is a drag circle for extended speed brakes.

ETOs and ETAs as calculated by the FMC are naturally correct when the actual winds match the forecast winds and the FMC Mach number is the actual one. Magnetic heading is shown, but True is available via the IRS.

If a VOR receiver fails, the associated magenta deviation bar and/or pointer is removed from the display.

PLAN

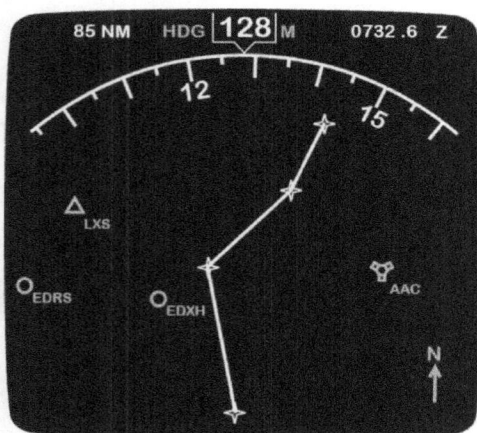

PLAN

The PLAN display provides an overview of the whole or parts of the route, but is not displayed in real time, except for the information at and above the expanded rose.

You cannot normally display wind and weather in this mode (depends on the manufacturer). You might use it to see the effects of changes in the route before entering

them into the FMC. Plan mode is always expanded, and oriented to True North (i.e. North up - watch for the arrow bottom right, though on some systems the arc may be set to N). There is also no aircraft symbol.

VOR/ILS

In full mode (also known as *centred*), you get an electronic representation of the traditional HSI. You will get wind, but not weather, information. In expanded mode, weather information is available on both EHSIs.

The full rose will change for the VOR and ILS according to the frequency selected. The full deflection is 20° for the VOR and 5° for the ILS.

DEAD RECKONING

DR mode is a backup for when the other navigation sensors are not working. It computes heading, airspeed, wind data, groundspeed and time.

OVERFLY FUNCTION

This makes the aircraft fly specifically over a waypoint, of which there are two types.

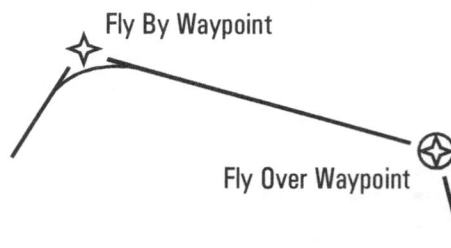

A *flyover waypoint* is one whose lat & long position* must be flown over before you can turn onto the next leg, typically used on standard departures to ensure that you don't make excessive bank angles that will interfere with performance calculations. You can fly *direct-to* any waypoint, or *direct/intercept*, where you can select a desired course to reach it. Waypoints can also have speed, altitude and time constraints (*not before*, etc.)

*Waypoints can be entered into all INSs as lat & long.

capt.gs

👍**Rule Of Thumb:** Anticipate the turn by 1 nm for every 30° change.

SYMBOLS AND COLOURS

Active flight plans and waypoints are *magenta* in MAP mode. Otherwise, general colours are:

- **GREEN**: Present situation, low priority info, light precipitation.

- **WHITE**: Static information, turbulence, current and armed data values (cyan can also be armed).

- **MAGENTA**: Command information (i.e. FD bar), weather radar, turbulence, selected heading, active routes or waypoints.

- **CYAN**: Non-active and background information, can also be armed mode.

- **RED**: Warnings (flight envelope or system limits).

- **YELLOW**: Caution or abnormal sources.

- **BLACK**: Off.

- **BLUE**: The sky.

- **TAN/BROWN.** The Earth.

The extensive use of yellow for other than caution/abnormal information is discouraged. In colour Set 1, magenta should be associated with analogue parameters that constitute *fly to* or *keep centred* information.

EICAS/ECAM

The *Engine Indicating and Crew Alerting System* (EICAS) shows you what all the systems around the aircraft are up to. EICAS & ECAM*, from Boeing & Airbus, respectively, are well known monitoring systems, but they all have an EFIS-type display at the front end.

Electronic Centralised Aircraft Monitoring. Engine parameters are on the upper display, and system/status information on the lower display. If a caution message appears, the system will display a diagrammatic view of the affected system.

Anyhow, the downward pointing arrows at the bottom left of the upper EICAS screen tell you there is information on the lower one - if you can't see anything, it is not working. If both displays fail, N_1, EGT and N_2 information is displayed on the standby engine indicator.

You only get a warning light if the ECAM display fails.

Although it primarily shows engine indications, EICAS also acts like a central warning panel. The upper screen is the primary display, and the lower is the secondary. The status portion is used to determine the readiness of an aircraft for dispatch.

EICAS Recall messages appear on the screen in white.

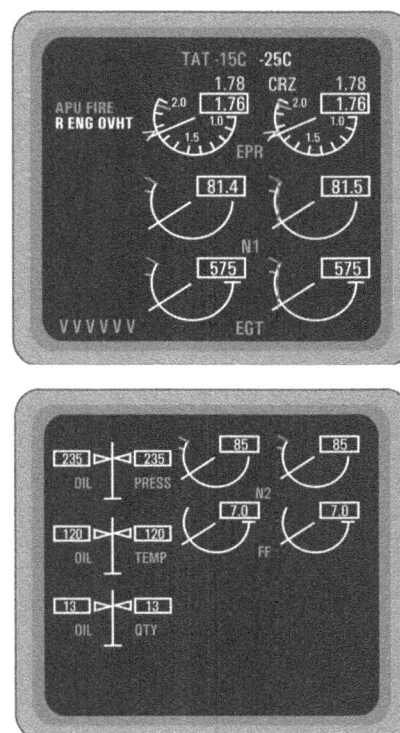

INERTIAL NAVIGATION

Inertial systems can provide continuous information on your position, true track, heading, groundspeed and height without any outside help, allegedly first designed for the V2 rocket, but also extremely useful for submarines. With TAS information from the ADC, they can calculate wind velocity - being self-contained, they can work anywhere and, as a bonus for the military, are undetectable.

Although they can operate in True at any latitude, inertial systems can apply local variation (between 73°N - 60°S*) from a lookup table in a database, so a flux detector is not required, although there is an area between 90°W to 120°W and 70°N to 72°N (in Canada) where the variation table cannot update the output from true to magnetic. Some sets show HDG FAIL in that case and need manual switching to TRUE, which others can do automatically. This is because it is too close to the North magnetic pole.

*At higher latitudes the variation is either unusable, unreliable, or has too high an annual rate of change.

Tip: INS/IRS navigation uses great circle tracks (i.e. the shortest distance between any two points - see *Navigation*), because they orient themselves in space (against the stars) and their data is converted into latitude & longitude through a mathematical model, typically WGS 84. When you see IRS/INS in a question, you know it involves a

Great Circle. The differences between WGS 84 and the proper shape of the Earth are why Schuler tuning is needed, discussed later.

The data provided and the equipment used can be made available for other systems - the high quality gyros will typically drive the artificial horizons and allow for accurate heading maintenance, which is the real trick - once the initial heading is calculated from the Earth's spin rate, no corrections should be required.

The principles are simple enough. Starting from a known (usually precisely surveyed) point (such as a departure gate), your present position is calculated from the directions and speeds you have used since then, so you have a continuously running **dead reckoning** position that will drift in proportion to the elapsed time, as will the accuracy of any computed altitude. The drift should be around 1 nm per hour for a strapdown system, but it could be 3 nm for the older stable platform. A drift of 0.1° per hour over 15 hours at 500 knots would therefore mean a position error of around 6 nm. If t is the elapsed time since switching to NAV, the azimuth gyro heading error is proportional to t. The main causes of such cumulative distance errors are wander in the levelling gyros and integration errors in the second stage of integration, as described below.

All this sounds wonderful but, as the accuracy degrades over time, you must supplement it with navaids or GPS, where it becomes subject to *bounded* errors based on the other system. Otherwise, in the dynamic situation (exam speak for *in flight*) the error normally continues to build, at differing rates as the velocity error varies, but it will never cancel itself. As the system error keeps growing, it is *unbounded*, and readings will therefore be inaccurate to some extent, especially at the top of the descent, because it has had the whole flight to drift off. It will also be inaccurate just after takeoff, because no updating takes place while you taxi (although the FMC position can often be updated on takeoff with the TO/GA button).

As a fix is obtained (say by being overhead a navaid), you can place the system on hold and tell it where it really is, or at least reset the drift to zero (*Map shift* occurs when the moving map changes position to show the updates).

However, manual updating is only allowed within 25 nm of a co-located VOR/DME, or above a visual fix below 5,000 feet. Auto updating can take place within 200 nm of 2 DMEs or 140 nm of a single DME. GPS, described elsewhere, is a lot more accurate, although it is actually a low bandwidth system, meaning that its update rate is very slow and will resemble a straight line between the start and end points of a journey. IRS and INS are high bandwidth systems that update a lot more often and will show a truer picture. Combining INS/IRS with GPS can therefore provide an accurate, drift-free system, by combining the short term accuracy of INS with the long term accuracy of GPS. The two can also provide redundancy, as INS can keep things going if GPS conditions are not ideal, say when less than 4 satellites are in view, or those that are badly positioned (if GPS data is less than optimal, its signals are verified for accuracy before being incorporated into the system, which is why there are two receivers, but this is only possible with a strapdown system). The GPS can be used for alignment (10 minutes) or navigation. The two systems can be *uncoupled*, *loosely* or *tightly coupled*.

There will normally be at least three INS/IRS systems on most modern aircraft to guard against error, working through the FMS. In the early days, they were standalone, so the only way to check for errors was to inspect each one against a position fix or your DR position (or readings from another aircraft), if you didn't have GPS. Errors would not necessarily be seen until the system pumped out the codes, from which you could tell which one it was. Now, each one's output is compared in a voting system, from which inaccuracies are detected. Having said that, on a triple-fit IRS system, the displayed present positions may differ as the information comes from different sources - and, having said that, a 10 nm difference or one of 8° drift could mean at least one is drifting.

Inertial systems have their own (28v DC) batteries which run for 20-30 minutes, or they may use the hot bus. *If power is lost, you cannot realign for the rest of the flight.*

Older systems were called Inertial *Navigation* Systems because that was their main function, but more modern versions are fully integrated with other parts of the aircraft, hence the name Inertial *Reference* Systems. The basic difference between the two is that an IRS has a reduced spin-up time and an insensitivity to g.

Note: All INS/IRS systems depend on the right information being inserted in the first place, which is why it is so important in the checklist. *Both* pilots must check the entries (see *Flight Management Systems*).

ACCELERATION

Newton's first law of motion is the basis behind inertial navigation. Very loosely, it states that bodies at rest or in motion tend to retain their current state unless acted upon by an external force. Put another way, if you want to change the inertial state of a body, you must use a force. All that is obvious to us, probably, but apparently not so to Aristotle and other great thinkers before Newton. After Newton, however, Mr Einstein added his own views in his Special Theory of Relativity, which are relevant here.

In the wider scheme of things, nothing is at rest. At least, a book on a table is "at rest" with regard to the table, but the book, table and the observer are actually sharing (curved) velocities in space, which brings us to Newton's second law which, in brief, states that the rate of change of velocity (acceleration) is directly proportional to the force making the body accelerate, and inversely proportional to the body's mass.

Acceleration is therefore a measure of how fast the speed of something is changing, being the time rate of change of velocity, or the time rate of change of the time rate of distance. That is, it is measured in feet (or metres) per second, per second. We know that velocity involves changes of distance over time, and acceleration involves changes of velocity over time. If you have a record of its history, an aircraft's accelerations in the vertical, horizontal and lateral planes in space can be integrated* over time to find the changes in its velocity, then again for how long it has been travelling at that velocity to find the distance travelled up, down or sideways. We use accelerations because we cannot measure velocity directly without external aids, which is not the point of the exercise.

*If you know how fast something is changing, you can find out by how much it has changed, in the same way that a fuel flow meter can work out how much has been used from the rate of flow, based on the measurement of infinitely small components. Thus, if you know by how much your speed has changed, you can find out what your speed is now, and from that deduce the distance travelled.

The data from the various integrations is used to calculate track and groundspeed and resolve distances into changes of latitude and longitude. Starting with speed, which is the rate of change of distance with time:

$$S = \frac{D}{T}$$

It is also called the *differentiation* of distance over time. Acceleration is the differentiation of speed with time:

$$A = \frac{S}{T}$$

Since we know that S = D over T (see first formula), the above can be written as:

$$A = \frac{D}{\frac{T}{T}} \quad or \quad A = \frac{D}{T^2}$$

Working backwards, you integrate acceleration once for your initial speed, then integrate speed for distance.

SYSTEM CONTENTS

A typical (early) system consists of:

- *Inertial Navigation Unit* (INU). In it, the Inertial Sensor System contains the stable platform, accelerometers and a computer to integrate the information and provide a value for distance travelled. The ISS is turned into an INS by the ability to manipulate waypoints and find the time and distance to go to reach them.

- *Mode Selector Unit* (MSU).

- *Control Display Unit* (CDU), or *Inertial System Display Unit*, ISDU, below) with a multi-line keypad. It is used for inputting information, such as your starting position and waypoints, as lat & long.

- *Battery Unit* (BU) as a backup.

The MSU and CDU are on the flight deck, and the INU and BU in the depths of the aircraft, where only engineers touch them. The MSU (shown below) is used to switch the thing on in the first place, and select the mode of operation, such as STBY, ALIGN, NAV, ATT, etc.

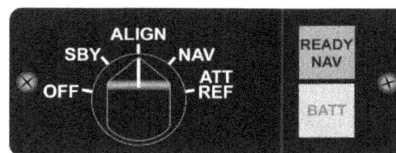

There are also a couple of warning lights. You get a red one when the battery is flat. An ALERT light may come on 2 minutes before a turn. The HOLD button freezes the display. You turn the system on by moving the switch to SBY (if present), so the oil in the gyros can warm up to a specific viscosity, then ALIGN after you have entered your present position, time and date.

Note: The aircraft must remain stationary!

During alignment, the direction of North can be detected from which way the Earth is moving, and the rate of movement provides the latitude. In other words, North alignment uses inputs from the accelerometers and the East gyro.

This process takes at least 2.5 minutes at the Equator and up to 10 minutes at 70° N or S. During initial alignment, an INS will not accept a 10° error in initial latitude, but will accept one in initial longitude.

Once everything is aligned, and before moving off, you must switch to NAV, which is the normal flight mode. At this stage, the outputs include acceleration (N/S & E/W), attitude and true heading.

ATT mode is a backup which retains just attitude and heading information while realignment takes place, so if the navigation computer fails, you can still use the artificial horizon, etc. Once a stable platform INS loses power in flight, it loses its level and alignment references and cannot be re-aligned, because it cannot discriminate between motion of the aircraft and rotation of the Earth, although a strapdown IRS (below) might be able to provide attitude and heading information - the procedure then is to switch to ALIGN and fly straight and level for a minute or two. If the FAIL flags disappear the system may be used for attitude information. If you then input the aircraft heading it may be used as a heading reference.

Having said all that, the equipment in the 787 can realign in flight if one GPS is working.

Picture: INS CDU & MSU for a twin system

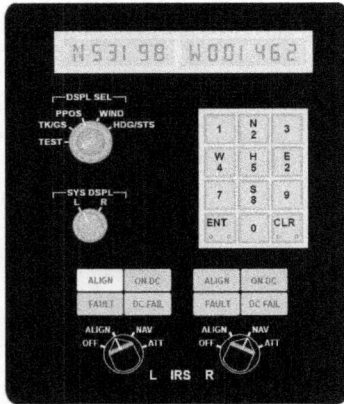

In the picture above, if the ALIGN light is steady, the IRS is in ALIGN mode, ATT mode, or is shutting down. If it is flashing, alignment cannot be completed due to a Code 3, 4 or 8 error. If it is not on, alignment may be complete (if the selector is at NAV) or the system may be off. The amber ALERT light illuminates steadily for 2 minutes before reaching the next way point.

If ON DC is illuminated, the IRS is working from the battery bus rather than AC. The right IRS is limited to 5 minutes. On the ground, a horn in the nose wheel well sounds, to indicate a possible battery drain.

STABLE PLATFORM

The *platform* (or *stable element*) is a gyro-stabilised cluster of linear accelerometers, in three circular gimbals (for the x, y and z axes), to keep them in the right position.

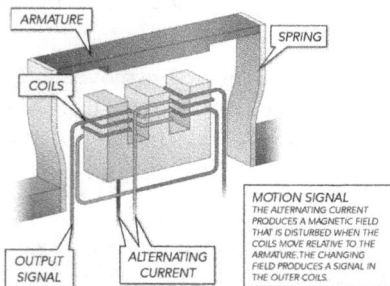

The basic system contains:

- **2 linear accelerometers** in the x and y axes (for LNAV sensing), with possibly another for the z axis. E & I bars may be used because they have minimal friction, otherwise some systems use pendulums. As with the arms on the flux detector, the bars are highly permeable, so a high flux density in proportion to the inducing field can be provided, with a rapid response to changes. The central arm is fed with 400 Hz AC, so the outer legs pick up a secondary induced AC voltage, which is affected by the gap between the bars. If there is no acceleration, the legs have the same voltage, but with opposite polarity. However, as the I bar moves away from the vertical (in the opposite direction to the acceleration), the secondary induced voltage is amplified, phase detected and rectified (to DC) so that a torque motor can try to restore the accelerometer to the null position - the amount of current involved is proportional to the acceleration experienced. The same signal also goes to the integrators.

  Phase detection ensures that the DC is of the right polarity so the I bar can be moved the right way.

- A **stable platform** that keeps the x and y axes oriented N-S and E-W and the z axis aligned with local gravity, so that the x and y accelerometers do not mistake gravity for acceleration. This isolates the aircraft's movements from the Earth's.

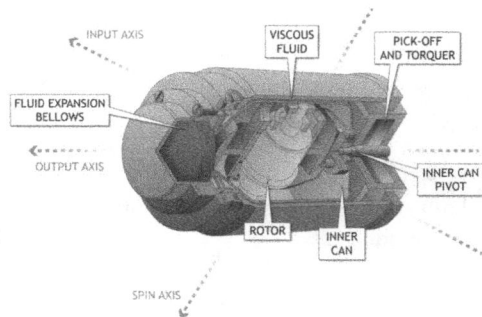

- **3 Rate Integrating Gyros** (for VNAV sensing) that measure and use changes in aircraft vectors to

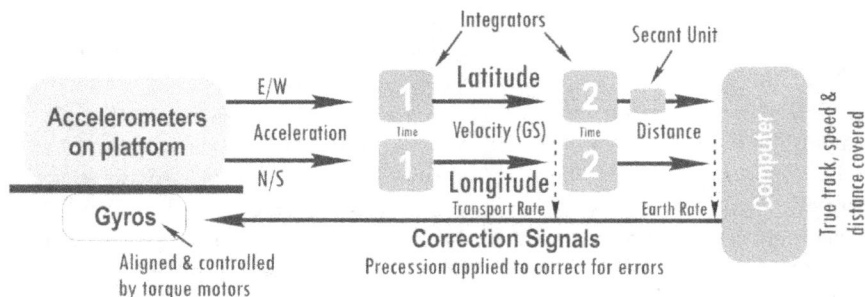

orient the stable platform (these have nothing to do with navigation - they are just there to keep the platform level, but they are highly sensitive). Rate integrating gyros provide a much higher output response for a given input than displacement gyros do. In other words, the output angle is proportional to the input angle, but it is not the same. As they only act about a single axis, three are needed to cover all bases. They are mounted inside cans, one inside the other, the outer one being fixed to the INS platform and the inner one rotating within it, behaving like a gimbal. They are surrounded with warm oil to eliminate friction and reduce bearing torques but, instead of stopping the gyros precessing or toppling, as would happen with a spring, the output axis continues turning as long as the input axis turns

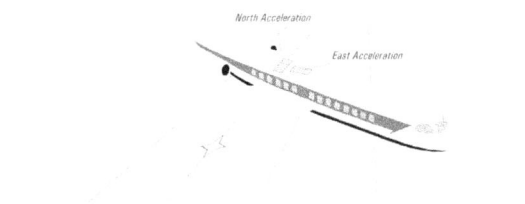

The rigidity of the gyro and the viscosity of the fluid determine the relationship between input and output. When such gyro gain is greater than 1, we have amplification of a displacement, hence the sensitivity. However, a torque motor can also be used to oppose the output. Because the electrical signal is proportional to the rate, it can be used as an input to a computer.

When a tilt from the level position occurs, the spin axes of the gyros remain fixed in space, but their cases move, and an error signal is measured to determine the rate of this movement, which is applied to the platform. Corrections are so quick that the platform does not rotate for more than 10 arcseconds before it is moved back to its original reference position. This also compensates for gravity being mistaken for acceleration, which is what Schuler tuning is for (below).

The RIG that senses the N/S axis is the *North Gyro*, the one for E/W is the *East Gyro*, and the vertical axis gyro (if there is one) is the *Azimuth Gyro*, the drift of which is proportional to time. Gyros are named for the sensitive axis. The platform is also forced to tilt (by torquing the gyros) in proportion to the Earth's rate of turn, based on the latitude. Transport wander is dealt with in the same way, and Coriolis and centrifugal force are also compensated for.

Gyro drift is the main source of error with an INS.

- **Integrators** to convert the acceleration data into velocity and distance information. The signals from the accelerometers go to the *1st stage integrators* which produce velocity information by multiplying the acceleration against time. The *2nd stage integrators* multiply the resulting velocity against time to work out a distance. For N/S, as each minute is 1 nm, this is easily converted into change of latitude which can be added to the start point to find the present latitude. The E/W distance, where a nautical mile is not always a minute of longitude, has to be calculated with the aid of a secant unit. Use of an INS (with its accelerometers aligned N/S and E/W) is limited to latitudes below about 82° because the secant and tangent corrections start to approach infinity and the computer (below) cannot handle the rapid changes involved.

- A **computer** to sort it all out and provide position information. Accelerometer signals are analogue, so there must also be an analogue-digital converter for the computer and displays.

SCHULER TUNING

If an INS is not moving, it assumes it is falling towards the centre of the Earth. If it isn't actually doing that, to register a zero change in position, gravity must removed from its calculations (you need it to measure acceleration).

However, the value of gravity changes with your position and height, what you are flying over, and even the weather. Only the latest systems can use a geometrically correct model of the Earth and its gravitational fields, so the INS must distinguish between the proper shape of the Earth and the mathematical one in its memory (WGS 84).

If the platform is only slightly away from the horizontal, there could be major errors in distance figures as gravity is mistaken for acceleration. If an accelerometer is out by just 1/100th of g, the error on a 1-hour flight would be 208,000 feet, or over 34 nm. Even when you are not moving, misalignment can produce similar effects, but as the velocity is in the system, the platform overcorrects, tilts in the opposite direction and senses a real acceleration to reduce the velocity back to zero. As the platform continues to apply the deceleration, the velocity increases in the opposite direction to produce correcting signals to stop the deceleration, and the increase in velocity. The process starts again because the system is now in full swing back to where it started.

The time taken for the disturbance to go from one extreme to the other (a pendulum effect) is the *Schuler period* of 84.4 minutes, named after Dr. Maximilian Schuler, who showed in 1923 that a pendulum whose length is the same as the radius of the Earth could help eliminate inadvertent acceleration errors because it will always point to the vertical (he was trying to figure out a way of stabilising sea compasses). Put another way, if you could build a pendulum the length of the Earth's radius, with its bob at the centre of the Earth, it would still point to the vertical wherever you moved the point of support (in our case, an aircraft). If the aircraft accelerates, the bob should stay where it is and the pendulum "cord" should stay vertical for all motions of the pivot point (the aircraft). Schuler determined that, if the bob were disturbed, the pendulum would oscillate over 84.4 minutes, so if a system is built with an identical period, it would indicate the local vertical regardless of any acceleration of a vehicle carrying it. It is ironic that he thought it was impossible to build an INS!

An INS platform behaves just like an Earth pendulum in that, when it is disturbed, it takes 84.4 minutes to settle down again, during which time you may be a bit off course. The Earth wobbles, not the INS, but it appears to, relative to the Earth. In other words, it wanders, as can be seen in crosstrack readouts which may increase, then return, in a certain period. The wobble is the Schuler cycle.

The relationship between a circle's angle in radians and its circumference is $^1/_R$ (based on 2π divided by $2\pi R$)*. Multiplying this by V (from the first stage integration) gives you an angular velocity over a surface distance, or the transport rate, which is used to torque the gyro and make the platform precess at the same rate that it is being moved over the Earth's surface.

Schuler tuning provides an undamped closed-loop corrective action to stop tilt errors, oscillating around a zero value over 84.4 minutes.

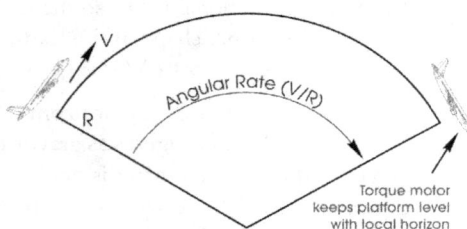

*To make allowances for altitude, $^1/_{R+H}$ is used.

Note: Although Schuler tuning prevents the accumulation of errors which would be caused by platform tilt and treating gravity as an acceleration, it will not compensate for errors from the precession of the steering gyro.

The Schuler tuned platform produces its maximum error at 21.1 and 63.3 minutes through each 84.4 minute cycle. The magnitude of the maximum error depends on the size of the disturbance that caused it, but the mean error remains at zero (assuming no accelerometer error).

Any error in the outputs of the accelerometers caused by Schuler tuning is bounded, meaning that the error does not increase with time beyond its original maximum value.

The output of the first stage integrator (velocity) will also be bounded. Strapped down systems are also considered to be Schuler tuned, and to suffer similar bounded errors.

ALIGNMENT

You cannot use the system until two tasks are accomplished. The platform (or rather the accelerometers) must be levelled*, then lined up with True North, also known as *gyrocompassing*. This is done over about eleven minutes by motoring the (level) platform until there is no topple output from the East gyro (when stationary on the ground, the only cause of topple would be the rotation of the Earth, so if there is none, the axis is assumed to be aligned N/S). The topple output of the North gyro should now equal the Earth rate, which is 15° x cos latitude, so this is impossible at high latitudes because of the torquing rates. Also the cosine value would be near zero. However, the INS cannot do this unless it has a latitude input.

*With coarse levelling, the pitch and roll gimbals are driven until they are at 90° to each other. The platform is then levelled to ± 10° against the aircraft frame or gravity using the horizontal accelerometers or gravity switches. Coarse azimuth alignment (± 2°) is achieved by turning the platform in azimuth until the heading output agrees with the aircraft's best known heading, normally obtained from the gyro-magnetic compass. This is followed by fine levelling, which is done by motoring the platform until no acceleration from gravity is sensed by the x and y accelerometers - this does not need lat & long input. It takes about 6 minutes. Fine levelling uses the accelerometer null technique - with the aircraft stationary there should be no output from the horizontal accelerometers if the platform is level. Fine levelling normally takes about 1.5 minutes.

Alignment is only done once, before the flight, because the outputs from the accelerometers and gyros are used differently, hence the separate ALIGN mode on the MSU (although alignment can be done in ALIGN or NAV mode). It takes about 17 minutes overall for a stable platform. However, with such a North pointing system, things get interesting when you go over a Pole, because the platform would have to turn through 180° almost instantly (in fact, the problems start several hundred miles away). A workaround is to keep the platform level, but not worry about aligning it to North necessarily - just detect how far out of alignment it is, and include it in future calculations. In this case, the accelerometers would be offset by the *wander angle*. Yet another is not to bother levelling (or aligning), but figure out how far out the accelerometers are at initialisation and monitor changes.

During alignment the aircraft must remain stationary. If there is excessive movement, the ALIGN annunciator will flash and the fault indicator will come on, so this is not possible during flight (the gyros cannot distinguish between acceleration due to aircraft movement and initial alignment errors). Switch the Mode Select switch off for at least 3 seconds then put it back to ALIGN. The ALIGN light will also flash if you do not enter the present position within the normal alignment time. Once aligned, the platform will be level, pointing along True North, and you can switch to NAV mode. If it is level, and the aircraft is not, the difference is measured and displayed as Pitch and Roll. The yaw difference between the longitudinal axis and the platform (North) is *Heading*. During alignment, most systems start passing attitude information to the FMS before being fully set up.

ERRORS

INS errors are *bounded*, *unbounded* and *inherent*.

Bounded errors are constant over time, such as track or groundspeed errors that start off at a fixed rate, but these can lead to unbounded errors that get larger with time. Otherwise, accelerometers cannot tell the difference between gravity and acceleration, hence levelling errors. The estimated local gravity (from a database) can be subtracted from vertical accelerations to compensate. The usual stuff also applies, like Earth rate and transport wander, which are predictable, because the computer knows your position. Thus, Coriolis effect and centripetal acceleration can also be calculated, and Schuler corrections applied to compensate for Transport rate (using the velocity signal from the first integration).

Real wander is compensated for on the ground, but can occur in turbulence, etc.

STRAPDOWN

The *strapdown system* is strapped directly to the aircraft structure. It has no gimbals, because it uses ring laser gyros (at least 3, with 3 accelerometers at 90° to each other), so the outputs are *rate* sensitive, as opposed to *displacement* sensitive. The "spinning mass" therefore follows the airframe and its alignment to true North is *calculated*. With no moving parts, the "stable platform" is maintained mathematically*, rather than mechanically. This provides more accuracy and reliability, aside from spinning up faster, but it can also suffer from laser lock.

*The strapdown has a bias signal to compensate for Schuler drift applied to the readouts. You may notice position variations of about 1 nm between systems when they are not on the same points of the Schuler cycle. Other potential errors, such as Coriolis, are allowed for, but not mentioned here.

The IRS contains:

- two **Air Data Inertial Reference Units**, with:

    - a **power supply**

    - an **Inertial Reference** (IR). This senses and computes linear accelerations and turning rates around each axis, to feed pitch and roll

displays and navigation calculations. The only other information needed is your start position, barometric altitude and TAS, which is obtained from the ADR, together with other useful information. Barometric altitude provides a reference for vertical navigation, and stabilises the vertical velocity and inertial altitude outputs. As an IRS doesn't need a platform, it needs three "accelerometers".

- an **Air Data Reference** (ADR), which is separate on some aircraft.

- a **display unit**

- a **mode select unit**

Rotation about an axis can be sensed with fibreoptic or ring laser gyros, as described earlier.

ALIGNMENT

This is a much faster process than with the stable platform, because the system moves with the Earth, although levelling and alignment are still done while stationary, because the only acceleration is from gravity and the only angular movement from the Earth's rotation. From its direction and magnitude, the position of True North can be sensed and the latitude can be estimated.

However, you have to enter your whole position (i.e. an **accurate lat & long**) because the present longitude cannot be worked out (the latitude input is used as a crosscheck for the calculated figure, while the longitude input is compared to the last stored one). Put in exam speak, *you need to position the computing trihedron with reference to the Earth*. Well, of course you do.

Without Earth rate compensation, the system would also think it is upside down after 12 hours at the Equator. Elsewhere, there would be pitch, roll and heading errors. If you put in the wrong latitude, the Earth rate calculations will be wrong and you won't be able to align to True North properly (if the ALIGN lights are flashing this is what has happened).

As with other systems, you must switch to ALIGN to set things up, although Boeing recommend selecting NAV directly if you're between the 70°S and 70°N latitudes (there is no STANDBY setting as there are no gyros to warm up). Alignment varies with latitude - 5 minutes at the Equator, 10 minutes at 70°N and 17 minutes between 70- 78°. Although, during turnarounds, it is best to turn the system off and allow it to realign completely, if time is tight (it usually is), a fast re-alignment can be done. Just switch to ALIGN and enter a new gate position. Reselect NAV once the ALIGN lights go out.

In NAV mode, the gyros measure the Earth's movement with respect to space, and your movement with respect to the Earth, in the form of Transport rate, because any movement over a sphere involves some sort of rotation.

AUTOMATIC CALIBRATION

- **Auto cal** maintains the calibration of the gyros and the longitudinal and lateral accelerometers to improve performance and reliability.

- **Gyro autocal** measures the position error after the flight and estimates the gyro errors that would have caused it.

- **Accelerometer autocal** picks up lateral bias errors found during taxi, because movement is generally forward.

ERRORS

A strapdown system suffers from lock-in errors caused by imperfect mirrors, which are reduced by wobbling, or vibrating with the *dither motor* and *spring*.

However, the system accuracy is around 2 nm/hour.

Otherwise errors include:

- **Schuler Tuning**. Platform oscillations cause errors to be propagated over a 84.4 minute cycle.

- **Levelling & Azimuth Gyro Drift**. Real Wander possibly 0.01°/hour - the largest errors in the system, distance error unbounded.

- **Initial Levelling** (Tilt). The accelerometers sense gravity - velocity and distance errors unbounded.

- **Initial Alignment**. Accelerometers misaligned N/S & E/W - velocity error bounded, distance error unbounded.

- **Accelerometer Errors**. Small random errors throughout the system.

- **Earth Shape**. The computer's spherical trigonometry is in error.

- **Altitude**. Earth rate/transport wander gyro corrections are calculated for ground level, giving small unbounded errors on long flights.

- **Coriolis** (Accelerometer). Earth rotation and transport wander cause a curved track in space - very small random errors.

- **Centripetal Acceleration** (Accelerometer). A constant altitude creates a curved track in space and acceleration towards the centre of the Earth.

As the readings from the INS/IRS drift over time, you need to check that the system is working within certain limits. For this reason, after the flight, you check your real position with where the system thinks it is. The idea is to check the *radial error rate*. For this you divide the distance off by the time the system has been in navigational mode.

The error rate history can be checked on the *IRS Monitor* page of the Flight Management System. A probable error of 1 nm/hour is the maximum that is commonly accepted (0.3 nm/hr is considered normal), in addition to initial

input errors, although you will usually see a spread of up to ½ nm. Vertical position is potentially not so accurate as horizontal position. If the end position is put in, some units can use it to self-correct for future flights (limits are 10° for base latitude and 30° base longitude).

$$\frac{Dist\ out\ (nm)}{Time\ (hours)}$$

Although the system uses spherical trigonometry, the departure formula (see *Navigation*) can be used to find your distance E-W. Combine that with your N-S distance in a normal Pythagoras calculation to find the distance you are out, which is the hypotenuse:

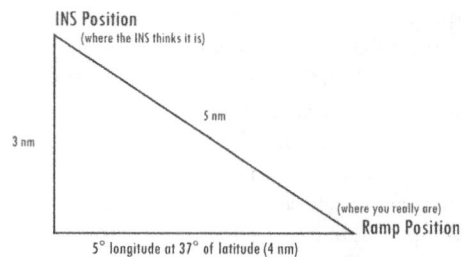

INS Position (where the INS thinks it is)

5 nm

3 nm

(where you really are)
Ramp Position

5° longitude at 37° of latitude (4 nm)

In the picture, the INS thinks you are 5 nm away from your real position, having flown for 2 hours. Your radial error rate is 2.5 nm per hour (the cosine of 37° is 0.8).

EXAMPLE

1. With an azimuth gyro drift of 0.03° per hour, what will be the lateral position error after 5 hours at,500 knots?

After 5 hours (2,500 nm), the error is 0.065° (0.13/2) for a 2.7 nm error, using the 1 in 60 rule.

AHRS

An AHRS (*Attitude and Heading Reference System*) replaces traditional gyros* and their problems, such as topple, drift or gimbal lock in aircraft that don't have a full IRS. It is a combination of inertial sensors in one package that can output attitude, heading and flight dynamics information to flight deck displays and other systems. A flux valve and Air Data Computer will be involved, and 3D orientation is obtained by integrating the gyroscopes with accelerometers and magnetometers (for the magnetic field vector). An AHRS also converts the raw data into standard units like feet or metres, etc., although it will not necessarily provide a True heading output, as this is associated with commercial and military inertial reference and flight management systems. Thus, an AHRS requires less power, less wiring, weighs less and has a smaller footprint, but it will probably cost a lot more.

*While fibreoptic or laser gyros provide very stable angular rate measurements, *Micro Electro-Mechanical System* (MEMS) gyroscopes have the advantage of low power requirements and costs by using Coriolis Effect to measure an angular rate. They are used in solid state accelerometers, rate sensor gyroscopes and magnetometers. Most use a tuning fork configuration, where two masses oscillate and move constantly in opposite directions. In any case, the AHRS is smaller, lighter, more accurate, more reliable and cheaper than traditional mechanical instruments.

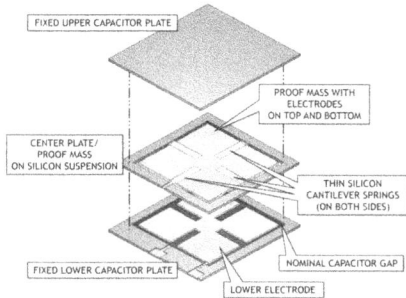

During linear acceleration, the two masses move in the same direction, so no change in capacitance will be detected. However, when angular velocity is applied, the Coriolis force on each mass produces a change in capacitance that is proportional to the angular velocity, which is then converted into output voltage for analog gyroscopes or LSBs for digital gyroscopes.

The magnetometer will usually be mounted remotely from the AHRS, where magnetic disturbances are minimal.

WARNING & RECORDING

Warnings should be attention-getting without being startling, while informing you of what is going on (or not). They should also guide you to the correct actions.

For example, if you need to be aware of something, but maybe have to take action afterwards, you will get an advisory message, which may be any colour except red, and preferably not amber. Red (warning) lights indicate hazards that require immediate corrective action. Amber lights signify that action is required, but not immediately.

Systems should be reliable, meaning they should respond to genuine problems without generating false alarms.

Alerting for important failures should be fulfilled by an audio warning. Ideally, there should be a single one to alert the crew and direct their attention to a single central warning panel that announces the nature of the problem with a suitably illuminated caption.

Otherwise, the standard methods of bringing unusual occurrences to the notice of pilots include:

- **visual** (lights, gauges, displays)
- **aural** (bells, sirens, and sometimes voice)
- **tactile** (stick shakers)

The three levels of alerting are:

- **Warnings** (Level A) - Red, could be flashing
- **Cautions** (Level B) - Amber
- **Advisory** (Level C) - White

Some warnings may be turned off (or muted) so as not to be a distraction during an emergency, or a nuisance during a normal procedure. This includes the Master Caution light, which can be cancelled so you can see if another warning appears on the Central Warning Panel.

Off flags signify whether an instrument is working properly. They might come on if:

- electrical power is lost.
- a gyro is at too low a speed.
- the signal received by a navigation instrument is non-existent or too weak.

GPWS
CAT.OP.MPA.290

A major cause of accidents is Controlled Flight Into Terrain (CFIT).

GPWS

The first attempt at stopping CFIT was the *Ground Proximity Warning System*, which is supposed to be able to give warning of your impending approach towards Terrain Impact Mode in five areas of flight, whereas the radio altimeter relies on the crew looking at it, although it does have an adjustable height bug which acts as a rudimentary warning, if your attention is not diverted. This is why an urgent-sounding audio low height warning was considered necessary (apart from a scream from the other pilot!)

Neither, however, provide a look-ahead function, so would not help if you were about to hit a mountain. The GPWS might get its information from the radio altimeter, the ADC, the Captain's ILS receiver, and gear and flap indicators, over a range of 50-2500 feet (the limits of the radio altimeter). When fitted, *a GPWS system should be switched on and used throughout the flight*, unless it is unserviceable, *and the MEL allows it to be so.*

The GPWS should have at least one sound alarm to which a visual alarm can be added, so a GPWS would provide visual and aural warning if an aircraft descend below 200' radio altitude with its flaps not in the landing position and its speed below Mach 0.28. Alert/warning information is provided by a radio altimeter with a downward transmitting beam whose dimensions are in the order of 30° and 60° in the fore/aft and the athwartship axes.

A GPWS will warn you in case of (amongst others):

The GPWS will warn you in case of (amongst others):

- dangerous proximity to the ground
- loss of altitude during takeoff or missed approach
- wrong landing configuration
- descent below the glidepath

The basic installation has five modes of operation:

- **Mode 1** - *excessive* (barometric) *rate of descent*, which operates when the barometric ROD is more than 3 times greater than the radio height or the clearance available. It uses two different warnings: an advisory, or soft warning, **Sinkrate**, **Sinkrate**, and a hard warning of **Whoop Whoop Pull Up**, repeated twice. Both stop outside the warning envelopes of between 50-2500 feet radio altimeter (the usual operating range of GPWS). The aural alert goes off when passing the first boundary.

- **Mode 2** - *excessive closure rate*, from a reducing radio altitude. This can be confused with Mode 1, but this means the ground is coming up rather than the aircraft going down, so it may even go off in level flight. Mode 2a is sounded if the flaps are not in the landing position, and 2b if they are. If the radio altitude, speed and rate of closure are within the warning envelope, the words **Pull Up, Pull Up** after a whooping sound are heard, which cannot be inhibited. Otherwise, the warning is *Terrain*.

- **Mode 3** - *negative climb rate* (for radio altitude), or *sinking after a takeoff or go-around* (i.e. height loss before achieving 700 feet terrain clearance). If the barometric altitude lost is around 10% of radio altitude gained, the continuous **Don't Sink, Don't Sink** aural warning will sound, with a second advisory of **Too Low Terrain** if the original radio altitude is over 150 ft AGL, then decreases by more than 25% of it. If you get a warning during takeoff or on a missed approach, you have started to lose altitude. Mode 3 activates between 30 and 667-1,333 feet radio altitude (depends on airspeed).

- **Mode 4** - *approaching too close to the ground with flaps or gear up*, so this is only active during the landing phase. There are two sub-modes (4a and 4b) and three alerts, depending on the phase of flight and aircraft configuration. Aural warnings will be either *Too Low Gear*, *Too Low Flap*, or *Too Low Terrain* (depends on aircraft speed).

- **Mode 5** - *going too far below the glideslope* (more than 1.3 dots), assuming you have tuned the correct ILS frequency. You may hear *Terrain*, *Too Low Glideslope*, *Glideslope* and *Pull Up*.

PULL UP

BELOW G/S

- **Mode 6** - *Miscellaneous* stuff like automatic height callout and bank angles, usually company-specific.

- **Mode 7** - *Windshear Mode*. A two-tone siren, plus the words **Windshear Windshear Windshear,** given once only, with a warning light, which are triggered if the predicted aircraft energy level falls below a safe threshold. Windshear warnings have a higher priority than other GPWS modes.

Alerts and warnings in Modes 1 and 2 are only given when you are less than 2,500 ft above local terrain, because this is in the normal operating range of the radio altimeter. Both modes are active in all flight phases.

A GPWS must generate at least one sound alarm, for which a visual alarm can be added. You can expect:

- An **alert**, which is just a caution, or

- A **warning**, which requires *immediate action*, because verifying warnings takes so long you may as well not have the device in the first place, and it takes a few seconds to get over the denial that you could be in the wrong position. Warnings could be:
  - *genuine*
  - a *nuisance* (when in a safe procedure), or
  - *false* (outside the validity area of a glideslope)

However, there are those who think that modes 1-5 have been "adjusted" so much to try to eliminate nuisance warnings that they have become ineffective. For example, to get a Mode 1 alert you need to exceed 3,000 feet per minute at,500', 1,200 fpm at 200' and 900' fpm at 10' - very high and very close, so the problems may well arise before the warnings! Typically, this will be for between 5-30 seconds beforehand, if at all over exceptionally rugged ground. Also, once an aircraft with GPWS has been configured for landing, there is very little protection against inadvertent proximity to terrain or water.

In summary, GPWS takes into account the aircraft's height as well as its descent rate and configuration. It has no terrain display or map, no predictive capability, and is radio altimeter based but, for all that it was a first generation attempt, GPWS marked a substantial decrease in hull loss rates in the 80s. Around 40% of fatal accidents were in aircraft without it.

TAWS

Terrain Awareness and Warning System is the generic term for altitude alerting systems of varying complexity, which includes GPWS and radio altimeters. The term therefore includes EGPWS, or Enhanced GPWS.

ENHANCED GPWS

GPWS was required for aircraft over 5700 kg and EGPWS became required for aircraft over 15,000 kg. It is linked to the instruments and can be updated with software. You get the basic GPWS modes and:

- **FLTA** (*Forward Looking Terrain Avoidance*), which checks for the absence of anything in the way within a preset search area (or volume, since it is vertical as well as horizontal). The search volume is curved in the direction of any turns

- **PDA** (*Premature Descent Alert*). Under normal circumstances, after the gear is lowered, if there is no ILS signal, an aircraft would be unprotected, so the internal database can be used to provide a protected area around each runway, which enhances Mode 4, described below.

To provide the FLTA function, the details in a **world terrain and obstacle database** are compared with your GPS vertical and horizontal position, but radar helps as well, if you have it. The system also takes account of your barometric altitude and predicted flight path, so a side benefit is improved situational awareness from the advanced warning of the surrounding terrain.

As it happens, EGPWS has 32 modes, including *Terrain Clearance Floor* (TCF), *Terrain Look Ahead Alerting* and *Terrain Alerting and Display* (TAD). TAD is affected if the computed aircraft position gets less accurate. The system first identifies the stage of flight, then selects the appropriate one, with the airborne value stored in memory and kept immune from power interruptions. A system will typically go *In Air* when the weight on wheels switch indicates that you are airborne.

Note: Since the system relies on databases, they must be kept up to date! This means internal company procedures for ensuring that this is done in a timely fashion!

Note also that, to save memory space, the terrain database is only high resolution within about 16 miles of an airport - areas between them are low resolution. Beyond 60 miles, it is typically an eighth (you should be in the cruise by then). So, EGPWS is a terrain based map system, which has a predictive capability that can determine your position and flight path based on information from the FMS/GPS, Air Data System, Radio Altimeter and VOR/ILS (plus flaps and the angle of attack), comparing your altitude with its internal database and, if there is a potential threat of hitting the ground, can generate warnings well before the classic GPWS could do.

It uses the same colours as weather radar, namely green, amber, red and magenta.

In spite of the above benefits, there are still limitations. First of all, as mentioned above, the system requires an up to date database, which may have errors and will, by definition, not know anything about mobile obstacles.

Secondly, protection will be limited if your navigational accuracy is degraded - there are still areas in which GPS reception is poor. There may also be delays in alerts being given, or even unwanted ones.

A caution alert is typically given 60 seconds ahead of a terrain/obstacle conflict and is repeated every 7 seconds as long as the conflict remains within the caution area.

BITE

Built In Test Equipment is a press-to-test function used to do part of the prestart checks. When pressed, the GPWS system lights come on in sequence with audio alerts and warnings. If the system is not functioning, they will not be complete (pushing the **PULL UP** light tests the system and illuminates all the lights). An **INOP** light will come on if the system fails or it loses a source of input.

Radio Altimeter

A radio altimeter is a self-contained on-board safety device that indicates the *true height* of the *lowest wheels* (with oleos extended) above the ground. Data supplied includes the distance between the ground and the altimeter. Radio altimeters (with audio) are required equipment over water. Low altitude radalts are used for precision approaches, with accuracy of ±2 ft between 0-500 feet or $\pm 1.5\%$, whichever is greater, and are only active below about 2,500 ft. High altitude ones work up to 50,000 feet above the surface.

A *continuous wave* FM radio beam in the SHF band (4200-4400 MHz)* is directed towards the ground in a 30° cone fore and aft, and 30° athwartships. The signal is reflected back to the aircraft. As the time delay for a pulsed signal is too small to measure properly (and the antennae cannot switch between transmit and receive that quickly), CW (as opposed to pulse) radar eliminates minimum range problems. You need separate transmit and receive aerials.

*Centimetric - see *Radio Navigation*. High altitude radalts use decimetric.

It takes around 6.1 microseconds for a wave to be reflected back from an object around 10,000 m away. With CW radar, we can arrange for a frequency change for that time period - say from 1,000 MHz to 1006.1. The difference of 6.1 MHz therefore represents 10,000 yards. You only have to measure the difference in frequency to find the range, so the system is frequency modulated. Although the frequencies change, the difference between them remains constant.

The transmitted frequency sweeps up and down through about 200 MHz either side of 4300 MHz. Compensation is made for aerial (residual) height and wiring, and to account for signal processing time, so the altimeter reads zero when the wheels touch down (placing the aerials near the gear means the radalt will also read zero when the nosewheel is on the ground). For most radio altimeters, when a system error occurs during approach, the height indication is removed.

In any case, below 1,000 feet, on an EFIS display, the readout changes to analogue.

When a system error occurs on approach, the height indication is usually removed.

Slope changes on a radio altimeter operating area should be avoided or kept to a minimum, being as gradual as practicable, with no abrupt changes or sudden reversals. The rate of change between two consecutive slopes should not exceed 2% per 30 m.

TCAS/ACAS

CAT.OP.MPA.295
ICAO Annex 10

If SSR can provide information to ground stations about aircraft carrying transponders, the same information can be provided to airborne stations.

Airborne Collision and Avoidance Systems (ACAS) provide you with an independent backup to your eyes and ATC by telling you if you are likely to hit another aircraft. The system was developed after the increased use of Area Navigation systems which allowed more direct routings away from specific airways.

An aircraft with such equipment is surrounded with three concentric envelopes of airspace that are monitored by radar. As the envelopes are defined by flight time, their size depends of the relative speeds of the aircraft involved. The space immediately around the aircraft is the **collision area**, then there is a **warning area** that represents 20-25 seconds of closing time. The largest envelope is the **caution area**, which expands outwards to allow for 45 seconds of response time.

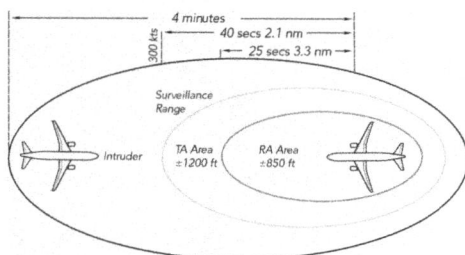

TCAS (the T stands for *Traffic*) is actually the system developed by the FAA, whilst ACAS is the generic name used by ICAO. Your aircraft's ACAS capability is not normally known to ATC, unless you mention it on a flight plan. Basic systems (TCAS I) just provide warnings of traffic without guidance.

However, TCAS II, the current equipment (version 7.1*), provides advice in the *vertical* plane, as a:

- **Traffic Advisory** (TA), or a warning, telling you where nearby *transponding aircraft* are, or a...
- **Resolution Advisory** (RA) which suggests avoiding action *in the pitch plane only*.

This is because all systems depend on azimuthal accuracy, which is not all that good, and why TCAS II makes you climb or descend to avoid traffic (TCAS I leaves any avoiding action up to you).

*For RVSM. A *Level Off* RA replaces the *Adjust Vertical Speed* one in version 7.0.

In view of the above, TCAS I can be regarded as a VMC aid, and TCAS II as an IMC aid, although it is possible, though not advisable, to use TCAS I in cloud. The system interrogates other aircraft, independent of ground aids, using four antennae, a computer *and a transponder* to continually survey the airspace around you and predict the flight paths of likely intruders, based on Mode C (TCAS I) or S (TCAS II) transponder signals from other traffic. If both aircraft have TCAS II, the bearing of the intruding aircraft is determined with a specific directional antenna.

It will not see obstacles or non-transponder equipped aircraft. Without Mode C, you will just get Traffic Advisories. The anti-collision logic of TCAS I is based on time. TCAS II will use inputs from the radio altimeter to inhibit RAs close to the ground.

The equipment scans a small amount of airspace around your aircraft in which it thinks a collision is possible. The range of intruding aircraft is determined by measuring the time lapse between the transmission of an interrogation signal and the reception of a reply from the intruder. Relative heights are measured by comparing Mode C transmissions.

An *intruder* will show up on the display with a symbol representing the grade of threat, plus numbers for their relative height above or below you in hundreds of feet (+ or - signs). An up or down arrow provides a vertical trend (over,500 fpm).

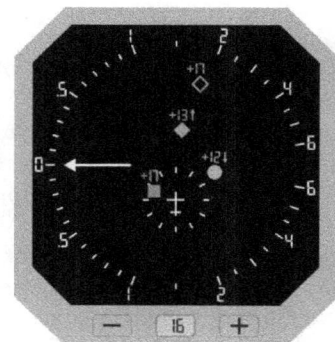

A hollow diamond (white on EFIS) indicates **non-threat** (other) traffic over 6 nm away horizontally. A shaded (solid) diamond indicates **proximate traffic** within 6 nm horizontally and 1 200 feet vertically. A Traffic Advisory (TA) is given when an intruder comes with 30 seconds of your aircraft (45 seconds for TCAS II), as a *potential* threat, when the symbol changes to a solid amber circle.

A Traffic Advisory (TA) is given when a close traffic intruder comes with 30 seconds of your aircraft (45 seconds for TCAS II), as a *potential* threat, when the symbol changes to a solid amber circle. When it becomes a red square (RA) the intruder is an *immediate* threat - red for danger and a box, because if you don't follow an RA that's where you will be. An RA would normally come about 20 seconds after the TA.

A *corrective advisory* calls for a change in vertical speed (or something different to what you are currently doing) and a *preventive* advisory restricts it. RAs are corrective except MONITOR VERTICAL SPEED, which is a *preventative* RA, during which you should avoid deviation from the current vertical rate, with no changes to that rate.

Note: RAs do not take stall margins into account!

An RA voice message CLIMB CLIMB NOW repeated twice is generated after a DESCEND RA when a reversal is needed.

The aural messages provided by TCAS II include *Climb, Descend, Increase climb, Increase Descent.*

TCAS MANOEUVRES

A TCAS manoeuvre is a valid reason for the inability to comply with a clearance. They should be reported to ATC, even after the action has been taken and the original clearance has been resumed (although ATC may issue a revised clearance). A response should be initiated immediately (not in the opposite direction), and crew members not involved should check for other traffic.

Because of past confusion when responding to a TCAS RA, the only radio call you now make includes your call sign followed by TCAS RA. When you are clear of conflict, you report back to ATC, but maintain the new altitude until ATC tells you otherwise. Do not resume the previous altitude without ATC clearance. An RA may be disregarded only when you visually identify conflicting traffic and decide that no deviation is necessary. If an RA and ATC conflict, the RA wins.

If an aircraft approaches from below, you would get an aural warning (CLIMB CLIMB CLIMB) and a visual one showing red for negative rates up to 15 fpm and green from 1500 fpm onwards (see right, above). Nuisance or false advisories should be treated as genuine unless the intruder has been positively identified and shown visually to be no longer a threat. TCAS II can display on its own screen, on weather radar, EFIS, a variometer (VSI) with an LCD display, and others. It uses two antennae, the upper one of which is directional.

POINTS TO WATCH

TCAS II can handle multiple intruders, and you could get multiple advisories when your workload is very high, which is why you can turn RAs off. Another time when you might want to do this is when operating with one engine inoperative (OEI), because a climb RA could demand a higher ROC than that available. Descent RAs are inhibited anyway when below 700 ft AGL, to avoid Controlled Flight Into terrain, or CFIT.

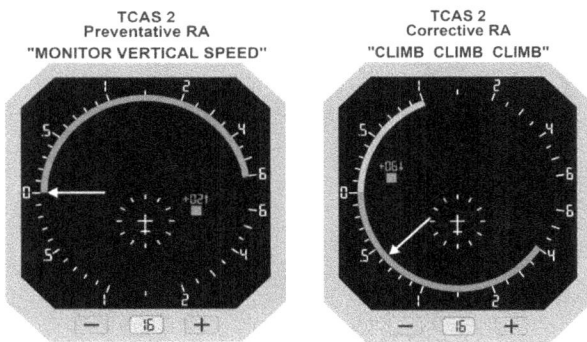

TCAS 2
Preventative RA
"MONITOR VERTICAL SPEED"

TCAS 2
Corrective RA
"CLIMB CLIMB CLIMB"

Resolution Advisory (RA)
30 Seconds From Collision
300-600 ft Vertical Separation
200 ft Above, Climbing

Non-Threat Aircraft
1700 ft Above
Less Than 500 fpm Change

Traffic Advisory (TA)
No Mode C
Altitude Unknown

Threat Aircraft
Traffic Advisory (TA)
1200 ft Above
Descending >500 fpm

Proximate Aircraft
Within 1200 ft & 6 nm
1300 ft Below
Climbing

FLIGHT RECORDING

Flight data must be recorded over at least 25 hours, and cockpit voice and sound warnings at least 30 minutes.

Cockpit Voice Recorders
CAT.IDE.A.185

CVRs are required for:

- aeroplanes with an MCTOM **over 5 700 kg**. When the individual C of A has been issued **on or after 1 April 1998**, it must record the following for the past 2 hours (if issued before, 30 minutes):

  - Voice communications transmitted from or received on the flight deck by radio

  - The aural environment of the flight deck

  - Voice communications of flight crew members on the flight deck using the interphone system

  - Voice or audio signals identifying navigation or approach aids introduced into a headset or speaker

  - Voice communications of flight crew members on the flight deck using the public address system, if installed

- multi-engined turbojets with an MCTOM of 5 700 kg or less, an MOPSC of more than nine and first issued with a C of A on or after 1 January 1990. It must record the preceding 30 minutes.

A CVR must start to record automatically before the aeroplane moves under its own power* and continue until the termination of the flight when the aeroplane is no longer capable of so doing.

*As early as possible during the cockpit checks before engine start until the cockpit checks immediately following engine shutdown at the end of the flight.

A CVR must have a device to assist with locating it in water.

Flight Data Recorders
CAT.IDE.A.190

- Aeroplanes with an MCTOM of more than 5 700 kg and first issued with a C of A on or after 1 June 1990

- Turbojets with an MCTOM of more than 5 700 kg and first issued with a C of A before 1 June 1990*

- Multi-engined turbojets with an MCTOM of 5 700 kg or less, with an MOPSC of more than nine and first issued with a C of A on or after 1 April 1998

require a digital FDR with a method of readily retrieving its data, positioned as far to the rear as practicable.

*For the previous 25 hours.

The FDR must start to record **before an aeroplane is capable of moving under its own power** and shall stop after it is incapable of so doing. It must be located as far to the rear of the aircraft as practicable.

Pushing the EVENT button on the control panel sets a mark on the recording, so it can be found quickly at the subsequent Board of Inquiry.

The FDR must have a device to assist locating it in water.

NAVIGATION (GENERAL)

Navigation involves taking an aircraft from place to place without excessive reference to the ground, except, perhaps, for checking that you've got the right destination! To do this without radio navigation aids, a system of calculation called *Dead Reckoning* is used, which is actually short for *Deduced Reckoning*, based on solving a *triangle of velocities* with a flight computer, discussed later in the book.

The biggest mistake people make when starting to fly is to confuse navigation with map reading (or *pilotage*), which is used when you need to know your position more precisely, as when doing survey, or as required by a customer. As far as navigation goes, however, you only really need your location in terms of something like "10 miles SE of a radio beacon", or similar. This allows you to sit back and enjoy the ride a bit more, or devote your attention to something slightly more useful. In fact, there are many ways of keeping track of where you are:

- **Pilotage** (visual reference to landmarks), typically used under VFR with.......

- **Dead Reckoning**, or calculating a heading that will take you to where you want to go, allowing for forecast winds. It is used where pilotage is hard to deal with, such as over the sea or a desert, and is often combined with it.

- **Radio Navigation** (with radio beacons).

- **Astral Navigation** (not on the syllabus!)

Usually, combinations are used, with pilotage getting you started on a trip, and helping you end it (as soon as you see the destination, head directly towards it). Pilotage is certainly used to confirm your DR position.

The first step, however, is to get acquainted with .....

THE EARTH

The Earth is the third planet away from the Sun and the fifth largest in the Solar System.

It is not round, but pear-shaped, with the greater of its mass in the Southern hemisphere. It is therefore a *geoid* (its actual shape), an *ellipsoid* (a smoother version, as a 3D ellipse) and a *sphere* (for convenience) in order of accuracy. It is also called an *oblate spheroid*.

The ellipsoid is easier to express mathematically, and the sphere will have the same volume. As it happens, the distortion caused by treating the Earth as a sphere is less than 5% in terms of distance and 12 minutes for direction.

Note: As the Earth is not a perfect sphere, its "radius" can mean many things. It is the distance from the centre to the *mean sea level* at a point, which can vary quite a bit (it is around 12 miles from the top of the tallest mountain to the bottom of the deepest ocean).

The value of the radius *at the Equator* (the *major semi axis*) is **6378.4** km (around 12 700 km in diameter) for an Equatorial circumference of 40 069 km (21 600 nm).

Between the Poles (the *minor semi axis*, around which the Earth revolves), it is **6356.6**, with a circumference of 39 943 km, so the Earth is larger round the Equator than it is through the Poles by just under 140 km, or 74 nm. The difference is called the *compression ratio*, and the value for the flattening is 1/298 (0.3%).

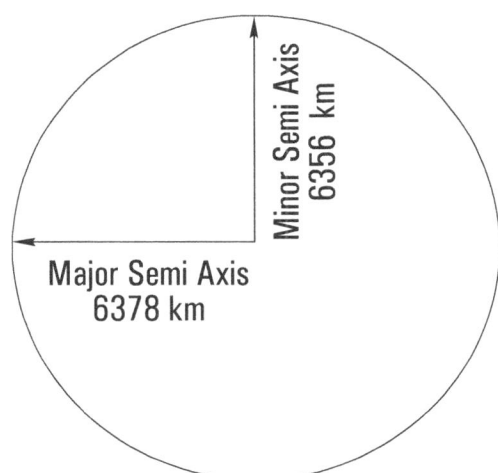

So, if the major (Equatorial) radius is 6378 km (3444 nm), the minor (Polar) axis is 1/298 shorter, or:

$$6378 - \frac{6378}{298} = 6356.6$$

The assumed radius of the Earth (as a sphere) is 6371 km. As this is a constant figure, you don't need to include it in any calculations, which allows us to use a 2D coordinate system, as described below.

POSITIONAL REFERENCE

A Positional Reference System identifies any position* on the surface of an object. The following can be used:

- A graticule system (latitude & longitude or a grid)
- A known point (a position fix)
- The bearing and range from a known point

*The word *position* means a place that can be positively identified, and which may be qualified by such terms as *estimated*, *nil wind*, etc. The distance between two points, or axes, on a sphere, is measured by angles which can be related to physical distances. Positions are related to others by the differences in latitude and longitude between them.

Longitude

We can find our position on a straight line graph by using just two parameters, *x* and *y*, otherwise known as *Cartesian coordinates*. As the Earth is a sphere (well, nearly, anyway) with no obvious place to start, we have to use *polar coordinates*, using the angles λ and ϕ, also known as *latitude* and *longitude*, respectively. As a starting point for finding your position, a series of imaginary lines is drawn from Pole to Pole through the Equator, called lines of *longitude*. The Poles are points about which the Earth rotates. The North Pole is the one at the top.

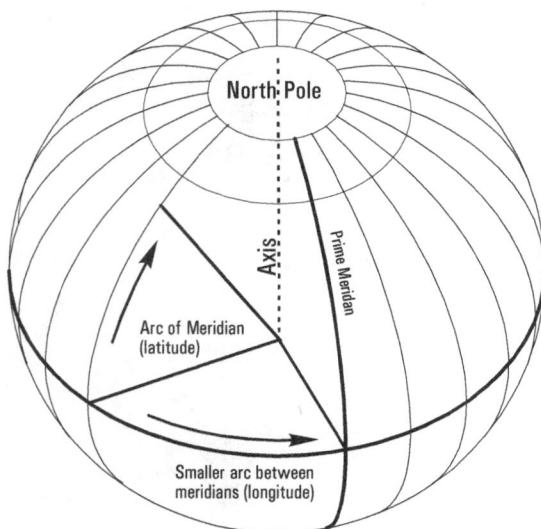

The lines are also called *meridians*, and by convention are drawn for every degree you go round the Equator, of which there are 360. Each meridian has its own

antimeridian on the other side of the Earth. The two together form a Great Circle, described later. Also, by convention, they start at Greenwich, in London (with the *Prime Meridian* at 0°). Longitude is the distance East or West from the Prime Meridian up to 179° E or W (180° is just called 180° longitude as it is neither). Technically, it is the *smaller arc of the Equator between the Prime Meridian and the one through the point concerned*. The angular difference between meridians is the *Change Of Longitude* (ch long).

As the Earth takes nearly 24 hours to spin on its N-S axis, 15 lines of longitude represent 1 hour, and it is noon when the Sun is overhead (*transiting*) any particular meridian (the day starts when it transits the antimeridian). The spinning is anticlockwise at 15.04° per hour when viewed from the top of the Earth (from West to East), so the Sun and other heavenly bodies will appear to move the other way, that is, to rise from the East and set in the West.

Latitude

Having only one vertical line, however, is not enough to find a position with, as you could be anywhere on it, so horizontal lines are also drawn, parallel to each other, North and South of the Equator, up to 90° each way, called *parallels of latitude*. The Equator is 0°.

Parallels go across lines of longitude, and indicate your position North or South of the Equator, up to whichever Pole. An aircraft travelling North in the Northern hemisphere and South in the Southern hemisphere is increasing its latitude, and *vice versa*.

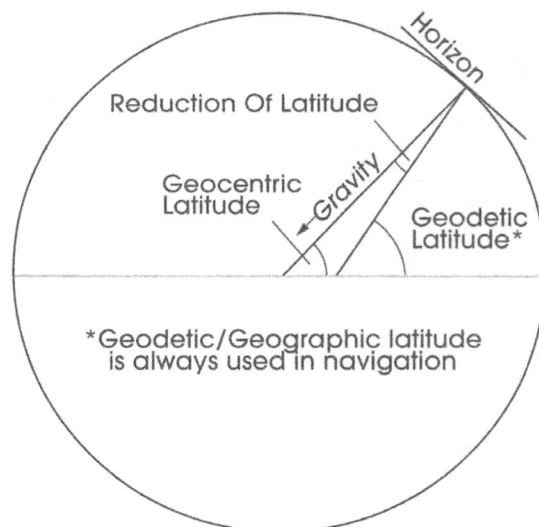

The latitude of any point is the *arc of the meridian between the Equator and the parallel through the point*, or that represented by the angle between the plane of the Equator and a line from the point of interest to the centre of the Earth. Just to confuse things, there's more than one way of defining this angle, because of the Earth's ellipsoid shape.

The angle between a line from the centre of the Earth to a point on its surface and the Equator, measured along a Meridian, is called **Geocentric Latitude**.

If the Earth were a sphere, the story would end there, but it isn't, so such a line is not always vertical, and its angle from the horizon can vary. Put another way, the angle can change with latitude, and it is not always perpendicular to the surface. **Geodetic latitude** is the angle between the normal (right angle) to the geoid, and the plane of the Equator. Geodetic (or geographic) latitude is used in all navigation, and different geoids give slightly different geodetic latitudes, longitudes and times. Most aviation charts use the WGS84 geoid, as used inside the GPS.

At the Poles and the Equator, a line from the centre of the geoid is normal to the surface anyway, so the geodetic and geocentric latitudes are both the same at those points.

The difference between the two (*Reduction of Latitude)*, is greatest half way between, at **45°N or 45°S**, where it is about **11.6'** (nm), almost $1/5$ of a degree.

Each degree of latitude represents 60 nautical miles, and each minute is 1 nautical mile, or 6080 feet. The difference between parallels is called *Change Of Latitude* (ch lat).

Lines of latitude are fixable by natural means - for example, the Tropics of Cancer and Capricorn represent the limits of the Sun's travel North and South as it rises and sets every day, based on the Earth's tilt.

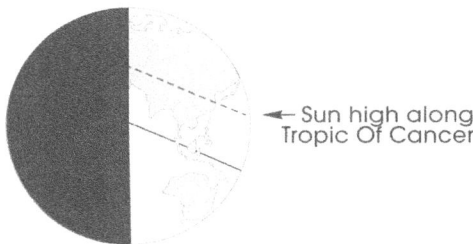

← Sun high along
Tropic Of Cancer

Important latitudes include the *Tropic of Cancer* (23° 27' N), the *Tropic of Capricorn* (23° 27' S), the *Arctic Circle* (66° 33' N), and the *Antarctic Circle* (66° 33' S).

Only between the two Tropics can the sun be at its zenith, and only North or South of the Arctic and Antarctic Circles, respectively, is the midnight sun possible.

Until the 1770s, however, when John Harrison invented a marine chronometer which only lost 5 seconds in two months, you could not fix longitude precisely, because time was measured by the cabin boy turning a glass with sand in it over and over. In other words, you only knew your longitude by calculation from when you left port, and if you knew what the time was. The Moon (against the fixed stars) was the only useful item in this respect as it orbited the Earth so quickly (13° of arc per day).

Ptolemy had plotted some sort of lat & long system by 150 AD, but he used the Canaries for the Prime (or zero) Meridian, which has also been at the Azores, Cape Verdi, Rome and Paris, to mention but a few (the Ancient Egyptians probably used the pyramids). It was placed at Greenwich in 1884 because the Royal Navy was the dominant naval power at the time, and there had been an observatory there since 1675 (Prince George was also a keen astronomer).

It may also have something to do with being part of the shortest Polar circumference.

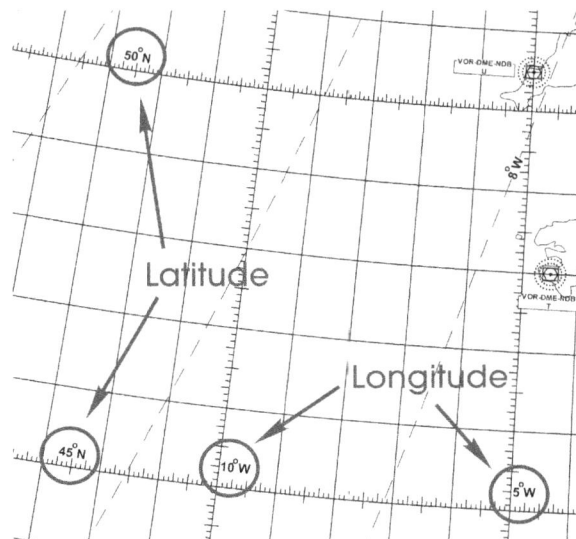

Latitude

Longitude

Trivia: A Great Circle that crosses the most sea and least land passes through the middle of Salisbury Plain in UK.

When giving position, latitude is always given first, as in 45°N, 163°W.

Great Circles (Orthodromes)

Great Circles have planes that go through the centre of the Earth, or, in other words, are circles whose centre and radius are the same as the Earth's, so they will divide it into two equal parts. The name comes from the fact that it is the largest circle you can obtain, so only one Great Circle can be drawn through two points on the surface of the Earth that are not diametrically opposed. *The shortest distance between any two points on the surface of a sphere is the smaller arc of the Great Circle joining them.*

Imagine a great circle as the path taken by a satellite, or a star over the Earth's surface. Radio waves follow Great Circle routes.

The definition includes lines of longitude and the Equator. As meridians are semi-great circles, a meridian and its antimeridian together make a Great Circle.

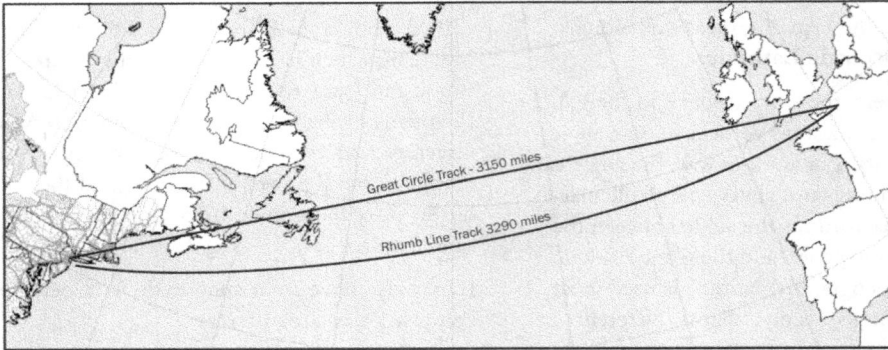

Great Circle Track - 3150 miles

Rhumb Line Track 3290 miles

Although the shorter arcs of great circles are the shortest distances between two points on the Earth's surface, as you change meridians during your travels, your relationship to True North is changing by the amount of *Convergency*, which is discussed later.

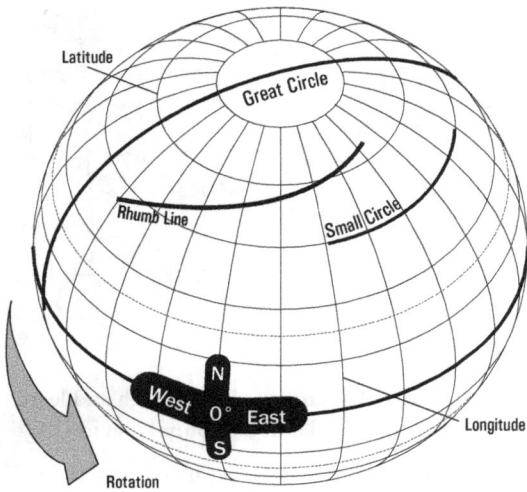

Thus, your track direction is defined by the local meridian, and you must keep altering track if you want to fly long distances along great circles. This, of course, is a pain, and there are solutions, discussed later.

THE VERTEX

This is the highest (and lowest) point of latitude that a Great Circle reaches, or its most Northerly and Southerly positions. It has the same value as its inclination where it crosses the Equator. In other words, if a Great Circle crosses the Equator at an angle of 76°, it will only reach 76° of latitude (its *direction* at the Equator will be plus or minus 90°, according to which way you are travelling.

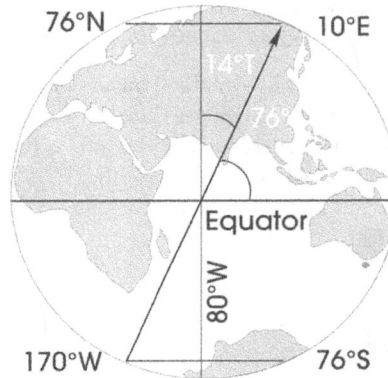

This has some relevance when trying to receive satellite signals, in that the orbit of a satellite will not take it higher than whatever inclination it has with the Equator. This is true even though the satellite's path over the Earth's surface does not trace a Great Circle (the Earth is spinning while the satellite traces its orbit in space).

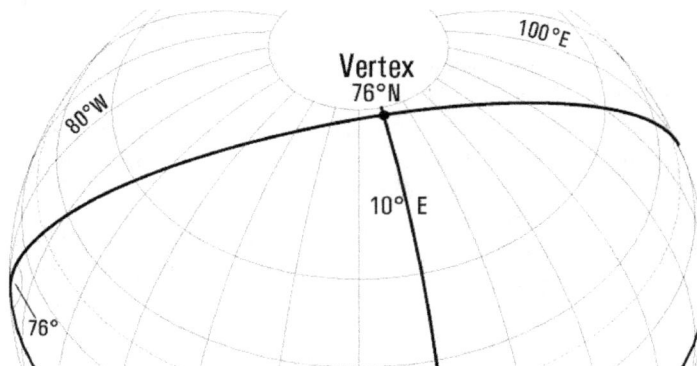

You can only go East or West at the vertex*. Put another way, if your great circle track includes East or West, that will be where the track passes closest to the Pole. The vertex is always 90° removed in terms of longitude from where it crosses the Equator. The Great Circle distance between vertices is 180° of arc, or 10,800 nm.

*The track direction when crossing the Equator is at an angle equal to the latitude of the vertices so, if you are heading East from the Northerly Vertex in our example, the track direction will be 090° + 76° = 166° when first crossing the Equator. At the second crossing, the track direction is 090° - 76° = 014°. Westward travel has the same crossing points but in reciprocal directions.

For example, if a Great Circle has a Northern vertex of 35°N 90°W, what is its Southern vertex? 35°S 90°E.

At what longitudes does it cross the Equator? 000°/180°.

What will be the track direction at each point if the initial track direction is 090°? 125°/305°.

If you know the convergence factor (n), the meridian of the vertex can be calculated if you don't know the inclination at the Equator. First find out how much of a bearing change it would take to convert the initial track to E or W, then divide it by the CF. Then add the result to the departure longitude to find that of the vertex.

For example, an initial track of 105° at 24°S 110°E in the Southern hemisphere produces 15° (105 - 90). Dividing 15 by the CF of 0.4 (the sine of 24), you get 37.5 which, when added to the original longitude gives 147.5°E.

What you have done is convert a bearing change to a change of longitude based on the fact that the track at the vertex will be 090°. See *Convergency*, below.

Alternatively, as the midpoint would be halfway, the distance of the vertex from the Equator in nautical miles can be found with:

$$\text{Vertex} = \frac{\tan \text{ECA} \times \frac{1}{2}\ \text{departure}}{2}$$

Divide the result by 60 to get the degrees of latitude.

Small Circles

These are circles on the surface of a sphere whose centre and radius are less than those of the sphere itself, so anything that is not a Great Circle is a Small Circle. You can have an infinite number of them between two points.

Parallels of latitude (except the Equator) are small circles constructed with reference to the Equator (they are also rhumb lines - see below). The angular distance between them along a meridian is *latitude*.

Rhumb Lines

Rhumb Lines are lines on the surface of the Earth that cross each meridian at the same angle, so they are lines of constant bearing. They are not straight (being concave to the nearer Pole), because meridians converge, so they are longer in distance than Great Circles between the same points. For example, over 2,000 miles a rhumb line may be 4 miles longer than a Great Circle at 20° latitude, 20 at 40°, and 100 miles longer at 60°. Over 500 miles, it is less than a mile longer, even at 60°, so long flights (say over the Atlantic) are usually plotted as Great Circles made up of a series of rhumb lines every 10° of longitude. At 60° latitude, this is only 300 nautical miles. Thus, the difference between rhumb lines and Great Circles is not worth worrying about below about 1,000 miles, for the convenience of steering one track, especially in low latitudes, and when they are close together.

The difference between Great Circles and Rhumb Lines is greatest E/W, and increases with latitude - it could easily be 600 nm near the Poles, as described in *Grid Navigation*.

Rhumb lines (or *loxodromes**) spiral toward a Pole unless they are going East, West, North, or South, in which case they close on themselves to form parallels of latitude or a pair of meridians. That is, lines of latitude are rhumb lines, as are meridians, but the Equator and meridian pairs are also great circles. Because a rhumb line appears as a straight line on a Mercator chart (later), following one is often called Mercator flying, or following Mercator tracks.

*A rhumb line is a course, a loxodrome is a curve.

SPEED & DISTANCE

Distance is the length of a line separating two points, although this becomes more complicated on a sphere, where the line becomes curved. As the Earth is considered to be a sphere for our purposes, and its radius is "constant", the distance between places on the Earth's surface can be expressed as an angular measurement.

The number of nautical miles between any two places is equal to the number of minutes in the shorter arc of the Great Circle that joins them. We take the distance between parallels of latitude as 60 nautical miles, although the physical distance varies between the Poles and the Equator because the Earth is not a sphere. The length of a nautical mile at these points is 6108 and 6046 feet, respectively, but the UK value of 6080 is used for calibration and navigation in general, and is only correct at 48° latitude*.

*The syllabus is limited to where 1 degree of arc = 60 nm - two points on the same meridian, or on a meridian and anti-meridian, or two on the Equator.

One minute of longitude, however (i.e. along a parallel of latitude), will only be 1 nm *at the Equator*, because every point on it is the same distance from the centre of the Earth. The distance between meridians gets smaller toward the Poles.

You can find the true length of a degree at any latitude by multiplying the change of longitude (in minutes) by the cosine of the latitude, so at 60°N, the distance between meridians is only 30 nm, or half of what it is at the Equator (this is the *departure formula*, which is accurate along one parallel).

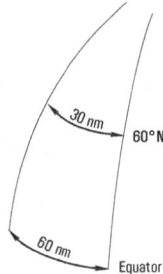

Horizontal distance is measured in kilometres or miles, and speed is a *rate of change of position expressed in those units* (per hour, minute, or whatever). For example, a **knot** is 1 **nautical mile** per hour. It was originally measured by allowing a rope with a log on the end to stretch out behind a ship. The rope had coloured rags tied in knots at regular intervals, which were counted over time. For aircraft, we need *airspeed*, *groundspeed* and *relative speed*, discussed later.

In navigation, a typical length can be expressed as:

- A **kilometre**, which is 1000 metres, and was originally 1/10,000 of the average distance between the Equator and either Pole on a meridian passing through Paris (thanks to Napoleon, although the Sumerians were there first). It is equivalent to 3280 feet, and 8 km equals 5 statute miles. As a rate, it is expressed in km/hour.

- 1 **nautical mile** (nm) is an angular distance taken as an average of 6080 feet, or 1852 m (as a reminder, check out your calculator - see right). However, 6046 feet is used in the USA, so be careful with their calculators.

- A **statute mile**, which is 5280 feet and an Imperial measurement introduced by Elizabeth I. In aviation, it is used only in visibility reports in some countries. 1 nautical mile is equal to 1.15 statute miles.

Relative Velocity

Subtract one speed from the other if aircraft are going the same way, or add them if they are travelling head-on.

BASIC EXAMPLES

1. At 12:00, an aeroplane flying at 105 kts is 30 miles behind a helicopter which is flying at 95 kts. When will the aeroplane overtake the helicopter? The difference in speeds is 10 knots, so it will take 3 hours to cover 30 miles. The answer is 15:00.

2. Two aircraft, each flying at 90 kts, are 120 nm apart and approaching head on. How much time is there for avoiding action? 40 minutes.

CASE 1

Overtaking a slower aircraft on the same track where you need to find when and where you will pass, or to a given separation distance. For example, aircraft A has a groundspeed of 280 kts and reports over an airfield at 10:20. Aircraft B on the same track has a groundspeed of 420 kts and reports overhead at 10:35. When will B overtake A and how far from the airfield will it be?

- Select a common time, such as 10:35

- Find out how far they are apart - B will be overhead the airfield at 10:35 and A will be 70 nm away. This is the **Closing Distance**.

- Find the closing speed:

  ```
  420 - 280 = 140 kts
  ```

- Find the **Closing Time** from the above:

  ```
  70 nm at 140 kts = 30 mins
  ```

- Add the closing time to the common time to find when the aircraft will pass each other.

  ```
  1035 + 30 = 1105
  ```

- How far will A have travelled from the airfield?

  ```
  45 mins at 280 kts = 210 nm
  ```

A variation may include an in-flight visibility so you can find out when you will catch sight of the first. If the visibility above was 7 nm:

- The closing distance becomes 63 nm (70-7)

- The closing speed is still 140 kts

- The closing time is 27 minutes (63 nm at 140 kts)

- You will see aircraft A at 11:02

CASE 2

Two aircraft approaching head on, where the time and position of the potential crash is required. Aircraft A has a groundspeed of 360 kts and reports overhead X at 14:00. Aircraft B reports overhead Y at 14:20 on its way to X at 480 kts. The distance between X and Y is 360 nm. When will the aircraft pass each other and how far will aircraft B be away from X?

- Select a common time, such as 14:20

- Find the closing distance at that time

  ```
  240 nm (360-120) at 1420
  ```

- Find the closing speed:

  ```
  360 + 480 = 840 kts
  ```

- Find the time to cover the closing distance

  ```
  240 nm at 840 kts = 17 mins
  ```

- Add the closing (elapsed) time to the common (clock) time to find when the aircraft will pass each other (or crash!):

  ```
  14:20 + 17 = 14:37
  ```

- At 480 kts, in the closing time (17 minutes) aircraft B will travel 136 nm

- Its distance from X will be 360 − 136 = 224 nm

CASE 3

When and/or where speed is reduced to effect a given delay to an original ETA, so you can ensure longitudinal separation. For example, an aircraft with a groundspeed of 360 kts must delay its ETA at a waypoint by 9 mins, which can be done by slowing down to 280 kts. How far from the waypoint should this be done?

- Find the percentage reduction in groundspeed

  ```
  280
  ─── x 100 = 22.2%
  360
  ```

- A 22.2% reduction in time is 9 minutes. At 280 kts, you will cover 42 nm, so the total distance covered will be 189 nm.

CASE 4

To find the change in speed to achieve a delay.

An aircraft is at FL310 at ISA −14°C and Mach 0.83. The distance between A and B is 800 nm and ATC needs you to slow down 360 nm away from B to achieve a delay of 3 minutes at B. What Mach number will achieve the delay?

If the aircraft is overhead A at 10:00, at what time will the slowdown take place and what will be the new ETA at B?

- Find the TAS from the Mach number and temperature (-61°C), 470 kts (assuming no wind). The time taken to travel 360 nm is 46 minutes. The delay is 3 minutes and the new time is 49 minutes. 360 nm in 49 minutes means a new TAS of 441 kts. The new Mach number is 0.78.

- The aircraft travels 440 nm at 470 kts, so it takes 56.2 minutes to get to the slowdown point. The ETA is 10:56.2, and for B is 10:56.2+49 = 11:45.2

And to prove it:

- 189 nm at 280 kts = 40.5 mins 189 nm at 360 kts = 31.5 mins. A 9 minute delay

CASE 5

You need to reduce speed from 300 to 250 knots and also delay your arrival by 6 minutes. How far back from the destination should you start to slow down?

- Find the distance that needs to be lost. The original ground speed of 300 knots over 6 minutes gives you 30 nm. The speed reduction is 50 knots. Travelling 30 nm will take 36 minutes.

- 36 minutes at the reduced groundspeed of 250 knots is 150 nm

OTHERS

An aircraft departs A at 09:00 anticipating a groundspeed of 330 kts. After 190 nm, it is 3 minutes behind schedule. What will be the new ETA for B if the distance between A and B is 520 nm?

- ATD 09:00

- 190 nm @ 330 kts = 34.5 mins + 3 = 37.5 mins

- Groundspeed is 190 nm in 37.5 mins = 304 kts

- 520 nm @ 304 kts = 102.6 mins

- ETA B = 10:42.6

An aircraft departs A at 11:00 anticipating a groundspeed of 275 kts. After 250 nm it is 2 minutes ahead of schedule. What will be the new ETA for D if the distance between C and D is 440 nm?

- ATD 11:00

- 250 nm @ 275 kts = 54.5 mins - 2 = 52.5 mins

- Groundspeed is 250 nm in 52.5 mins = 286 kts

- 440 nm @ 286 kts = 92.3 mins

- ETA D = 12:32.3

An aircraft departs E at 12:30 anticipating a groundspeed of 460 kts. After 307 nm it is 4 minutes behind schedule. What will be the new ETA for F if the distance between E and F is 750 nm?

- ATD 12:30

- 307 nms @ 460 kts = 40 mins + 4 = 44 mins

- Groundspeed is 307 nms in 44 mins = 418 kts

- 750 nms @ 418 kts = 107.7 mins

- ETA F = 14:17.7

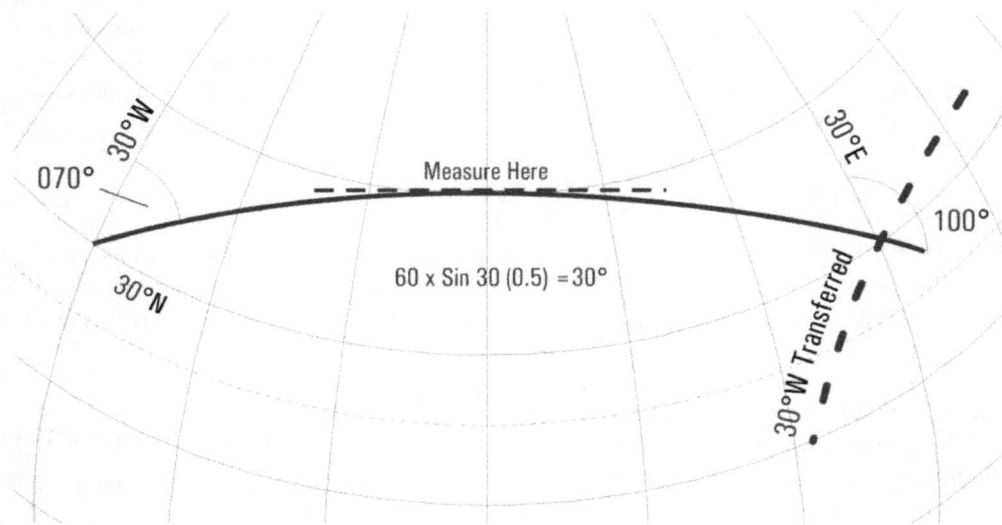

CONVERGENCY

Meridians are only parallel to each other when they cross the Equator. Elsewhere, they get closer (converge) as you go toward the Poles. This means that, as you fly a great circle track to the East in the Northern hemisphere (and West in the Southern hemisphere), your true direction will increase, as can be seen in the picture above, where you start off at 070° and end up at 100° (remember each meridian points to North).

This change can be calculated, which is often more accurate than measuring it.

Finding the distance travelled, on the other hand, involves the departure formula, used for calculating distance between two points on the same latitude, discussed later.

Earth Convergence

This is the angle between the tangents to two meridians.

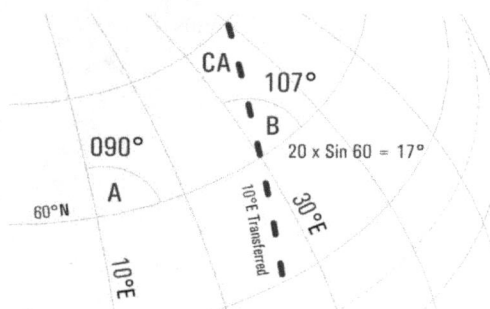

It is zero at the Equator, and is equal to the difference in longitude between them at the Poles - in general terms, Earth convergence is the difference in Great Circle bearings between two meridians, varying with the **sine** of the latitude because the maximum change is at the Poles.

On the right hand side of the diagram below, the 10°E meridian has been transferred from its original position, so we have the original direction of 090° plus a little bit. The difference between A & B is the *Convergency Angle*.

The approximate formula for convergency is:

```
ch long x sin mean lat
```

where *ch long* means the change in longitude between the meridians. In the example given, the difference between 10°E and 30°E is 20°, and the sine of 60° is 0.866*, so:

```
20 x 0.866 = 17
```

Add 17 to the original direction to obtain 107°.

*get used to this figure, it is used a lot. Also remember the cosine value, which is 0.5.

Chart Convergence

As charts are based on the Earth's surface, they suffer from convergency as well - chart convergence is the angle made between meridians *on a projection*. The convergence factor is the number of degrees change in track bearing per degree travelled. It, too, is zero at the Equator, and 1° at the Poles, and varies at the *sine* of the latitude, but as the meridians are straight, the value stays constant over the chart, instead of changing between latitudes. This means you can use a factor for the whole chart instead.

On a Mercator projection, the chart convergence is zero everywhere because the meridians are parallel. On a Lambert, chart convergence equals Earth convergence at the Parallel of Origin but otherwise remains constant everywhere. The sine of the PO is the *constant of the cone*. On a Polar Stereographic, chart convergence equals Earth convergence at the Poles and is constant everywhere.

Direction & Variation

These have already been covered in *Instruments*.

Departure

Distance along a parallel of latitude is also known as *departure**. Here is the formula:

α (nm) = ch long (mins) x cos lat

In English, it means that the distance between two points on the Earth's surface **in nautical miles** is equal to the difference in longitude between them **in minutes** multiplied by the cosine of the latitude. The cosine is used because the meridians converge towards the Poles and the distance between them gets shorter - in this case, the maximum change is at the Equator.

*Change of longitude (d´long) is an *angle* measured in minutes at the Equator, and departure is a *distance* in nautical miles elsewhere. More technically, *departure is the distance made good in an E-W direction along a rhumb line.*

If you are going N or S of track, you take the mid latitude, or the mean for short distances. This is because the departures above and below the track are of different lengths due to convergency.

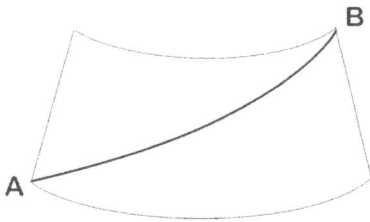

To find a mid-latitude, add them, then divide by 2.

Once you know the positions of two places, you can work out the rhumb line direction and distance between them, approximately enough for our purposes. The trick is to divide the vertical distance by the horizontal distance, having worked out the changes in latitude and longitude, respectively. For short distances, these become the two (non-hypotenuse) sides of a right-angled plane triangle:

$$\frac{departure}{d'lat} = \tan (course)$$

For example, you have to fly from 54°N 100°W to 56°N 110°W. You can already see that you are going a little bit North and quite a bit West, judging by the angles (2°N, 10°W). To work it out more accurately, the mean latitude is 55°N, so the departure is:

α (nm) = 600 x cos 55

or:

α (nm) = 600 x 0.5736 = 344 nm

so:

$$\frac{344}{120} = \tan (course)$$

or:

$$\frac{344}{120} = 2.868$$

This is 71°. Subtract from 360° to get 289° as a course to steer. The distance is the hypotenuse which can be found (accurately enough for our purposes) by dividing the departure by the sine of the course (0.9455) to get 375.5 nm, or dividing the d´lat by the cosine of the course (0.3256) to get 368.5. The accurate calculation is 374.74!

This is the kind of mental calculation you can get involved in all the time while flying. All you need to know is where you are in terms of lat & long (GPS!) and the cosine of your latitude, which won't vary enough to make a difference. Very often you can head more or less in the right direction straight away and refine it on the way.

Note: Always assume the shortest route. For a change of longitude between *different* hemispheres (one value is E and one W), just add the values. In the *same* hemisphere, subtract the lowest value from the higher. If the answer is more than 180°, subtract the result from 360° for the shortest route. If the longitudes equal 180°, the shortest way is over the Pole, as they make a Great Circle based on a meridian and its antimeridian.

Note: For Local Mean Time calculations (see later) you take the longest route.

On the Jeppesen CR-3, you can find out departure quite easily. Say from York (roughly 54°N), you need to find a ship just East of the Isle Of Man, which is more or less on the same latitude, but 3° to the West, or 180 minutes, which at the Equator would be 180 nm. The cosine of 54° is the same as the sine of 36°, so you have 106 nm to go.

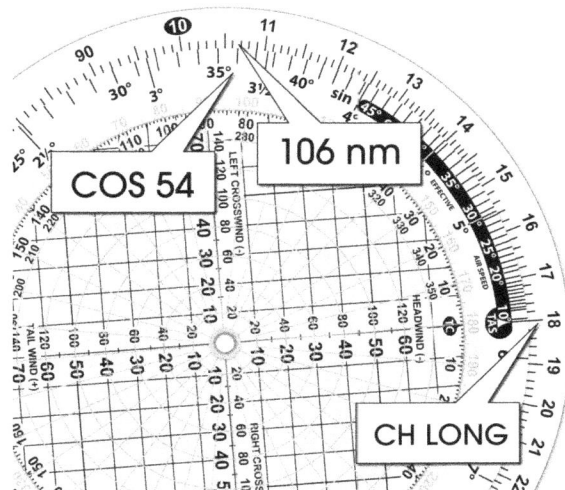

EXAMPLES

1. In what latitude will a d´long of 3°40´ correspond to a departure of 120 nm?

We know that the difference in longitude refers to the Equator, where 3°40´ (3 x 60 + 40) equates to 220 nm.

The other distance is 120 nm, so divide that by 220 to get 0.5455 for which the cosecant means 56°56.5´, N or S

2. What is the approximate rhumb line track between 45° 00'N 010° 00'W and 48°30'N 015°00'W?

    (a)   270

    (b)   245

    (c)   315

    (d)   350

Given the spread of the answers, this can easily be solved by just drawing a simple diagram, but the line from 45°N 010'W to 45°N 015'W is the base of a triangle, and the distance along it can be found with the departure formula:

```
212.132 = 300 x cos 45
```

From 010°W to 015°W is 5° x 60 = 300 minutes. The change of latitude is 3° 30' or 210', or 210 nm.

The tangent of the angle at 45°N 010'W is 210/212.132 nm, or 0.9899, or 44.71°. Adding this to 270° gives you 314.7°. The nearest answer is 315°.

3. What is the distance between 35°25'W and 28°53' W at 41°S?

The d'long is 6°32' or 392', multiplied by 0.7547 (the cosine of 41°), so the distance is 296 nm.

4. You fly North from a position at latitude 60°N for 90 nm. Then you fly another 90 nm to the East, South and West. How far away are you from where you started?

At the end of the first leg, you arrive at 61°30'N. You also go South for the same distance on the third leg, so you arrive right back at 60°. However, the distance at 61°30'N. gives you a larger d'long than the distance at 60°. The distance from where you started will simply be the difference in departures for the two latitudes, or 4.31 nm.

Tip: The North and South legs cancel each other out.

5. Two aircraft 45 nm apart at 40°30'S fly North at the same speed until the distance between them is 55 nm. How far did each one fly?

The d'long will be the same on both parallels. Working backwards, this is 59.1794' or 59 nm. Divided into 55, this gives 0.9294, the cosecant of 21° 40'.

6. At 24°N, with a departure of 32 nm, what is the change of longitude?

The cosine of 24 is 0.91. Divide that into the mileage to get 35 minutes.

7. If you fly on a track of 300° for 400 nm, what is the departure and change of longitude?

347 nm and 200 minutes to the North. **Hint:** 400 nm is the length of the hypotenuse.

8. A is at 40°N 120°E and B is at 60°N 086°E. The initial great circle track is 315°(T). What is it measured at B?

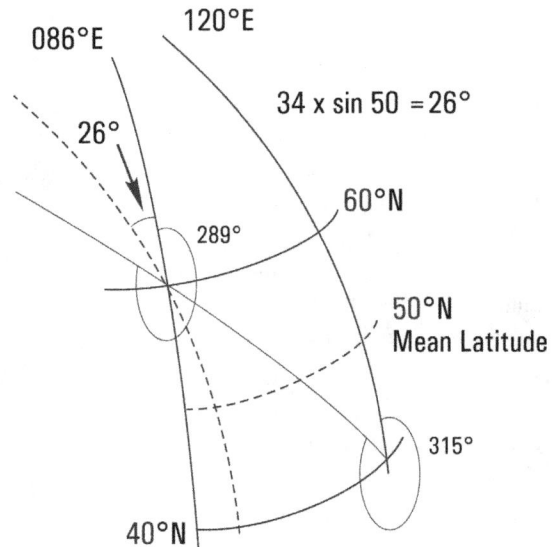

The change of longitude is 34°, and the sine of the mean latitude of 50° is 0.77, so the convergency angle is 26°, to be *subtracted* from the original track of 315° (see the transferred meridian of 120°E). The answer is 289°.

9. What is the final great circle track between 60°S 169°W and 40°S 173°E if the initial track is 290°(T)?

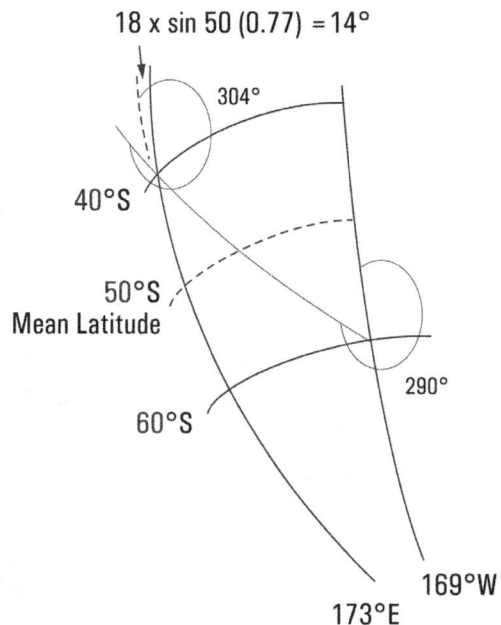

The ch long is 18°, so the CA is 14°. Added to 290°, we get 304°.

10. The initial and final tracks between A (30°N 18°W) and B (50°N) are 060°(T) and 082°(T). What is B's longitude?

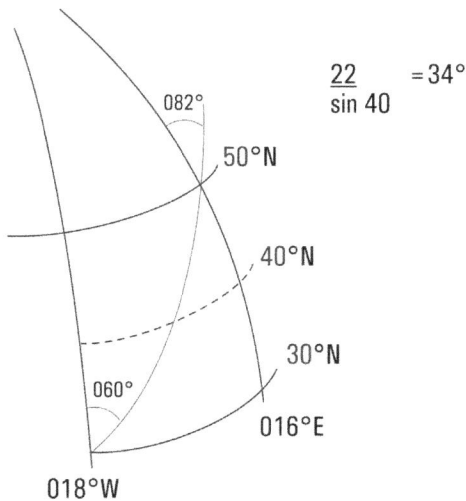

$$\frac{22}{\sin 40} = 34°$$

We know the CA (22°) so divide it by the sine of the mean latitude to get 34°. Subtract 18° (you are going past the Prime Meridian), and the remainder is 16°.

11. What is the distance and track between 58°N 13°W to 66°N 2°E?

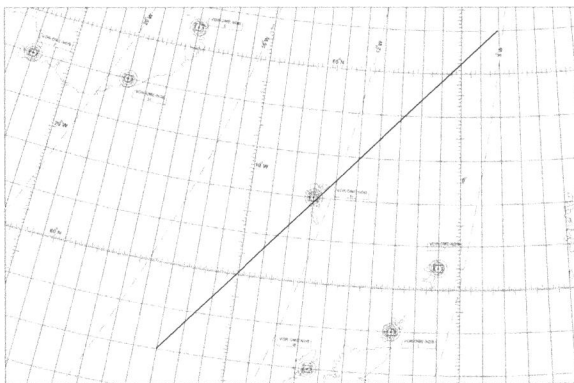

The track of 042° can simply be measured (at the mid point) if you have the map. However, it can also be calculated with the tangent value (opposite over adjacent).

The change of latitude can easily be figured out from 8° x 60 = 480 nm.

The change of longitude is 15° which, multiplied by 60 is 900 nm. The cosine of the mean latitude (62°N) is 0.4, so the departure is 423 nm.

You could now use Pythagoras and obtain the track distance of 639 nm, but you could also use the variation scale on the wind side of the CR-3:

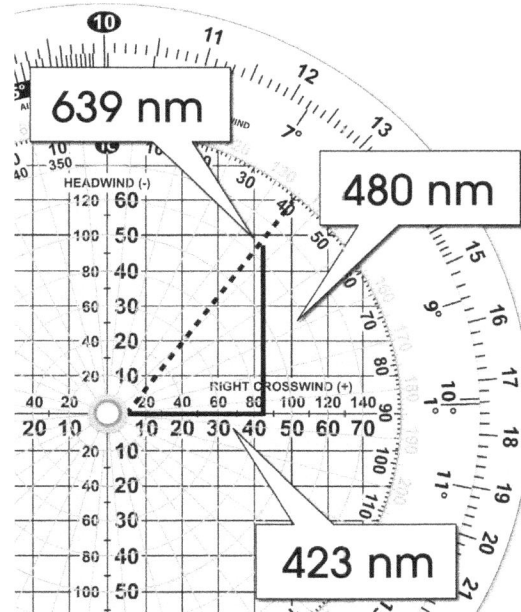

Apply the change of longitude horizontally, then go vertically for the change of latitude, according to scale. The average track direction (042°)can be read on the degree scale and the distance (639) just past the green line marked 60.

Conversion Angle

Sometimes, you need to convert between rhumb lines and great circles, especially when plotting radio bearings on Mercator charts. It may be best to come back here after having read about their properties, later.

Note: The conversion angle is irrelevant close to the Equator, where it is almost zero and only possibly relevant to helicopters close to the Poles. - aside from the fact that the ranges involved with helicopters are so short that, except in the highest latitudes it is going to be very small.

Radio bearings take the Great Circle route, which is a curved line on a Mercator chart. As these are difficult to plot when finding your position, you must convert Great Circle tracks into rhumb lines, which are straight. Complications also arise from whether the plot is done at the aircraft (ADF) or the station (VOR/VDF), and where you apply variation and conversion angles.

The conversion angle is the difference between a rhumb line (or a Mercator track) and a great circle at each end of a line joining two points - it happens to be half the convergency because the difference between them would be full convergency. At the halfway point, the two lines are parallel, so the change must be half, and their bearings would be the same, so you should measure your track **at the mid-point** if you use a chart where straight lines are great circles (i.e. most flight planning charts). If the average true course of a great circle is 130°, for example, the true course of the rhumb line will be the same.

Conversion angle is applied to bearings at the point of measurement, towards the Equator.

Both variation and conversion angle must be applied wherever the bearing is measured. For example, the ADF measures the bearing, so both must be applied at the aircraft. A VOR signal gives the bearing measured at the VOR, so only variation needs to be applied at the VOR. See *Plotting*, below).

THE NDB

You estimate your position as 50°N 6°W at 10:00, and an NDB at 56°N 3°E bears 058°. Variation (at the aircraft) is 8½°W. What bearing would you plot from the meridian passing through the station? The sine of 53° (the mean) is 0.7986 (0.8).

Tip: Always draw a diagram!

Find the rhumb line bearing from the aircraft to the station by applying the conversion angle *towards the Equator*. Then add or subtract 180° to find the True rhumb line bearing from the station.

The NDB is North East of you. Its True bearing is 49½° (058° - 8½°). The conversion angle is:

```
½ x 9 x .8

4½ x .8

3.6°, or 3½°

49½° + 3½° = 53°
```

So you would add 053° and plot 233°.

THE VOR

Find the rhumb line bearing from the station to the aircraft by applying the conversion angle towards the Equator.

Using the example above, with a co-located VOR, you see 062° on the display, and the variation is 5½°W, so:

```
242° - 5½° = 236½° - 3½° CA
```

You would still plot 233°.

EXAMPLES

1. What is the direction of the Great Circle track at each end of a line joining 30°S 130°E and 30°S 160°E?

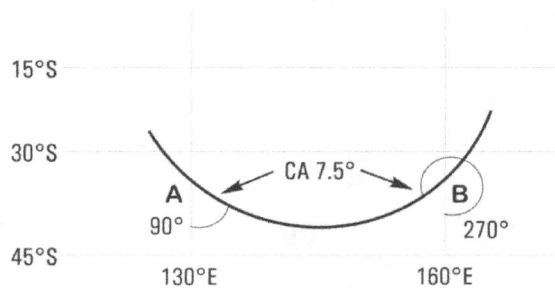

These are both on the same latitude, to make it easy, so the rhumb line track is 090° or 270°, depending on which way you go. The picture below is based on Mercator (with parallel meridians), since this is where the difference between Great Circles and Rhumb Lines is most relevant.

The formula for convergency is:

```
ch long x sin mean lat
```

or:

```
30 x sin 30
```

Conversion angle is half that value, so:

```
½ x 30 x 0.5 = 7.5°
```

The Great Circle Tracks are 097½° and 262½°.

2. A flight is made from 51°N 001°W where the local variation is 8°W, to 51°N 006°W, where the local variation is 9°W. The constant of the cone is 0.8, and radials are maintained with 7°S of drift.

What are the magnetic headings on departure and arrival?

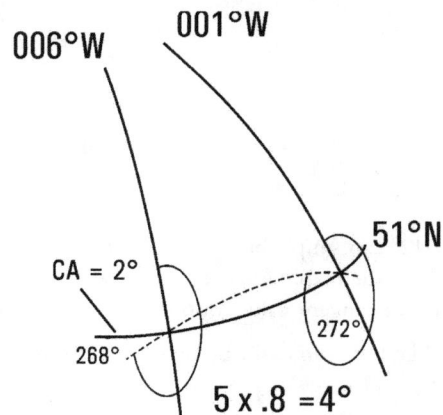

The GC track at the start is 270° + 2° = 272°(T)

```
Hdg (T) = 272°-7° (drift) = 265° (T)

Hdg (M) = 265° + 8° = 273° (M)
```

Plotting

A bearing from a VOR or NDB is called a *Line Of Position* (LOP). You need at least 2 LOPs to obtain a position fix.

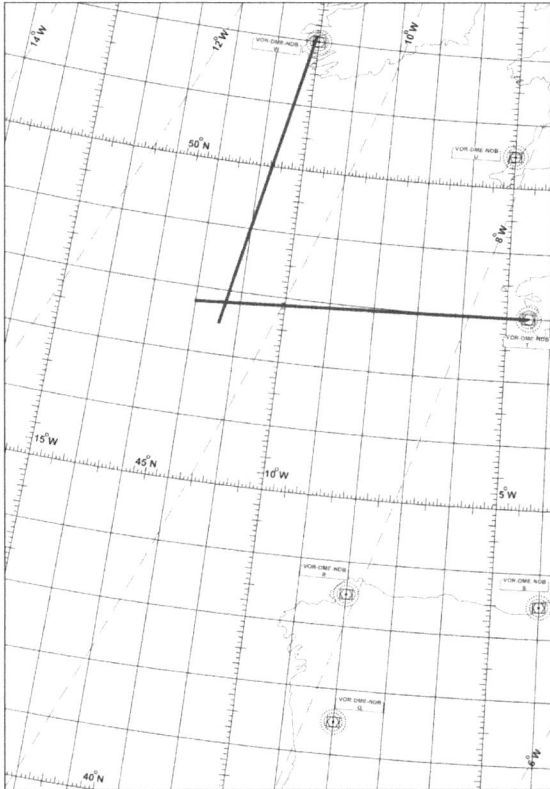

When plotting LOPs, you might have to use True bearings, so if the reading is from a VOR (which is normally aligned to Magnetic North, except in the Arctic), it must be converted to True before you draw the line.

In the chart above, two LOPs have been drawn from 2 VORs and where they cross is your position fix. The radial from the most Northern VOR is (for example) 195°, while the one from the most Eastern is 265°. Remember that the CDI must be centred with a FROM indication!

If required, you must apply the variation at the VORs first - but notice that each one is lying next to a different isogonal. Also make sure that one VOR is not in the Arctic, where its readings will be True anyway.

Note: Sometimes isogonals are given for a particular date, which will be on the chart.

The Northerly VOR in this case must therefore be adjusted by 12° and the Easterly one by 8°. The process is similar for NDBs, but the bearings are not the same - both must be adjusted by 10°, which is the value of the isogonal at your position fix.

VOR EXAMPLE

A VOR is at 60°S 20°W, and the variation there is 10°E. The DR position of the aircraft is 62°S 9°W, sitting on the radial (QDR) of 145°. What true bearing would you plot from the beacon?

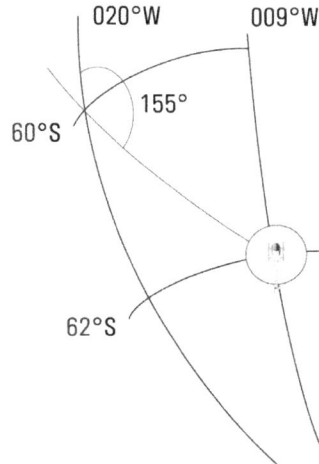

The lat & long figures are irrelevant when it comes to the VOR, because the variation is applied at the beacon. In this case, just apply the variation to get 155°.

ADF/NDB

An NDB is at 70°S 175°E, with a variation of 10°E. An aircraft is at 72°S 172°W, where the variation is 8°E. If the QDM is 325° and the sine of the Parallel of Origin is 0.75, what is the true bearing plotted from the beacon?

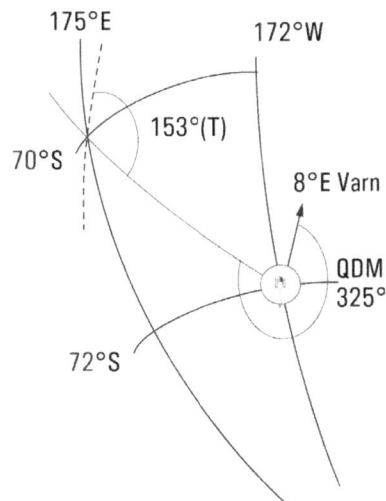

Things get more complex with NDBs, as you must apply the variation at the aircraft, then account for convergency, because you must transfer the aircraft's meridian (where the variation is measured), so the QDM now becomes 333°. The ch long (13°) x 0.75 = 10° for the CA, so 333 + 10 = 343 − 180 = 163° to plot.

capt.gs

Maps & Charts

A map is a graphical representation of part of the Earth's surface drawn to a scale, as seen from above. On them, features found on the ground are represented by symbols, which are larger than the items they represent, so you can see them without a magnifying glass*. A map's purpose is to provide information on the existence and location of, and distance between, ground features.

*Not everything on a map is done to its scale; if it were, you would hardly see roads and railways, so they are artificially expanded to be visible. The centre of any object is its actual position.

Technically, a chart is a representation of a small part of the surface of the Earth on a plane, where distortion from any curvature of the surface is practically absent. In the marine world, a chart refers to the ground features underneath the sea. In aviation, the words *map* and *chart* are interchangeable, as an aviation chart will show parallels and meridians with minimal topographical features:

A map will show greater detail of the Earth's surface, so maps are for looking at, and charts are for working on!

You can use a chart as a map, but not necessarily the other way round.

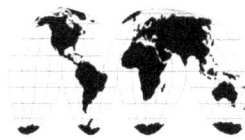

The point about them both is that they are small scale representations of the Earth's surface that are only accurate within a relatively small area, since you are trying to show a 3 dimensional object on a 2 dimensional surface. The further from the *centre of projection* you go, the more the distortion you get but, to all intents and purposes, it can mostly be ignored in its general area. You can see the problem if you try to flatten a globe (left), and the Equator and poles pose special problems because their meridians are parallel and converging, respectively.

Distortion can be minimised, but not eliminated, and there are many ways of adjusting for it, each suiting a different purpose, so lines drawn on maps based on different projections will not necessarily cross through the same places (watch those danger areas!) When producing maps and charts, a reduced model of the Earth is used, which means that the compression factor is so small that it can be ignored.

Projections

The term *projection* means that an imaginary light is placed inside a model of the Earth and the shapes of the land masses are projected onto a developable surface, which is one that can be flattened without being torn, stretched or wrinkled. This does not include a sphere.

The type of surface primarily determines a projection's classification, but the source of the imaginary light is also a factor. The main ones used in aviation are *conical* (Lambert), *cylindrical* (Mercator) or *flat* (stereographic). All projections require sophisticated maths to be effective, in order to keep any distortions under control.

The quality of *orthomorphism*, or *conformality*, which is the more modern term, that all charts should strive for, means the scale is correct in all directions, or at least within a very small area if the scale varies, and bearings are correctly represented. That is, the scale at any point is independent of azimuth, so, for a short distance in any direction, it will be equal. The outlines of the areas to be portrayed must conform, or be free from angular distortion. As well, parallels must cross meridians at right angles. If a chart were not orthomorphic, compass roses around VORs would appear as ellipses.

The scale on orthomorphic charts does not have to be the same all over - it only has to be constant in all directions at each point.

Otherwise, no chart is perfect, as you will find when you try to fold them!

Lambert's Conformal

Imagine the Earth with a light shining at its centre, then place a cone on top. If it could shine through the crust, an image of the Earth's surface will be projected onto the cone. Where the cone meets the Earth, the shadows of the land formations will be accurate, but will be out of shape the further North and South you go. This is the *conic projection*, and the latitude at which the cone touches the Earth is known as the *Standard Parallel*. All points on it are the same distance from the top of the cone, so distance is also the radius of the arc produced by the parallel when the cone is unrolled. The shape unrolled will be a circle with a wedge missing - the amount remaining (*n*) bears a direct relationship to the location of the Parallel of Origin.

If the missing wedge is 25%, 75% (0.75) remains. This is the *Constant Of the Cone*, or the *Chart Convergence Factor (n)**. It is the same as the sine of the Standard Parallel, which is important for calculating convergence on Lambert Charts.

The inverse sine of 0.75 is 48° 35', which is the Standard Parallel for this chart.

*The rate of change of a great circle track depends on the convergence factor (n) of a chart, which in turn depends on latitude. n is the number of degrees of change in track bearing for each degree of longitude travelled. 0.8 means that the change will be 0.8 for every degree.

In the simple conic projection with one parallel, the scale is correct only along that parallel and expands away from it, which limits the use of that chart in the N-S sense as it is not orthomorphic.

Johannes Lambert improved on the problem in the 18th century by mathematically pushing the imaginary cone into the Earth's surface, to cut it in two places instead of one. This produces two *Standard Parallels*, where scale is correctly shown (and where the nominal scale is). The original SP now becomes the *Parallel Of Origin*.

There is a slight contraction between them, but this is insignificant (1% or less) if two-thirds of the chart is between Standard Parallels that are less than 16° apart. The Parallel of Origin (or Parallel of Tangency) is almost midway between them (slightly closer to the Pole), where

the scale will be smallest. Outside the standard parallels, the scale expands, and will be greatest at the top and bottom of the chart. Thus, although the scale is not constant, the chart is used as if it is, the variation being less than 1%.

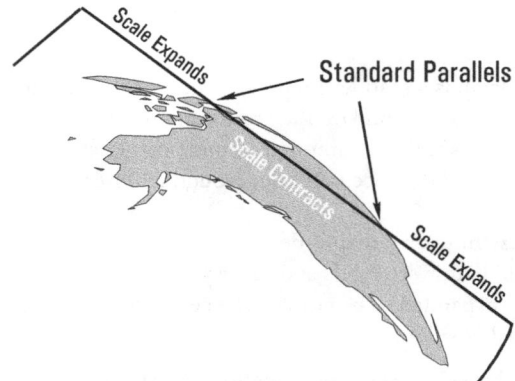

The thirds rule governs how a section of Earth on a Lambert Chart is displayed, where $^2/_3$ of the chart is within the Standard Parallels, which should not be more than 14° apart. Distortion is acceptable within these limits:

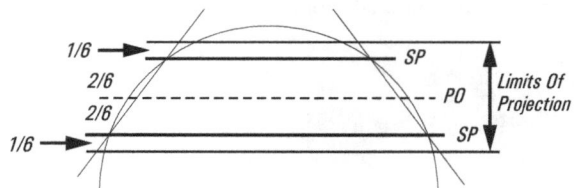

The Lambert Conformal is what most of today's aeronautical charts are based on, as all latitudes apart from those close to the Poles can be represented fairly accurately with well-chosen Standard Parallels.

Great Circles drawn on a Lambert are (nearly) straight lines, so they are good for plotting radio bearings although, to be precise, Great Circles that are not meridians are curves concave to the Parallel of Origin. Rhumb lines will be curves concave to the nearer Pole (parallels are rhumb lines!)

Here is a good example of a Lambert Projection.

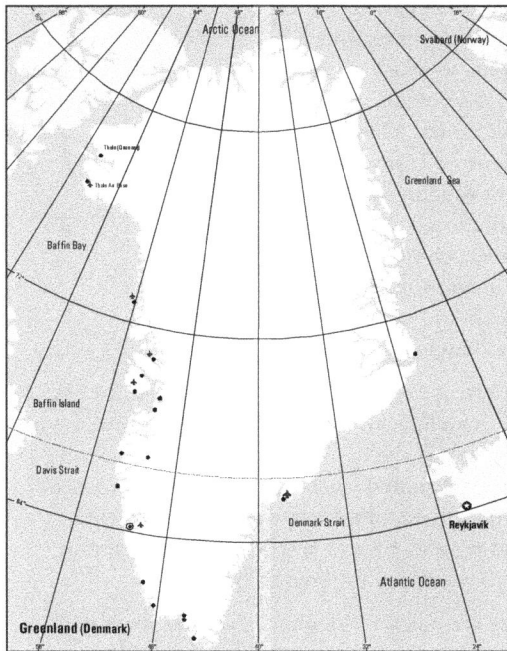

Note the converging meridians, and the curved parallels of latitude.

Remember:

- The sine of the parallel of origin is also the constant of the cone

- There are 2 standard parallels at which the *scale* is correct

- There is one parallel of origin where *convergency* is correct

- The scale is constant within 1% if the Standard Parallels are up to 16° apart

- Two thirds of the chart is between the Standard Parallels so the maximum spread of latitudes is 24°

- Great Circles are nearly straight, but are concave to the parallel of origin

- Rhumb Lines are concave to the Pole

Mercator

The Mercator projection does things differently. Instead of being capped by a cone, the Earth is imagined to be surrounded by a vertical cylinder, which touches it at the Equator (the chart is actually constructed mathematically).

Archimedes did it first, but Mercator varied the vertical scale inversely to the cosine of the latitude to make the chart orthomorphic. This is because the light projection becomes very distorted near the Poles. Mercator's trick was to figure out how to space the parallels to make rhumb lines appear as straight lines, which they will do if the meridians become straight.

Meridians on a Mercator chart are therefore *parallel, equally spaced, vertical straight lines* (compare this with those on the Lambert), and the distance between latitudes increases away from the centre. Up to around 600 m either side of the Equator, this can be ignored.

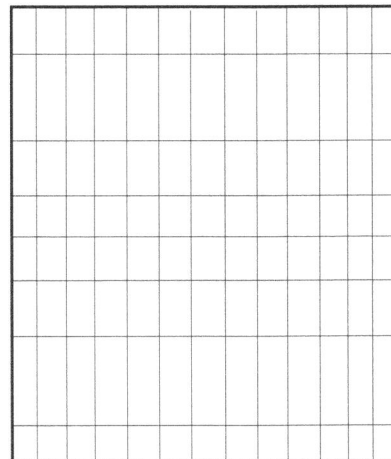

As the scale varies greatly away from central parts of the map (with the secant of the latitude), it does not show equal areas. An island at 60° latitude on a Mercator will have the same shape as it would at the Equator, but it will be twice the size, because of the scale expansion.

The Mercator is relatively accurate within about 500 nm (about 8° latitude) of the Equator because that is where the chart paper touches and is parallel to the reduced Earth. Scale there is roughly correct and great circles plot as almost straight lines. This is actually the only region a Mercator chart would be used for plotting these days.

As rhumb lines on this projection are straight lines, it follows that great circles must be curved, in this case, concave to the Equator, and convex to the direction of the increase in scale (except for meridians and the Equator itself). This curvature increases away from the Equator.

Note: The rhumb line is always nearer the Equator.

The rhumb line looks shorter than the great circle because of the scale expansion that occurs as you move away from the Equator.

MERCATOR PROPERTIES

- No convergence
- Rectangular graticule
- Scale correct at the Equator, expands with secant of the latitude
- Scale roughly constant within 8° N/S
- Rhumb lines are exactly straight lines
- Great circles are curves concave to the Equator

TRANSVERSE MERCATOR*

Within 10° or so of the Equator, scale error on a direct Mercator is only 1% or so, but there's no reason that the cylinder has to touch at the Equator.

The Transverse Mercator is a *horizontal* cylinder projection, on which a rhumb line is no longer straight, a straight line represents a great circle, and, with the exception of the Equator, parallels of latitude appear as *ellipses*. The *Central Meridian* (CM), or Meridian Of Tangency, which can be any meridian, where the cylinder touches the sphere, coincides with the relevant longitude, so True North and Grid North are the same along it, and the scale is exactly correct. However, because rectangular grid lines are based on the CM, moving East or West means applying some sort of *grivation* (see *Grid Navigation*, below). A scale factor also has to be applied as you move around to convert ground distances to measured distances. To reduce this, the projection uses two North-South lines with a scale factor of 1, so in the centre the correction is less than 1 (0.9996 for the UTM, below), while outer parts have it greater than 1. Parallels, except for the Equator, are ellipses. Convergency is correct at the CM and along the Equator, and the chart is usable within 350 nm of the CM.

The Transverse Mercator's advantages include accuracy, over small areas, at least, and it is used for long, narrow areas, such as countries with a great N-S extent, or which are not very wide. Wide countries are split into zones, for which see......

UNIVERSAL TRANSVERSE MERCATOR

Because the Transverse Mercator is very accurate in narrow zones, it has become the basis for a global system, in which the globe is subdivided into narrow longitudinal zones, which are projected onto a Transverse Mercator projection. A grid is then superimposed on the projection, which is actually what is used to define your position (grids are easier to use than latitude and longitude).

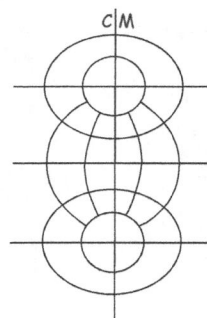

Note: Knowledge of the UTM is not required for EASA exams, but is included because you will come across it in your career, as it is the basis of Ordnance Survey grid references. It all started when the US military imposed standards on a system that was already in use by the British, Portuguese, French and Belgians for mapping Africa, since they were the colonial powers.

The system uses sixty 6° longitude *zones* and twenty 8° latitude *bands* between 80° S to 84° N, giving 1200 areas overall (you have to go up to 84°N to get to a point north of Greenland).

Longitude zones are numbered 1-60 starting at 180°W, and can be thought of as individual strips of the Earth's surface that have been cut at the poles and peeled back, so they can be "laid flat" as the basis for smaller maps.

See also *Grid Navigation.*

OBLIQUE MERCATOR

This projection is used specifically to produce charts of a great circle route between two points, i.e. strip charts. The *Meridian Of Tangency* is any great circle other than a meridian. The cylinder round the Earth is neither vertical nor horizontal, but is skewed, hence the name *oblique.*

Polar Stereographic

These charts are used in polar regions (between 50°-90°), because the others cannot cope with convergence that well. To get the details correct, the paper is held flat over the top of the Pole and the imaginary light projected straight up from the centre or the other side of the Earth.

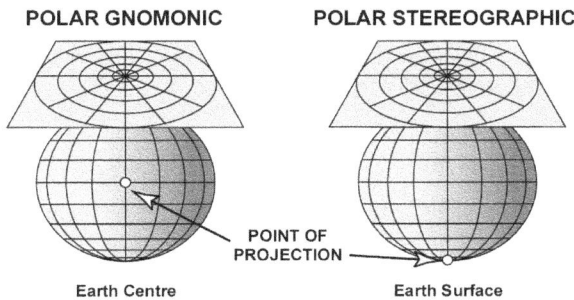

POLAR GNOMONIC **POLAR STEREOGRAPHIC**

POINT OF PROJECTION

Earth Centre   Earth Surface

Note: The Polar Gnomonic is only used for planning. It is not used in flight. Probably because you can't include the Equator if you project from the centre of the Earth.

The Parallel Of Origin is at the Pole.

PROPERTIES

Parallels of latitude are shown as concentric circles, and the spacing between them *increases* away from the Pole, so the scale expands, like it does with Mercator. As the scale and convergency are correct at the Pole, the chart is accurate in the Polar region, with its scale within 1% of the reduced Earth scale from the Pole down to about 78° of latitude, although the chart is often used beyond this. It is mostly used for general navigation and plotting in the polar region, or for trans-polar, long-haul flights.

Meridians are straight lines, radiating from the Pole. Great Circles, except meridians, are (very) slightly concave to the Pole but more closely approximate a straight line at higher latitudes. Rhumb lines, except meridians, are curves concave to the Pole.

As the value of the convergence factor is 1, convergence is always equal to the change of longitude. That is, there are no sines involved (see *Convergency*, later).

CALCULATIONS

The simple geometry of the Polar Stereographic allows you to make calculations that might be more difficult on other charts. For example, parallels plot as circles, so a track with both ends at the same latitude makes an isosceles triangle with the Pole at the third apex, so we can calculate (as well as measure) the initial bearing of a track from A 80°N 070°W to B 80°N 040°E, plotted as a straight line.

Tip: When drawing diagrams, select the Prime Meridian for your North direction, so that the Western Hemisphere is on the left, and the Eastern Hemisphere on the right.

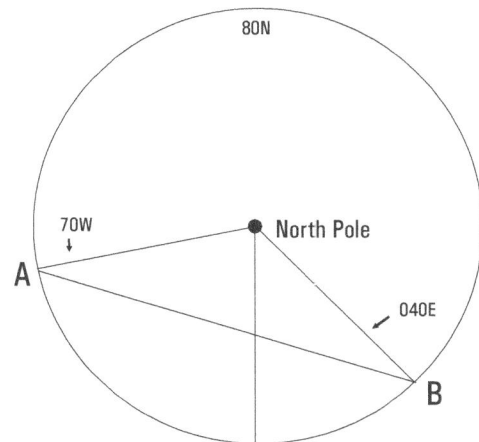

In the picture, the angle at the Pole between the 070°W and 040°E meridians is the same as chart convergence between the meridians, which is 110°. The angles in the triangle between these two and the track must add up to 180°, so the other two add up to 70°. As it is an isosceles triangle, and the angles are the same, each must be 35°.

In this case, the track from A to B, measured at A, is 35° right of North, or 035°T. Of course, this does not remain the same due to convergence, but the same figures can be used to find the track at B, which is 35° left of South, or 145°. The difference between the two is 110°T, which is the convergence between A and B. So, once you know one bearing, the one crossing any other meridian can be calculated with convergence.

Looking at the track, it reaches its most Northerly point, and is closest to the Pole, half way between A and B at 015°W. Given the convergence between A and 015°W the track here is 090°T. This is hardly surprising as any track would run 090° or 270° at its South or North vertex.

POLAR NAVIGATION

At the Poles, it's darker for longer and there are fewer navaids (those that do exist are oriented towards True directions). The compass is unreliable because of the dip and the change in the rate of magnetic variation nearer the Poles, and there is increased deviation from the aircraft's own magnetic field, so realigning the DGI is also a problem, especially as it wanders in the long term (many pilots align it by flying down a runway or other feature with a known bearing).

Tip: Another way to determine true heading is to ask your GPS (if it is capable) for the true bearing to an NDB. Then subtract your relative bearing for the true heading.

The two main problems are excessive compass dip, and the meridians converging at acute angles, where you cross them more rapidly, discussed under *Grid Navigation*, below.

Areas above 65° latitude are officially known as *high latitudes*. A *polar track* exists where part of it crosses an area where the horizontal component of the earth's magnetic field is less than 6 micro-teslas. Inertial Reference Systems are used to overcome these problems.

Tip: If an aircraft is at the North Pole itself, every direction is South, and every direction is North at the South Pole. This means that direction must be specified either as a grid direction (see below) or stating which meridian is to be followed. If a grid direction is given, measure bearings off the grid, which might not be straight up on the map. If a meridian is given, count around from the Prime Meridian, in the correct hemisphere.

GRID NAVIGATION

In higher latitudes, the difference between a rhumb line track and a great circle is very much greater than it is at low latitudes, as can be seen in the picture below:

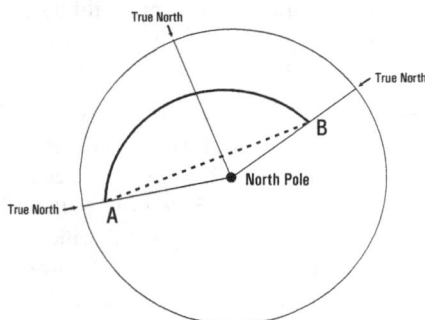

It is obvious that the shortest track lies near the pole on a great circle track that is nearly a straight line on a Polar Stereographic chart. However, the magnetic field is weak (so North is hard to detect), meridians converge greatly, and isogonals are very close together, so true track and magnetic variation are changing all the time. However, the transport drift is the same as convergence, so they cancel each other out and you can keep a constant gyro heading.

Note: Grid Nav requires a stable gyro (i.e. one with very little random wander), so your alignment with reference to Grid North can be maintained for as long as possible - for every degree of compass error, you will drift around 5 miles off per hour at 300 kts. This is where the high quality gyros in the Inertial Navigation/Reference System become useful.

The nearer you get to the poles, the quicker things happen. In the picture, you can see the angular differences in starting and ending points relative to the poles. At A, the initial True track is around 350°, whereas near the pole it is 270°. At B, it's around 190°. In other words, you start

off nearly Northbound, but end up nearly Southbound in a very short space of time!

So how can you navigate under these conditions?

The answer is to use an artificial grid of parallel lines about 60 nm apart on a chart that can be aligned with any meridian (the *Datum Meridian*), although, in practice, it is almost always aligned with the Prime Meridian. This is called a *Standard Grid*. Anyone using the UK Ordnance Survey maps will already be familiar with using a grid over a UTM projection - see *Map Reading*, later.

Tip: The Douglas protractor has a useful grid that can be superimposed on a map.

Using a grid therefore compensates for massive changes in variation and convergency where the meridians disappear up their own orifice. Although the original purpose of grid navigation was to help with navigation at the poles, it can be used at any latitude, and the process can be illustrated on a Lambert chart*. You can see below that the transposed 0° line (which is also the grid) creates a greater angle to True North as you go West.

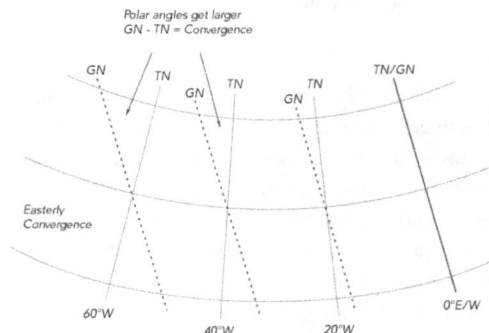

If True North is pointing East of Grid North, you have Easterly convergence, and *vice versa*.

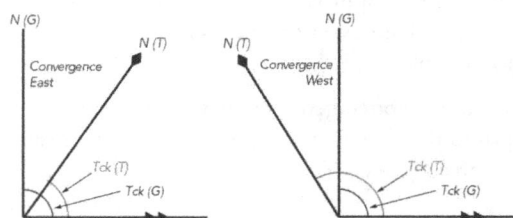

Easterly or Westerly convergence does not necessarily mean that the aircraft is in the respective hemisphere. This will only be the case on a South Polar chart. In the Northern hemisphere, therefore, if the local meridian is West of the Datum Meridian (as in the picture), convergency is East.

*Grid works best on Polar Stereographic and Lambert charts, because (nearly) straight lines on those charts represent great circles (you can use a Transverse Mercator as well). A grid track is therefore (nearly) a great circle.

The angle between Grid and True North is governed by longitude and the convergence factor of the chart*. It is called *Grid Convergence**, or the *Convergence Angle*. With a CF of 1, it is equal to the convergence between the Datum and the local meridians, and it can be calculated with the normal convergency formula. For example, in the Northern hemisphere, at 30°W, GN is 30° West of TN, as adjusted by the convergence factor, if any.

*Convergency at the poles is equal to the change of longitude, but as you move away, the rate of convergency decreases. However, you could probably go down to as much as 80° of latitude before you noticed any real difference, so, over a whole Polar Stereographic chart, the convergence angle is taken to equal longitude.

**Convergency is the angular difference between any two meridians - convergence is that between the datum meridian and another (where grid North is parallel to the datum, and True North will have changed by the amount of chart convergence). They therefore have the same numerical value as the change in longitude, as the angular difference is 1° for every degree of ch long. If your position is at 100E, that is your convergence angle.

The convergence angle is treated in the same way as variation. From True to Grid, add Westerly convergence and subtract Easterly (and apply the convergence factor!). Do the reverse when going from Grid to True.

```
GH = TH +W -E
TH = GH -W +E
```

For example, in the diagram below, the True track to B is about 350°T at A which is 075°W. Adding 75° to 350° gives a grid track of around 065°.

At B, true track is around 190°, but B is at 125°E, and the grid track is still 065°.

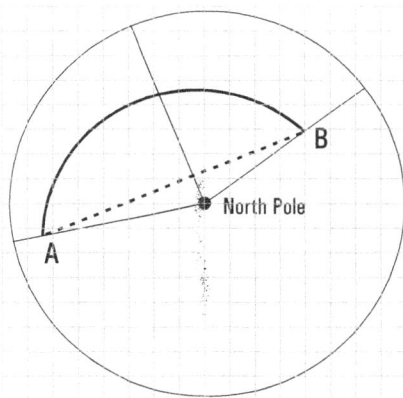

Note that, in moving away from the centre of the chart, although you are heading "Northwards" on the grid, you are actually going South as you move away from the pole.

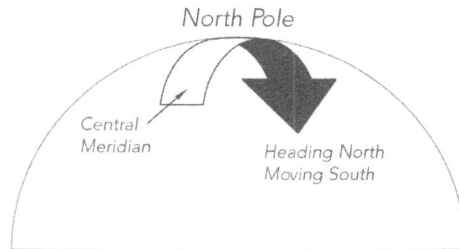

This visualisation is important! You set the DGI against Grid North instead of Magnetic North.

In the picture below, the Grid North line to the East of A is pointing to the left of the True North meridian at 40°W.

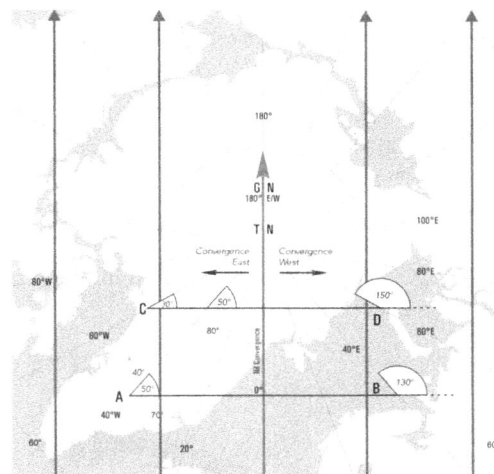

Grid direction is equal to the true direction plus the polar angle, which is measured clockwise from GN to TN. The grid track here is 090°G, based on 40 + 50. Grid and True tracks are the same at the alignment point.

A is at 40°W, so the Convergence is East, True track is least and the calculation becomes:

```
090° - 40° = 050°T
```

At B, on the other hand, which is at 40°E, you get:

```
090° + 40° = 130°T
```

It's a problem that is simply solved on the CR-3:

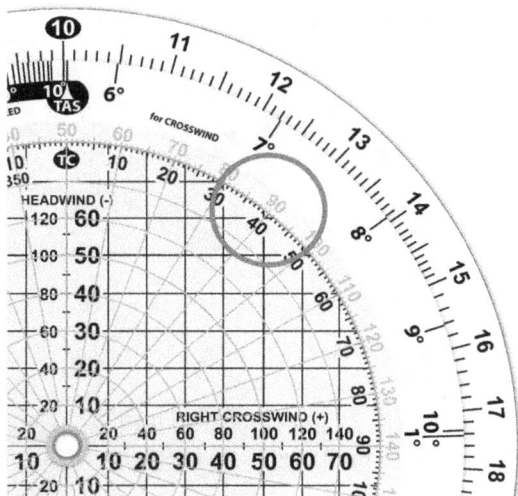

For A, simply set up the True Course against the TC index, and opposite the longitude* (40°W) you will find the Grid Track of 90°.

*On a Polar Stereographic, chart convergence is considered to be 1, so convergence = longitude. If you were using a Lambert, you would need to involve the convergence factor of the chart.

For B, place 90° against 40°E and you will find the True Course of 130° against the TC index.

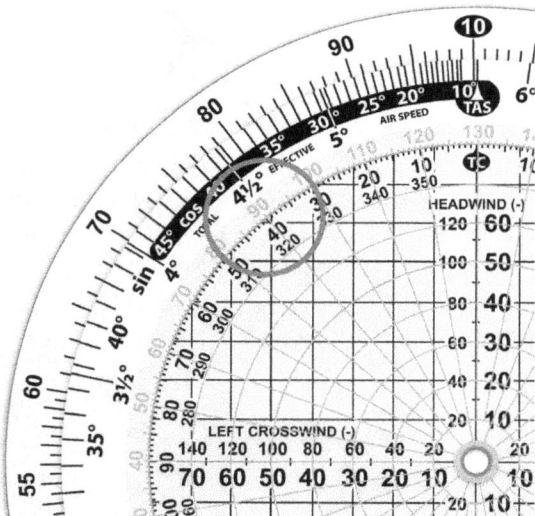

For a standard grid (North Polar chart) grid convergence is W for Easterly longitudes, E for Westerly longitudes, and the opposite for a South Polar chart.

If the grid is aligned with the Greenwich anti-meridian, meaning what they call a non-standard grid where the Grid Datum points down, work out the convergence for standard grid and subtract 180°. The result is negative which reverses E and W, but the figure is correct.

Another option is to calculate with standard grid then take the reciprocal of the answer.

You can also subtract the longitude from 180° and work with the result as a standard grid. For example, if a grid is printed on a South Polar stereographic chart, with Grid North aligned with geographical North, aligned with the 180° meridian, the true track of an aircraft at 80°S 100°E flying on a grid track of 280° would be 000°.

$$180° - 100°E = 80 + 280 = 360$$

In the picture below, the aircraft has a left drift of 6°, so it is heading slightly right of True North for a grid heading of 101°. This is the result of True North being along 95°W (check the lat & long figures) plus the 6° correction.

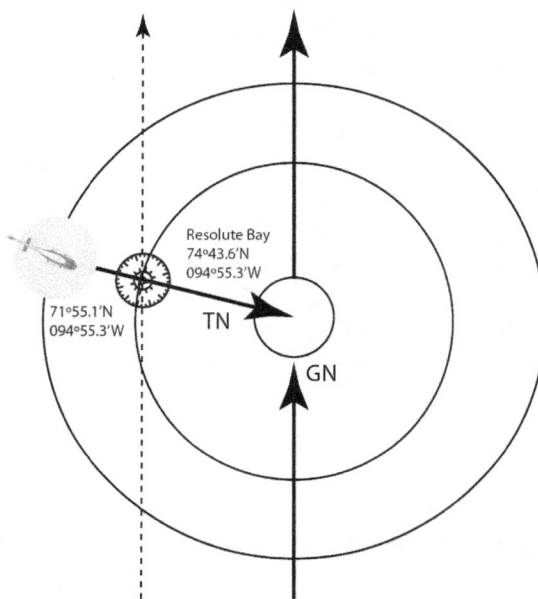

The next picture shows what the RMI would look like.

GRIVATION

This is the difference between Grid and *Magnetic* direction or the sum of Grid convergence and variation. As the difference between True and Grid tracks is longitude, so Grivation is longitude + variation. Whereas normal variations make the compass point along meridians, grivations make it point along the artificial grid lines (this is not needed if you have inertial navigation).

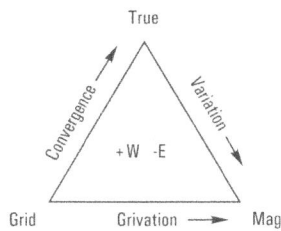

You can either convert Grid to True, then apply variation, or combine convergency and variation in one step.

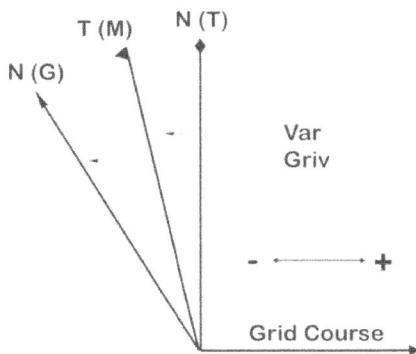

Grivation East, Magnetic Least

Grivation West, Magnetic Best.

So, if your Grid Heading is 90° and the Grivation is 30°E, the magnetic heading is 60°.

Isogrivs join points with the same value of grivation.

Scale

Because a map is a representation of the Earth's surface, you need to know to what proportion it has been drawn to gauge distances accurately.

Assuming a constant scale, the ratio between distances on a map and the Earth's surface is expressed as a scale based on the map's size. For a scale of 1:500,000 (commonly referred to as a half-mil), one inch on the map is equal to 500,000 inches on the Earth:

Picture: CAA 1:500,000 map (small scale)

There are 63,360 inches to the mile, so an inch on a half-mil map is 7.89 statute miles. A "one-inch map" is one that uses one inch for one mile. A "quarter inch map" has 4 miles to the inch (about the length of the distance between the joint on your thumb and the tip, for quick reference).

Picture: CAA 1:250,000 map (larger scale)

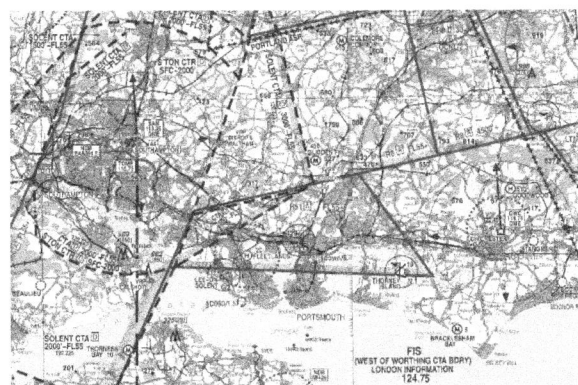

You can tell which chart has a larger scale by looking at the *representative fractions*, obtained by dividing chart distance by Earth distance. Thus, a chart distance of one inch divided by its Earth equivalent of 13.7 nm would be a 1:1000000 map, and of a smaller scale than a 1:500000 (the bigger the number after the colon, or under the dividing line, the smaller the scale is). The representative fraction is always written with the map distance (as the numerator, on top) as 1, regardless of the measurement units.

To find out what Earth distance is represented by a chart distance, multiply the chart distance by the scale so, taking the 1:500,000 scale above, 5 units on the map would be 2,500,000 units of ground distance. If asked what distance is represented by 25 cm on a 1/1,000,000 chart, multiply 25 x 1,000,000 to get 25 million centimetres. Divide that by 100 to get metres (250,000), then by another 100 to get 250 km.

To find the distance on the map, take the ground distance and divide by the denominator, or apply the line against a marking like this:

Tip: To find the scale at a particular latitude, multiply the scale at the Equator by the cosine of the latitude concerned. The RF at the Equator will be bigger!

MERCATOR

As the chart distance between parallels of latitude stays the same and the Earth distance reduces, the *scale* of a Mercator chart *becomes larger* at higher latitudes, expanding as the *secant* of the latitude, or the reciprocal of the cosine. This is not significant below about 300 nm, but you should always use the scale near the distance to be measured.

The easiest way to calculate the scale at different latitudes is to use the cosine of the latitude on the denominator (the large number, ignoring the 1 to the left of the scale ratio - so on a 1:5 000 000 chart the denominator is 5 000 000).

To convert from a scale at any latitude to that at the Equator, divide the denominator by the cosine of the latitude. To convert the Equatorial scale to that at the new latitude, multiply the denominator by the cosine of the latitude. Thus, if you have the scale at any latitude, it can be found for any other latitude.

For example, if the scale at 30°N is 1:5 000 000, what is the scale at 45°N?

$$\frac{5\ 000\ 000}{\cos 30} = 5\ 774\ 000$$

so the scale at the Equator is 1:5 774 000.

$$5\ 774\ 000 \times \cos 45 = 40\ 852\ 387$$

which means that the scale at 45°N is 1:40852387.

A quicker way is to use:

$$\frac{\text{Denominator} \times \text{Cos B}}{\text{Cos A}}$$

Note that it doesn't matter if the new latitude is North or South of the Equator.

EXAMPLES

- If the scale of a Mercator chart is 1:500,000 at the Equator, what is the scale at 15°N?

  The cosine of 15° is 0.97, so 500,000 x 0.97 = 482963. Since the scale will have expanded, the denominator should be smaller.

- If the scale of a Mercator chart is 1:600,000 at 30°N, what is the scale at the Equator?

  This time, divide the denominator by the cosine of the known scale, so: 600,000/0.87 = 689655.

- What is the chart distance between longitudes 179°E and 175°W on a direct Mercator chart with a scale of 1:5 000 000 at the equator?

  It's 6° (assume the shortest route) or 360 nm, or 26,265,600 inches. Divide by the scale for 5.25 ins.

- On a Direct Mercator chart at 15°S, a certain length represents 120 nm on the Earth. The same length on the chart will represent on the Earth, at 10° N, a distance of:

  The original line is at 15S, so to go to 10 (doesn't matter N or S) the distance represented will be slightly longer, for one thing (often you can see the answer just with this type of logic). Anyhow, 120 nm at 15S means 123.7 at the Equator (cos 15 = .97 - divide into 120 to get larger number). The cosine of 10 is .98, so multiply the new number by that to get 121.2 nm

- If the chart distance between 150°W & 150°E on a Mercator at 25°S is 25 cm, what is the scale at the Equator?

  At the Equator, the distance between the meridians is the same (they are parallel lines). The Earth distance at 25°S is 60 x 60, or 3600 nm, so 1 cm = 144 nm or 266 km, or 26600000 cm. The scale is 1/26600000.

- If the scale of a Mercator at 50°N is 1/5000000, what is the chart distance between 150°W & 150°E at 20°N?

  The distance between 150°W & 150°E at 50°N is 60 x 60 x .64 (cos 50) = 2314 nm or 4300 km, or 430000000/5000000. The chart length is 86 cm.

Relief

Information about high ground is given in various ways. *Contours* are lines on a map joining points of equal height (or elevation) above sea level, so they are like isobars (the closer they are, the steeper the slope they represent).

Spot Heights show the elevation of prominent peaks with small dots, with the actual height shown next to them. The highest one will be distinguished in some way, possibly surrounded by a square, or printed in bold.

Tip: Add 300 feet to spot heights for obstacle clearance, because obstacles up to 299 feet can be built without lighting. Also, round up to start with, and add 1000 feet!

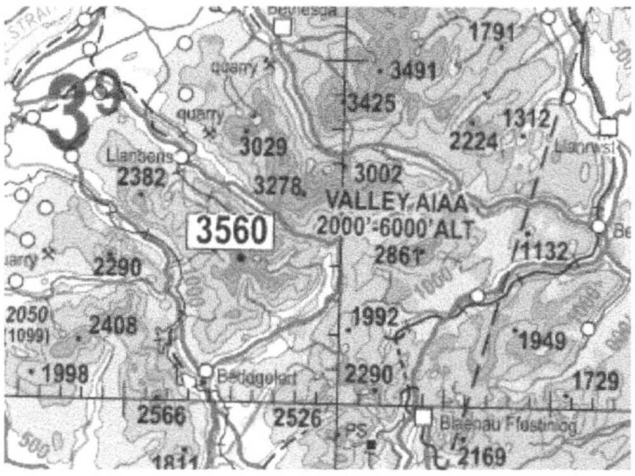

A bold italic figure next to an obstruction is the height AMSL of the top.

1850 (995)

The smaller figure (often in brackets) is the height of the top of the obstruction above ground level. Subtract it from the bold figure to get the elevation of the ground AMSL.

Note: The Minimum Safe Altitude (MSA) will be at least 1800 feet in the UK. This is because ground lower than 499 feet is not shown on the charts, so we start at 500 feet. Add the theoretical height for obstacles of 299 feet, making 800 feet, rounded up. Then add the safety margin of 1000 feet to get 1800. The big blue figure 3^9 in the picture above is NOT an MSA value, it is a **Maximum Elevation Figure**, which represents the maximum elevation of an obstruction within half a degree of latitude and longitude. You need to add 1000 feet to the MEF to get the MSA. Check the maps - in Germany, the big blue figure is an MSA.

Some maps may give different colours or shading to various layers to make things more obvious, known as *Layer* or *Hypsometric Tinting* (see below).

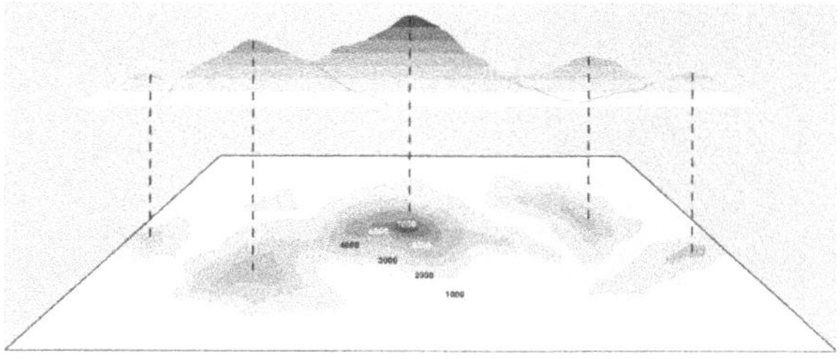

Otherwise, on a map, expect water to be blue, vegetation to be green, and railways and power lines to be black.

Picture: Example Of Hypsometric Tinting

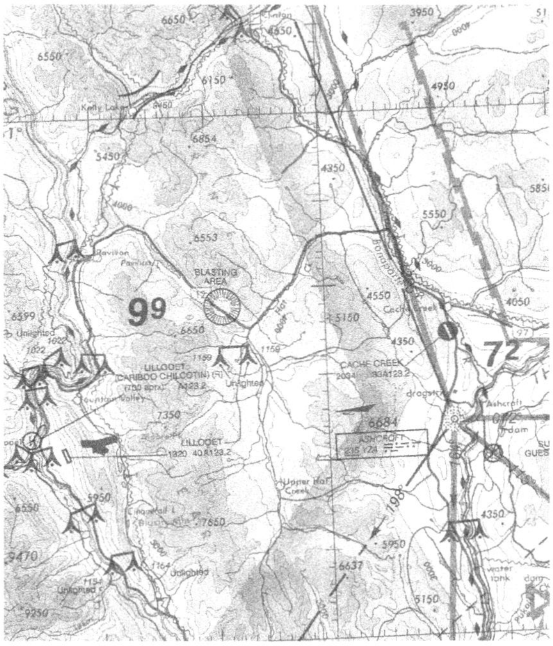

TIME & TIME ZONES

A s it happens, the principles of modern time-keeping have evolved from the needs of navigation, in particular finding your longitude when at sea, as it is not fixable by natural means. The standard used is the interval between two transits of the same heavenly body over some place on the Earth, otherwise known as a **sidereal day**, or one which is related to the stars.

All other methods of recording time (clocks, watches, eggtimers, etc.) reflect regular divisions between those transits. However, sidereal time is only used in observatories, because it doesn't fit naturally with the Sun's motion, which is what we base our lives on. The Solar day is longer than the sidereal day by about 4 minutes (it varies), and it is noon when the Sun is over the meridian you are on. This is *local time* unless you know when it is noon at a standard meridian, like Greenwich.

To recap, a sidereal day concerns one revolution of the Earth against a particular star. A solar day relates to one revolution against the Sun, and it is longest in February (+14 mins), and shortest in November (-16). This is the result of several circumstances, one being the *obliquity of the ecliptic*, and another being the Earth's orbit.

The Earth does not spin vertically, but is inclined at 23½° from the vertical over a 41,000-year cycle, so the Equator is not in line with the Celestial Equator (for the fixed stars). This obliquity of the ecliptic actually ranges over 22.1-24.5°, so the Earth, in this respect, behaves rather like a ship caught in the swell of the sea as it nods back and forth. When the inclination points towards the Sun, the Northern Hemisphere days are long and the nights are short - it's Summer. The day when this is at its maximum value is the *Summer Solstice* on June 21 (Solstice is Latin for *Sun Stand Still*). In other words, the Sun sets further South each day, until, on December 21st, it stops, then starts moving North again about 3 days later. On June 21st, it stops going North to go South.

The highest latitude at which the Sun will reach an altitude of 90° above the horizon is 23.5°. The highest latitude at which it will rise and set above the horizon every day is 66.5°.

The Earth takes 365 days, 5 hours, 48 minutes and 45 seconds to orbit around the Sun.

Kepler's Laws Of Planetary Motion

We know that the Earth, with 8 other planets (making 9), revolves round the Sun although, to be picky, Pluto is no longer considered to be a real planet, because its orbit intersects with Neptune's - it is referred to by astronomers as a dwarf planet. There are also about 2000 minor planets and asteroids. 1 year is the time it takes a planet to go once round the Sun, in the Earth's case being 365¼ days (the odd quarters are consolidated every four years into one day in a leap year, and 3 leap years are suppressed every 4 centuries). While it is going round the Sun, the Earth spins on its axis once nearly every 24 hours, and the speed of the Earth's orbit is 66,600 mph, or 18.5 miles per second,

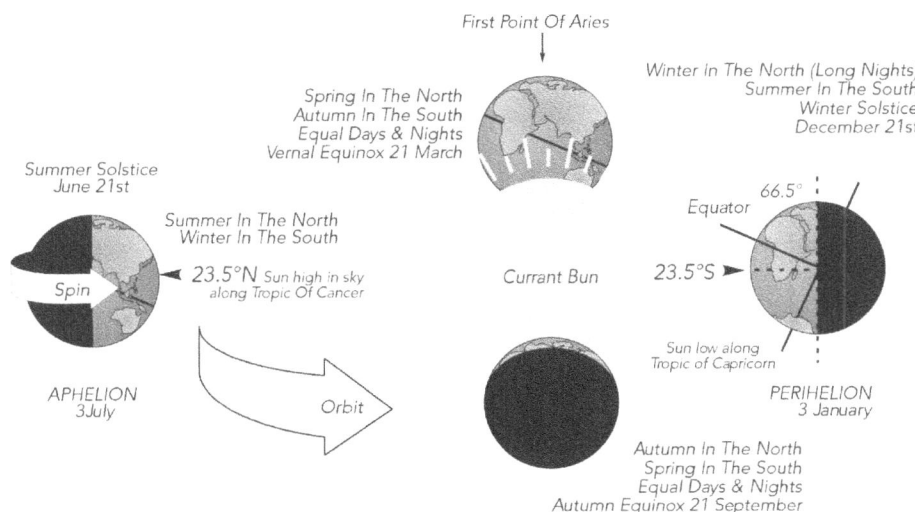

First Point Of Aries

Spring In The North
Autumn In The South
Equal Days & Nights
Vernal Equinox 21 March

Winter In The North (Long Nights)
Summer In The South
Winter Solstice
December 21st

Summer Solstice
June 21st

Summer In The North
Winter In The South

66.5°

Equator

Spin

23.5°N Sun high in sky
along Tropic Of Cancer

Currant Bun

23.5°S

APHELION
3 July

Orbit

Sun low along
Tropic of Capricorn

PERIHELION
3 January

Autumn In The North
Spring In The South
Equal Days & Nights
Autumn Equinox 21 September

capt.gs

much faster than a bullet. Because the Earth rotates from West to East, the heavenly bodies appear to revolve about the Earth from East to West.

Copernicus first proposed that the planets revolved around the Sun but, using 3 laws, Johannes Kepler (after Tycho Brahe) determined that:

- **1.** Each one moves in an ellipse*, with the Sun at one focus (it's an ellipse rather than a circle due to influences from outside the solar system).

  *But the Moon's orbit around the Earth is nearly circular.

- **2.** the radius vector (the straight line joining the Sun and any planet) sweeps **equal areas in equal time**, so planets speed up and slow down to compensate (they are fastest near the Sun).

- **3.** The squares of the periods of revolution of any two planets are proportional to the cubes of their mean distances from the Sun. That is, their orbital speed increases with distance away from the Sun.

Essentially, the planets move in their orbits because they follow a mean line between two forces, and such a line is a curve (Carpenter, 1896). This is a corollary of Kepler's third law. True, the mean looks like a straight line, but the curve is so large that small segments would look straight.

The two forces are centripetal and centrifugal force, which could be regarded as attraction and repulsion. In fact, it was Kepler, and not Newton, who discovered that gravity varies inversely with the square of the distance between bodies. In simple terms, a phrase like "the square of the distance" just means that any attraction at two feet is a quarter of the attraction at one foot, etc.

Similarly, "the squares of the times as the cubes of the distance" refers to the square of repulsion being equal to the cube of the attraction. With only two bodies, you end up with a circle. With many, you get an ellipse, as with a typical planetary orbit, as per the second law, above.

The Earth's orbit, then, is the result of a balance between gravity (centripetal force, attraction) from the Sun, and centrifugal force (repulsion) due to the Earth's movement around it. You can find the distance of any planet from the Sun by inspecting its orbital speed (time) and vice versa.

For example, if a new planet were to revolve round the Sun every two years, its distance from the Sun would be 1.6 times that of the Earth, 1.6 being the cube root of 4, the result of doubling the time involved, namely two years. Similarly, if a planet took 6 months to go round the Sun (and was therefore nearer), you would divide the Earth's distance by 1.6.

The *perihelion* (1-10 Jan) is where the Earth is closest to the Sun, and the *aphelion* (1-10 Jul) is where it is furthest away. Having said that, at perihelion, Earth is about 91 million miles from the Sun; it moves outward to around 95 million miles at aphelion, so the difference in distance is only about 3%.

The problem with the elliptical orbit and the different speeds is that the length of the apparent solar day varies. For example, in Summer in the UK, a sundial in Cornwall could be as much as an hour and a half away from the UTC value, so your watch must keep changing its speed to keep up with the real, or apparent (visible) Sun.

Local Mean Time

We use the *mean solar day* at 24 hours as the average between the longest and shortest Solar days. Thus, a (non-existent) Mean Sun actually transits any meridian at noon, hence the expression *Local Mean Time* (LMT), which is an averaged time referenced from the lower branch (2400) of the observer's meridian. Greenwich Mean Time, or GMT, now called UTC, is referenced from the meridian at Greenwich. If you are sitting at Greenwich, GMT is LMT.

A sundial does, however, indicate the proper time of the upper transit of the real Sun over a meridian at *Local Apparent Noon*, and the lower transit on the other side of the Earth at midnight 12 hours before (the observer is considered to be in the upper branch of the meridian concerned - the lower branch is the antimeridian).

Remember: The Mean Sun is a fictitious (or hypothetical) Sun moving at a uniform rate along the Celestial Equator at the *average (uniform) speed* of the real Sun's movement along the Ecliptic. It coincides with the Apparent Sun at the Spring Equinox (below).

The difference between solar and mean days less than a minute, but the results are cumulative - the real Sun is around 16 minutes **ahead of the mean Sun in November** and 14 minutes **behind it in February**. The difference between clock and apparent solar times (or a clock and a sundial) is the *Equation Of Time* to be added to or subtracted from civil time for apparent time.

In summary, the word *transit* means the passage of a heavenly body over the meridian of a place on the Earth (actually across the face of the Sun) - the time difference between two transits is called a *day*, and we have to cope with transits of the Sun and the fixed stars, so we have two types of day. *Sidereal time* (star time) is kept with regard to the fixed stars, which appear to be fixed only because of their distance from us (it's actually time measured by the apparent diurnal motion of the vernal equinox*, which is very close to, but not identical with, the motion of stars. They differ by the precession of the vernal equinox relative to the stars, but you knew that already ☺).

*The word *equinox* is Latin for *equal night* - when the apparent path of the Sun round the Earth (Ecliptic) passes over the Equator on its way North or South (that is, it has a declination of zero), the days and nights are of equal length everywhere, at the Spring and Autumn Equinoxes, which are the times in the year when the relationship between the length of day and night, as well as the rate of change of declination of the Sun, are changing at the greatest rate in mid-latitudes. They are also points where the Sun rises and sets due East and West, respectively.

Because the position of the Sun on the longest and shortest days of the year shifts Westward amongst the stars, and some stars move relative to others anyway, the best point from which to locate stars with reference to East and West, and to start the year from, is the position of the Sun when the days and nights are of equal length, in this case the Vernal Equinox (the one that happens in Spring), also known as the First Point of Aries.

The Sun increases its declination (latitude) until it reaches the Solstice point, on June or December 21st, North or South of the Equator, respectively. The Solstice is the point where the Sun stops travelling and starts to go the other way. Having stopped going South on December 21st, for example, three days later, it starts North again.

To all intents and purposes, therefore, the Earth rotates by 360° in one *sidereal day*, which is regarded as a constant figure against the stars, even though, technically, it isn't. A sidereal day lasts 23 hours and 56 minutes (of solar time), which is about 4 minutes less than a solar day, because the Earth's direction of rotation and its orbit round the Sun are the same. To make up the time, the Earth must rotate an extra 0.986° between solar transits so, in 24 hours of solar time, the Earth will actually rotate 360.986°. In other words, during the course of one (solar) day, the Earth has moved a short distance along its orbit around the sun, and must rotate a little bit more before the Sun reaches its highest point again at any given place.

Using the sidereal day removes this anomaly.

The Earth spins slower every day, enough to be detected by the atomic clocks in satellites which must be resynchronised every 20 years or so (1000 weeks).

Time

In navigation, time can mean a specific hour of the day, or a time interval. After Einstein, the state of motion and location of the clock used to measure time became an important part of its measurement (see *Satellites*).

Days and nights are of equal length on the Spring and Autumn *Equinoxes*, March 21 and September 23 (Equinox means *Equal Night*), because the spin axis is vertical to the Earth's orbit. The Equinoxes are the times in the year when the relationship between the length of day and night, as well as the rate of change of declination of the Sun, are changing at the greatest rate. They are also points where the Sun rises and sets due East and West, respectively.

Note: The claim that night and day are symmetric is based on the definition that the day starts or ends when the middle of the centre of the Sun's disk touches the horizon, ignoring the effects of the atmosphere.

Trivia: The Moon rises and sets at the same points as the Sun, but at opposite solstices. For example, it rises at midwinter at the same place the Sun does at midsummer. The Earth and Moon also rotate round each other, round some pivotal point, as they proceed on their way around the Sun. Even more strange is that the Moon fits exactly over the Sun when superimposed on it.

The beginning of the day at any location is when the Mean Sun is in transit with its anti-meridian, on the opposite side of the Earth to the point in question. This would be midnight, or 0000 hours *Local Mean Time* (LMT). Similarly, when the Sun is in transit with the meridian concerned, it will be Noon, or 12:00 hours. The angle between a meridian over which a heavenly body is located and where you are is the *Local Hour Angle*, or LHA. It serves a similar purpose to longitude.

In fact, the Hour Angle is measured Westwards (from the meridian to the celestial body), based on three datums:

- Greenwich
- Local
- Sidereal

The *Prime Meridian* is the standard to which local mean time is referred - it is currently in the UK. *Greenwich Mean Time* (GMT) is now referred to as *Universal Coordinated Time*, or UTC, which is more accurately calculated, but can be regarded as the same for our purposes (GMT itself only came about because of the railways - previously, every part of Britain ran its own time scheme). The Greenwich day starts when the mean Sun transits the anti-meridian (180° away), and transits the Easterly ones before it reaches Greenwich. The local mean time in those places will therefore be *ahead* of UTC, and that of those West will be *behind*. When calculating, reduce everything to UTC first, and don't forget the date!

THE INTERNATIONAL DATE LINE

This is where a change of date is officially made, mainly the 180° meridian which bends to accommodate certain islands in the South Sea and parts of Siberia, but otherwise it over the sea. As you cross it, you can gain or lose a day, depending on which way you are going. When solving time problems, however, calculating in UTC usually sorts things out automatically.

Since we take (more or less) 24 hours to go round the Sun, in one hour we move through 15°, or we take 4 minutes to go through 1°. Similarly, in 1 minute we transit 15 minutes, or take 4 seconds to go through 1 minute (just to remind you, a degree is split up into minutes, which in turn are split into seconds).

STANDARD TIMES

To save you adjusting your watch constantly as you move round the Earth, some countries adopt standard times, as established in the UK in 1880 and the US in 1883. That is to say, legal authorities allocate a standard amount of time East or West of Greenwich, based on meridians 15° apart. For example, Canadian time zones are:

Zone	Convert (UTC-)
Newfoundland	3.5
Atlantic	4
Eastern	5
Central	6
Mountain	7
Pacific	8

The standard meridian for Eastern time is 75°, or 5 hours West - Central is 90° (6 hours) and so on. In theory, all places within 7½° either side of a standard meridian should keep the same time, but some zones are aligned with other boundaries for convenience (some towns in Northern BC actually keep Alberta time).

There can be a **13-hour time difference** between countries around the world.

To convert standard time to LMT, multiply the degrees distance from the standard meridian by 4 to get minutes, then subtract if you are West and add if you are East.

Picture: Time Zones across the USA.

DAYLIGHT SAVING (DST)

This was originally set up in UK during the First World War (actually 1916) in an attempt to keep people out of pubs during working hours, or to save fuel in munitions factories (it depends on which book you read) and to get people up earlier so they could use the daylight.

Essentially, clocks go forward one hour for the summer - in *Spring* they go *forward*, in *Fall*, they *fall back* (Windows will tell you automatically!)

INTERNATIONAL ATOMIC TIME

Since 1 January 1972, UTC has been linked to IAT, which is based on an atomic clock, and which has shown that the length of the average day is increasing by about 2 milliseconds per century, due to tides, winds and other types of friction. That is, atomic seconds are all the same, whereas astronomical seconds are inconsistent because of the Earth's wobble. To compensate for all this, a leap second is inserted or omitted on a day decided by the International Time Bureau. It last happened in 1989.

Remember:

- The length of a day varies because the Earth's orbit is not symmetrical
- The Mean Solar Day is an average of the variations
- The Equation Of Time is the difference between the Mean and Solar days
- At 66.6° (N or S), there is no sunrise in Winter
- At 64.5° latitude (N or S), there is no sunset in Summer
- At 60.5° latitude (N or S), there is continuous twilight as the centre of the Sun's disk does not reach 6° below the horizon

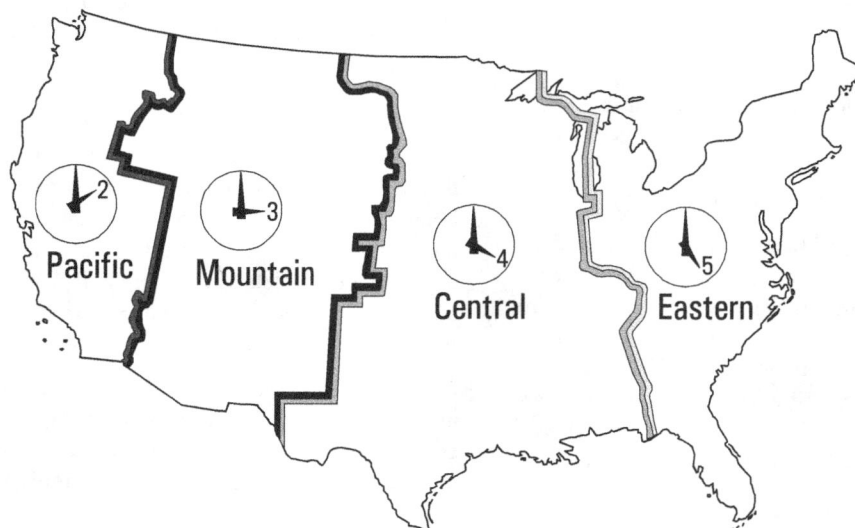

capt.gs

The Air Almanac

Standard times around the world are in three lists on pages A20-A23, *Fast on GMT, Slow on GMT,* and *Keeping GMT.*

List I - PLACES FAST ON G.M.T. (mainly those EAST OF GREENWICH)

The times given below should be }		added to G.M.T. to give Standard Time. subtracted from Standard Time to give G.M.T.		
	h	m		h	m
Admiralty Islands ...	10		Estonia	03	
Afghanistan	04	30	Ethiopia	03	
Albania*	01		Finland	02	
Algeria*	01		France*	01	
Bangladesh	06		Iran‡	04	

*Summer time may be kept in these countries
‡ The legal time may differ from that given here

Check the footnotes!

List III - PLACES SLOW ON G.M.T. (WEST OF GREENWICH)

The times given below should be }		subtracted from G.M.T. to give Standard Time. added to Standard Time to give G.M.T.		
	h	m		h	m
Argentina ...	03		Chile‡	03	
Azores	01		Colombia	05	
Bermuda*	04		Cuba*	05	
Canada			Ecuador	05	
Alberta*	07		Grenada	04	

At 105° 45' E, at noon LMT, what is the GMT?

105/15 = 420 mins, or 7 hours. 45 divided by 15' = 3 mins. Greenwich is least because the location is East, so 12 (noon) - 7 hrs 3 mins is 04:57 GMT

At 147° 28' W, at 1327 LMT, what is the GMT?

147/15 = 588 mins, or 9 hours 48 mins. 28 divided by 15' = 2 mins. Greenwich is best as the location is West, so 1327 + 9:50 23:17 GMT

SUNRISE, SUNSET

There are also tables for specific days and latitudes in LMT that tell you when the Sun rises and sets, varying with date and latitude (between 60°S to 72°N). There are no calculations involved - the tables have been made up from observations over hundreds of years. Sunrise or Sunset occurs when the Sun's upper edge is on the viewer's horizon, which will be affected by atmospheric refraction - when you see the Sun for the first time, it is still half a degree below the horizon, but this will not affect the figures as they are based on visible phenomena.

At the Equator, Sunrise is always 0600 and Sunset at 1800. Except in high latitudes, the times of Sunrise and Sunset vary only a little each day, so they may be taken as the same for all latitudes. Notice that the Sun rises later and sets earlier as latitude increases in Winter, but it rises earlier and sets later in Summer. However, outside the latitudes above, the Sun will not set in Summer, or rise in Winter. An open square box at the top of a column means the Sun is visible, and a filled in box means it isn't. 4 hash marks (////) means continuous civil twilight. This is representative of a Sunset table from the Air Almanac:

Lat	July							
	1	4	7	10	13	16	19	22
°	h m	h m	h m	h m	h m	h m	h m	h m
N 72	■	■	■	■	■	■	■	■
70	□	□	□	□	□	□	□	□
68	□	□	□	□	□	□	////	////
66	////	////	////	////	////	////	////	////
64	////	////	////	////	////	////	////	////
62	////	////	////	////	00 19	00 51	01 11	01 27
N 60	01 01	01 09	01 17	01 26	01 36	01 45	01 55	02 05
58	01 47	01 52	01 57	02 03	02 09	02 16	02 24	02 31
56	02 16	02 19	02 24	02 28	02 33	02 39	02 45	02 51
54	02 38	02 41	02 44	02 48	02 52	02 57	03 02	03 08
52	02 55	02 58	03 01	03 04	03 08	03 12	03 17	03 22

The readings depend on latitude and time only. To find the time of sunset at 55°N on July 12th in the table, first interpolate for the latitude, so you end up with 02 38 on the 10th, and 02 42 and a bit on the 13th. With 4 minutes between them, the answer is 02 40

The Almanac also has tables for Sunrise and Twilight, but the process is the same. It deals with the real Sun, but the times are in LMT.

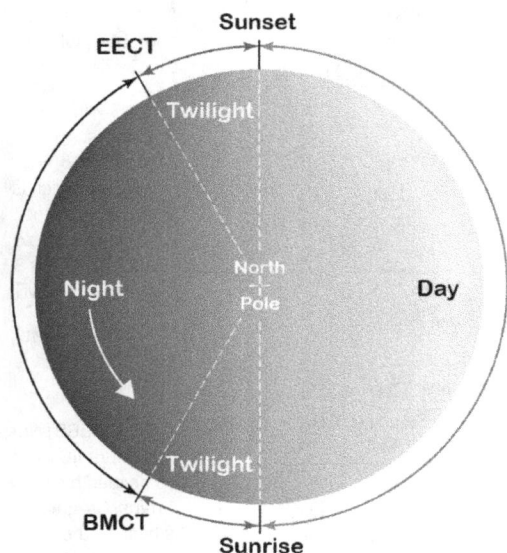

In fact, it is refraction that accounts for twilight (which is longer at higher latitudes). *Civil twilight* exists when the centre of the Sun's disk is within 6° of the horizon, during which you still have a distinct horizon (this is the Sun's actual position when its top is on the horizon). *Nautical twilight* exists when the Sun's centre is between 6-12° below the horizon. Between 12-18° below, you get *astronomical twilight*, and *legal twilight* happens 30 minutes before sunrise and 30 minutes after sunset.

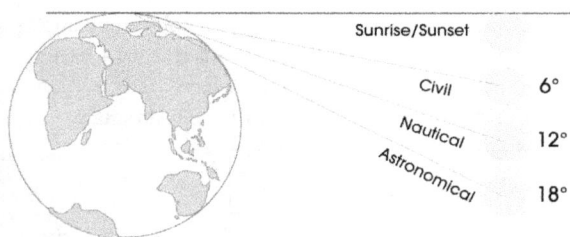

Remember that the figures are tabulated according to *local mean time*, which is based on the mean Sun, which doesn't exist. You will also have to interpolate, since not every day is shown, or every latitude.

Note: You have to be above 66° 33' N or S before the sun is above or below the horizon for a full 24 hours at some time during the year. However, the atmosphere plays tricks with light. In summer the midnight sun is actually visible at 66°. In winter, you need to go beyond 67° so as not to see the sun on the winter solstice. The onset of darkness is more sudden at the Equator because the Sun is setting perpendicular to the horizon, while at higher latitudes, it

can set more obliquely, allowing it to remain close to the horizon for longer.

The Sun is also used, with other tables, to get a True Bearing, with which to set your DGI, which is very handy when up North. You could also use the heading of a known feature, such as a runway.

Radio depends on the movement of electric and magnetic waves, which depend on the movement of electricity, which ultimately depends on the activities of electrons inside an atom. If you are wondering why you need to know this stuff as a pilot, it is because it is also part of the syllabus for an amateur radio licence, of which a pilot's radio licence is a cut-down version.

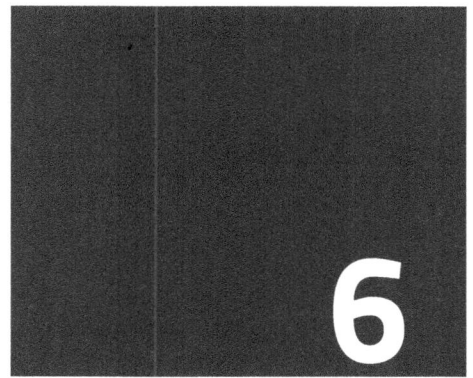

RADIO NAVIGATION

6

Alternating current is also the basis of radio waves, which we use to convey information or find our way. The sound of a rotor blade slap from 1100 feet will take one second to reach your ears, but air travelling at that speed would be ten times more powerful than a hurricane, so the sound you hear is not *in* the air - it changes the characteristics of the air instead.

The effect is like the example of electrons moving down a cable. One pushed in at one end affects the others in line until one falls out at the other, so it is easier to imagine a wave of compression pushing air particles in front of it before it affects your eardrums. If this is done too slowly, though, the air particles have a chance to get out of the way, so the effect is not noticeable below a certain rate of vibration, or *frequency*.

WAVE MOTION   062 01

A wave is a progressive disturbance in a medium that itself is not displaced permanently, although electromagnetic waves do not need a medium. Either way, waves can be transmitted without affecting matter.

The usual example is dropping a stone into water, where the water only moves up and down, but there is forward movement of energy, which comes in the first place from the loss of kinetic energy as the stone hits the water.

Making electrons move along an antenna can set an electromagnetic wave in motion in the air in the same way.

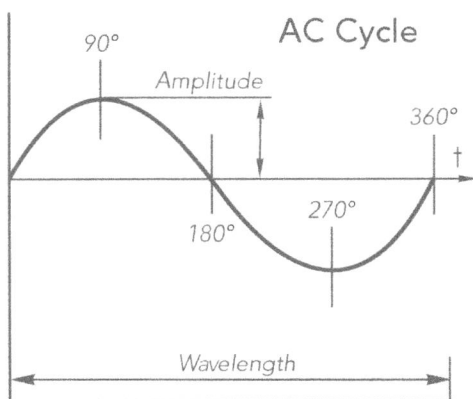

The qualities associated with any type of wave motion are:

- **Velocity**.
- **Frequency**. The rate of oscillation, *or the number of waves that pass a fixed point in one second, measured in hertz (hz).
- **Wavelength**. The least distance between two consecutive points on two consecutive waves with the same displacement and velocity, represented by the symbol λ.
- **Period**. The time between successive waves.
- **Amplitude**. The maximum displacement of a moving particle from its mean position, labelled positive or negative. Loosely termed *volume*.

Radio waves were originally classified by wavelength, but it is more convenient to use frequency (see table overleaf).

Where the particles of the transmitting medium move at right angles to the direction of propagation (say up and down on the surface of water), you have a *transverse* wave. Where particles move back and forth in the same direction as the propagation (sound), you have a *longitudinal* wave.

Polarisation

Electromagnetic radiation is made up from E and H fields, which stand for *electric* and *magnetic*, respectively. In other words, radio waves have electrical and magnetic axes, acting at right angles to each other. The electric field arises from voltage, and the magnetic one from the current.

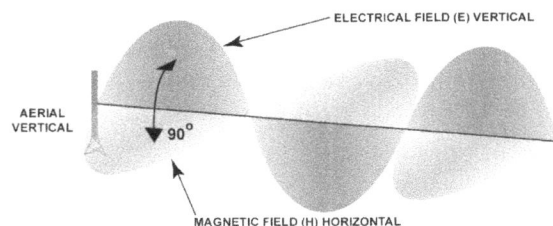

A wave's polarisation is noted (by convention) with reference to the electrical field, which is parallel with its antenna, so a vertically polarised wave has a vertical electric field, which will come from a vertical aerial. For efficiency, the receiving antenna must have the same orientation. For example, NDBs (and weather-based static) are vertically polarised, and VORs and ILS localisers are horizontally polarised.

In theory, or in perfect conditions, a vertically polarised antenna should not couple with a horizontally polarised one, but the signals are not always at 90° to each other, and there will be some reflection involved from obstacles along the signal path. Despite that, however, VHF/UHF signals can easily get 20 db of isolation, or a 100 times difference in signal strength. Thus, you can transmit two signals on the same frequency that won't interfere with each other (receiving both on two receivers is called *Diversity Reception*).

With such linear polarisation, the plane of oscillation is fixed in space, whereas with circular polarisation, the plane is rotating - the electrical and magnetic components of the wave spin about the axis of the advance at a rate equal to the frequency. Circular polarisation is often used (with helical antennae) where the relative orientation of the transmitting and receiving antennae cannot be easily controlled, as with GPS, or where the polarisation of the signal may change, as with reflections from the ionosphere. It can reduce rain clutter with radar.

In general, polarisation does not change over short distances, but over long distances, especially at high frequencies, it can change drastically.

Calculations

In free space (or a vacuum), electromagnetic waves move at the speed of light, which is taken to be 300,000,000 metres per second, abbreviated as *C*. The number of waves that will arrive per second at a radio antenna (the frequency) depends on dividing C by the length of the wave concerned. Put another way, over 1 Hz (i.e. 1 cycle), a wave will travel for 300,000 km.

For radar purposes, this is **300 m per microsecond**. In nautical miles, try 161,800.

Frequency and wavelength are related as follows:

$$\lambda = \frac{C}{F}$$

F is the frequency in cycles per second. Wavelength is given in metres. So, to find the length of a wave with a frequency of 300 Khz:

$$\lambda = \frac{300000000}{300000}$$

The answer is 1000 m, or 1 km.

Wavebands

The range of electromagnetic waves is quite large, but radio waves only occupy a small part of it, actually between about 3 Khz to 3,000 GHz.

This area is split up by International agreement between the people who wish to use it, and consists of frequency ranges, or bands, that share similar characteristics.

Trivia: Wavelengths below 100m (i.e. short wave, or HF) used to be thought of by scientists as useless for long distance communications until amateur operators proved them wrong!

Band	Frequency	Wavelength	Aids	Notes
VLF	3-30 Khz Kilo = Thousand	10-100 km Myriametric		This needs high power and large antennas, so it is used for long ranges, where no transmissions are required from the aircraft - the signal travels as a ground wave for several thousand miles and can penetrate the ocean. Has the least attenuation.
LF	30-300 Khz	1-10 km Kilometric	NDB, Decca, LORAN	Distances of around 1500 miles, with minor attenuation
MF	300-3,000 Khz	100-1000 m Hectometric		Can cover 100-300 miles over land, but the range increases at night as the ionosphere merges back into one layer. Fading and static are problems, so can be unreliable at night. Needs fairly high power and fairly large antennas.
HF Short Wave	3-30 MHz Mega = Million	10-100 m Decametric	HF/RT	Longer distances (100-2000 miles) but only after refraction from the ionosphere - it doesn't go as far by itself as LF can (i.e. 30-100 nm), but you can use a transmitter in the aircraft. This band also suffers from fading and static, and you need to choose the frequency carefully according to the time of day, season and direction of transmission. Severe attenuation. Affected by sunspots
VHF	30-300 MHz	1-10 m Metric	VOR, VDF, ILS Localiser, Marker	Line of sight, is meant for local services, say up to 50 miles. It gives more precise results, and is not really affected by static.
UHF	300-3,000 MHz	10-100 cm Decimetric	Radio Altimeter (High Alt), SSR, DME, GPS, Glidepath	Short range line of sight, but there is little interference and antennas are small
SHF	3-30 GHz Giga = Trillion	1-10 cm Centimetric	Radio Altimeter (Low Alt), MLS, Radar, AWR, Doppler	Short range line of sight, but there is little interference and antennas are small
EHF	30-300 GHz	1-10 mm Millimetric		

HOW IT ALL WORKS

A sound wave will only travel so far by itself, which is why it needs help, in the shape of a *carrier wave*, to move over longer distances (if you could transmit a sound wave, it would be so long that huge aerials and large coils and capacitors would be needed). The carrier wave is created at radio frequency (the RF carrier), and a sound wave (the AF signal) is added to it, so that an electronic copy of the original signal is made. In other words, we are transferring energy with an electromagnetic wave. The process of frequency shifting is called *modulation*, described below.

Trivia: Although Marconi transmitted the first CW signal, a Canadian, Reginald Fessenden, transmitted the first *voice* signal from Massachusetts to ships along the Eastern Seaboard, and later across the Atlantic. He also invented the principles of heterodyning, mentioned later. However, Nikola Tesla was ahead of both - Marconi used 17 of Tesla's patents. The original effects were demonstrated by Heinrich Hertz in 1887, after James Clark Maxwell in 1864. He also determined the speed of the waves and the relationship between frequency and wavelength.

Radio waves are the product of the changing fields that result from alternating current. The backward and forward flow of electrons produces electrical and magnetic fields along a cable.

If the cable forms a closed circuit, the fields tend to cancel each other out, but you can still induce AC in an open circuit that ends in a bare wire. If the frequency is high enough, the fields will propagate at 90° to it. If the wire, or antenna, has the right length (half the wavelength, or multiples thereof), the fields will resonate and send continuous alternating waves of energy (radio waves) outwards, at the same frequency as the AC. If a wire of the same length as the transmitter is placed in the same orientation in space some distance away, the propagating fields will induce an identical alternating current along it.

The Transmitter

Radio transmitters are based around high frequency oscillators (mechanical devices such as alternators are too slow), but applying lots of power directly to an oscillator (above about 100 MHz) reduces its stability, so a relatively weak signal is used, then amplified for the later stages. The audio signal is treated the same way. A *modulator's* job is to combine the signals from the radio and audio amplifiers by superimposing the amplified speech signal on the RF carrier with a transformer.

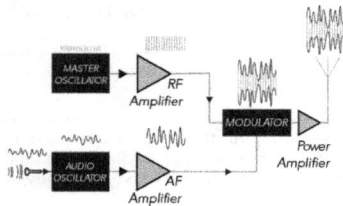

MODULATION

The process of imposing information on to a carrier wave by changing its characteristics is called modulation. That is, the information to be sent *modulates**, or varies, the carrier wave, although an unmodulated signal travels further than a modulated one for the same power, hence their use with long range NDBs.

*You can't just add the voltages together because the antenna would only transmit the radio signal.

The *Depth Of Modulation* is the extent to which a carrier wave is modulated by another frequency, as expressed by a percentage. Such modulation is actually done at just below 100% (typically 90% for voice) because there is a danger of over-modulation that will cause distortion. If the modulation is too low, the signal may be hidden by noise.

AMPLITUDE MODULATION (A3)

With AM, the amplitude, or power, of a carrier wave is varied according to the strength of an audio (or video) signal applied to it. Its shape changes as the AF signal distorts it.

The top part of the picture shows an RF carrier with alternating cycles above and below the line of nil current flow. The middle part shows a fluctuating DC waveform representing speech from a microphone (it is positive because it is all above the nil current line). When

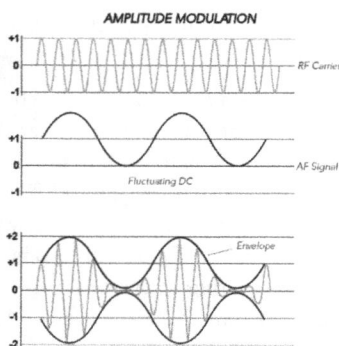

the two are merged together (in the bottom part) the RF carrier takes on the shape of the distorting AF signal.

AM suffers from two practical defects, one being noise, and the other lack of quality. Almost all natural and man-made electrical disturbances, such as atmospheric static, or electrical equipment, radiate amplitude-disturbed energy. In addition, the air gets more positively charged as you climb higher, as described under *The Ionosphere*, later, especially when it is wet. This may cause sudden leaks or discharges that produce electromagnetic waves called *precipitation static*, that interfere with radio transmissions, which is a factor when you want reliability in bad weather.

A quick look at a rainfall map of the world will tell you where it is worst, namely the tropics.

The lowest frequency where freedom from static interference can be guaranteed is 30 MHz.

*This ionisation of the air creates a layer around the Earth called the ionosphere which has less resistance to the flow of electricity. It is useful for getting longer ranges with certain frequencies (HF) and is discussed later on.

AM transmissions can therefore be noisy because the receiver cannot distinguish between the signals you want to hear and the ones you don't. This has led to the use of systems such as SELCAL (*Selective Calling*), which mutes the receiver until a special code is sent, so you don't have to listen to the background noise all the time.

Also, for a quality signal, you need to transmit all the audio frequencies in the range of human hearing. AM channels are not wide enough to do that, for historical reasons. This is why a contralto female voice is used for VOLMET - it fits the frequency spectrum better than a soprano does.

SIDEBANDS   062 01 01 03

When a carrier is modified by a frequency lower than itself, you get a band of frequencies either side of the carrier. The boundaries are effectively two extra frequencies, being the equivalent of the *sum* and *difference* frequencies of the carrier and the modulator, so you get three in total, from the carrier *plus* the audio and the carrier *minus* the audio (there are way more with FM transmissions). The extras are called *upper* and *lower* sidebands, which are exact mirrors of each other, in terms of the information carried, with half the original strength.

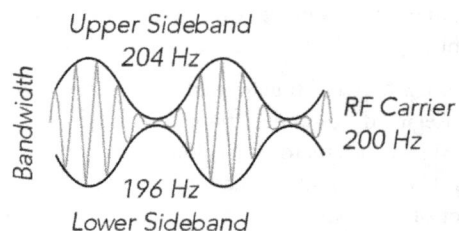

A receiver would normally need to pick up all the frequencies involved, but this can waste bandwidth (and power) as you are transmitting two identical sidebands and the carrier, which is there even if nothing is being transmitted - it is simply something to hang the sidebands on. In addition, the efficiency is limited to 33% to prevent distortion in the receiver when demodulating.

Because 80% of the power of an AM signal is in the carrier wave, which is essentially wasted, a neat trick is to suppress the carrier and one sideband, to transmit just the other one, *adding what was taken away at the receiver*. This means that you need less than half the power to transmit* (for the same distance), and the signal doesn't take up as much space, so you get to use more channels, although your receiver now needs an oscillator. In effect, you can transmit with narrower bandwidths. This is *Single Sideband Transmission*, or SSB. As there is no carrier, there is no transmission unless information is being sent.

*SSB can do with 250 watts what AM requires 1000 watts for, so the ratio is 4:1, or 16 times more efficiency.

Traditionally, the upper sideband is used above 10 Khz, and the lower one below (it is a modified form of A3). HF upper sideband is used for aeronautical voice communications over the N Atlantic - now replaced with satellite communications or ADS-B. HF VOLMET signals are also single sideband, as are HF two-way communications.

FREQUENCY MODULATION

Here, the frequency is changed instead of the amplitude, so FM does not suffer from man-made interference. As well, because the signal to noise ratio for FM is lower than it needs to be for AM, you don't need as much power for the same quality of reception. It is also steadier, although FM receivers are more complex to produce.

The whole audio range is covered because they were able to allocate a wider bandwidth to FM transmissions.

FREQUENCY MODULATION

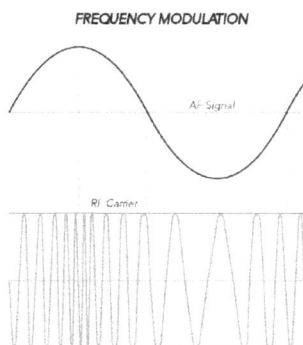

When the amplitude is positive, the frequency increases above the mean carrier frequency, and *vice versa*. The amount of change is called the *deviation*. The maximum limit is typically ±5 Khz for speech.

PULSE MODULATION

This is used for radar, where the superimposed information is the time of transmission. See *Radar*, later.

FREQUENCY SHIFT KEYING

For data, as used with satellites, where the carrier frequency is shifted above and below the mean (as 1 and 0) to represent bits of information.

Input is in FM with a very small deviation.

RESONANCE (TUNED CIRCUIT)

Radio waves must oscillate at a frequency high enough to excite the air molecules surrounding an antenna. This needs *inertia* and *elasticity*, so that energy can be stored and released. A capacitor and inductor (coil) in parallel is the simplest kind of electrical oscillating system, which behaves in a similar way to a weight on a spring, or an electrical pendulum. The problem is that, left to itself, the energy dissipates over time and the oscillations will stop, so we need a way of making sure that they keep going. With a weight on the end of a spring, all you need to do is pull the weight at its lowest point by just enough to cover for the losses caused by friction. In a watch, the main spring is timed to release just enough energy to the balance wheel to keep it moving.

In our case, friction is replaced by resistance, and we have to produce undamped (continuous) oscillations. Because of their ability to amplify, transistors are very good at doing this - the amplification creates energy that can be fed back into the system at the right moments to keep it going (otherwise called regenerative feedback).

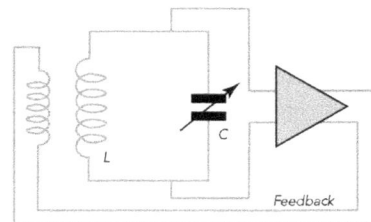

A *tank (LC) circuit* (so called because it stores energy) consists of a capacitor and inductance coil (see above). Depending on their electrical values, an alternating current can go back and forth between them in a periodic cycle.

The capacitor discharges through the coil as the excess electrons try to move from one of its plates to the other. However, back emf from the coil slows this down, and keeps the movement of the electrons going, where it would normally die away (the polarity reverses each cycle).

Current in a capacitor leads the applied voltage by 90°, while through an inductor it lags by 90°. With both in a circuit, the current flowing through the capacitor leads that in the inductor by 180°, so they cancel each other out, and only a little current is needed to keep things going. The resonant frequency is the one where reactance is zero, meaning that the circuit is operating on pure resistance. This provides a significant rise in voltage.

The coil and capacitor between them therefore behave like a flywheel and a spring. The energy is alternately stored in the electric field of the capacitor and the magnetic field of the coil, and we have an oscillator.

The Receiver

As the signal at the receiving antenna is very weak, a receiver must not only provide gain, but also be selective. The antenna picks up all the waves that are passing it, but the tuner makes the radio respond to the one you want to listen to.

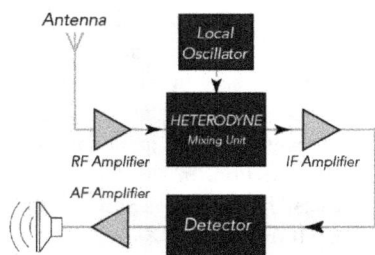

In a straight receiver (above), an RF amplifier at the end of the antenna produces a stronger copy of the transmitted signal (from about a millionth of a volt at the antenna to around a tenth of a volt). The signal is then demodulated, and amplified again on its way to the speaker.

However, early radio sets had many amplifiers and filters, which had to be tuned separately. In 1917, Edwin H Armstrong, a Major in the US Army Signal Corps, converted the received signals to a single, fixed, fairly low one (rather like mixing red and blue to get purple), at which most of the receiver's gain and selectivity could be obtained (it is easier to amplify a lower frequency). As it is between the AF and RF signals, it is called the *Intermediate Frequency*. 455 Khz has been used since the 1930s.

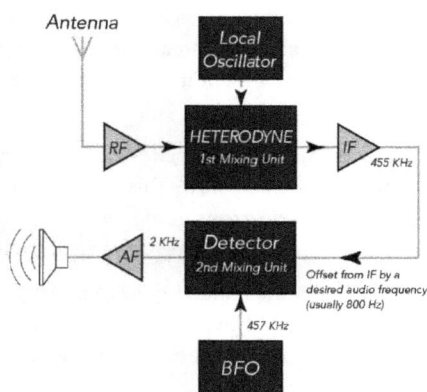

Frequencies were now easier to tune over a wide range and the filters could also be preset and not require tuning at all, hence one tuning knob. This was called a *superhet*, short for **superheterodyne**, or *supersonic heterodyne*, because the received and oscillator signals are mixed (heterodyned) to form a supersonic frequency. Almost every radio now is a superhet, constructed like two direct conversion receivers* in line.

*A direct conversion receiver demodulates by mixing with a locally generated frequency. It is mainly used for SSB.

To get audio output from a direct conversion receiver, the signal is mixed with one from a Beat Frequency Oscillator.

BEAT FREQUENCY OSCILLATOR

To hear a signal, it must naturally be inside the audio range of between 300 - 3000 Hz. Beat notes are created when any waves of different frequencies are mixed.

On the ADF (later), the BFO produces a small AC current which differs from the IF by around 2 Khz. The IF and BFO outputs are fed to the frequency mixer (heterodyne), where they are subtracted from one another to produce four frequencies, only one of which can be heard - the *difference* or *beat* frequency, which is amplified and fed to a loudspeaker which produces a steady AF of 2 Khz, within the human hearing range. If the incoming RF stops, no sound is heard from the loudspeaker. On modern aircraft the BFO is activated automatically (in the early days of SSB, a BFO system was used to establish the missing carrier. Now they use the Automatic Gain Control, where the BFO beats against the SSB signal).

The **squelch circuit** eliminates background noise when nothing is being transmitted. It is automatic on modern sets above a certain noise level.

DEMODULATION

Demodulation involves using a rectifier to ensure that only signal pulses moving in one direction get through.

For example, the picture below represents a very basic resonant circuit, containing a coil and a capacitor.

Between them, the coil and capacitor have a natural resonance which must match that of the transmitter. In other words, the amount of inductance from the coil

(L) and capacitance (C) must be the same for transmission and reception - the individual amounts can vary, but their product must be the same. The resonance can be altered by varying the inductance, but the most practical way is to adjust the capacitance with the tuning knob.

Anyhow, in its present form, the above circuit will not work, because AC has an average power of zero, meaning that the diaphragms in the earphones will simply move in sympathy with it and not actually vibrate.

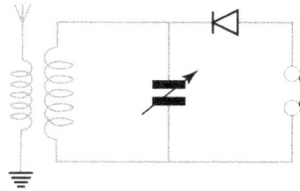

We need to introduce a device that only allows current to flow in one direction, namely a diode (or a "cat's whisker").

Now, the positive pulses pull the diaphragm towards the magnets, but the spaces in between the pulses (which replace the negative current) allow the diaphragm to try and spring back to its neutral position, and hence vibrate so you can hear the original speech. This is a *pulsating* direct current with a varying amplitude, with the same envelope (and effect) that was sent in the first place.

It is interesting to note that decoding an AM signal can only be done with a non linear circuit, in which the current is not directly proportional to the applied voltage - that is, it does not obey Ohm's Law.

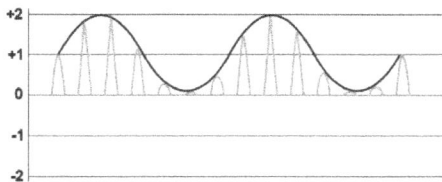

In practice, the circuit will be sensitive to a *range* of frequencies, due to the ratio of resistance to inductance, so the less resistance there is, the better the spike of voltage impressed upon the circuit. The antenna circuit can be decoupled to send its current into the circuit via a transformer, so that resistance is reduced to make the circuit tune more sharply. A step up transformer is used to give the signal a boost.

Finally, the audio-only signal goes into an audio amplifier for a quick boost before an exact copy of the original speech comes out of the loudspeaker.

Bandwidth

The "width" of any signal is known as its *bandwidth*, but a transmission medium also has a bandwidth, and here, the term is twisted slightly to mean the width it is *able to provide*, rather than the *width it occupies*. The aim, when matching signals to media, is to ensure that the signal bandwidth does not exceed that of the intended link, or that your car is not too wide for the road so, officially, the bandwidth is the difference between the highest and the lowest range of frequencies that a signal occupies. As an example, 3,000 Hz is a wide enough spread to carry voice information, and if you used it to modify a carrier wave of 3 MHz (3,000,000 Hz), your bandwidth will range from 2,997,000-3,003,000 Hz (see *Sidebands*, above). Unofficially (and more commonly), the term defines the amount of information that can be carried by any media, or signal, (that is, capacity) in a given time.

Emissions

The simplest method of transmitting information is to turn a signal on and off in a recognisable code, as used by older NDBs which break the carrier wave in a pattern matching the Morse code ID of the station, called *Telegraphy*, or CW (or even *keying*). This is an A1 transmission, whereas a carrier wave only would be A0.

Otherwise, we use *telephony*, or ordinary speech, where an audio signal modifies, or modulates, a carrier wave. Sending Morse as an audio signal creates an A2 signal.

When describing the emissions from a station, three symbols are used. The first is a letter describing the type of modulation, the second is a number for the nature of the modulation signal, and the third is a letter for the type of information transmitted.

For example, the VOR, discussed later, is A9W, because its carrier wave is frequency and amplitude modulated.

Table: Types Of Emission

Code	Modulation Type	No	Nature Of Modulating Signal	Code	Information Type
N	Unmodulated	0	Unmodulated CW	N	None
A	AM double sideband	1	Keyed CW (Morse)	A	Telegraphy (aural)
J	Single sideband, suppressed carrier	2	Modulated CW	B	Telegraphy (automatic)
H	Single sideband, full carrier	3	AM Modulated	E	Telegraphy (inc sound)
F	Frequency modulated	7	2 or more channels, Digital	D	Data
G	Phase Modulation	8	2 or more channels, Analogue	W	Combinations of the above
P	Unmodulated Pulse	9	Composite (digital/analogue)		
K	AM Pulse				

capt.gs

EXAMPLES

Class	Aid
N0NA1A	NDB (BFO on)*
N0NA2A	NDB (BFO on for tuning only)
A2A	NDB
J3E	HF (Communication)
A3E	VHF/VDF
A8W	ILS
A9W	VOR
P0N	DME, SSR
N0X/G1D	MLS (DPSK)

*Produces peak power all the time for better range.

Propagation

Although undisturbed waves travel through space in straight lines at a constant speed, the Earth is an uneven mass of solids and liquids surrounded by gases with varying densities and electrical charges, all of which affect the propagation of radio waves, or the means by which they travel between a transmitter and a receiver. They normally take the scenic Great Circle route (see *Navigation*), but they can be helped along by the weather - because of a rapidly rising pressure tendency at both ends, for example, in August 2013, NDBs in Canada were received in Europe. The trouble is that propagation is not an exact science, which doesn't help when you are trying to talk to a base station from a remote place. The fact that you can get through on one day does not mean that you can do it on another.

The Earth has a rhythm called a *Diurnal Cycle*, or a pattern that recurs every 24 hours (see also *Meteorology*). Propagation is affected by what the Sun does. In fact, it is the driving force behind much of HF propagation, simply because more energy and particles arrive on the surface of the Earth during the day. As a rule, the more illumination there is, the easier propagation will be. There is less in the morning and evening than there would be at noon, which is easily proven with a lightmeter. Very simply, the higher the Sun is in the sky, the higher the frequency you can expect HF signals to be refracted back to Earth.

The complication is that more energy arrives per square mile at the Equator than anywhere else.

THE IONOSPHERE

This is a region surrounding the Earth where the Sun's rays dislodge electrons from the gas molecules, making them ionised (and positively charged) and creating several conductive layers a couple of hundred miles thick around the Earth, starting about 60 miles up (but lower during the day) and varying with the seasons (they are not spheres, but change their shape constantly).

This is because the gases involved have different densities, so the molecules will settle out at different heights, as described below.

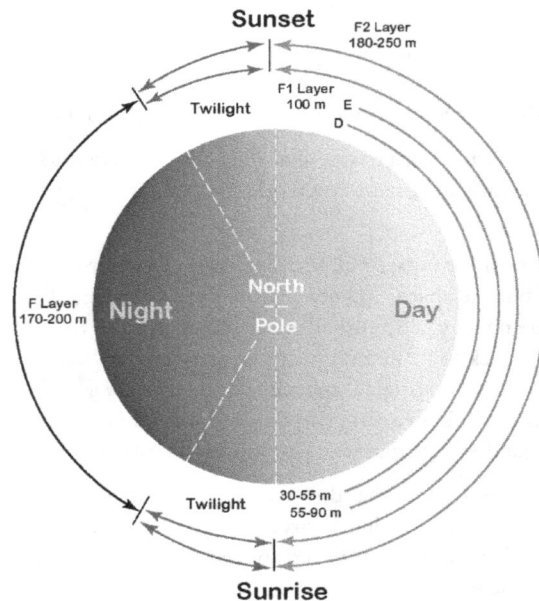

The ionisation stops the Sun's most violent radiation from reaching the Earth (ultraviolet light is dealt with by the production of ozone in the Stratosphere). It also makes the gases (nitrogen and oxygen) conductive. The nitrogen is ionised at the higher levels - lower down it is the oxygen. This happens mostly in daytime and is least just before sunrise, so air is a good insulator in the lower parts of the atmosphere, but ionisation makes it more conductive as you go up. *Recombination* is the process that gets electrons and atoms back together again, starting in the late afternoon and early evening, and continuing overnight.

As the ionosphere depends directly on the Sun's radiation, the way the Earth moves around the Sun affects its characteristics. As the ionosphere is warmed up, its ionisation level increases, so it will reflect signals better. Things tend to be better towards the East in the mornings because that part of the world has been in daylight for longer (more about this in *Navigation*). Signals paths to the South tend to be stronger around midday, and those to the West will be stronger in the afternoons and evenings. Contrary to popular belief, the weather doesn't have much of an influence at all.

The higher HF bands are daytime bands which tend to close soon after sunset. The lower bands, however, propagate towards the dark side of the Earth, so they open from just before sunset towards stations in the East that are already in darkness, and close soon after sunrise to work Westerly stations that are already in the dark. This is because the E and F layers described below remain ionised, while the D layer has disappeared.

As an example, in Europe, you won't receive many transmissions from America in the morning because it is still dark there. The best time is late afternoon, before Europe gets so dark that the signals start to fade away. In the picture above, reception times are related to specific frequency bands.

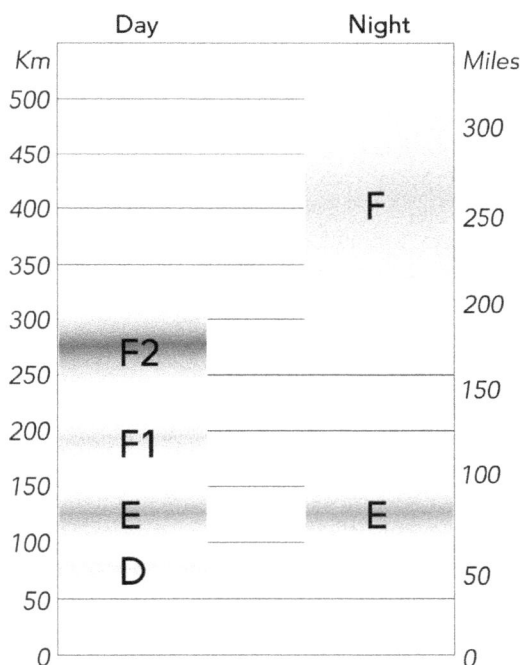

Some ionospheric changes are predictable, and some are not, but all of them affect radio propagation. Regular variations can be 27-day, daily and 11-yearly (from sunspots), but the daily ones have most effect on aviation. As the atmosphere is bombarded by waves with different frequencies, 4 cloud-like layers of electrically charged gas atoms are produced between 50-300 km above the Earth: The D, E (Heaviside), and F1 & F2 layers (Appleton). The first was discovered by James Van Allen in 1957, hence its naming as the Van Allen belt. UV rays with higher frequencies can penetrate deeper into the atmosphere so they create the lowest ionised layers.

- The **D layer** sits between 50-100 km high **during daylight hours**, so it starts to form at dawn and fades away after sunset. Ionisation is low because fewer UV waves penetrate to this level. The D layer can **refract VLF**, if large antennas and high power transmitters are used, but it is mainly responsible for **absorbing and blocking** (or at least attenuating) **LF* and MF waves**, while being transparent to HF. As the D layer fades, MF (NDB) signals can reach the higher layers where they may be reflected back.

  *Although the sky wave may be blocked, if the transmitter is powerful enough to have one, and the frequency is low enough, a ground wave can still travel for hundreds or even thousands of miles. Between 700-1000 Khz would appear to be the upper limit for ground wave propagation.

- The **E layer** is higher, between 100-150 km. It returns **LF and HF bands**, or waves longer than 100 m, and is normally transparent to VHF signals, but **Sporadic E** involves patches of strong ionisation that can return them, naturally more in Summer than at other times. It is weak at night but, because of its lower altitude, it gets less interference and therefore has more consistent critical and maximum usable frequencies, discussed later.

- In daylight, the **F layer** splits into the **F1** and **F2 layers**, F2 being the stronger and the higher of the two. It is responsible for most **HF long-distance** communication (waves shorter than 100 m). During maximum sunspot activity, F layer atoms can stay ionised all night because the process is a lot slower. For horizontal waves, the single-hop capability can be up to 3000 miles, and more with multiple hops.

Trivia: The Twilight Ring is called the Greyline because it is neither day nor night - greyline propagation is for very long distances. The line separating the dark side of the Earth from the sunlit side is called the Terminator.

TRANSMISSIONS

As, in a transmitter, the energy is alternately stored in the electric field of a capacitor and the magnetic field of a coil, an antenna connected to the circuit would alternately radiate electric and magnetic fields. In fact, they surround the antenna at all times, as there is a crossover where each field builds up and dies down.

As electrons rush up and down the antenna (as alternating current), they form an electric field between the antenna and Earth, as the relationship between them is capacitive. The movement of the electrons also creates a magnetic field. Both radiate outwards and synchronise together about a quarter of a mile away. When a transmitter is feeding an omnidirectional antenna, the waves will spread out equally in all directions.

Picture: Typical Propagation from a vertical antenna

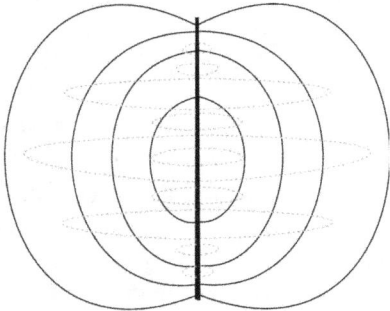

As the circumference of a wave front increases, its energy reduces per unit of length (see *Attenuation*, below). The signal strength at any point is called the *field strength*, and it is usually measured in volts.

Point B in the picture is 3 times the distance from the antenna than Point A is, and the circumference is three times larger, so the field strength at B a third of A's. Field strength in volts is therefore inversely proportional to distance.

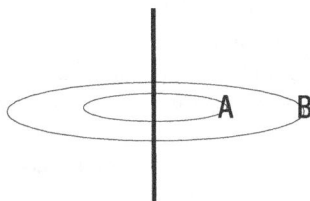

However, the signal also moves vertically and the signal has to spread out over the area of the resulting sphere. This measure of strength now is the *power* of the signal which is measured in watts. As Point B is on the surface of a sphere with 9 times the surface area of the one at Point A, it will receive a ninth of the power. Thus, the power of a signal fades in an inverse square relationship, meaning that a signal 2 nm from its source will have a quarter of the strength of one only 1 nm away. Put another way, you need 4 times the power to double the range of transmission, as a radio wave is an expanding circle, so its area depends on the square of the radius. With radar, described later, doubling the range would involve increasing power by a factor of 16 as the wave has to go there and back again.

This has important implications for radar, described later.

ATTENUATION

This concerns the loss of energy and velocity in various parts of a radio wave as energy is absorbed by the Earth and/or the atmosphere and ionosphere, on top of the normal decrease of power with range described above. If a signal's path is obstructed by rain, fog or a hill (for example), there will be a noticeable weakening of the signal behind the obstruction as a radio shadow is created.

The only way of combatting attenuation that we have any control over is with the frequency. The higher it is, the greater will be the attenuation.

- **Surface attenuation** increases with frequency.

- **Ionospheric attenuation** increases with a decrease in frequency.

- **Radar attenuation** increases with frequency, but is affected by water droplets which can also absorb and reflect the signal.

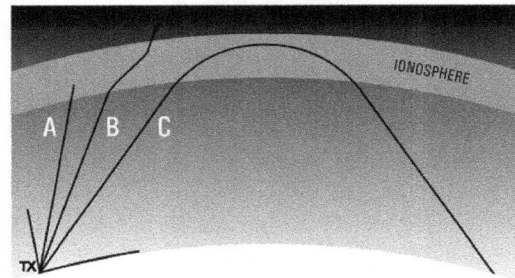

Radio waves generally travel pretty much in a straight line, but they may change direction because of:

- **Refraction (B)**, which is the change of speed and/or bending of a wave as it travels across different media, such as land or sea (as discussed under *ADF/NDB*, later). This also happens at the ionosphere, with HF, according to temperature, pressure and humidity. See *Sky Waves*, overleaf. The frequency does not change when refraction occurs.

- **Reflection (C)**, from a flat surface such as the Earth, or an aircraft (radar), like light off a mirror (where the initial and reflected waves have the same angle), but after reflection, a phase shift occurs, which will depend on the angle at which the surface was struck, and the wave polarisation.

- **Diffraction** (scattering). This is the spreading of a wave as it passes through a gap or round an edge, and is a problem with narrow beam signals, but it is also one reason why a radio wave follows the shape of the Earth (see *Ground Waves*).

This means that, if you rely on radio waves for approaches to airfields, you should be aware that they bend at certain times of the day (e.g. dawn/dusk) and over certain terrain, such as mountains, where you could also get multipath propagation*, as signals are received from many sources and will be out of phase with each other at the antenna. Such waves can cancel each other out and you end up with no guidance at all.

*In the above pictures, signals being received off the ionosphere have been shown as single refractions for simplicity. In reality, as the ionosphere is not uniform in terms of thickness, density or altitude, it is quite common for signals to be reflected from more than one layer to arrive at one point at different times. In other words, they are out of phase with each other, which is a characteristic of AM, but it can happen with line of sight signals such as VHF as they bounce off mountains and other terrain.

It barely affects SSB, but it can badly affect the PSK modulation used by GPS satellites, although problems with accuracy tend not to occur at the mid-latitudes occupied by Europe.

GROUND (SURFACE) WAVES

Ground waves are sometimes called *Surface Waves*. They are associated with VLF and LF, and often MF, and may go directly to their destination (if it is close enough), or curve to follow the Earth's surface, depending on the frequency (they don't leave the lower atmosphere). The two factors involved in the curving are diffraction and scattering mentioned above, and attenuation.

Radio waves tend to be reflected by objects that are larger than about half their wavelength. At centimetric wavelengths (SHF), this will involve reflection or absorption, and radio shadows behind the obstacles concerned but, at lower frequencies, the waves will curve round small obstacles, such as hills. The obstacle slows down the part of the wave that is closest to it, making the wave curve towards it as it passes. Similarly, the bottom surface of the wave is slowed down close to the surface and the wave will tilt into it.

As the H field cuts the Earth's surface, currents are created, the energy for which must come from the wave itself, so contact with the surface and the widening circumference of the wave eventually weakens its power (attenuation), causes it to curve downwards and eventually be absorbed. Once a ground wave starts to die away, it does so very quickly. Over 300 miles, for example, it may only die away in proportion for the first 200 miles - then it halves its strength for each hundred miles after that until it is undetectable.

The approximate lengths of LF/MF ground waves are 1000/500 nm, respectively, although MF suffers more from atmospheric attenuation. Ground waves must be vertically polarised to induce ground currents, and their range depends on:

- **Wavelength**. The lower the frequency (and the longer the wavelength), the better the reception over long distances. Put another way, the higher the frequency, the greater the attenuation. Below 500 Khz, you can obtain over 1000 miles just with a ground wave.

- **Type of ground**. The attenuation rate of a surface wave is around 3 times greater over land than over the sea. Typical figures for maximum range are 100 and 300 nm respectively, with high power.

- **Polarisation**. Vertically polarised waves normally have the least attenuation.

A *ground-reflected wave* bounces off the ground on its way to the receiver (which is why Distance Measuring Equipment uses an echo protection circuit). As it is not subject to continuous absorption by the Earth, it travels further than the ground wave, but the phase can be reversed at the point of reflection.

DIRECT (SPACE) WAVES (A3E)

These are contained within the troposphere, and are otherwise known as *tropospheric, or space wave*s. Being direct, they are known as *line-of-sight*, meaning that anything in the way, like hills or buildings, will affect the transmission (direct waves will not bounce like HF waves do).

VHF/SHF/UHF waves will not curve to follow the Earth's surface, so you have to be high enough to receive your selected station at a particular distance. As an example, when crossing the Irish Sea, you must be above 3000 feet to hear either Shannon or London Information. However, when using the VOR at high altitudes, you might get station overlap and erroneous readings, so don't use VOR bearing information beyond the published protection range (see the AIP). Air-ground transmissions are limited to 25 nm in the UK, up to 4,000 feet for tower frequencies and 10,000 feet for approach.

The (theoretical) reception range for line of sight transmissions can be estimated with this formula:

$$NM = (1.23 \times \sqrt{H}) + (1.23 \times \sqrt{h})$$

STOP Despite the fact that the value of 1.23 has been used since at least the 1950s, some questions in the EASA exams use 1.25.

H is the height of the aircraft antenna and h is that of the one on the ground. Do not be tempted to combine them into one calculation - the square roots won't work. The picture shows the reason why.

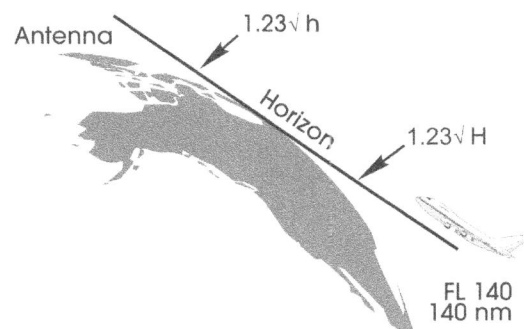

The short cut is to use Pythagoras and add a bit, or to multiply the square root of the flight level of the aircraft by 12. In real life, however, the results will vary if the transmitter is weak, there is something in the way, or the receiver is not working properly. The actual figure is greater by around $^4/_3$ due to diffraction.

The actual figure is greater by around 4/3 due to diffraction. Here are some samples:

Height	Range (nm)
1 500	50
5 000	87
10 000	123

SKY WAVES (J3E)

A *sky wave* reflects off the ionosphere, to reach further distances (on HF).

The HF frequencies allocated to commercial aviation range from 2 - 22 MHz, but not all of it is used. Details about ATC units using it will be found in Flight Information Publications. Transmissions are AM and SSB, coded J3E.

REFRACTION/REFLECTION

Anyhow, HF waves that hit the ionosphere can be bent if the angle is right, as the side of the wave that hits one of its layers first starts to speed up, because of the reduced *dielectric constant from ionisation**, which makes it turn. The effect is similar to that of light refraction in water which makes an object appear to be displaced.

*The speed of radio waves in the atmosphere is determined by its dielectric property, which ultimately depends on pressure, temperature and relative humidity. As pressure and relative humidity decrease with altitude, so does the Dielectric Constant**, but it increases as temperature decreases. Their combined lapse rates make radio waves increase their speed with height, so that, when a radio wave moves away from the Earth at less than a 90° angle, its upper part moves faster than its lower part. In essence, as you climb, the refractive index decreases uniformly (as does the ISA lapse rate). Radio waves can therefore be bent, particularly in a downward curve towards the surface of the Earth.

**The *dielectric constant* is the ratio of the capacity of a condenser in a given medium, i.e. air, to its capacity in a vacuum. It can also be thought of as a measure of the resistance of the air to wave propagation, and vertical changes in the Dielectric Constant determine the path of a radio wave, typically following a curved path with a radius of 1.3 times the radius of the Earth. This makes the normal range of VHF/UHF (line of sight) transmissions 1.3 times the visual horizon.

The angle at which the bending of a wave first happens is the *critical angle*, or the smallest angle that will allow a wave to be reflected back to Earth. Any rays more vertical than this are *escape rays*, typically bound for satellites.

The *critical frequency*, or foF2 (at which bending occurs) depends on the density of the layer concerned, so it changes all the time. If a wave manages to pass through one, it can still be reflected from higher up if its frequency is lower than that layer's critical frequency.

Trivia: foF2 is determined with the help of a worldwide network of ionosondes, which beam signals upwards and wait for an answer from the ionosphere. As its frequency keeps changing it is also known as a chirp transmitter, which is what it sounds like on an SSB receiver as it moves past the frequency you are listening on.

The ionosonde's purpose is to determine the frequency at which no signal is returned from straight above by the F2 layer of the ionosphere (it can get confusing signals from the E layer which can produce false signals with higher frequencies). Above foF2, the upwards signal goes out to space. Below it, at least some of it is returned. The rate at which foF2 drops after dusk is about the same, regardless of the season. Thus, the ionosphere behaves like a pane of glass above, and more like a mirror towards the horizon.

The first wave to reach the ground after being refracted or reflected is called the *First Returning Sky Wave*, until the maximum range is reached. When a wave leaves an antenna, the ground wave will be detected until it fades, or attenuates. Between that point, and where the first sky wave comes back from the ionosphere, is an area where nothing is heard, called a *skip zone*, or *dead space*.

Note that the antenna will be radiating the above signals in all directions of the compass, so some will be going to the left of the diagram, as a mirror image.

The **skip distance** is the Earth distance taken by a signal after each reflection, or the distance covered by the first sky wave. 30 MHz signals do not return because they are too high in frequency, being at the bottom of the VHF band (15-25 MHz is more typical for bouncing). You can reflect off the ionosphere and back off the ground several times for multiple hops (skip).

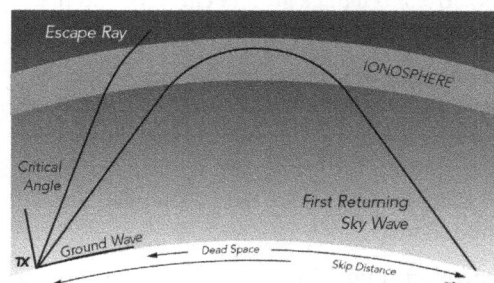

The size of the skip zone changes with frequency*, and it doesn't always stay constant, even when you are using only one. If the ionisation gets stronger, the ionosphere will behave more like a mirror, and you will get what is called Short Skip propagation, where the skip zone gets much narrower. If high angle signals reflect back very close to the transmitter, they could meet or overlap the ground wave and provide coverage out to a thousand miles or so.

*The lower the frequency of a wave, the longer its wavelength, the more rapidly it is reflected, and the larger will be its critical angle, but the less the distance it will travel. A 20 MHz wave will be detected further from the transmitter than a 5 MHz one. The absolute maximum that a wave can be reflected back from the F2 layer as one hop is around 4000 km, which is why the BBC has a relay station in Singapore to cover the Far East.

Thus, the skip zone of HF transmission will increase with higher frequencies and higher reflecting ionospheric layers. At night, if you use the same frequency, the skip distance will increase.

So what can you do if you are not getting through to a station but are receiving another from a greater distance away? Should you change to a higher or lower frequency? A lower one reduces the critical angle to make the skywave return at a shorter range and reduce the dead space. Skip is usually best when the Sun is about halfway between you and the area you are transmitting to or receiving from. You will normally hear skip from the East in the morning and the West in the afternoon with that from the North or South at any time. *Long path skip* takes the long way round the Earth, usually because ionospheric conditions are better that way. We therefore depend on the ionosphere for all HF contacts beyond the ground-wave zone. It moves all the time, itself being dependent on the intensity of particle and wave emissions from the Sun, so propagation is affected considerably by the ionosphere's movement, which is why the ADF suffers from what is called *night effect* just after sunset and before sunrise when the needle swings erratically as the plane of polarisation changes after reflections (on the other hand, during the night is when you will receive distant stations best).

Generally, HF communication is always possible when the frequency is low enough to be reflected and high enough not to be attenuated. Unfortunately, the only information we have about the above changes usually comes from statistical sources. It's not something you can work out.

HF DATALINK

This uses the upper sideband of a selected frequency to send phase modulated digital information, or voice transmissions having been converted to digital form. Once established, the link the link can be maintained continuously without flight crew interaction.

ANOMALOUS PROPAGATION

Within the Earth's atmosphere, the velocity of a wave is less than it would be in free space, because of atmospheric conditions. Normal refractivity, which exists for around 50% of the time, will cause a wave to be bent downward from its usual straight line. It exists when moisture, pressure and temperature all decrease with altitude.

However, when lapse rates depart significantly from normal, VHF, UHF and SHF waves (particularly radar) can follow different curved paths. A rapid increase of temperature with height (an inversion) and a rapid decrease of relative humidity (a steep lapse rate) can bend the wave more toward the surface of the Earth and increase propagation distances with little attenuation (although fading* can occur) for a condition of **super refraction**. This means that radar coverage, for example, can be extended for up to 50% above the normal range.

*During twilight.

If the waves curve more than the Earth does, because conditions are more intense, radio waves can become trapped between the surface and the negative gradient causing the refraction. Because the waves also bounce off the surface, they can travel for much longer distances.

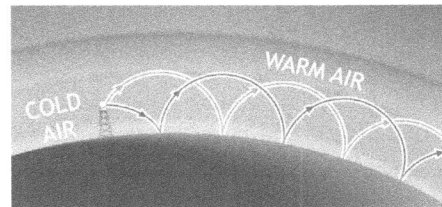

Such **ducts** are associated with regions of high pressure, over flattish terrain and the sea - not normally over hilly ground. Semi-permanent ducts can be found around the Earth in the major areas of high pressure, usually in meteorological conditions associated with tropical and subtropical latitudes (i.e. hot by day, and cool by night), near the Equator. In the Trade Winds (see *Meteorology*), ducting over 3 000 miles can occur, off the surface and below about 5 000 feet.

The depth of the duct required increases with the wavelength, such as 50 feet for wavelengths of 3 cm, and 600 feet for wavelengths of 1 metre, but they are normally less than 1 000 feet deep. Elevated ducts (between two layers of the atmosphere) can occur at height, so they may be present at more than one level, so if you are experiencing radio/radar reception difficulties, you can fly towards the destination, descend, or try a lower frequency.

Under an inversion, especially over the sea, the air can become warm and very moist, which allows for steep refraction. Thus, ducting is most common over the sea in tropical and subtropical areas. Propagation distances can reduce (*sub refraction*) with opposing conditions. Radar can also suffer from **ghosting**, or false echoes. A **shadow zone,** or **radar hole**, can make an object be invisible electronically. With radar, ducting will increase ground clutter.

- More moisture means more refraction.
- Higher temperatures mean less refraction.

Pressure by itself has little effect.

VLF signals can travel long distances through a similar process involving the ionospheric layers and a *conduit wave*, which is *reflected* rather than *refracted*.

FREQUENCY SELECTION

With HF, frequencies need to be higher during the day or when you are at greater range from the station. Because the ionosphere is higher at night, you can use lower ones, generally about half (that is, use *Double During Day*), which is something to be aware of when you are operating at a remote base and you use HF to keep in touch with the Operations office. Generally, you might leave for camp with a selection of five frequencies you can use depending on the time of day. Otherwise, for successful communication on HF between two given points, there is a maximum frequency, a lowest frequency and an optimum frequency.

LOWEST USABLE FREQUENCY

This is the point below which refraction cannot start.

MAXIMUM USABLE FREQUENCY

The point at which refraction is no longer possible. As the level of ionisation is less in the ionosphere by night than it is by day, you have to lower the frequency to get the same type of refraction. Luckily, attenuation is reduced at night as well, so this is offset slightly. The MUF not only varies with path length and between day and night, but also with the seasons, meteor trails, sunspots, etc., so it is usually higher in the tropics than the poles, and around the middle of the day. This is why HF transmitters use a wide range of frequencies between about 2-20 MHz to get through. The MUF is solely to do with the F layer. To stand any chance of getting a single-hop signal through up to 4000 km, the MUF needs to be above the frequency you wish to use at the refraction point (halfway).

OPTIMUM WORKING FREQUENCY

The *optimum* usable frequency, where attenuation is minimum for the range obtained, or where you have the least number of problems, is the best theoretical frequency that brings the skywave back to the receiver. It is the one that causes the first returning sky wave to fall just short of the receiving station, so that when it drifts, the station will still pick it up. This frequency should be high enough to avoid the disadvantages from multipath fading, absorption and noise, but not so high as to be affected by rapid changes in the ionosphere. It is about 85% of the MUF.

Antennas

Aircraft radios use 760 channels that are spaced 25 Khz apart with a power rating of between 2-25 watts, but power won't help without a good antenna.

An antenna is a conductor (or a group of them) that can radiate or collect electromagnetic waves. Put another way, it is a device that can convert electrical (AC) energy into electromagnetic energy and *vice versa*. The relationship between an antenna and the Earth is a capacitive one, with the air between them acting as a dielectric.

A certain length of straight wire will possess a natural amount of inductance and capacitance, which will correspond to a particular wavelength, as the length of a radiated wave depends on their product. For example, a half-wave dipole* for 18 MHz should be 8.33 m long (as the name implies, the optimum length for an antenna is half the wavelength, or multiples thereof).

*A dipole is an antenna that is split at the centre, with each section a quarter-wavelength long. More correctly, two equal lengths of wire connected to a combined feedpoint in the centre and suspended horizontally above ground is called a doublet. Radio waves passing by will induce voltage and current along the wires equal in amplitude but opposite in phase to each other. At the frequency where half a wavelength forms on the two wires there will be a low impedance at the feedpoint and a dipole is formed. The impedance will always be high at the ends because the current is close to zero.

In practice, the wires are about 5% shorter than the correct length (pruned), to allow for electric current in a conductor being slower than a radio wave, and to remove unwanted inductance. The physical length is therefore shorter than the electrical length - as it is not practical to carry around a range of antennas, adding a capacitor or coil (inductor) to the mix (*loading*) will allow you to artificially adjust its natural wavelength to suit the circumstances. A coil increases the inductance of an antenna and reduces its natural frequency, while a capacitor in series reduces the capacitance and raises the natural frequency (the same as reducing the wavelength). As an example, a normal VHF antenna would be about 15 cm long, but using complex circuitry allows you to electronically shorten it.

However, airborne systems do not use dipoles, as they tend to be large and their energy is not directional. A unipole, on the other hand, is a quarter length conductor mounted vertically on the fuselage, which acts as the other half, so one used for VHF communications can be less than 60 cm long. Two unipoles can often be seen back to back on a vertical stabiliser to behave like a dipole with VOR or ILS transmissions.

At higher frequencies, the antenna will be too long to be resonant, and will be inductive as well as resistive. At a lower frequency, it will be too short and will show capacitance (as a reminder, anything other than exact resonance will involve reactance and resistance, known collectively as impedance). An antenna tuning unit will tune out unwanted reactance - the classic way of making a piece of wire seem longer is to add a coil to it, but a lot of the energy is lost in heating the coil up, and it decreases the impedance anyway. Capacitive loading is a better solution that doesn't actually use capacitors, but just another piece of wire perpendicular to the original. The capacitance lies between them.

At frequencies between around 2 - 30 MHz (HF), a dipole would be between 5 - 75 m long. As the aircraft itself is around that length, its fuselage can be used as the radiating or receiving element. A tuned notch or slot in the base of the vertical stabiliser with a large oscillating voltage applied across it can drive current through the fuselage, which then radiates. A slot aerial is a rectangular shaped hole resonant at half a wavelength long that works like a dipole. A notch is a hole cut into a rounded part of the aircraft skin, covered with insulating material to preserve the aerodynamic shape. RF energy is fed to both sides of the aperture to produce skin currents.

However, for frequencies between 10 - 100 Khz, even the largest aircraft would be too small, so capacitive antennae are more suitable, with one "plate" being the airframe, but the receive-only systems they would be used for are now largely redundant. The ADF uses an alternative, though, in the shape of the loop antenna, described later.

At much higher frequencies (3,000 MHz), a **waveguide** may be used, as described under *Radar*.

In summary, there are two basic types of antennae, the *Hertz* (half-wave) or *Marconi* (quarter wave). Hertz types are also known as *dipoles*, and are usually positioned well above ground, radiating horizontally or vertically (see *Polarisation*) for frequencies of 2 MHz and above. Marconis are perpendicular to the Earth and have one end grounded to it, used for frequencies below 2 MHz.

The location of an antenna should provide a line of sight path for the signals concerned, so a GPS antenna (for example) should not be placed underneath a fuselage. The spacing between them should be at least ½ wavelength, but at least 36 inches, taking account of cable runs.

DIRECTIONALITY (DIRECTIVITY)

Most people know they have to turn a domestic radio round in order to get the best signal. This works the other way round as well - it is possible, with simple procedures, to transmit radio waves in certain directions, which can be useful if the wave attenuates quickly, as the power can be concentrated - using a directional aerial can boost

transmission in a particular quarter and increase the gain in that direction for longer range. Some directionality can be achieved with just two elements, or dipoles.

A rod slightly shorter than an antenna placed just less than a quarter wavelength away from it will strengthen the signal in that direction. Similarly, a slightly longer rod placed a bit further away will strengthen it in the opposite direction, effectively reflecting the signal. Thus, if a second rod, not fed with power, and slightly longer, is placed a quarter of a wavelength behind a **driven element** (the one radiating all the power) it behaves like a resonant coupled circuit which has oscillatory currents induced in it. The currents re-radiate, and the quarter-wave spacing causes it to be in such a phasing as to cancel out the original radiation on that side, and to reinforce it on the opposite side, so the second dipole has the same effect as a reflector (see *Radar*), and gives you a marked gain in signal strength in one direction. The more the number of dipoles in an array, the narrower and more intense will be the beam of radiation.

A shorter antenna called a *Director* in front of the driven element will behave like a lens which concentrates the energy. Directors and reflectors are called *parasites*, but a series of them is generally known as a Yagi array (like a TV aerial). It can create spurious side beams (or lobes) as well as the main beam.

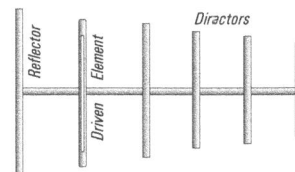

The Yagi is used with radar instead of parabolic arrays.

THE LOOP

Before metric and centimetric waves came on the scene, direction finding was based on the simple loop aerial, or vertical ones spaced apart (the Adcock).

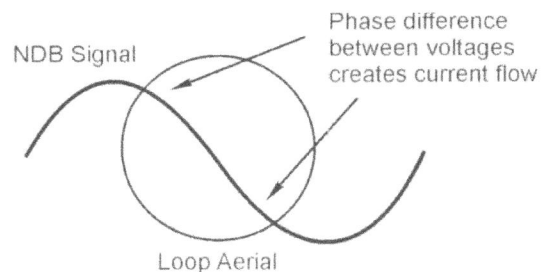

Remembering that there must be a *difference* in electrical pressures between two points for electrons to flow*, the maximum signal is found when the loop is in line with the transmission (i.e. sideways-on), when the points of contact are out of phase, so a current is generated, which drives an electric motor to continually seek the null position, when the loop is square (across the signal). As the vertically polarised signal now reaches both sides of the loop at the same time, no signal is detected. The null signal point is used for direction finding because it is easier to detect (it is much more sharply defined).

Various stages of magnification inside the receiver help this along, but they need not concern us here. Because the current flows in the opposite direction depending on the position of the loop, you also need some way of determining which end is what, otherwise you could be 180° out. A single vertical aerial called a *sense antenna* helps here - the signals are combined algebraically and the magnitude and polarity of the sense aerial arranged to be identical to the loop. The result is a polar diagram* called a *cardioid*, with only one null point:

*A polar diagram shows what happens to a signal after it leaves an antenna, as a map. It shows the position of points around it where the signal has reduced to (in general) half of its original strength. For most aids, a polar diagram is designed to be a particular shape, as with the cardioid, above, or the limacon with the VOR. The strength of a transmission in a particular direction is shown by a vector drawn from the antenna to the edge of the polar diagram.

Thus, loop aerials receive a signal, but the sense aerial is there to resolve ambiguities. It is placed vertically in the middle of the loop. By using a transformer, the electrons flowing in the sense aerial set a second stream flowing in one of the vertical parts of the loop.

So, on one side of the loop, the polar diagrams are positive and combine, but on the other, one is positive and the other negative, so they cancel out, hence the null point on one side. The modern (and more stylish) equivalent of the loop antenna is a small housing with two coils at right angles to each other, wound on ferrite cores, one fore and aft and the other athwartships. The sense aerial resolves the two null points. There is another pair with a search coil in the middle that reacts to its influence and drives a needle as it searches for the null point.

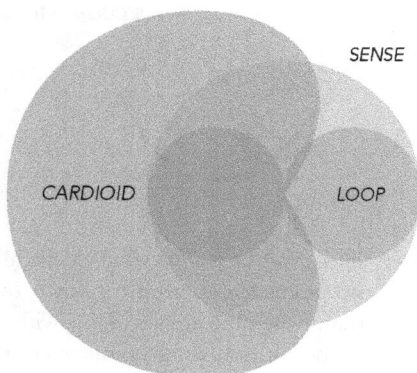

The Helical Antenna

A helical antenna, as used with GPS, allows you to use smaller equipment.

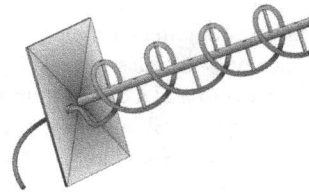

It can be used like a normal antenna, with maximum radiation at right angles to the axis of the helix. The radiation is linearly polarised parallel to the axis.

In the axial mode, however, the radiation comes out of the end (i.e. along the axis), and it works as a directional antenna radiating circularly polarised waves.

Parabolic

Parabolic dishes are used with radar systems and are described in that section.

The Slotted Planar Array

As used with most modern weather radar systems, this is flat (i.e. a plane), with slots that act as waveguides (in fact, they have the same effect as a dipole antenna). By stacking them, as shown, the beamwidth of the E (vertical) plane can be reduced. This gets round a problem caused by slotted waveguides which are long but thin, creating a wave that is wide in the E plane but narrow in the H plane.

Sidelobes are also reduced.

Gain

The ratio between the amount of energy propagated in a particular direction and that which would be propagated if the antenna were not directional is called antenna gain.

An antenna with a gain of 3 decibels, for example, could put out around double the power of a quarter wave antenna, which has no gain (referred to as *unity*). An antenna with a gain of 6 db hooked on to the back of an amplifier pushing 4 watts into it would put out the equivalent of 16 watts, or 80 if the gain were 13 db.

The gain control for Airborne Weather Radar adjusts the sensitivity of the receiver for optimum target acquisition.

STOP Gain is not amplification, but making the best use of the energy available.

In an omnidirectional antenna, the gain can come from spreading the RF energy closer and flatter to the ground, creating stronger ground waves, as is found by using a five-eighths antenna, for a 3-4.5 db gain (i.e. the power is taken from the higher angles). The increase in range can be up to 10 km or more.

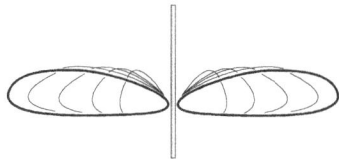

RECIPROCITY

This is the ability of an antenna to be used for transmitting and receiving.

TRANSMITTING SIGNALS

When an alternating current is applied to one end of a straight antenna, the wave travels to the other end, where it can go no further. This is a point of high impedance, so the wave bounces back towards where it came from. Although there is some loss from resistance, the wave is reinforced at the start point with more energy, which results in continuous oscillations that are sustained with suitably timed impulses. There is also a high voltage at the *start* point, so the centre of the wire has minimum voltage. The maximum movement of electrons is also in the centre, so it has a low impedance there. The meeting of these two stresses sets up a standing wave which makes the particles oscillate all the time. Standing waves can be kept going with the minimum expenditure of energy.

The length of the antenna must allow the wave to travel from one end to the other and back within one cycle, and the wavelength is the distance travelled within that cycle.

RECEIVING SIGNALS

In simple terms, the antenna catches a radio wave and a small electrical current with the same waveform as the incoming signal is induced in it through an electronic tide. In practice a *selection* of frequencies is captured because an antenna is cut for the middle of the frequency band.

The signal passed on to the radio set after being received is at the resonant frequency of the antenna, with a few on either side for good measure. This signal is amplified and selectivity improved with a tuned circuit, where capacitive reactance cancels out the inductive reactance. Some other signals do get through however, so filters eliminate them in later stages. In the end, all radio frequencies will finally be extracted, leaving only a low-level audio signal to be amplified and sent to your headset.

A receiver's ability to reject signals outside the relevant bandwidth is called its *sensitivity*.

Doppler

The Doppler effect is a change of frequency that comes from relative motion between the sender and receiver. It works on the principle that radio waves compress when directed to a station and elongate when going away (in other words, as two objects get closer together, the frequency of any radio wave between them will increase artificially because of their relative speed). The usual example given is listening to the change in the noise of a train approaching you, and passing by. The pitch is higher than normal at first, and becomes lower than normal when it has passed.

Picture: Doppler Effect

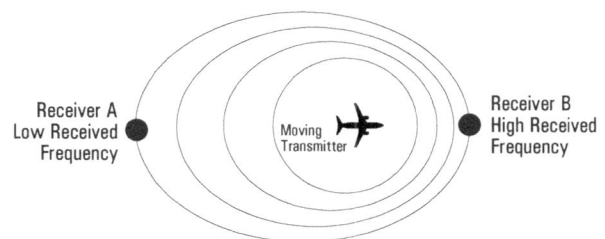

This is because the forward speed means that the sound waves have to fit into a smaller space, and therefore have shorter wavelengths, and a higher pitch, so the receiver will intercept more waves in a given time.

The opposite is true after the train passes - they have more room to fit into, and the wavelength becomes longer, to produce the lower sound. Apply that to radar, since both sound and radio travel as sine waves, and you have the basics of a good navigation system that can compute groundspeed and drift - in helicopters, it can provide auto-hover capabilities, amongst other things, although it has almost entirely disappeared, except for its use with GPS. The change in frequency is called *Doppler Shift*, which is given a positive (+) quality when a closing relative velocity produces an increase in frequency, and a negative quality when otherwise.

Discharge Detectors

Otherwise known as *Stormscopes*, after one manufacturer, these detect lightning discharges and display them on a green screen in the cockpit. They work in a similar way to an ADF with its needle pointing towards a storm.

RADIO NAVIGATION

Most radio aids just give you information about your position - only landing aids tell you what to do with it. Your position can be given in four ways as:

- A relative bearing *to* a radio station relative to the longitudinal axis of the aircraft (ADF, VOR)

- A radial *from* a station (VOR)

- A distance from a station (DME)

- An actual position (GPS, RNAV, INS)

For the first three, you need a chart with which to compute your position.

🛑 As a point of airmanship, equipment not directly required for navigation should be tuned to ground stations to check accuracy or ground speed, so errors can be detected and the equipment be available in an emergency. Also, **do not rely on a beacon until it has been identified**.

VOR   062 02 03

Very High Frequency Omnidirectional Range is a ground-based short range navigational aid that broadcasts two signals on VHF, using the *phase difference comparison* between them to signify your direction from the transmitting station as one of 360 radials *from* it*. The usable frequency range is between **108-117.975 MHz** (metric), which is just below aviation voice channels.

*An infinite number of tracks is theoretically available, but 360 is easier to manage.

Low-powered VORs (as used near terminals) and ILS localisers occupy the space between 108-112, with 50 Hz spacing, so there is room for 40 ILS and 40 VOR channels. The VORs usually use even decimals, plus even tenths to prevent confusion with the ILS, which uses odd tenths. For example, an ILS might use 108.1, while a Terminal VOR might use 108.2.

136
Voice
720 Channels
118
117.975
Hi Pwr VOR
120 Channels
112
Lo Pwr VOR
ILS
80 Channels
108 MHz

Higher powered VORs, as needed for aircraft at higher altitudes, operate between 112-118 (112-117.975) on odd and even tenths, for another 120 channels. They can be received up to 100 nm away.

In total, there are 40 ILS and 160 VOR channels.

VORs represented on maps have a compass rose round them, aligned with Magnetic North, except in Northern Canada, where they are aligned to True North. They are a pain to shut down and realign, which is why a VOR's variation will often be different from its aerodrome.

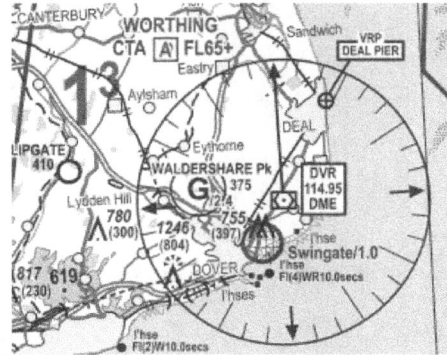

VORs are not sensitive to heading, as is the ADF (below), because they show *track*, although most pilots set the OBS to the heading anyway for neatness so that the left/right needle reads correctly. Neither do they suffer from many of the other problems associated with the ADF, especially night effect.

The *Station Identifier* is transmitted in Morse every 15 seconds (4 times a minute), and you must confirm the frequency and ID before using a VOR for navigation. If there is no ID, but behaviour is otherwise normal, the system is on maintenance (you may sometimes hear a Morse test code of ▬ ••• ▬).

Theory Of Operation

The radiation from a conventional VOR (CVOR) is a complex horizontally polarised VHF wave. Because the signal is frequency and amplitude modulated, it is classed as an A9W signal (Doppler VOR, mentioned later, has its modulations the other way round).

The equipment electronically measures an angle, having transmitted a signal with three components. There is a 30 Hz FM omniphase signal, received by all stations at a constant phase, and a variable phase (variphase) signal whose phase changes according to its bearing from North, lagging behind the reference signal. The variphase signal is a 30 Hz tone that modulates the amplitude of the carrier, and its sidebands are used to make the phase angle of the modulation equal to the azimuth angle.

To make separation easier (or to detect which signal is which), the reference signal frequency-modulates a sub-carrier (at 9960 Hz), because the carrier is already modulated by the variphase signal. The result is that an apparently AM signal (rotating at 30 Hz or 1800 RPM) is eventually received at the aircraft in terms of varying *power* (amplitude) levels. After demodulation, the signals have their phases compared to derive a bearing.

There is also a voice/ID channel that can carry 1020 Hz Morse and voice signals.

So, both signals are in phase when the "rotating" signal passes Magnetic North, but they get more out of phase by the number of degrees you go round the circle. Your receiver picks up the reference signal first and the maximum point of the variphase signal a little bit later. If the phase difference is 30° at your receiver, you are on the 030° radial from the VOR.

However, the information presented in the cockpit is the bearing *to* the station rather than from, in this case 050°.

As the radial information depends only on the phase difference between the modulating signals, and is independent of the aircraft heading, you may fly the long way round without heading information.

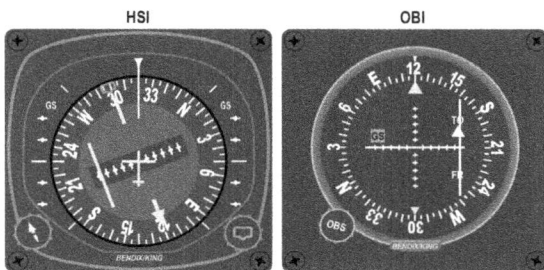

As an example, above is a comparison of the HSI against the OBI - you are heading 320°, and both have a setting of 120° *inbound*. Notice how the HSI presents the information clearly, but the OBI says something quite different - With no heading information, you could be going either way! Thus, to get the best results, the heading should approximately follow the OBS setting. In any case, you need to set the desired track according to the TO flag.

The situation shown above is typically found during a procedure turn - it's not a normal tracking scenario.

All this produces a polar diagram called a *limacon*, which has been inherited from an earlier navigation system, and is similar in shape to the cardioid used by the ADF (later), but without an absolute null point, rotating electrically at 30 times/second.

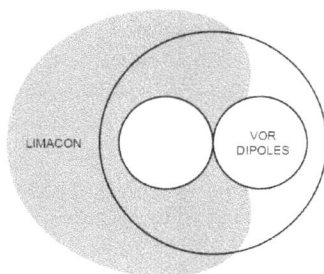

There is no null point because transmission is momentarily interrupted when the maximum point of the limacon passes through North. If it were otherwise, you would get a false North indication.

In your aircraft, the signals are received by a horizontally polarised V-dipole antenna, then mixed, converted to an intermediate frequency, amplified, detected and demodulated. Then the audio part of the signal is fed into a low-pass filter which allows the reference signal to enter one part of the circuit and the rotating one to enter another, through a 10 Khz bandpass filter, eventually to become 30 Hz AC.

The rotating signal is also fed into a calibrated phase shifter which is controlled by the OBS on the front of the instrument in the cockpit. It is turned until the two signals are in phase and the Course Deviation Indicator (CDI) is in the centre.

The TO indicator is driven by another phase shifter and phase detector operating in parallel. Because of the nature of VOR transmissions and the way they are used for direction finding, there is a 180° ambiguity, so the CDI is equally sensitive to signals coming from either of two opposite directions (i.e. two radials, 180° apart, from the same VOR). To resolve this an additional circuit indicates TO or FROM with a flag. The reference signal is shifted by another 90° and compared again to the rotating one, to tell whether it is leading or lagging the rotating signal, to make the indicator show the relevant direction.

The TO indicator will move when the difference between the selected course and the measured radial passes 90° in either direction.

Over the beacon, you will be in a *cone of confusion*, the same as you would be with any antenna - this is an area where no signal is received, so the TO/FROM flags disappear and the alarm flag comes up. The ICAO limit for the cone is 100° across, and the width can be worked out by finding the tangent of the angle and multiplying it by your height, to get the answer in feet (FL 360 = 6 nm).

During this *station passage*, just ignore the signal or use something else.

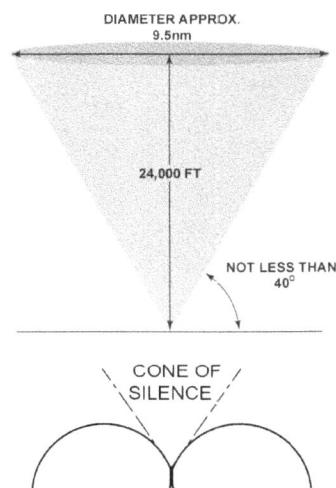

There are also ambiguities *abeam* the beacon - 90° either side of the selected radial there is a *zone of ambiguity* up to 10° across where the flag will not show at all, and the indications should therefore not be relied upon.

In the bowels of the aircraft will be a large black box, connected to a *remote indicator* in the cockpit, that might also double as an ILS display.

This one is a 5-dot display, using 4 dots plus a circle, so each one is 2°, for an overall width of 10°. For 3 dots plus a circle, each is 2.5°.

Once you select a radial by turning the *Omni Bearing Selector* (the knob under the dial), the *Course Deviation Indicator* (CDI) needle will be in the centre, or either side of it.

When the needle is in the middle, you will be on the selected radial, which is *from* the station when on the same side, shown by TO/FROM Flag, which, on later instruments, will be a small white triangle pointing in the relevant direction*. If the indicator shows *TO*, you are on the *reciprocal*, or going the other way. In the example above, the radial selected is S, or 180°, because the *To* flag is showing (as the needle is showing you are three dots left, you are on the 186° radial). Thus, when holding *inbound* on the 240 radial, your heading should be 060°. This is a common trap in exam questions (and check rides) - if you are tracking inbound on a radial, set the reciprocal at the top of the display, as radials go *from* a station.

Tip: The dots either side of the centre are useful for drift correction. If you are 2 dots off, or 4°, kick the nose into wind by 8° and see what happens.

*The changeover sector is within 10° either side of the abeam position. The TO/FROM indicator is independent of the heading. On the side of the radial you have selected, FROM is displayed. On the other side, you get TO.

All you have to do then is watch the needle - if the needle is pointing left, then you fly left until it centres.

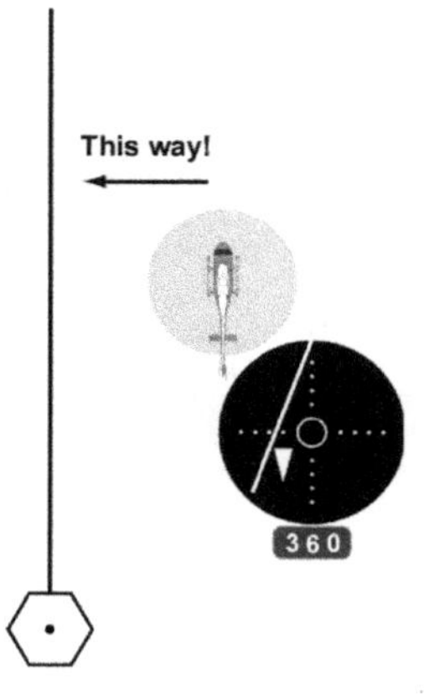

The thing to remember is that the needle always points to *where the radial is*, which has *nothing to do with the heading of the aircraft* (on the RMI, the tail of the needle shows the radial*), and you do not necessarily turn that way to get to it - sometimes, having the needle on the left means turn right! *Only if your heading is the same direction as the OBS will it be on the correct side.*

This way!

*VORs cannot indicate their relative bearing from the aircraft. An RMI (see picture) can only point to a VOR accurately if the heading indicator is accurate because the calculation is done within the instrument (see *RMI* under *ADF*, below). **If the heading indicator fails or is not set correctly, an RMI will not point to the VOR, but will just show you the radial you are on** (watch the tail of the needle*). The ADF, on the other hand will always point to the station, so you can still get to it even if the heading indication is not working.

*The pointer indicates the radial plus 180°.

For any radial, there are boundaries formed by the CDI and the TO/FROM indicator, creating quadrants around the station (that is, four distinct areas). You will be in one of them. In the picture below, which displays would the pilot see, and in what order, for a helicopter moving from A to B?

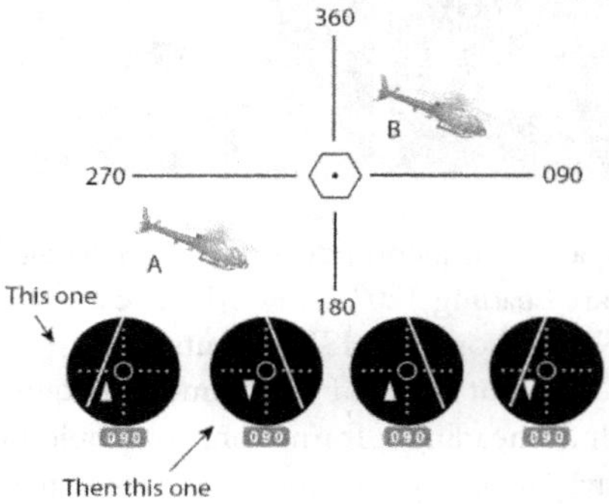

To intercept a radial inbound, tune and identify the VOR station, then select the reciprocal of the desired radial by turning the OBS until you get a TO reading. Fly to whichever side the needle is displaced, turning the shortest way to a heading 90° away from it, until the needle starts to move, at which point reduce the intercept angle to 45°. As the needle centres, reduce the intercept angle again and maintain the track with suitable adjustments for drift. Do the same outbound, except look for a FROM reading. A good rule (inbound and outbound) is to subtract the intercept angle if the needle goes left, and add if it goes right to find the heading to steer. For example, 280°-90°=190°.

Thus, if a VOR needle is centered when 200 is selected, with TO indicated, to intercept a radial of 100° inbound at 90°, the aircraft must turn to a heading of 190°. As you are going to the station, you are on the 080° radial*, so you must turn left. Subtract 90 for the intercept to get 190°.

*Read the radial from the bottom of the instrument. With a FROM flag you read it from the top.

With a heading of 140° and the needle centered with a TO indication when 120° is selected on the OBS, what heading should be steered to in zero wind conditions to intercept the 240° radial outbound at an angle of 45°?

The TO flag means that the aircraft is on the 300° radial, or NW of the VOR. To intercept the 240° radial it must move South, so to cut the 240° radial by 45°, subtract 45 from 240 to get 195° as a heading.

Here are the needle movements and responses of an aircraft drifting off to the left and coming back on course:

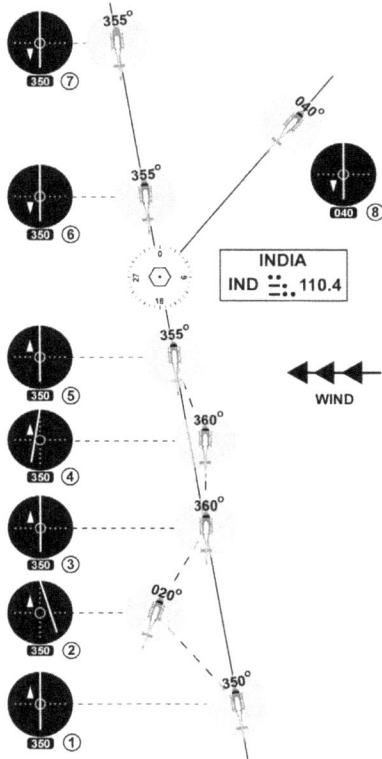

To bracket for drift, turn onto a zero wind heading and see what the drift actually is. Make a large correction the opposite way and see what happens. Then half the original correction. Keep going until the correct heading is found.

When tracking along an airway, tune and identify the station you are going from, track the selected radial until near the mid-point, then tune and identify the next station. The TO/FROM flag should change over.

If you have to use another VOR for a fix as a reporting point along the airway, select the required radial, and when the needle is centred you are over the fix:

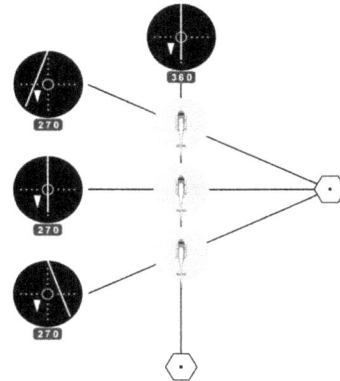

Range

As for standard VHF.

Time to Station

You often need to know the time (and distance) it will take to get to a station (well, you will in the exam, anyway), which is simply found by turning abeam the station and noting the time taken to go through a number of radials. For example, if it takes 13 minutes to fly from A to B, how long will take to get to the VOR?

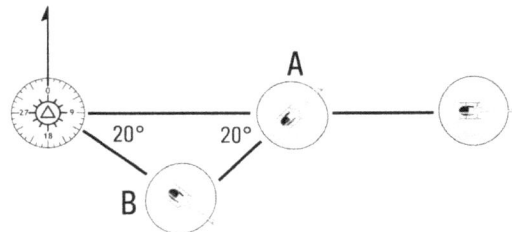

Rotate the OBS 20° to the right, turn left 20° and note the time. Keep the heading constant until the CDI centres. The time to the station is the same as the time just elapsed. There is no need to calculate anything, because we are simply working with an isosceles triangle.

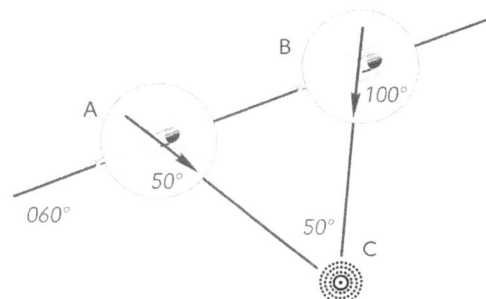

Tip: For a station between 10-45° off the nose, if you wait until you double the original relative bearing, your distance to the station will be the same as the distance just travelled (that is, A-B and B-C in the picture below will be two sides of an isosceles triangle), which you can work out with your groundspeed.

All you need do then is use the groundspeed (or TAS in an emergency) to find your distance. It is a variation of the 1 in 60 rule, as explained in *Navigation*. In short, for every 1° left or right of track, you will be 1 nm off track for every 60 travelled or, conversely, if you are 2 nm left of track having travelled 60 nm, you have drifted by 2°.

The logic behind finding the time to a station by measuring the number of degrees passed through lies with radians, which are a scientific method of measuring angles.

A radian is an angle that subtends an arc of the same length as the radius of a circle (360° = 2π radians).

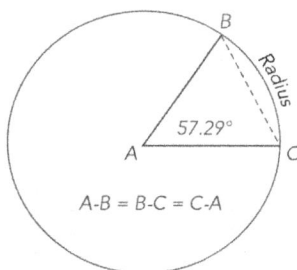

There is an equilateral triangle inside the circle, except that one side of it is an arc, which sweeps through 57.29°, or 60° for government work (the difference is less than 5% anyway). As the arc is the same length as the radius of the circle, the time taken to fly the arc is the same as it takes to fly to the centre.

If you set up any proportion of distance over time on the flight computer, as in the example below, the speed at which you fly round the arc is shown against the 60 marker, and therefore is the time to get to the station.

For example, your relative bearing to a fix is 315°, which 3 minutes later is 270°.

The formula is:

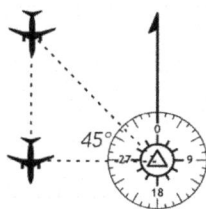

$$\text{Time (mins)} = \frac{\text{Seconds}}{\text{Degrees}}$$

$$4 = \frac{180}{45}$$

Or working with minutes:

$$\text{Time (mins)} = \frac{3 \times 60}{45}$$

On the flight computer, just set up a ratio of time over degrees passed through ($^3/_{45}$) and look for the answer (4 minutes) against the 60 marker:

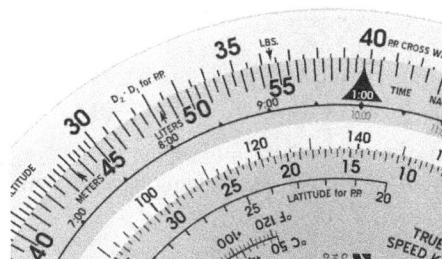

4 minutes is the time it would take to fly the straight line between B and C above, although the accurate answer is 3.8 minutes if you look opposite 57.29.

The front face of the Jeppesen CR-3 can give you the time to fly the arc, which can be handy with approaches:

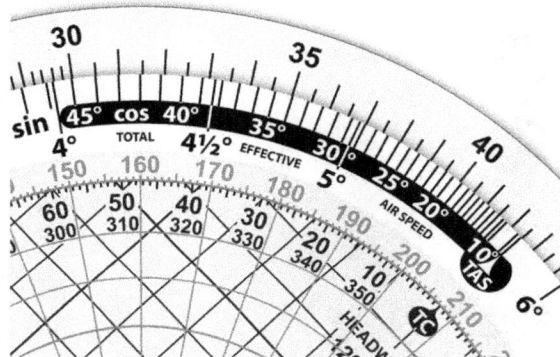

The Lead Radial (where you start turning) of an arc based procedure is 2 nm before intercepting the final approach course. Of course, it is printed on the approach chart, but if you want to work it out yourself, remember that 57.29° of arc is equal to the DME value which, for the sake of argument, we will take as 7 nm. So, set up $^7/_{57.29}$ on the flight computer and look opposite 2 on the outer scale to find the amount to add to or subtract from 16.4. The answer would have been 17 had you used $^7/_{60}$.

You can use the same logic to find the point at which you might want to slow down and collect your thoughts. If you want to start preparing 5 nm away, just use that instead.

However, it is more logical to want to know the distance to a station, as it is a handy way of finding out whether you are inside an airway as you fly along it, where no crosscuts are available and the DME isn't working (or there isn't one), as you might find in the open spaces of Canada.

You need to know the groundspeed for this one:

$$\text{Distance} = \frac{\text{Mins} \times \text{GS}}{\text{Degrees}}$$

Using the situation above, how far West of the VOR would you be with a ground speed of 180 knots? 12 miles.

Again, on the flight computer, set up the $^3/_{45}$ ratio and look for the answer (12 miles) against the grounsdpeed.

Logic check: 4 minutes at 3 miles per minute is 12 miles.

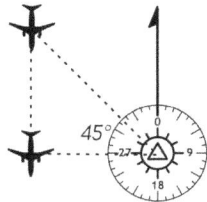

Airways

Question: If you are 100 nm from a VOR, and if 1 dot = 2°, how many dots deviation from the centreline of the instrument represent the limits of the airway boundary?

Airways are normally 5 nm wide either side of the centreline, so, applying a variation of the 1 in 60 rule:

$$\frac{5 \times 60}{100}$$

The answer is 3°, or 1.5 dots deviation.

At 200 nm you would be 3.5 nm off track, with a 1° error.

Question: An airway 10 nm wide is defined by two VORs with a bearing accuracy of ± 5.5°. To ensure accurate track guidance within the airway, what is the maximum distance between the transmitters? **Answer:** About 109 nm.

Tip: You change over halfway so there are two triangles.

The greatest acceptable cross track error is 5 nm off the airway centreline. If you fly out of one beacon and switch over halfway, the greatest error occurs at the halfway point, where the maximum distance off track is 5 nm, and the track error angle is 5.5°, so:

$$\frac{5 \times 60}{5.5} = 54.5$$

Multiply by 2 to get 109 nm. Use this formula as well:

$$\frac{\text{airway width} \times 60}{\text{accuracy}}$$

Testing

Some airfields have low power test equipment (2 watts) transmitting on 114.8 (usually, but you might get 108.0 from a repair station), identified with the ATIS, so have a pen ready to save you writing it down again later (the ID may just be a series of dots). The VOT is intended for ground use, although it can be used when airborne (there will be certified airborne check points), but you could always get to a position on a known radial and check the readings. As you move the OBS, you can expect the usual indications relating to the bearing selected (which is why two transmitters are used, to save you moving the aircraft to the radials). With the needle centred, the instrument should read 000° FROM or 180° TO at any point in the airport, with an accuracy of ± 4° (± 6° when airborne).

In fact, propagation error (or FM/AM synchronisation, at least) should be within ±1°. The system should shut down automatically if it gets outside that (the monitor will remove the ID once the measured bearing changes by more than 1°). Phase comparison (equipment) error should not be more than ±3°, and station (site) errors should be within ±1° (at 200 nm this is 3 nm). The nominal accuracy is ±5° within the published protection range, based on a 95% probability rate.

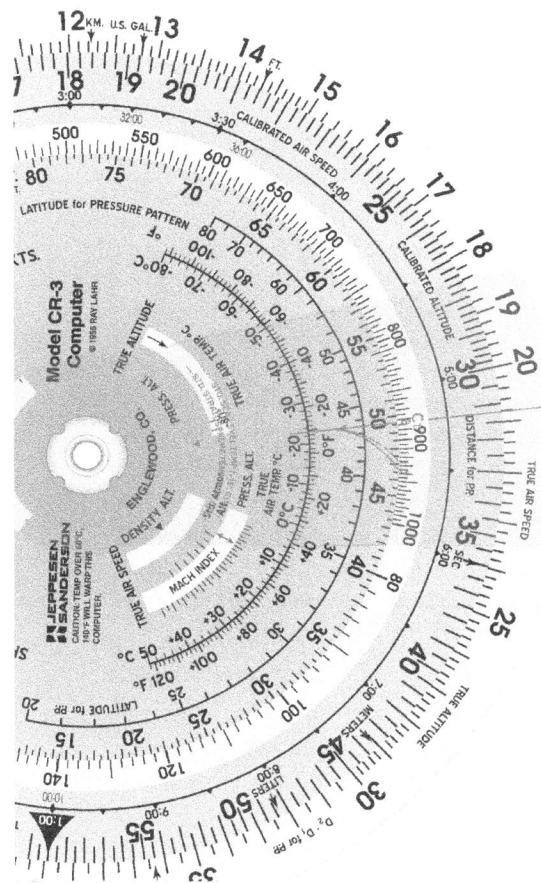

Problems

Although the VOR is less subject to static and other interference than an NDB (there is no night effect), and it is more accurate, the transmissions depend on line of sight, and there are suspect areas at 90° to a radial (zones of ambiguity), and overhead (cone of confusion), as mentioned above. In addition, certain rotor or propeller RPM settings can cause fluctuations up to ±6° (change them slightly before saying the instrument is not working!) Transmissions may be adversely affected by uneven propagation over irregular ground surfaces (scalloping), and if bearing information is used beyond published ranges, you may get interference from other transmitters.

If the transmitting station cannot stay within required limits, the identification is suppressed and the navigation components from the carrier wave will cease.

Doppler VOR

Using Doppler allows the frequency of a signal to decrease when the distance between the beacon and aircraft increases, and *vice versa*. It removes site errors and allows you to use a VOR in hilly country (it also needs less of a clear radius around the station). Range is also improved.

The reference signal is AM and the FM variphase signal rotates **anticlockwise**. A wide-aperture antenna averages out the local distortions that would normally be much more noticeable with the more narrowly focussed CVOR antenna (which uses about half a wavelength as opposed to about 5), so a theoretical tenfold reduction in site errors is possible (something to do with space diversity).

The Doppler shift comes from the relative motion of the antenna and the receiver. It is used because the wide aperture system needs Doppler to work properly, in that it creates the direction-dependent **FM signal** which allows you to detect a frequency change (in proportion to the azimuth) as the antenna rotates.

Thus, the Doppler shift makes the transmitter look as if it is advancing and retreating 30 times a second. The aircraft sees a varying frequency rather than varying power. The end result is signals that are the opposite way round to a normal VOR, but the equipment in the aircraft doesn't notice because the signals still have the right phase and they are rotating the other way.

ADF/NDB   062 02 02

An *Automatic Direction Finder* (ADF), also known as a *radio compass*, is a device in an aircraft that picks up vertically polarised signals broadcast on the Medium wave band (LF/MF) by *Non Directional Beacons* (NDBs), so called because they radiate in all directions, using mainly surface waves as modified by indirect waves.

You can only depend on the range when the ground wave is dominant, as with low powered beacons that cannot manage a space wave. At higher powers, sky waves can reach the E layer of the ionosphere and make the readings inaccurate. If the needle is hunting and the signal gets louder and fades away, the ground wave is being contaminated by sky waves. Medium frequencies are used because their range is good, and the aircraft dimensions

are not similar to the wavelength. The term *automatic* means that you do not have to turn a loop antenna.

Although there are a few problems (see overleaf), you can get 1,000 nm range over the sea and 300 nm over land if the power is high enough, but NDBs tend now to be used as *Locators*, or enroute navaids on airways, homing beacons for instrument approaches and markers for the Instrument Landing System (ILS), with a typical power of 15W and a range of about 10-25 nm.

A long range (LF) NDB could put out 200 watts for a range of between 50-60 nm. To help with the range, they could be **N0NA1A** (the most common), which uses less power but will need the BFO to be selected because the information will be keyed Morse. The problem is that, during the breaks when the ID is transmitted, there is no navigation signal, and the needle will wander around.

A N0N A2A transmission remains a carrier wave for most of the time, but the ID is amplitude modulated when required. The BFO is needed only for initial tuning. Plain A2A transmissions that are continuously modulated do not need a BFO.

The approved ICAO frequency range for aeronautical NDBs is between **190-1750 Khz** (hecto- or kilometric), but that part of the radio spectrum includes commercial radio stations, whose use in IFR work is not allowed because of the problems involved with quality control, and there are no guarantees of consistency of service. If there is no ID, but the system otherwise appears to behave normally, it is undergoing calibration or maintenance - instead you will hear T or TST (in Morse).

The minimum signal to noise ratio is 3:1. ICAO also requires ±7° accuracy for 95% of the time by day. Bearings in the published protection range should be accurate to within ±5° **by day**.

The tracking accuracy for an NDB approach is within ±5°.

NDBs are dual systems, using main and standby transmitters, plus two monitors to ensure continuous service. If the power falls by more than 50%, or a monitor or the ID fails, an automated telephone message creates an alarm. Standby transmitters have an E at the end of their identification so you know it is a standby.

Errors

The most common error is failing to recognise *station passage* - if you are directly over the beacon, it will swing around all over the place and be confused with one of the errors below, or failure of the instrument, where the needle just rotates to the right. This is the same cone of confusion effect that is experienced with a VOR (above).

This is useful knowledge for an NDB approach to a coastal aerodrome in mountains as the sun is setting!

Limitations*

Limitations of the system include:

- **static**, including local thunderstorm activity, which is likely to cause the greatest inaccuracy and make the needle point towards a storm.

- **night effect,** where the needle swings erratically, at its strongest just after sunset and before sunrise. The loop is designed to receive surface waves - any sky waves will be out of phase and distorted, because they energise the horizontal parts of the loop, hence the Adcock antenna (waves change their polarisation when reflecting off the ionosphere). If the ionosphere is not parallel with the Earth's surface, they will also arrive from different directions. Low power beacons are virtually unaffected by this as they can only produce a ground wave. Check for an unsteady needle and a fading audio signal.

- **station overlap**, when NDBs have the same frequency. Because this is more pronounced at night, it can easily be confused with *night effect*, below (promulgated ranges are not valid at night for this reason). **This will have the greatest effect on ADF accuracy, particularly at night.**

- **mountain effect**, or variations caused by **reflections** from high ground, where two signals might be received at once from different paths.

- **quadrantal error**, or variations from the aircraft itself, in the same way as it might affect a compass. The signal is reradiated by the airframe and the receiver gets an additional (much weaker) signal to contend with. The greatest error lies at 45° to the fore and aft axis, hence the term *quadrantal*. Modern systems have corrector boxes for this.

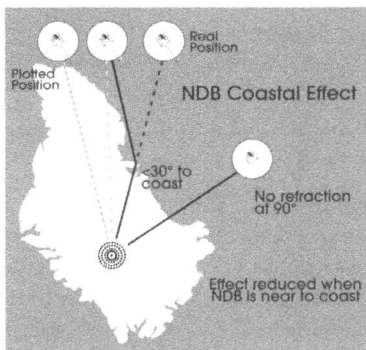

NDB Coastal Effect

- coastal refraction (diffraction), from radio waves in transit from land to sea, because they travel slightly faster over water, which makes your aircraft appear closer to the shore. This effect is most noticeable at less than 30° to the coastline (i.e. an acute angle), and at lower frequencies, so expect errors if you are using an NDB inland directly in front of or behind you. With two NDBs, one 20 nm, and the other 50 nm inland from the coast, and if the coastal error is the same for both, the error seen by an aircraft will be greater from the beacon that is further away. Your altitude has an effect.

- **Identification**. As an NDB has no flag indication of failure, as there is with the VOR, you should continuously monitor the station ID when relying on the instrument. Aside from that, the only way of knowing about problems is seeing the needle rotate to the right if the signal is not received.

Use

The ADF is normally tuned with the function switch in the ANT position (it stands for *antenna*). This removes the needle from the loop (that is, receiving is done through the sense antenna) and saves wear and tear as it tries to point at every station you tune through - here, the sense antenna is used by itself to obtain the ID. Once there, return the switch to the ADF position.

As always, check - in this case, ensure that the needle points vaguely where you expect it to.

The TEST button spins the needle 90° from its tuned position, and back, to indicate a good signal. The BFO switch also uses the sense aerial by itself to detect the modulated Morse identifier.

While most NDBs use a modulated continuous wave, some use a plain carrier wave, which may be interrupted. The giveaway on a chart is an underlined frequency:

<u>395</u>

This requires the BFO (Beat Frequency Oscillator) to identify the station (it is used for A1A transmissions), but this is automatic on modern aircraft.

N0NA2A transmissions amplitude modulate the carrier for identification.

The fixed card display (*goniometer*) has a compass rose with 0° representing the nose of the aircraft at the top of the instrument, and a needle that points to where the signal is coming *from*, in this case a QDM of 165° (including thunderstorms if the strength of their output is greater than that of the NDB to which you are tuned).

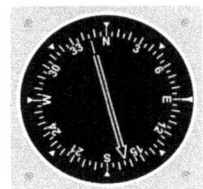

Thus, if a station is ahead, the needle will point to 0°, or 180° if it is behind. However, if you made no allowance for wind, and just pointed the nose of the aircraft at the station (*homing*, as opposed to *tracking*), you would actually follow a curved path of pursuit towards it (also known as *bird-dogging*).

Allowing for drift lets you keep a straight track, which is needed for airways (see *Tracking*), and which is why homing is unacceptable for IFR work (it takes you away from the centreline of an airway). If you are heading to a beacon with a relative bearing of zero, and the magnetic heading decreases, you have some right drift, and *vice versa*. Unfortunately, working with fixed cards involves maths!

First of all, though, some definitions:

- **Magnetic Heading** - the angle between the aircraft's longitudinal axis and magnetic North

- **Relative Bearing** - the angle between the longitudinal axis and the NDB, which is what you read directly from a fixed card ADF

- **Magnetic Track** or **Bearing** - the angle between the aircraft position and the NDB, To or From

Take note of this formula (you will need it in the exam):

$$MH + RB = BTS \ (MB)$$

The magnetic heading plus the relative bearing gives you the bearing to the station.

Taking the example below, the formula would read:

$$324 + 46 = 010$$

MB = MH + RB

My **B**uddy
Must **H**ave
Red **B**lood

You can get the relative bearing like this:

$$BTS - MH = RB$$

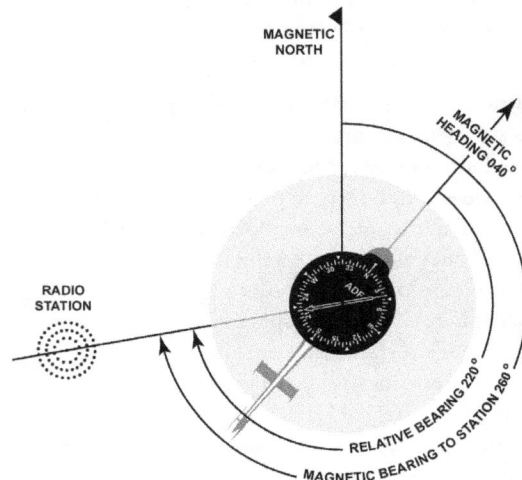

RMI

The *Radio Magnetic Indicator* is a combination of ADF indicator and slaved compass. The top of the instrument represents the aircraft's compass heading (which includes deviation) and the needle points to the QDM (or QDR, if you look at the other end), which saves you doing the calculations above in your head. In other words, it always displays the present heading and bearing, and does some of the work required by a fixed display. There may also be a repeater needle from the VORs giving you the same information relative to the stations they are tuned to.

In the picture, the heading is 139°, and the ADF QDM is 077°. The VOR needle is pointing to a QDM of 210°.

The RMI does not need a TO/FROM flag, as there is no 180-degree ambiguity. With the VOR, the tail of the needle on the RMI shows the radial. Change it to True by using the variation at the VOR.

As a point of interest, the VOR needle on an RMI will always read correctly if any deviation occurs, but headings and ADF readings will be in error by the deviation. This is because the ADF needle will naturally point towards the transmitting station, regardless of what the compass rose does. The VOR QDM, on the other hand, is created *within the instrument* by subtracting the aircraft heading from the QDM and applying the difference clockwise round the dial from the lubber line. Deviations are automatically applied because the number cruncher ensures that the VOR needle moves in the same direction for the same amount as the compass rose.

Put another way, the tail of the VOR needle always points to the radial even if the heading indication is wrong. The ADF needle always points to the station, so you will be on the wrong course if the Heading Indicator is not accurate, although you will always be able to find the station.

For either needle, however, if it is off to the left, you fly left, and *vice versa*.

Position Fix

For a fixed card ADF, find the relative bearing to each station and add them to your heading to get the tracks to the stations. Then find the reciprocals and plot them outwards (using variation at the aircraft). Along an airway, to find where you are in relation to an intersection, you will already know the bearing to station (BTS), because it will be on the map.

Time to Station

As with the VOR.

Tracking

When drifting, the needle will always point to the side of the aircraft the wind is coming from, so corrections should always be made that way, ensuring that the needle goes to the *other* side of the lubber line* once a corrected heading is established.

If needle moves right, aircraft is drifting left

Turn right to bring needle left of lubber line

*When tracking inbound.

For example, if the wind is coming from the left, you need the heading to be an equal amount of degrees the other side of the lubber line as the needle is, such as a heading of 350° (*minus* 10 of the lubber line), looking for a 010° relative bearing (*plus* 10 of the lubber line). If you just turned left enough to point the nose to the beacon, you would follow the curve of pursuit described above. Taking the needle across the lubber line means that you can make an attempt at regaining track as well. In other words, you are adding the drift to the track correction. If you were off track on the windward side, it may be possible to just turn to a heading that is equal to the track and let the wind do the work.

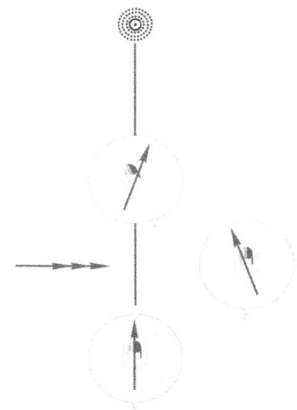

The relative bearing of the NDB should be equal (in magnitude and sign) to the angle of drift.

How far you are away from the beacon determines how large the intercept angle can be. It should be smaller as you get closer to the beacon. As you probably won't know how far away you are, the trick is to watch the speed of the needle as it moves - it rotates faster when you are close. In fact, it gets very sensitive in the overhead - you should not be correcting by more than 10° in that area, if any.

A good ploy is to allow the drift to happen until you get a positive reading, say 10° port, double it the other way (go 20° starboard), and when you are back on track, reduce it by half (10° in this case) to hold it. This is *bracketing*, and the process may have to be repeated several times in smaller amounts until you get it right. *Do not chase the needle - hold it steady so you can see the effects of adjustments.*

In fact, bracketing can be done simply with as few as two heading changes, and you should rarely need more than six. It is essentially a game between you and whatever needle you are using. Starting with your heading matching your track, at some point you will start to drift off if there is any wind at all. If you were heading 270°, your next heading could be 250° or 290°, according to the direction of the drift. Now you wait for the results, and your next heading change will be 10°. So, had we encountered left drift and turned onto 290°, if the needle moves to the right again, you would now select 300°, or if it moved left, you could select 280°. You should rarely need to go down to 5° changes.

Anticipation is the key! Do not wait until you have passed through your track until turning back on to it. Using 5° as a lead angle is good enough. The closer you are to the beacon the greater that angle will be.

When tracking *outbound*, you need the needle on the same side as the wind, so, although you are still looking for the plus 20, minus 20 equation, the needle would be pointing at 160° RB (when you make your initial turn, the needle looks like it's going the wrong way, but you get used to it).

If needle moves right, aircraft is drifting left

Turn right to bring tail further left of lubber line

In short, if the pointy end moves to the right of a line between 0° and 180°, fly right, as drift is to the left, and *vice versa*. This is true going to or from an NDB.

If you split the display into two halves, on a line between 0° and 180°, and call the right half plus, and the left minus (if going to a station), you can use the needle's position to find the track to a station. For example, if the needle is in the right half (the + segment), add the heading to the relative bearing to get the track. If it is in the left, take it away (work the needle back from zero). Whilst turning right, the aircraft heading will increase while the relative bearing decreases, and *vice versa*. If you remain on the same bearing, the heading change will always equal the change of ADF indication. When outbound, reverse the signs.

INTERCEPTION

To intercept a QDM or QDR, it's usual to use 90° inbound and 45° outbound, but 90° takes you no closer to the beacon, and involves large heading changes, and an angle that is too shallow takes you no closer to the track, so use what ATC and circumstances (or exam questions) dictate. 30° is nice. In the picture below, to intercept the 090° QDM, you need to turn **the other way** (e.g. left), the same number of degrees the **other side** of the lubber line

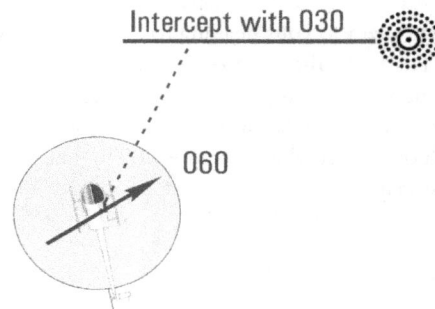

Intercept with 030

060

This is assuming zero wind conditions!

Remember: Going to a station, if the desired track is to the right of the QDM (in this case 090°), intercept to the left by the same difference in degrees, and vice versa.

Now the heading is 030°, and the ADF needle shows a relative bearing of 30°. The QDM is still 060°.

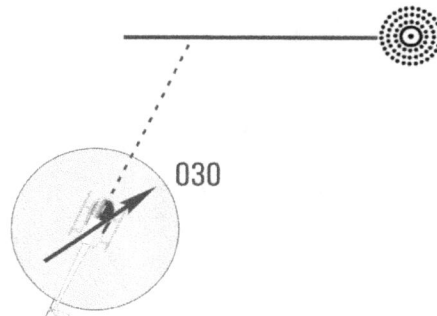

030

Now wait (on the same heading) until the needle moves a further 30°, which is double the original difference, or the sum of the angles either side of the lubber line.

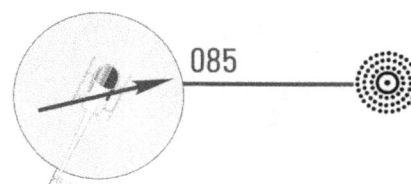

085

Start a rate one turn 5° before reaching the desired track, in this case at 085° Relative Bearing.

Going from a beacon, if the desired track is to the right, intercept to the right, and vice versa. In the picture below, the intercept heading is on the opposite side of the QDR to what the tail is showing, then turn the shortest way.

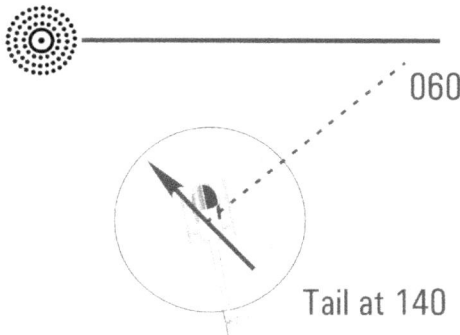

060

Tail at 140

EXAMPLES

1. An NDB bears 279° relative from an aircraft whose heading is 209°. If deviation is -7° and variation is 18°E, what is the bearing (M) of the aircraft from the NDB?

```
C = 209°C D = -7° M = 202°M
```

HDG(M) + RB = QDM:

```
202°M + 279° = 481° (-360°) = 121°M
```

QDR from NDB to aircraft = 121°M + 180° = 301°M. For a True Bearing:

```
C = 209°C

D = -7°

M = 202°M

V = 18°E

T = 220°T
```

HDG(T) + RB = QUJ

```
220°T + 279° = 499° (-360°) = 139°T
```

The QTE from NDB to aircraft = 139°T + 180° = 319°T

2. If the magnetic heading is 120°, and variation is 17°W, and there is an island 15° to the left, what is your True bearing from the island? The heading is:

```
120 - 17 = 103
```

And the relative bearing of the island is 345°:

```
103 + 345 = 448 - 360 = 088

088 + 180 = 268
```

AIRWAYS

The information from navaids becomes less reliable the further away you get from them, so corridors are defined, within which the signals can be counted on.

For VORs, the corridor width starts 5 nm either side, diverging at 4° for 70 nm, until 20 nm wide. The width remains constant between 70-140 nm, where it diverges again at 4° until a width of 40 nm is reached at 280 nm out, at which point it remains constant.

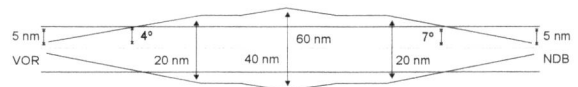

For NDBs, the corridor starts 5 nm either side, diverging at 7° until a width of 20 nm at 40 nm out, remaining constant between 40-80 nm out, thereafter diverging at 7° until 60 nm wide at 245 nm, then remaining constant.

TACAN

This is a pulse-based military navigation system operating in the UHF band (*Tactical Air Navigation*), which can be used by the DME in your aircraft (*not* the VOR - military aircraft have a display which is not compatible). When a TACAN is co-located with a VOR, the VORTAC will show DME readouts automatically when you tune the VOR, as the frequencies are paired. Of course, a military machine can pick up the complete TACAN signal, which provides range, radial speed and bearing information.

The maximum distance between VOR and DME/TACAN ground installations if they share the same Morse ID is 600 metres.

FANS

Future Air Navigation Systems relate to developing the necessary equipment and procedures to manage air traffic in a more efficient manner, using new technology, although much of it has already arrived.

Improvements relate to:

- **Communication**, and the use of data links rather than voice communications to transmit complex ATC clearances, plus 8.33 Khz spacing for radios. This can be done automatically by the FMS, using HF, VHF, Mode S transponders, ADS-A & B and satellite links.

- **Navigation**, and the use of GPS with other aids to improve accuracy and make better use of airspace. This would include Performance Based Navigation, using RNP and ANP, plus RVSM, WAAS, the ILS and MLS, all discussed below.

- **Surveillance**, and the use of datalinks to signal the position of aircraft and the intentions of their crews to the ground and other users.

All are commonly referred to as CNS.

RNAV   062 05

Airways normally use ground-based navigation aids, but these days you don't necessarily need them to maintain an accurate track.

Area Navigation is a generic term for systems that allow navigation over wide areas - it was originally coined for a way of electronically moving navaids, VORs in particular, to other places enroute (they became *phantom waypoints*), which implies that you must be within range of the navaids concerned in order to use them. If the system does not receive radial or distance information, it goes into *Dead Reckoning* mode.

For example, you could tell the black box the distance and bearing of your house from the nearest VOR and it would present all the signals as if the aid was at your house.

In the above case, waypoint 6 in the device's memory has been programmed with the frequency 114.1, and the VOR concerned has been offset by 14.1 nm on the 210 radial (the 737 FMS can store 46 navaids). When in range of the VOR, the readings would base themselves around the new location, and you can fly directly to it.

On a direct route with no specific navaids to aim for, you could shift all nearby ones to fit on your direct track for a series of phantom waypoints, typically displaying cross-track and along-track distance with reference to the phantoms, and not the navaids on which they are based. The concept is illustrated in the picture below, where the direct route is 24 nm less than using the airways.

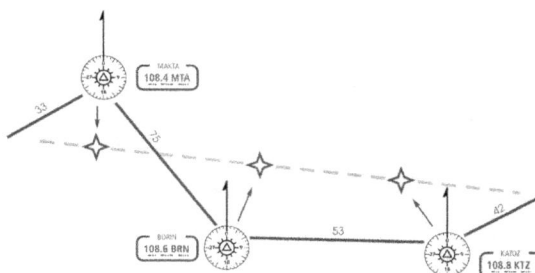

You could also fly parallel to a track at a chosen offset distance*, or fly approaches involving turns that do not depend on the location of navigation aids.

*If a fast aircraft is following a slow one on the same track, an instruction to *fly offset by X nautical miles* can allow it to overtake and climb/descend through the level of the slower aircraft, an alternative to radar vectoring.

Strategic Lateral Offset Procedures (SLOPs) provide for emergencies that require immediate descent, including avoiding wake turbulence.

Thus, RNAV describes ways of flying directly across country without doglegging all over the place, or having to pass over radio fixes, which saves fuel and makes better use of airspace, as you don't pack more aircraft into a relatively small portion of the airspace, i.e airways. You can also eliminate procedure turns because you don't care where the ground-based aids are (indeed, straight-in approaches can often be the norm, with arrival at the threshold in a specific time window). Lower minima and increased capacity are also available.

The FMS can also provide ideal vertical flight paths for climb and descent to arrive over positions at particular altitudes. The FMS, using the autopilot, can fly the whole route in three dimensions, and even airspeed adjustments can be made to achieve arrivals at required times.

As far as pilots are concerned, RNAV means a reduction in workload and increased safety, as the navigation is undertaken by accurate and sophisticated equipment, and the reliance on navigation aids that lose their effectiveness over distance (splay areas) is lessened. ATC can also use straighter routings and use them instead of radar vectoring, which reduces their workload as well.

ICAO Annex 11 defines Area Navigation (RNAV) as "a method of navigation which permits aircraft operation on any desired flight path within the coverage of station-referenced navigation aids or within the limits of the capability of self-contained aids, or a combination."

An RNAV waypoint could be a geographical position derived from a VOR radial and DME distance but, in the USA at least, RNAV is no longer VOR-based. Otherwise, RNAV can use VOR/DME and/or GPS to update an FMS position that was originally based on Inertial Reference Systems. It does not use NDBs!

In RNAV mode, the horizontal dots on the instrument face represent not an angular displacement from a radial, but a *distance* to the side of a track. Each dot represents one nautical mile, so a full scale deviation on a 5-dot CDI in enroute mode means a deviation from the desired track of 5 nm. On a 2-dot display, the deviation per dot is 5 nm. In approach mode, it becomes 1.25 nm for a 5-dot display (1 dot represents 0.25 nm in approach mode on a 5-dot display) and 0.5° per dot for a 2-dot display.

Standards

There are nearly as many RNAV standards as there are varieties of airspace. For example, Basic and Precision RNAV are used in ECAC (Europe), MNPS* over the North Atlantic and RNAV 1 and 5 internationally (RNAV 1 = P-RNAV). RNP 4 (and RNAV 10) are used over oceanic and remote continental airspace - although both rely on GNSS, RNAV 10 does not need ATS surveillance. In the US, RNAV 2 is the basis of navigation in enroute continental airspace.

*MNPS tends to be excluded from these definitions due to its mandatory nature, and the fact that no changes are expected anyway. It is otherwise called RNAV 10.

Under RNAV 10, aircraft operating in oceanic and remote areas must have at least two independent and serviceable LRNSs comprising an INS, an IRS FMS or a GNSS. Aircraft with dual INS/IRU installations have a standard time limitation. Operators may extend their RNAV10 navigation capability time by updating.

The above terms are used interchangeably here, especially as the ECAC specifications will migrate to RNAV 1 & 5. Note that P-RNAV does not have the same functionality as RNP 1, even though it shares the same accuracy.

Otherwise:

- RNAV 5 is used in the enroute and arrival phases.
- RNP 2 (RNP requires monitoring - see below) is used in enroute, and oceanic/remote phases.

- RNAV 1 and RNP 1 are used in the arrival and departure phases.
- RNP APCH and RNP AR APCH are used in the approach phase.
- RNP 0.3 (for helicopters) is used in all phases of flight except for oceanic/remote and final approach.
- RNAV 1, RNP 1 & RNP 0.3 may also be used in the en-route phases of low level IFR helicopter flights.
- RNAV 2 and RNP 2 are also used as navigation specifications.

There are no RNAV approach specifications.

In Europe, **B-RNAV** is the basic system, with an accuracy of ± 5 nm for at least 95% of the time, as for RNP 5 (see below). B-RNAV is needed for flights in Europe above FL 95, using VOR/VOR or VOR/DME fixing. One of the course line computer's jobs is to transform the information from a VOR/DME station into tracking and distance information to any phantom waypoint.

Precision Area Navigation (**P-RNAV**), used for SIDs and STARs, has the same accuracy as RNP 1, meaning ±1 nm on 95% of occasions*, and will be controlled by the FMS (the FMC will automatically select and tune stations based on their relative accuracy). You need P-RNAV to use DME/DME fixing, which gives you the best accuracy.

*P-RNAV requires a track-keeping accuracy of 0.5 nm standard deviation or better, referenced to WGS 84.

The aircraft will fly as accurately as it can, which is mostly down to around 0.02 nm (Actual Navigation Performance). The difference between systems is how happy the aircraft is to be off track, or how much its ANP can degrade before you get warnings. Thus, if the GPS fails and the ANP gradually rises to 2.0, the aircraft will still navigate in RNAV 5 airspace, but not RNAV 1.

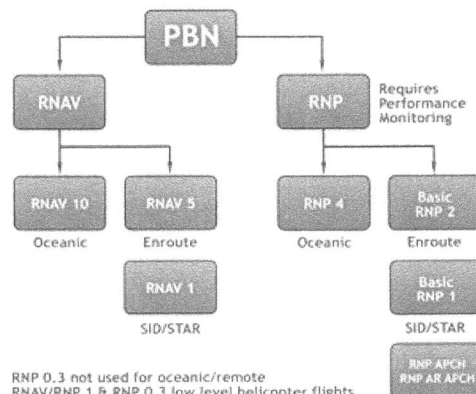

RNP 0.3 not used for oceanic/remote
RNAV/RNP 1 & RNP 0.3 low level helicopter flights

2D systems provide information in the horizontal plane only. 3D RNAV adds guidance in the vertical plane, and 4D has a timing function, which would be needed if ATC ask you to be at a waypoint at a particular time.

RNAV2 and RNP2 are also used as navigation specifications.

System Capabilities

RNAV equipment should at least be able to:

- Display the present position as latitude/longitude or a distance and bearing to a selected waypoint.

- Allow you to select or enter the required flight plan through the CDU.

- Allow review and modification of navigation data for any part of a flight plan at any stage of a flight and store enough to carry out the active flight plan.

- Review, assemble, modify or verify a flight plan in flight, without affecting the guidance output.

- Execute a modified flight plan only after positive action by the flight crew.

- Where provided, assemble and verify an alternative flight plan without affecting the active one.

- Assemble a flight plan, either by identifier or selection/creation of individual waypoints from the database, or defined by latitude/longitude, bearing/distance parameters or other parameters.

- Assemble flight plans by joining routes or route segments.

- Allow verification or adjustment of the displayed position.

- Provide automatic sequencing through waypoints with turn anticipation. Manual sequencing should also allow flight over, and return to, waypoints.

- Display cross-track error on the CDU.

- Provide time to waypoints on the CDU.

- Execute a direct clearance to any waypoint.

- Fly parallel tracks at a selected offset distance (offset mode should be clearly indicated).

- Purge previous radio updates.

- Carry out RNAV holding procedures.

- Make available estimates of positional uncertainty, either as a quality factor or by reference to sensor differences from the computed position.

- Conform to WGS-84.

- Indicate navigation equipment failure.

NAVIGATION PERFORMANCE

Navigation performance is only one factor to be considered when determining minimum route spacing, but certain standards must also be met before a system can be a sole means navigation system for IFR purposes:

- **Accuracy** in terms of *position error*, or the difference between estimated and actual positions.

- **Integrity** - the measure of trust that can be placed in the information supplied by the system. *The ability of a system to provide timely warnings as to when it should not be used for navigation.*

- **Continuity** (Reliability) - the system's capability to perform. There must be a high probability that guidance information to the appropriate level of RNP will continue to be provided for an acceptable period of time after the loss of a sensor.

- **Availability** - the time during which the system can deliver for a specific phase of flight. Sole means navigation systems require 99% availability.

- **Coverage**.

- **Functionality**. RNP airspace may have different requirements for varying types of RNP, in terms of continuous indication of lateral deviation, distance/bearing or groundspeed/time to an active waypoint, failure indications, etc. For example, RNP airspace with a high accuracy requirement may need parallel offset capability, whereas less accurate airspace may only require a point-to-point facility.

Safety is contingent upon the accuracy, resolution and integrity of the data, which in turn depends upon the processes applied during its origination.

The Actual Navigation Performance of a system is represented by a circle defining its accuracy for 95% of the time, derived from the output all the navigation sensors and weighing them statistically. It is then compared with the Required Navigation Performance.

RNP is a measure of the standards needed to operate within certain airspace, or within which the ANP needs to be constrained. This commonly means the lateral accuracy in nautical miles that must be maintained for 95% of the time, relative to a desired flight path (technically, a Total System Error* of X nm or less for over 95% of total flight time). In practice, a system's capability is determined by the most limiting of the characteristics described above.

*TSE is the vector sum of:

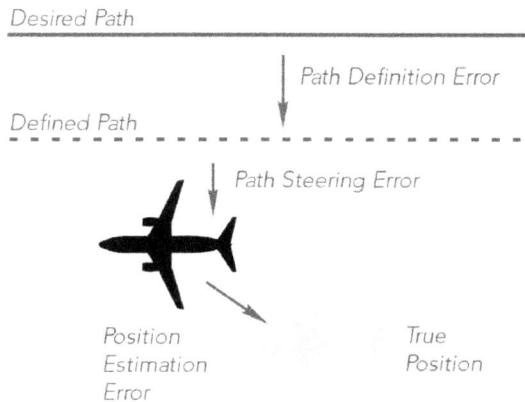

- **Path Definition Error**, or the difference between the intended path and the actual path. On board performance monitoring and alerting is managed by *gross reasonableness checks of navigation data.*

- **Path Steering Error**, from steering the course, either manually or by autopilot, not including human error (this is the biggest factor). In simple terms, the ability to follow the defined path. Also known as *Flight Technical Error*. On board performance monitoring and alerting is managed by on board systems or crew procedures.

- **Position Estimation Error**, the combination of system or sensor errors and computation error. Also known as *Navigation System Error*. On board performance monitoring and alerting is a requirement of on-board equipment for RNP.

Otherwise, the system accuracy takes after the specification - for example, RNP 4 means within 4 nm along or across track. This would typically be used en route, whereas you would need RNP 1 or 2 around terminals, which are busy. The lowest value is 0.10.

RNAV and RNP systems are essentially the same, but RNP requires on-board performance monitoring and alerting, so it can warn you if you are likely to stray outside airspace boundaries, which are equal to twice the RNP value - for example, RNP 4 has corridors 8 nm wide.

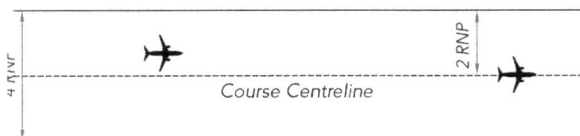

The warning given to crews means that ATC can have greater confidence in track keeping performance, which mean that routes can be placed closer together.

As monitoring is already incorporated within satellite systems, the distinction is essentially the requirement for GNSS, which can support very low RNP values, if you consider position accuracy alone*. So, with some exceptions (where you cannot monitor cross-track deviations), RNP operations are satellite based.

*Accuracy also depends on Path Steering Errors, otherwise known as *Flight Technical Error*, or FTE, which is actually the most dominant factor. This term tends to be irrelevant for the PBN operations described below, as cross track errors are commonly managed by the system rather than by pilots moving the controls.

Thus, although many RNAV systems are very accurate, if they cannot provide assurance of their performance, they cannot be used in RNP airspace. Having said that, RNP 10 is inconsistent because it does not require monitoring, so it is often referred to as RNAV 10 as it is too much of a pain to change all the charts - it is not an RNP operation, but the term is already used in current documentation.

Aircraft approved for higher standards are not necessarily approved in airspace with lesser standards. This is because lateral navigation accuracy is not the only criterion for approval. For example, to meet the RNAV 1 specification, you can usually use any of GNSS, DME/DME/IRU or simply DME/DME. However, one state may specify GNSS and another may disallow it.

At least two LRNSs, capable of navigating to RNP 4, and in the flight manual, must be operational at the entry point of the RNP airspace as well as ADS/CPDLC capability.

RNP is a measure of the probability that the aircraft (or at least the FMC) will think it is somewhere that it isn't. As a result, the term *performance* refers to the abilities of the complete navigational system, including satellite data accuracy, transmission accuracy, and the receiving component's ability to interpret the data properly.

Any breakdowns will create an alert that the ANP is not acceptable for whatever RNP you are trying to use so, if a satellite is missing, your flight plan may contain a warning of an ANP limitation around your ETA.

That is, with a satellite off line, if the ANP is within the RNP, the chances that the system is confused are within acceptable limits, although you could be half a mile off track during the approach and you will not get an ANP alert. The concept depends on average risk, where most pilot training is based on specific risks.

PERFORMANCE BASED NAVIGATION

062 07

Specific approval to use conventional navigation equipment such as VOR/DME on airways is generally not required, but you may sometimes need to use older equipment (even specific models, which may or may not be available), even though newer and better systems are around, which means unnecessary expense.

To help with this situation, the emphasis is now on performance capability, in that, as long as the equipment you propose to use meets the requirement of the airspace, it doesn't matter who made it, or where you got it, provided it passes the usual safety checks. In other words, PBN is **not sensor specific**, although it does require on-board performance monitoring and alerting so, instead of depending on the accuracy of the raw data from specific navigation aids, PBN systems integrate that data into a computed solution. Under PBN, navigation requirements are based on operational requirements*, and operators can select the most cost-effective option. Technology can then evolve as fast as it likes without slowing the system down.

*Communication, surveillance and ATM environments, the availability of navigation aids (ground- and space-based), and redundancy.

Thus, two fundamental aspects of any PBN operation are the requirements in the relevant navigation specification and the navigation aids available (the infrastructure). A navigation specification sets out the requirements to be met by aircraft and aircrew to support a navigation application* by defining the performance required from the RNAV systems as well as any specifics, such as the ability to fly curved paths or parallel offset routes.

*The application of a navigation specification and the supporting navaid infrastructure, to routes, procedures, and/or defined airspace volume, in accordance with the intended airspace concept.

When you meet the airspace requirements, you must include /R in Item 10 of the ICAO flight plan form. If you are not so equipped, ATC need to know so, in Box 18, insert STS/NONRNAV. Also mention it on your initial contact with them.

For RNP legacy reasons, in oceanic/remote, en-route and terminal phases, PBN is limited to operations with linear lateral performance requirements and time constraints. In the approach phase, PBN accommodates linear and angular* laterally guided operations.

*Approach and landing operations with vertical guidance for APV-I and APV-II GNSS performance levels, as well as ILS/MLS/GLS precision approach and landing.

In other words, PBN is a range of operations based on two types of navigation specification, RNAV and RNP. As such, it allows aircraft separation to be built in to the airspace design, on which hinges the *airspace concept*, or what you plan to do with it.

For example, Europe's current airspace concept, which extends well beyond PBN, has these characteristics:

- A parallel network of ATS routes, based on B-RNAV, across the continent.

- A system of feeder or link routes based mainly on B-RNAV which connect to P-RNAV or Conventional SIDs and STARs, starting at the nominal TMA boundary.

- An organised track system (OTS) in the North Atlantic based on MNPS, which is due to change to RNP 2 or RNAV 10.

- The use of RVSM between FLs 290 and 410.

- Class C airspace above FL195.

- Extensive use of the *Flexible Use of Airspace* concept.

- Some use of Free Routes.

- Evolution from State managed upper airspace to Functional Airspace Blocks (FABs).

Europe's Airspace Concept will eventually use Advanced RNP (discussed below) in en-route and terminal operations, and RNP APCH* on the Approach.

*The RNP APCH is known as an RNAV Approach even though the specification requires on-board performance monitoring and alerting. There are four versions:

- RNP APCH LNAV (LNAV only, relying on GPS).

- RNP APCH LNAV/VNAV (with VNAV added, relying on GPS and Baro VNAV). This is also referred to as an APV Baro.

- RNP APCH LP (Localiser Performance only, relying on GPS and EGNOS (see *Satellites*).

- RNP APCH LPV (with VNAV added, relying on GPS and EGNOS). Also called an APV SBAS.

In en-route operations, the European starting point was the European-wide 1998 mandate for B-RNAV, which is now known as RNAV 5. For terminal area operations, this was followed through with the 2001 introduction of P-RNAV, which is closest to RNAV 1*, and the subsequent introduction of RNP APCH - RNP APCH to LNAV and LNAV/VNAV minima from 2009 and RNP APCH to LPV minima since 2011.

*In Europe, the main difference between P-RNAV and RNAV 1 is that P-RNAV permits the use of VOR/DME in limited circumstances.

You cannot fly an approach if it is not correct as published on the charts (i.e. with a waypoint missing on the chart). You should request another type of approach.

Reading the official PBN manual (ICAO Doc 9613) is cruel and unusual punishment but, in summary:

- PBN needs an on-board RNAV or RNP system.

- You need airworthiness certification and operational approval to use RNAV in the airspace concerned.

- The RNAV system must not only be accurate within a certain range, but must also perform other tasks, such as BaroVNAV, RF, FRT, etc.

In short, both aircraft and crew must be qualified for the airspace concerned.

CONDITIONS OF USE

Abnormal and contingency procedures must be used if PBN capability is lost.

STOP Unless otherwise specified in ops documentation or an AMC, the navigational database must be valid for the current AIRAC cycle.

SIDs or STARs based on RNAV1, RNAV2, RNP1 or RNP2 may not be flown unless they are retrievable by route name from the onboard navigation database, and conform to the charted route, which may subsequently be modified through the insertion (from the database) or deletion of specific waypoints in response to ATC clearances. The manual entry, or creation of new waypoints by manual entry, of latitude and longitude or place/bearing/distance values is not permitted, although manual data entry is acceptable for RNAV 5.

ADVANCED RNP

Advanced RNP (the successor to B & P-RNAV) is an ECAC-wide navigation specification used in enroute and terminal airspace, including the approach, missed approach and departure phases, which have gaps in them. For example, P-RNAV stopped at the FAF and started again at the MAP. Although RNP APCH covered the missing Final Approach, it only started just before the IAF and finished halfway up the missed approach.

A-RNP therefore can apply to all flight phases. It incorporates RNAV 5, RNAV 2, RNAV 1, RNP 2, RNP 1 and RNP APCH, although it may be associated with other functional elements.

One of the main requirements is the need for track repeatability and predictability in the turn, which is why Radius to Fix (RF) functionality is required, together with Fixed Radius Transition (FRT).

RF is a path terminator used for SIDs, STARs and Approach. FRT is a leg transition used when the FMS is in en-route mode. In PBN, both functionalities are associated only with RNP specifications.

Approaches

Most RNAV approaches default to 0.3, down to which you can hand fly - autopilots are needed below that.

An RNP APCH must not be flown unless it is retrievable by procedure name from the on-board navigation database and conforms to the charted procedure.

An RNP APCH to **LNAV minima** is a **non-precision** instrument approach designed for 2D operations. An RNP APCH to **LNAV/VNAV minima** is a 3D operation with lateral guidance based on GNSS and (certified) vertical guidance based on SBAS or BaroVNAV. The latter may only be conducted when the aerodrome temperature is within a promulgated range.

STOP The correct altimeter setting is critical for the safe conduct of an RNP APCH using BaroVNAV, as well as for LNAV and any other 2D operation.

An RNP APCH to **LPV minima** is a 3D operation that requires a FAS datablock.

An RNP AR APCH requires authorisation (the *AR* stands for *Authorisation Required*).

RNP AR approaches are designed with BaroVNAV capability in mind*. They are characterised by:

- RNP values of 0.3 nm.

- Curved flight paths before and after the FAF or Final Approach Point.

- Protection areas laterally limited to a value of 2 x RNP without additional buffers.

RNP AR operations may include missed approach procedures and instrument departures with reduced RNP (<1 nm).

*BaroVNAV is a function of the FMS that computes vertical guidance referenced to a specified vertical path, based on barometric altitude. This means that the Altimetry System Error (ASE) is also a component of the vertical Total System Error (TSEz). Aircraft operating in airspace where vertical performance is specified must have a TSE in the vertical direction (TSEz) that is less than the specified performance limit for 99.7% of the flying time. For example, the specified performance at or below 5000 ft in ED-75/DO-236 is 160 ft.

There is no integrity and continuity requirement for vertical navigation.

Flight Paths & Terminators

In its simplest form, the system will compute the track between two waypoints, but life is not that simple! More complex flight paths are needed, both lateral and vertical.

Combinations of path types and terminators (e.g. track and beacon, respectively) are used to describe around 23 path/terminators. They are described in ARINC 424 code, with the terminator (or end statement) providing the RNAV system with the information it needs to connect the current segment with the next.

In other words, the system uses a library of leg types to create your flight path. One of the most common is a series of **TF** legs (Track to/from Fix), or straight lines*, during which the system normally interprets the coding to fly by a waypoint with a curved flight path.

*Although they are regarded as straight lines, TF legs are great circle tracks over the ground between known fixes.

An **RF** leg (Radius to Fix) allows you to fly a circle with a specified radius **relative to the Earth's surface*** rather than the undefined curve shown above. RF segments provide a large amount of flexibility, especially when it comes to avoiding mountains or reducing noise footprints.

*The radius of the turn is now limited by the *groundspeed* and angle of bank, as opposed to the TAS. Thus, there will be a maximum tailwind limit. If the IAS is not managed properly, the limiting bank angle may be reached at less than that limit, so it is important to respect the guidance from the flight director. This is an RNP function.

👍 **Rule Of Thumb:** Anticipate the turn by 1 nm for every 30° change.

The fix in path/terminator legs can be based on radio aids or be an RNAV waypoint.

A **CA** (Course to Altitude) leg allows you to follow a course until you get to a specified altitude, commonly used (if supported by the equipment) to specify the initial leg of a departure. It may then, for example, change to a DF (Direct to Fix) leg. The termination of a CA leg will be automatic if you have an integrated VNAV system, otherwise it must be terminated manually.

- **First Letter** (path): V = heading, C = course/track, F = course from a fix, H = hold, D = direct, P = procedure turn, T = track, I = initial, A = arc, R = radius.

- **Second Letter** (terminator): A = altitude, D = DME distance, I = intercept (next leg), R = radial, F = to fix/at fix, M = manual termination, C = distance from fix.

Terminators that may be used for PBN include:

- **VA** = Heading to an altitude (often used off parallel runways).

- **VI** = Heading to intercept next leg (used with Localisers).

- **VM** = Heading to a manual termination (e.g. end of STAR for radar vectors).

- **CA** = Course to an altitude (more accurate ground path than VA).

- **CF** = Course to a fix (the original path/terminator).

- **TF** = Track between fixes (most accurate leg type).

- **IF** = Initial fix (begins a series of path-terminators, used for some SIDs, and for all STARs/APCHs).

- **DF** = Track from present position direct to a fix.

- **RF** = Constant radius to a fix.

- **HM** = Hold to a manual termination.

- **HA** = Hold to an altitude (climb in the hold).

- **HF** = Hold to a fix (1 circuit in hold then continue).

OVERFLY FUNCTION

This function in the FMS makes the aircraft fly over a waypoint. Although they tend to be avoided because they are less controllable, *flyover waypoints* are those whose lat & long position* must be flown over before you can turn onto the next leg, typically used on standard departures to ensure that you don't make excessive bank angles that will interfere with performance calculations. You can fly *direct-to* any waypoint, or *direct/intercept,* where you can select a desired course to reach it. Waypoints can also have speed, altitude and time constraints (*not before,* etc.)

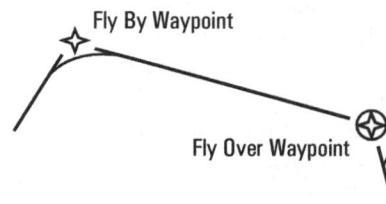

*Waypoints can be entered into all INSs as lat & long.

The start of the turn is based on the current groundspeed and a programmed bank angle, which will normally allow enough radius to provide a smooth interception. As such anticipation does not provide track guidance during the turn, the crosstrack error cannot be monitored, and crew intervention may sometimes be required.

The RNAV computer needs the heading and TAS input so it can work out the wind velocity.

Short Range Systems (2D RNAV)

Traditional instruments display only one position line, such as an arc from the DME, or bearing from a VOR, and you have to combine several to get any meaningful information. They can now be combined on one instrument for ease of interpretation, and interfaced with other equipment. Short range systems are typically based on line-of-sight navigation aids, such as VOR or DME.

For best results, the area you fly over must necessarily have a reasonable density of them (the FMC will have a database, including their frequencies, and it will tune those required for you). In normal NAV mode, with at least four stations (and position lines), the accuracy will typically be around 2 nm.

VOR/DME (RHO-THETA)

Here, you can get a fix from only one position line, so with the proper computer (such as the original KNS-80), this is the simplest form of RNAV. One of the functions of the Course-Line Computer is to transfer the information from a VOR/DME station into track and distance indications to any chosen phantom waypoint.

As mentioned above, the VOR/DME station can be offset electronically to any desired position within its range of promulgation. A VOR does not have to be in range when its details are entered into the system, but must be when used, otherwise erratic indications may be experienced when flying towards a Phantom Station at low altitudes close to the limits of reception. In fact, the system will go into DR (*Dead Reckoning*) mode when receiving only one VOR, or if there is no bearing and distance information, using whatever TAS is coming from the ADC, the heading from the compass and the last computed wind velocity (to calculate the wind, the system needs radials and distances from various VOR/DMEs, heading and TAS).

Filters limit the rate of change of VOR bearings, where they arise from multi-path reflections (site error). Close to the beacon, DME range sets the maximum rate, as the bearings change fast anyway, and errors might occur. On approach, 1 dot's deviation is equal to ¼ nm, and 1 nm en route, where 5 dots span half the airway.

Trivia: The Greek letter R (*Rho*) stands for range, and *Theta* is an angle, so a Rho-Theta fix involves a range and an angle, as you would get from VOR/DME.

DME/DME (RHO-RHO)

Also called *direct ranging*, DME receivers are used with a microprocessor to measure the distance from two DME receivers for a position fix. Some systems have their own tuners and can automatically set up DMEs, etc. according to signal strength for best position lines (the most accurate RNAV fixes come from DME/DME).

Long Range Systems

Long range systems do not rely on short-range navigation aids. These would include GPS, Loran, Decca, etc.

INERTIAL NAVIGATION SYSTEMS

These are long-range area navigation systems that have already been described under *Instruments*.

Global Navigation Satellite System

062 06

The original satellite systems were based partly on hyperbolic navigation aids such as Decca Navigator or LORAN, and Doppler. By measuring the distortions from Sputnik in 1957, it was realised that a satellite's position could be established with some accuracy. It wasn't too hard to reverse the situation.

There are two systems currently available, with another one coming. The USA one is **NAVSTAR/GPS** (GNSS is the generic ICAO term), and the Russian system is **GLONASS**, which is only just operational, so it is not approved even for B-RNAV, although smartphones can use it. Each can produce extreme accuracy at a much reduced cost compared to, say, Inertial Navigation, with better approach paths, etc.

These days, satellite signals are not only used for navigation, but also for specialised clock systems in various earthbound systems, such as cell phone networks and TV stations, since the satellites all have atomic clocks on board. ATC use it for this purpose as well (GPS is a legal source of accurate time).

A satellite system can calculate distance, track and speed from your changing position. It can also provide your altitude, but such 3D readouts require 4 satellites. In any case, the datum for altitude information when under IFR or conducting approaches is **barometric altitude**, because the Earth is not a true sphere and there may be wide differences between its actual shape and the WGS 84 model inside the GPS receiver.

GPS reliability approaches 100%, within 100 m of the true horizontal position for 95% of the time and 300 m for 99%. However, it can be affected by atmospheric interference, satellite positioning and tuning inaccuracies.

Each satellite has three sections, for timing, signal generation and transmitting.

GALILEO

Although the American GPS system is still usable, it is old technology and originally designed for military use so, for modern purposes, continual workarounds have to be employed, which often turn out to be more expensive than starting from scratch. *Galileo* is a European system whose first satellite was launched on the 28th December 2005. It will start with five types of signal - one being available to everyone, like the GPS C/A code, a more precise commercial signal, a *safety of life* service for critical applications, a *public regulated service* (PRS) for government use, and one combined with a distress signal, for rescues.

2 types of clock have been developed for it - a Rubidium Frequency Standard clock and a Passive Hydrogen Maser. In other words, they are non-identical atomic clocks.

Galileo should use **30 satellites**, with **9 and a spare** in each of **3 planes** in a near circular orbit at **23 222 km** inclined at 56° to the Equator. Orbits will take 14 hours. The signals will be transmitted on two bands, 1164-1215 MHz and 1559-1591 MHz. The overlap with GPS will use *spread spectrum technology* to unscramble the mess.

The frequency band is 1164 - 1215 MHz, 1260 - 1300 MHz and 1559 - 1591 MHz.

NAVSTAR/GPS

The Global Positioning System was originally set up by the US military in 1977 to help submarines get lost more accurately, based on Doppler Shift, as one of six satellites passed overhead, although how they received the signals beats me. Now the system is managed by an executive board that ensures that all users' needs, including civilians, are considered. This was after flight KAL 007 hit a Russian missile that was on a peaceful mission.

GPS is supposed to use 24 (21 + 3) satellites, in 6 groups of 4 (60° apart), with at least 21 operational at any time, although there are now over 31 on line, to allow for orbital manoeuvres and maintenance. The idea is that the transmissions from as many satellites as possible, but at least 4 for best results, are received by a device that is permanently tuned to 1575.42 MHz, although there is another frequency used by the military for precision positioning*. Satellite transmissions include atomic time in their signals so the receiver can calculate its distance from them. The phrase *Full Operational Capability* means that all 24 satellites are working. *All In View* means that a receiver is tracking all the satellites it can find (not the ones that it wants), and can instantly replace a lost signal with another that is already being monitored. *Search The Sky* is a procedure that starts after switching on a receiver to check that no stored satellite data is available. It typically occurs after you move the GPS some distance since its last use. A pseudo satellite (*pseudolite*) is a ground beacon that transmits similar information to a satellite.

*The 95% position accuracy should be 30 metres horizontally under ICAO.

The centre of the Earth can be used in the same way.

The satellites fly high enough to avoid the problems encountered by other navigation systems. They operate (at 7500 mph) between **6 circular planes, 20 200 km above the Earth, with 4 in each plane**, optimised for wide coverage. Each one should have a 28° view of the Earth, and at least 5 should be in line of sight from any point on Earth (in view), provided they are more than 7.5° above the horizon (satellites are *in view* when over 5° above). The most satellites are visible round the Equator, but this varies, according to the time and your location. A good combination would be 3 satellites with a low elevation

above the horizon with a 120° spread between them, and a fourth directly overhead.

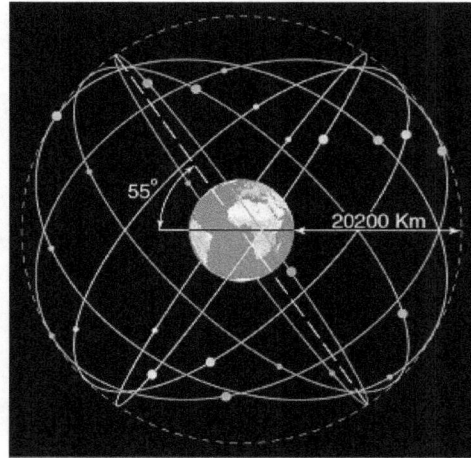

Any errors in satellite orbits are down to solar winds and the gravitational effects from the sun, moon and planets.

Their orbits cross the Equator at a **55° angle** (or, rather, the inclination* of the satellite's orbit to the Equatorial plane is 55°), so you won't see a satellite directly overhead when North of 55° N or South of 55° S. In other words, the maximum latitude of the ground track of a satellite is 55° N/S (see *Vortices* in *Navigation*).

This does not affect polar service, because, at high latitudes, receivers can see satellites over the other side, so more can actually be visible than elsewhere (they never go right over the Poles). Where the satellite goes South to North it is in the *ascending node*, and vice versa. The *mask angle* is the lowest angle above the horizon from where a satellite can be used, due to possible range errors.

*The inclination is the angle between the orbital and Equatorial planes.

The satellites move once around the Earth, from W-E, every 11 hours 58 minutes (that is, twice a day, getting 4 minutes earlier each day, actually half of a sidereal day). That's 14 times faster than a 747! The height used gives the best coverage with the least number of satellites, though you could get a problem flying through the odd ravine, especially as their transmitting power is only around 50 watts, or rather less than the average light bulb, which allows you to use smaller antennas.

The signals themselves have less strength than a Christmas tree light.

GLONASS, in contrast, uses 3 planes with 8 satellites equally displaced by 45° of latitude. To stop them hitting US satellites, they fly lower, in a near circular orbit at **19 100 km** at an inclination of 64.8° to the Equator. Each orbit is completed in 11 hours and 15 minutes. The time reference is UTC Russian time, and the datum is PZ-90

Earth-centred, Earth-fixed. Navigation signals are transmitted on two frequencies on the L band (UHF), L1 at around 1.6 GHz and L2 around 1.2 GHz. The navigation message is 2 seconds long, with "immediate" data relating to the satellite transmitting the signal and "non-immediate" data relating to the other satellites.

Although it is guaranteed to be kept running for the foreseeable future, in (US) National Emergencies NAVSTAR may be unavailable, which is why you still need radio-based navigation aids, at least under EASA*. In addition, the satellites are not always in an optimal position, and interference can affect their signals, including jamming, which can be done with minimal equipment.

*If a position fix from GPS differs from conventional systems by an unacceptable amount, the flight may be continued with those systems, so prescribed IFR equipment must still be installed and operational.

The system consists of three basic elements:

- The **Space Segment**, which contains the satellites, transmitting signals that are used by the receivers.

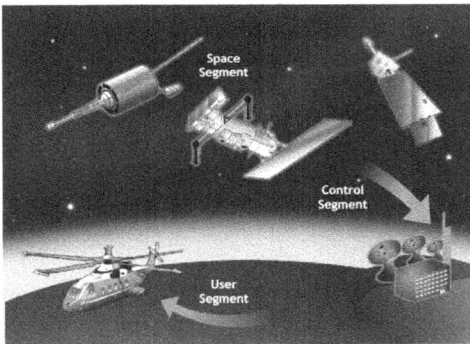

- The **Control Segment** has the ground stations and systems that track the satellites and monitor their status. It includes a **Master Control Station** in Colorado, its backup and 5 **monitoring stations** around the world, including their **ground antennas**. Their data is sent to and processed at the MCS, then used to refine and update satellite navigational signals, including the sending of new ephemeris and clock data to the satellites. Otherwise, its main tasks are to:

  - manage performance

  - upload navigation data

  - monitor satellites

- The **User Segment** includes the receivers that select satellites automatically, track their signals and calculate the time taken for them to reach the receiver. *Single channel* receivers move from one

satellite to the next in sequence. Although this can be very quick, it is not fast enough for navigation. *Multi-channel* receivers (most suitable for aircraft) continuously monitor position data whilst locking on to the next satellites. *Continuous receivers*, with up to 12 channels, can eliminate GDOP problems (see *Errors*) by watching more than four satellites. GPS receiver antennas are semi-omnidirectional, and the active element is a quarter wavelength of 1.6 GHz, or approximately 2.5 cm.

GPS signals are line-of-sight, and will not pass through water, buildings or solid objects in general, although they do pass through clouds, glass and plastic (regardless of that, though, the best conditions for reception are in clear areas with open skies). In simple terms, each satellite transmits a signal composed of a noise-like digital code (a Gold code) modulated on a microwave carrier frequency known as L1, whose timing is precisely controlled by an atomic clock. A GPS receiver can tune into a satellite signal by generating ts own copy of the Gold code and carrier, then matching their timings to the incoming signal. The differences are then converted to distance.

In more detail, satellites transmit a **Coarse Acquisition** (C/A) code, with a **navigation data message** encoded in it. Navigation data is transmitted every 30 seconds as frames, that contain 5 subframes.

Clock	Ephemeris	Ephemeris	Almanac	Almanac

Because even atomic clocks can drift, the first frame tells the receiver the difference between satellite and true GPS time, as defined by the ground stations. Subframes 2 and 3 include details of that satellite's exact orbital path for the next 4 hours or so, which is called the **Ephemeris**, and unique to that satellite (it is used to correct for small disturbances). The last 2 subframes make up the **Almanac**, which has less precise positioning details of the other satellites, valid for around 6 months. Thus, the receiver knows which ones should be in view and searches for their C/A codes. It can then establish the elevation and azimuth of a satellite and your range from it. The speed of light is assumed, as the signals come from space.

The C/A code is the ranging code used by the receiver to measure the distance (also called *Standard Positioning Service*, or SPS, as distinct from the military P code). It is a 1023-bit pseudorandom number (PRN) that is transmitted at 1.023 Mbits/second, so it is repeated every millisecond.

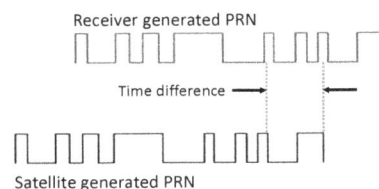

The receiver knows the PRN code of each satellite and is able to generate them internally. As the satellite includes a time tag (referenced to GPS time) in its signal, indicating when the PRN started, on reception, the receiver can compare when its own version started with the arrival time of the satellite's PRN. The difference in time (in nanoseconds) corresponds to the distance between the satellite and receiver. The result is a pseudo random range.

The system depends very much on precise timing between satellites and receivers. Although they generate time-codes together, satellite signals lag behind due to their distance. If they are out by 0.6 seconds, the satellite will be 11 160 miles away. 0.7 seconds will be 13 020 miles, and so on.

Time measurement therefore consists of:

- The transit time of the signal

- The time offset between transmitter and receiver

The timing accuracy is actually down to one billionth of a second. The General Theory of Relativity predicts that time runs slower with more gravity, and the atomic clocks in satellites indeed run slightly faster (2 seconds over UTC) than they would on the surface, so corrections have to be made continually. If you are off by even 1 millisecond, your position would be in error by over 300 km, so, for 1 m accuracy, time measurement must be accurate to within 3 nanoseconds. Satellites therefore use atomic clocks for high precision, and continuously transmit their positions, plus a code number in a set code, at exactly the same time. The signal is modulated with a pseudo-random code that allows the time of the transmission to be recovered by the receiver. Instead of trying to distinguish the signal from the Earth's background noise, it is sent as Pseudo Random Noise because it is not really as random as normal noise.

Although noise will change randomly, the GPS signal will have the same sequence. Over time, more matches will be found for the PRN than for the noise, so the GPS signal can be found. This technique allows all satellites to use the same frequency, with individual ones being identified by their Pseudo-Random Noise code (PRN).

The system thus works loosely like DME, except that is it passive - the time it takes for a signal to travel from a satellite to your receiver is multiplied by the speed of light to obtain a distance measurement, which gives you a *Line Of Position* (LOP). One, of course, is no good by itself, and you actually need 4 LOPs* to determine your position in terms of latitude, longitude and altitude.

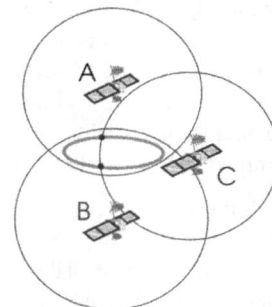

*The job can actually be done with three satellites - the fourth is there to correct for timing errors by calculating the position a second time, and the results will differ by an amount equal to the timing error. As calculations are involved, and are therefore subject to receiver clock error, the distance is called a pseudorange.

For example, you must be somewhere on the surface of a sphere centred on Satellite A, and similarly for Satellite B. In fact, you must be somewhere on the circle formed where they intersect. With Satellite C, the three spheres intersect at only two points, and you must logically be at one of them, which is where the fourth satellite comes in - there are techniques for deciding which one, using "bad mathematics" according to Garmin. Mostly the wrong one is discarded because it puts you somewhere completely weird, like 100 miles out in space.

The basic elements transmitted from a satellite are:

- clock offset from UTC

- ephemeris data

- almanac data

- ionospheric delays (see *Errors*, later)

- satellite health data

- satellite clock corrections

As each satellite contains **almanac** data for the entire constellation, a GPS receiver only needs to download it from one satellite to figure out the approximate location of them all. Almanac information is transmitted every 12.5 minutes and takes **12.5 minutes to download** (30 seconds per data frame), so it will take at least that time before accurate fixes can be determined (the initial setup is known as a *cold start*). This data becomes stale over time or if you move the receiver to another location more than several hundred kilometers away. The Almanac covers:

- Satellites that are operating normally

- The PRN codes of available satellites

- Predicted positions of satellites in their orbits

The receiver can then determine which satellites are in view and their relative geometry, then which are the four best ones to track for the best lines of position.

As each satellite transmits only its own **ephemeris** data, the receiver must get it from each one in view. Ephemeris data is transmitted every 30 seconds, and takes 12 seconds to download. It is valid for up to 4-6 hours.

Normally, when two PRNs are multiplied together, they give a value of near zero. A satellite's PRN is multiplied by the L1 carrier (described below) at different time shift intervals, until it finds a lock-on, when a particular time shift results in a high multiplication value. Thus, all the other satellites are filtered out and the time-shift required for the lock-on is used to calculate the satellite's range and extract the navigation message from the C/A code.

By decoding the navigation message, the receiver gets the data it needs to correct the pseudo range. When the two code patterns match, the satellite and receiver can be synchronised, which is the first step in finding an LOP (*initial acquisition*). The receiver in your aircraft can generate the same pseudo random code as the satellite because it has its own code book with them all in. The code sequence is started when the local clock says the satellite should have started transmitting its PRN.

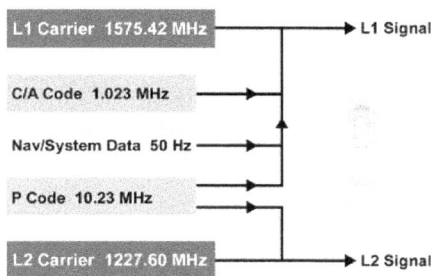

The x, y, z position from the centre of the Earth is translated into latitude and longitude using the WGS 84 model, and GPS time is translated into UTC. Your velocity is calculated with a combination of your rate of change of position and Doppler shift from the L1 frequencies of different satellites, compared to the receiver's L1 oscillation frequency.

In fact, two UHF frequencies are used, L1 and L2*. The (higher) L1 frequency is 1575.42 MHz and L2 is 1227.60 MHz. Both are multiples of a base frequency of 10.23 MHz (L1 is 10.23 x 154) which is generated by a crystal controlled by an atomic clock. All satellites transmit on both frequencies, but their outputs are multiplexed so they can share the same carrier.

The higher frequency transmits the C/A and P codes.

*L2C (and M for the military) was added in 2005 so that cheaper receivers could use proper signals instead of having to make do with the carrier, because they couldn't decrypt the military code. L5 was coming in 2015.

L5 is a civilian frequency that allows the avionics to compute ionospheric corrections without the need for a separate SBAS, like WAAS or EGNOS.

The (digital) information is superimposed on the carriers with BPSK modulation (*Binary Phase Key Shifting*), where

code changes cause a 180° phase shift in the carrier (i.e. phase modulation reverses the carrier wave). Being digital, the data exists as strings of 1s and 0s, which are simpler to transmit, more reliable, and less prone to jamming because redundancy checking can be used. The P (Precise) code is transmitted on L1 and L2. As it runs at 10.23 MHz, it is ten times more accurate than C/A. It can be encrypted (as Y Code) and is therefore almost impossible to jam. Comparing the L1 and L2 frequencies at the receiver can compensate for ionospheric propagation errors. In other words, differences between the frequencies tell you what the ionosphere is doing - radio waves change speed as they pass through it. As the delay is inversely proportional to frequency, it can be calculated and virtually eliminated.

SIGNAL AUGMENTATION

The majority of PBN operations can be conducted using unaugmented satellite signals.

GROUND BASED

Ground Based Augmentation Systems (GBAS) are the practical application of Local Area Differential GPS. Differential GPS was a workaround (by the US Coastguard!) for the intentional errors in the C/A code for unauthorised (non-military) users of the GPS system using a LORAN data channel. It uses a fifth signal from a precisely surveyed ground based transmitter whose position can be compared against that of the receiver. The difference is the intentional error. The nearer the receiver is to a DGPS ground station, the more accurate is the fix.

In other words, corrections are sent **directly to aircraft receivers** from ground stations at airports, typically within about 20-30 nm (the closer the better). The VDB signal provides error correction & integrity data, and approach data for more than one runway. The coverage is within 35° of the final approach path up to 15 nm from the landing threshold, and within 10° between 15 - 20 nm.

When even that is not enough, extra GPS transmitters nearby (pseudolites) can increase the accuracy right down to less than the size of a manhole cover (GBAS + GPS is also called *Local Area Augmentation System* in the US). The 787 can do a GLS down to and along the runway.

In summary, GBAS can provide two services:

- Precision approach - down to 200 feet at Sydney.

- Horizontal Positioning for RNAV operations in terminal areas.

SATELLITE BASED

Here, Differential GPS is extended to cover a larger area. The idea is to measure the signal errors from the satellites and provide separate corrections for ranging, ephemeris, clock and ionospheric errors. Correction data is then transmitted directly to **geostationary** satellites, and re-transmitted to the user (the frequency band of the data link is identical to that of the GPS signals). Pseudorange measurements to the geostationary satellites can also be made as if they were GPS satellites. SBAS regionally augments GPS and GLONASS by making them suitable (as a standalone navigation aid) for safety critical procedures such as landing.

The FAA's **Wide Area Augmentation System** (WAAS) allows GPS to be used throughout a flight, including a Cat I precision approach. Satellite signals are received by precisely surveyed ground stations, which detect errors and send them to a Master Station (WMS), which in turn adds correction information based on geographical area (which is fairly constant) and uplinks a correction message to geostationary satellites (around the Equator and way above the other satellites) for rebroadcast, from which pseudorange measurements can be made, as with normal satellites. This improves the 95% signal accuracy from 100m to 7m, but it can be better than 2 m. *Lateral Precision Vertical* (LPV) has a lateral accuracy as good as ILS, with vertical capability. Unlike BARO VNAV, SBAS vertical guidance is not subject to altimeter errors, non-standard temperatures or lapse rates.

When SBAS integrity messages are used, the additional satellites that would be required for RAIM are not needed, because the messages are available wherever the satellite signal can be received. WAAS currently uses two satellites over the Atlantic and Pacific Oceans.

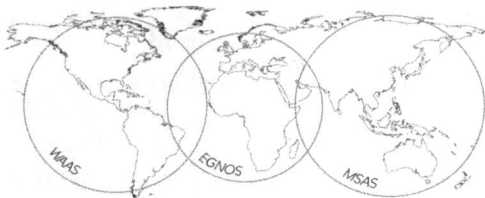

EGNOS, or the *European Geostationary Navigation Overlay Service* is the European equivalent to WAAS (there is also MSAS in Japan and GAGAN in India). It has INMARSAT satellites broadcasting GPS look-alike signals (on UHF), so the coverage is limited to between 80N and 80S (EGNOS has a primary service area further North than WAAS). It is designed to improve accuracy to **1-2 m horizontally** and **3-5 m vertically**. Integrity and safety are improved by alerting users within 6 seconds of a malfunction, as opposed to the normal 3 hours.

AIRCRAFT BASED (ABAS)

This uses redundant elements (i.e. excess information that is not otherwise needed) within the GNSS constellation to develop integrity control (ABAS does not improve positioning accuracy, as you get with GBAS and SBAS). ABAS using GNSS information only is RAIM (*Receiver Autonomous Integrity Monitoring*), described below.

A system using information from additional on-board sensors is AAIM (*Aircraft Autonomous Integrity Monitoring*).

Typical sensors used are barometric altimeters, clocks and inertial navigation systems.

Although the ground stations monitor satellites and detect faults, it can take up to two hours for an error to be corrected. **Receiver Autonomous Integrity Monitoring** (RAIM) is a bit quicker than that. It is achieved within the receiver, which monitors satellites and verifies their signals, so an extra satellite is needed to detect corrupt information. For the bad signal to be isolated as well, you need one more. Without RAIM, accuracy is not assured, and you still need 4 satellites for a 3D fix. Thus, Basic RAIM (fault detection) needs 5 satellites in order to work, and 6 (with good positioning) to continue working after a failure is detected (*Fault Detection & Exclusion*, or FDE). If a satellite is excluded, the system works as Basic RAIM and can be used as an independent means of navigation.

If RAIM is available, the integrity limits are 4 nm for oceanic, 2 nm for enroute, 1 nm for terminal work and 0.3 nm for GPS approaches. If RAIM is not available, the GPS must be integrated with other systems, such as DME/DME fixing, with traditional equipment (VOR, etc.) as backup. If the GPS is the only equipment meeting the B-RNAV standards, RAIM availability must be confirmed before flight.

5 positions are calculated using 4 of the 5 visible satellites:

> ABCD
> ABCE
> ABDE
> ACDE
> BCDE

The signal is assumed to be reliable if they all agree within a certain tolerance.

RAIM can be assisted with *baroaiding* (barometric aiding), which uses barometric information from the aircraft's altitude encoder to reduce the number of real satellites required by one. Barometric altitude is the datum for altitude information such as MDA. The idea is to convert the aircraft's altitude to a range from the centre of the Earth, which can then be used for consistency checks with the pseudo ranges from the satellites that are used to create the fix.

Another technique is *clock coasting*, which uses atomic clocks in the user segment to reduce clock bias (below).

ERRORS

The effects of the errors below are smallest when the satellites are directly overhead and greatest when they are near the horizon, as the signal is affected for a longer time. Having said that, the most accurate fix comes from 3 satellites with a low elevation above the horizon, 120° from each other and a fourth directly overhead.

- **Clock Bias**. As the receiver's clock is not as precise as the atomic clocks in the satellites, there can be a large difference in the measurements, which can introduce a ranging error. When a receiver starts up, its own code is inaccurate by an unknown error called clock bias, or clock offset, against GPS reference time. In addition, the size of the atomic clocks in satellites are necessarily smaller than ground-based ones would be. The receiver corrects by running a series of simultaneous equations. It must be aware of the satellite's position, which is where the ephemeris comes in. Signals are monitored by control segment ground stations and the corrections sent to the Master station, which makes the necessary corrections then relays them to the satellites.

- Satellite **clock drift**. Although the orbital paths of GPS satellites could theoretically be predicted under Kepler's laws of planetary motion, the assumption that the Earth is a perfect sphere of uniform density is not correct, and gravity from other heavenly bodies (e.g. the Moon and the Sun) have their own effects on top of Earth gravity. There is also very slight atmospheric drag, because satellites are not travelling in a perfect vacuum, plus the impact of photons of light emitted by the sun both directly and reflected off the Earth and Moon. This solar radiation pressure is a function of a satellite's size and orientation, distance from the sun, etc., but the end result is that satellites headed towards the Sun are slowed down, and accelerated when headed away. This *clock drift* is virtually impossible to estimate accurately, and is the largest unmeasurable source of error.

- **Ephemeris** (position) **error**. This error is caused by the satellite not being where the receiver thinks it is. That is, there are errors in the satellite's calculation of its own position due to the gravitational effects mentioned above from the sun, moon and other planets. Ground monitoring stations check satellite positions every 12 hours, so the maximum error is 2.5 metres. The computers at the master control station can predict the satellite's future position at a specific time, which is compared with its actual position from the monitor stations. Updated information on future positions is then uploaded.

- **Ionospheric Propagation**. UHF signals are not normally refractable by the ionosphere, but even the very small amount that they suffer from increases the time taken for the signal to reach the receiver as it bends through a shallow angle, as shown above. The total distance covered by the red signal is greater than the (correct) green line, especially when they pass through the layers of the ionosphere at a shallow angle (this is less of a problem when the satellite is overhead the receiver). The signal is also subject to attenuation as it passes through the layer of ions, which is effectively thicker and therefore has more effect at a shallow angle. The combined error is called the *ionospheric group delay* which, when combined with the delay from other satellites can produce a total position error of around 5 m. Ionospheric group delay is inversely proportional to the square of the frequency so, if two frequencies are received, as with military systems, by noting the time delay between the L1 and L2 signals, much of the effect of atmospheric propagation can be removed internally by the receiver (as determined from the satellite navigation message). The corrections are imperfect, although they are slow and can be averaged over time. The model of the ionosphere is corrected by the ground stations every 12 hours, so the maximum position error is 5 metres. This is the worst natural error.

- **Receiver noise**. Internal noise within receiver circuits can cause position errors of up to 0.3 m.

- **Signal noise**. Similar to Receiver noise.

- **Tropospheric**. Water vapour in the atmosphere affects refraction. The maximum error from tropospheric propagation is between 0.3 - 0.5 m.

- **Multi-path reflection.** Antennas should be fitted on the upper fuselage near the Centre of Gravity, as shadowing by parts of an aircraft may stop signals from being received or cause them to come from different directions. Some frequencies, such as 109.5 MHz, have been known to cause the GPS not to work if the antenna is not sited properly. The maximum error is 0.6 m.

- **C/A Selective Availability**. Now discontinued, but it used to be done by dithering satellite clocks.

- **Manoeuvring Errors**. Caused by aircraft attitudes and similar to Multi-path reflection.

- **GDOP/PDOP**. When satellites are too close to each other, vertical and horizontal position accuracy is degraded, because the lines of constant range do not cut cleanly (the optimum is 60°) resulting in *Geometric (Position) Dilution of Precision*, where you end up anywhere inside a range of positions rather than just one. ICAO requires a PDOP/GDOP of less than 6 for en-route navigation, and 3 or less for non-precision approaches (4 is considered to be good). The normal accuracy of 100 m for 95% of the time assumes a PDOP of 3 and a range error of 33.3 m (range errors are multiplied by PDOP to obtain stated accuracies). GDOP is minimised by RAIM.

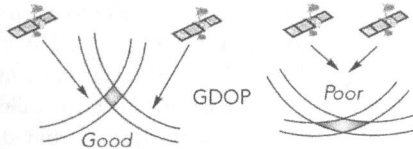

OPERATION

Although it is tempting to use GPS all the time, remember that it is electrical, and therefore reserves the right to go offline at any moment, without warning. The antenna in a GPS is live as well, and equally liable to stop working. A GPS may also have a database of airspace and frequencies inside - although not so important for VFR use, it is still the mark of a professional to keep it up to date.

For GPS approaches, you use a CDI in the same way as you would for an ILS, except that the needle deflection is measured in terms of distance rather than degrees off course. This means that the instrument's sensitivity is fixed all the way down through the approach, and is not so sensitive in the final stages. However, the sensitivity does vary according to the age of your receiver. For a non-WAAS capable one, you have three levels. In *en-route mode* (more than 30 miles from the destination or departure point), one dot is equal to 1 nautical mile. Inside those figures, it reduces to *terminal mode*, which is one fifth, so *full deflection* is now 1 nm. In *approach mode* (within 2 nm of the FAF), full deflection is 0.3 nm left or right of the centreline. At the MAP, the sensitivity returns to the terminal level.

WAAS capable receivers have a CDI sensitivity of only 2 nm in en route mode. The terminal level remains the same, but approach mode reduces to the *lesser* of 0.2 nm or 2°. The sensitivity of an LPV approach is 350 feet either side of the centreline at the threshold, or 70 feet per dot!

DIRECTION FINDING   062 02 01

Direction finding is the process of determining the straight line (Great Circle) along which a transmitter is located, so you need a chart that allows straight lines to represent Great Circles as closely as possible, so you can measure the angles correctly. For aviation purposes, this is

normally a Lambert projection. By using more than one transmitter, you can get a series of position lines with which you should be able to determine where you are. The accuracy is not brilliant, but it is enough to be a supplement for dead reckoning navigation, so it is useful when the weather is bad and you can't see much, assuming that you identify the correct station.

The most basic method is to turn a directional antenna round until the signal disappears.

VDF

The purpose of *VHF Direction Finding* is to provide directional assistance in times of difficulty, rather than for general navigation, so a typical frequency it might be used on is 121.5 MHz (the full range is between **118-137 MHz**, or metric), although military stations tend to use UHF. One or more ATC stations can get a bearing for you to steer (QDM) to get to their location from your transmissions, so the minimum equipment is a VHF radio. On its own, a direction-finding station can only find your position in relation to itself - for an exact position, you need two or even three more, who will all report to a Master Station. As well, you must work out the headings needed from the information given.

Being based on VHF, VDF is subject to the usual limitations (line of sight, multipath, etc.), so the higher you are, the better the results you will get. You must transmit for a few seconds for a bright line to spread from the centre of a screen to the outside which is marked with compass bearings at the ground station.

The full range of services available could include:

- Emergency Cloudbreak
- Emergency No-compass Homing
- Homing
- Fix - only on 121.5 MHz
- Track-out Assistance
- Time & Distance Estimates

However, ICAO only recognizes homing, with no compensation for wind, which is actually the only element that most pilots are aware of, receive training on, or use.

The following services are available, assuming no wind:

- **QDM** - magnetic bearing *to* (with no wind)
- **QDR** - magnetic bearing *from*
- **QUJ** - true bearing *to* (to be steered, with no wind)
- **QTE** - true bearing *from*

The QTE & QDM are the only serious ones - a QTE allows you to plot a line on a map from the station and the QDM gives you a magnetic heading to steer.

When a position is given in relation to another point, or in lat & long, it is a **QTF**. When positions are given by heading or bearing & distance from a known point that is not the station making the report, the known point shall be from the centre of an aerodrome, a prominent town or geographic feature, in that order.

A series of bearings is a QDL (so QDL QDM means several QDMs). QGE is the distance from the relevant point. A VDF letdown exists where ATC give you QDMs, and you work out the headings to steer, so the responsibility lies with the pilot. A QGH is an approach based on VDF bearings, where a VDF unit is prepared to give you assistance, based on VDF bearings (the responsibility lies with the controller). Older equipment uses a cathode ray tube on which the line appears (like a radar sweep) pointing to where your transmission is coming from. More modern digital equipment uses a circle of LEDs at 10° intervals, which will show the same information, with a digital readout in the centre (see left). The controller can store the last transmission, if busy with something else at the time.

Accuracy comes in these classes, in relation to bearing or position, and will be included in the transmission:

Class	Bearing	Position
A	±2°	5 nm
B	±5°	20 nm
C	±10°	50 nm
D	<C	<C

Multipath signals may result in bearing errors.

The Adcock RDF Antenna

The Adcock antenna has been used for many years for Radio Direction Finding. It is basically an interferometer, and was originally developed to overcome Night Effect, which creates spurious signals in the horizontal parts of an ADF loop. With the Adcock, the top part of the loop has been dispensed with and the bottom part is sometimes shielded with an earthed metallic covering.

If the antenna is lined up on the four cardinal points, and an aircraft is to the North, the N-S poles will pick up the maximum signals, and the E-W ones will pick up none. As the aircraft moves to the East or West, the E-W poles will pick up a signal strength and move the needle accordingly (the N-S poles are connected to the upper & lower plates of a CRT and the E-W poles to the left & right ones). The system works on phase difference, and directionality can be changed electronically.

Since this antenna only responds to vertically polarized components, poor performance can occur when the signal is horizontal or nearly horizontal.

A series of such antennas is used for VDF operations, in a circle round a pole.

RADAR

Although technology has improved matters, radar is still quite a crude instrument which requires an understanding of how it works in order to understand its information correctly, especially when you consider the speed of the waves against the ranges involved. Very short intervals of time in the order of millionths of a second have to be measured with considerable accuracy for the best results.

The use of radar improves aircraft spacing and safety - the word stands for *Radio Direction and Ranging*, but the system was called RDF (*Radio Direction Finding*) until 1943, when the name was changed to harmonise with the Americans (in those days it just about got the distance right). It works on the basis that microwave pulses can be reflected (or echoed) off suitable objects, and the time between transmission and reflection can be used to calculate the distance because the speed of transmission is known (the reflection of signals is called scattering. Reflections in the exact opposite direction are called *backscatter*). The "blips" representing the objects are displayed on a video monitor and a controller can see the relative positions of aircraft reflecting any pulses.

The radar beam is rather like that from a lighthouse, as the antenna focusses the pulses in one direction with the most energy concentrated in the centre. VHF does not provide the bandwidth required for the short pulses that allow good target definition*, so SHF bands are currently used. Thus, radar is limited to line of sight.

*For accuracy, the leading edge of the pulse must be sharp, so it needs to jump to its maximum value suddenly. This is a serious matter when using longer waves, because radio waves with different frequencies have to be mixed, so the process is better done with very short (centimetric) waves.

In most countries, outside of terminal control areas, radar is used more as a monitoring device but, in others, you are more or less under radar control all the time and you may very rarely follow a flight planned route. You will be given details of other traffic according to the clock system, such as "fast mover at 6 o'clock".

The word *pulses*, mentioned above, means that short bursts of electromagnetic energy are mixed with relatively long periods of silence (*relatively long*, in electronic terms, means less than a thousandth of a second). *Continuous Wave radar* is used in radio altimeters and the Doppler system.

Pulses were used originally because early radar sets used thermionic valves as opposed to the transistors of today. A valve small enough to produce the short waves required would overheat when used continuously, so using pulses allowed them suitable periods to cool off.

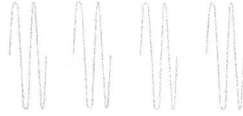

RF energy is created with magnetrons, which bunch together electrons that fly past alternately charged grids (essentially diodes that are influenced by a magnetic field). The energy is released at intervals (the PRF), which are determined by the range required, and discussed later.

The range of a target is determined by measuring the time taken for a pulse of energy to travel there and back. It takes around 3 microseconds for a wave to travel around 1 000 m, but it has to get back so, between transmission and reception there will be a time interval of around 6 m/s for every 1 000 m of (slant) range. This is *primary radar*.

Radio signals weaken over distance and, as the pulses must make two journeys (there and back), the range is necessarily limited. The blip on the screen is also quite large, and aircraft very close together cannot be told apart, unless the beam is narrow enough to pass between them (a 1 millisecond pulse takes up 300 m of space). Finally, radio waves can be bent by the atmosphere or screened by mountains or buildings, and different aircraft return signals differently, in terms of shape or surface (long wavelength is required to penetrate cloud).

The strength of an echo received back at a radar set varies with the size of the target and its distance. As the returning pulse is not reflected, but re-radiated*, it decreases in strength in the same way as it did on its way out, so the received signal in this case has one third of one third of its original strength, meaning one ninth. As power is proportional to the square of the field strength, echo power is inversely proportional to the distance of the target[4]. So every time you double the range of a target, you reduce the power of its echo by 2^4 or 16 times (or, to double the effective range of primary radar, the power output must be increased by a factor of 16). Trebling the range reduces it by 3^4 or 81 times.

*Pulses make valence electrons ripple and release energy.

The transmitter has to:

- Generate very high power at high frequencies. The radio frequency (RF) energy is produced inside the **HF oscillator** by a *magnetron*, which is a piece of copper in which there are cavities surrounded by a strong magnet. The electrons are made to spin within the cavities and set up the microwaves, hence their use in microwave ovens.

- Be capable of being switched on and off rapidly to produce pulses. This is done by the **modulator**.

- Send out the pulses at regular intervals (as per the *pulse recurrence rate)* via the **synchroniser**, which regulates the rate at which pulses are sent (i.e. sets the PRF) and resets the timing clock for range determination for each pulse. Signals from the synchronizer are sent simultaneously to the transmitter, which sends a new pulse, and to the display, which resets the return sweep.

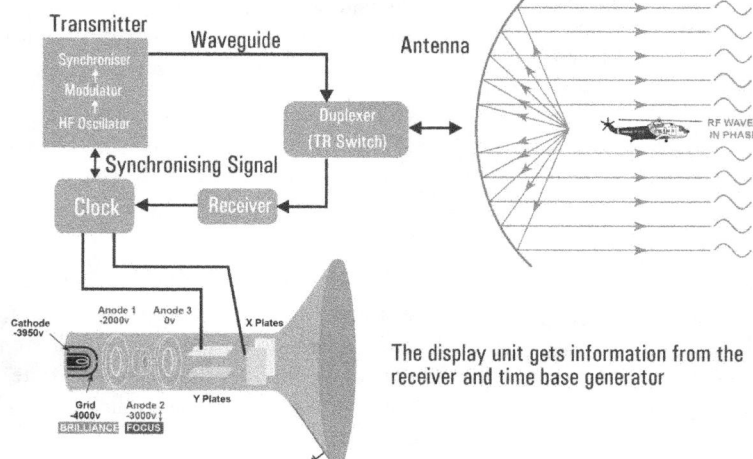

The display unit gets information from the receiver and time base generator

capt.gs

The generated pulses travel through either coaxial cable or a hollow, generally rectangular, metal tube called a *wave guide,* which prevents excessive power loss because it is tuned to the wavelength. The RF energy is injected into the waveguide by a probe, which is simply an antenna that only radiates into the waveguide.

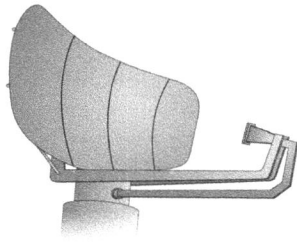

A waveguide is not required for weather radar because it uses slots on a flat (planar) array.

The clock drives the deflector plates of the screen used for the display. It oscillates at a very exact frequency, geared down by dividers. The clock also ensures that the spot of light that moves around the screen is cut off at appropriate moments to keep the screen clear (blacking out flyback - by making the grid (brilliance) negative, the fly-back is suppressed, meaning that you won't see the lines where the pulse flies back from the end of one line to the beginning of the new line). Range markers are displayed with a saw-tooth wave.

The problem is that the signals are very different - the transmitted signal is very strong, but the received one is very weak and the system must be sensitive enough to detect it. In other words, the receiver circuits must be protected against the high energy from the transmitted signals, otherwise they would be fried when the system is switched on. The solution is not necessarily to switch between transmit and receive, but to route the signals to the appropriate places, which is where the **duplexer** comes in. It is a routing device that directs outgoing pulses to the antenna and incoming pulses from the antenna to the receiver. The speed at which it returns to the receive position helps to determine minimum range.

The antenna is a parabolic dish, shaped according to its function. For example, the orange peel produces a wide narrow beam. A parabolic dish produces a focussed beam, but it spreads with distance. A phase array has a series of conducting elements like small dipoles that are arranged in a line and fed with signals that are in phase with each other. The interference patterns produce a pencil beam.

Truncated Paraboloid	Paraboloid	Orange Peel Paraboloid	Parabolic Cylinder
2D Surveillance	Target Tracking	Height Finding	2D Surveillance

There is a protruding radiating element (a probe) somewhere in the middle, which beams the signals to the face of the dish, to form the beam into the desired shape and go in the direction required.

The dish and element work in the reverse sense when receiving signals - the larger the dish, the more of the weak signal can be received. If the width of the main beam is taken from where the signal strength drops to half of what it is at the centre, you can find the beam width with this formula:

$$\text{Beam Width}° = \frac{2 \times \text{wavelength in cm}}{\text{diameter (ft)}}$$

So a reflector 4 feet wide using 3 cm waves would have a beam width of around 1.5°. Here are some common sizes:

Dish Size	Beam Width
10″	9.5°
12″	7.5°
18″	5°

Advantages of a narrow beam are:

- getting bearings more easily
- greater concentration of energy
- more range
- target definition

A *short pulse length* with a *narrow beam* gets the best picture.

As the antenna is expected to work with a transmitter (horizontally) and a receiver (vertically), it should be able to produce a thin beam, and receive a wide one, respectively. A perfectly directional antenna would be very large and unwieldy so, to use small ones, we have to live with unwanted radiations known as sidelobes, which can show multiple targets for one aircraft at close range.

The advantage of using a slotted antenna is to virtually eliminate lateral lobes, and to concentrate more energy in the main beam. The receiver converts the microwave returns into electrical signals that are amplified, because they have only a fraction of the power that was sent originally. Thus, the receiver should have a high overall gain, with little random noise in its circuitry. Because of this high amplification capability, no RF stage is required.

Finally, the signal is sent to the *Plan Position Indicator* (PPI), which is called that because it displays the returns as if you were looking from the top, as opposed to the original display, which showed the returns from the side.

The display's timebase (the frequency with which the picture is repainted) is linked to the antenna, in that when it passes through North, so does the beam painted on the display. As a pulse is fired off, a spot of light moves from

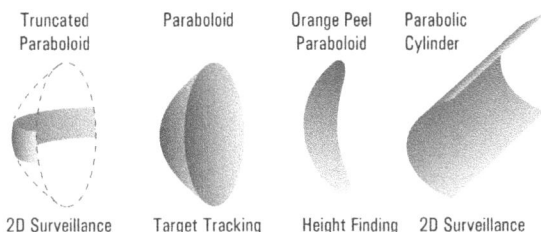

the centre of the tube to the outside, reaching the circumference before the next pulse goes. The effect is a line of light rotating round the screen.

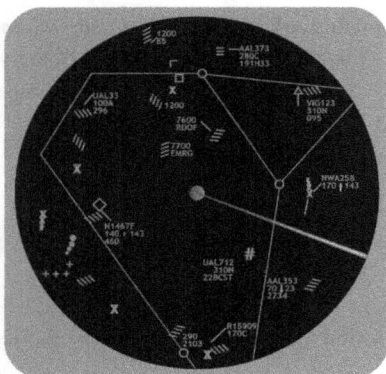

When a return is received, the electron flow is increased and the intensity of the display increases to a spot which fades away slowly as the line moves on.

Calculations

You can calculate the distance between the transmitter and the target because the speed of the radio wave is known, and the direction the antenna is pointing at the time supplies the bearing. It takes 12.36 microseconds for a radio wave to travel out and back for each nautical mile of range (radar mile), or 123.6 microseconds for each 10 nm.

Given that radar speed is 300 m per microsecond, the leading edge of the average pulse is already several hundred metres on its way when the transmitting stops.

Put more mathematically, if the time delay is Dt, then you can find the range (R) with:

$$R = \frac{cDt}{2}$$

where c = the speed of light, and it is divided by 2 because the pulse train has to get to the target and back again.

Using C as the speed of light, 299,700 km/sec, the *Maximum Theoretical Unambiguous Range** will be determined firstly by the *Pulse Repetition Frequency* (PRF)**, because pulses have to return to the transmitter before the next ones are sent, plus the *Pulse Interval* (PI).

*If an echo is received from a long range target after the pulse following the one it relates to, the radar uses the very much shorter time between the second pulse and the echo, and calculates a shorter range. Range ambiguity occurs when the time taken for an echo to return from a target is greater than the Pulse Repetition Time. For example, if the interval between pulses is 1000 microseconds, and the return time of a pulse from a distant target is 1200 microseconds, the apparent distance of the target is only 200 microseconds.

To increase the unambiguous range, you have to increase the PRT, which means increasing the PRF.

**It is more correct to say that the PRF is limited by range. To see targets up to say, 25 nm, the maximum PRF is around 3000 pulses per second. It can be determined by:

$$Max\ PRF = \frac{80\ 000}{nm}$$

Simply replace the letters *nm* with the distance required. 80,000 represents half the speed of light in nautical miles.

In fact, the range is determined by the time *between* pulses (the *Pulse Recurrence Period* or *Interval*), which must be long enough for a pulse to go out to the target and return. It follows that, if it is too short, this cannot happen. As the number of pulses per second depends on the length of the interval, we say that maximum range depends on PRF. As an example, the maximum range of Long Range Surveillance Radar is between 200 - 300 nm.

The number of pulses per second is the Pulse Repetition Frequency (PRF), so the further the target is away, the longer must be the PRP and, by extension, the PRF. A shorter PRP means more pulses per second and a higher PRF. The two are related:

$$PRF = \frac{1}{PI\ (PRP)}$$

With this formula, make sure you use the right numbers!

In between pulses, you also need some dead (rest) time.

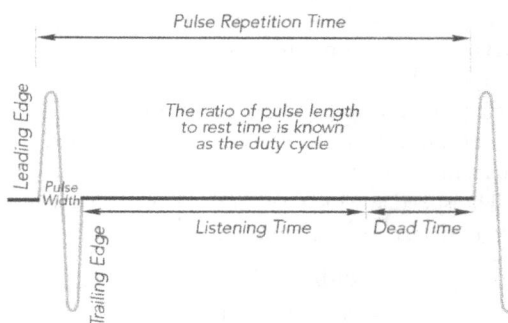

This is because a pulsed wave doesn't just stop when it hits a target, but carries on, and may be reflected from other objects way back. At 100 000 yards, for example, it would take around 610 microseconds to travel out and back from the target. If the time interval between pulses is only 610 microseconds, any reflected pulses from further away would be received after the next pulse and produce confusing results, such as a false echo near to the station.

Thus, the interval between pulses needs to be made a little bit wider to allow all possible echoes to be received. The sweep of the beam will still take 610 microseconds, but the spot on the screen will be held at the start during the dead time until the next pulse is ready.

MAXIMUM RANGE

Although it mostly affects the minimum range (see below), the pulse width can also affect the maximum detection range, as the energy depends on pulse width and output power (a long pulse has more energy and returns a stronger signal). *Maximum Theoretical Unambiguous Range* (MTR) in km is found by:

$$MTR = \frac{C}{2 \times PRF}$$

PRF (if you know the range) is found by:

$$PRF = \frac{C}{2 \times Range\ (km)}$$

Example: Assuming transmission power is enough, the maximum range of a ground radar with a PRF of 450 pulses per second is 333 km.

MINIMUM RANGE

This (or, more technically, the dead zone at close range) is set by the pulse width (plus the recovery time of the duplexer), because a long pulse could still be receiving part of an echo from one target while starting to get the information from a second, if they are close together (with continuous wave radar, the minimum range restriction is removed, so you can measure short distances, hence its use with radio altimeters). Put more simply, the receiver is switched off while the pulse is being transmitted.

The minimum range is around half the pulse width, as is range resolution. As a pulse width of a microsecond will cover over 300 m, two aircraft within 150 m of each other will appear on the screen as one, so the pulse width can also affect the ability to discriminate between targets that are close together. Based on the scale in the diagram above, if the duty cycle was 1:1000, and the pulse was 1 microsecond, the next one would be over 10 feet away. The transmitter is idle a lot of the time.

Moving Target Indication

Strong radar returns from stationary objects (e.g. terrain and buildings) can mask a primary radar return from an aircraft, especially if it is at low level. MTI uses Doppler to eliminate returns from fixed objects. That is, only returns that show a Doppler shift (moving targets) will be shown, but **targets at constant range will not show up**.

Secondary Surveillance Radar

This is a development of a system introduced during the Second World War called *Identification Friend or Foe* (IFF), which was supposed to distinguish between friendly and enemy aircraft. Friendly aircraft had a small transmitter that produced a longer blip on the screen, so anything shorter was an enemy. It was codenamed Parrot (or Canary) by the British, which probably has something to do with the current use of the word *Squawk* to mean *transmit the relevant codes*, which you dial up on the transponder and which will appear next to your blip with your height readout, depending on the type of transponder you have.

SSR improves on primary radar* by using double-pulse secondary equipment to provide more information, hence the name. An interrogating ground station sends a rotating beam of pulse modulated signals in all directions in a form that is recognised as a request for information. Participating aircraft carry a *transponder* (for *transmitter/responder*) that receives the interrogation pulse (1030 MHz ±0.2 MHz), superimposes information on it and sends it right back on another paired frequency (1090 MHz). Aside from being 60 MHz apart, this means, first of all, that the range of operation can be doubled (the power of the echoed pulse has nothing to do with range, so is only subject to normal radio range limitations) and that the blip on the screen can be made much smaller, together with information that makes it more easily identifiable to ATC, because the pulses can be coded. As well, there is no storm clutter, as the principle of echo return is not used. Computers can provide predicted tracks and collision warnings, etc.

*Primary radar is more accurate in terms of bearing and distance.

The following can be presented on the radar screen:

- Squawk Code
- Flight Level
- Callsign, Flight Number or Registration
- Groundspeed

You cannot set the number 8! Watch for this in questions that ask you to choose between valid codes

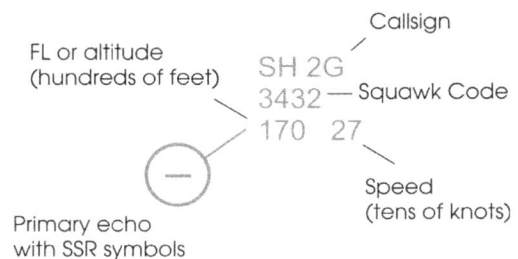

Primary echo with SSR symbols

There are standard numbers to squawk, when not otherwise instructed, which are:

- 2000 - from non-SSR area
- 7000 - conspicuity code

In emergency, squawk:

- 7500 - Hijack*

- 7600 - Comms failure

- 7700 - Emergency

*Absence of a reply is confirmation that the selection is not accidental

STOP When making routine code changes, you should avoid inadvertent selection of 7500, 7600 or 7700 (**do not** switch the transponder to standby during the change to avoid it, as senior pilots often do, because this removes your display from ATC's screen and creates all sorts of alarms). For example, when switching from 2700 to 7200, switch first to 2200 then to 7200, not to 7700 and then 7200. This applies to 7500 and all discrete codes in the 7600 and 7700 series (i.e. 7600-7677, 7700-7777) which will trigger special indicators in automated facilities.

When fitted, transponders should be used **all the time**.

Elementary Surveillance provides a controller with aircraft position, altitude and identification. It is based on ground initiated Comm-B protocols and needs a Mode S transponder with Surveillance identifier (SI) code capacity and automatic reporting of aircraft identification, known as ICAO Level 2s. SI codes must correspond to the aircraft ID in the flight plan, or the registration mark. On the other hand, *Enhanced Surveillance* extracts additional information from the aircraft, known as *Downlink Additional Parameters* (DAP).

Such information, being automatically extracted, reduces controller workload so that they can concentrate on safety. Because radio calls can be reduced, it also makes things easier for pilots.

MODES & CODES

Modes are used to ask questions, such as "Who are you?" (Mode 3/A) or "How high are you?" (Mode C) in the form of pairs of interrogative pulses and a control pulse (they are never sent together). The answer comes back as a code, of which there can be up to **4096** (8^4), but not Mode S, which has nearly 17 million.

The decoding of time between interrogation pulses determines the operating mode of the transponder (a spacing for transmission and reception is called a mode).

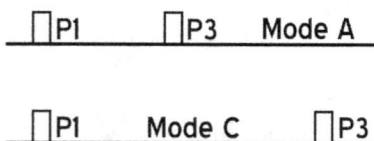

For modes 3/A and C, a pair of pulses called P1 and P3 are sent out to the aircraft (the interval between them decides which one it is). An omnidirectional antenna sends out another one called P2, which is weaker than the

others but stronger than any sidelobes so, if the transponder sees P1 and P3, it knows it is receiving the main lobe. If it sees P2, it's a side lobe, so responses from aircraft near them are avoided (in fact, the transponder's responses will be suppressed for a short while). Mode S also uses a short P4 pulse. A long P4 pulse means that the interrogator is transmitting a Mode A/C/S all call.

A Special Position Identification (SPI) pulse is sent by using the IDENT switch.

MODE A/B

Mode A is the regular variety, based on the original IFF, which just displays the code you select in the aircraft - you get this just by turning the switch to ON. In other words, it is for basic identification (Mode B is occasionally used in place of Mode A in some countries, but has been superseded by Mode S).

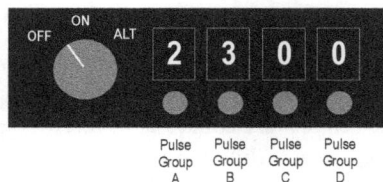

In answer to an interrogation, a Mode A transponder will transmit up to 14 pulses 8 microseconds apart (17 for B), the first and last ones being *frame pulses* (F1 and F2), which are always there and enclose the whole signal so it doesn't get confused with others. The 12 that are left can be there or not in up to 4096 (2^{12}) combinations, from 0000 to 7777. The *ident pulse* is transmitted for up to 20 seconds, 4.35 microseconds after the last frame pulse when you press the button.

Each number selection knob controls 3 pulses (pulse groups A, B, C & D). 2300 (for example) produces the binary codes of 010, 110, 000 and 000. 0 means Off, or no signal, so selecting 2 means that only pulse 2 of Pulse Group A is transmitted. Selecting 3 requires pulse 1 plus pulse 2 of the B group (refer to *Binary Arithmetic* under *Computers, Etc.* for more information). There would therefore only be 3 pulses between the frame pulses, which saves on transmission bandwidth.

MODE C

"Mode C" is selected by switching to ALT, after switching on for Mode A, so it is separate (being actually A + altitude reporting - it is not a mode in the proper sense). You should always use Mode C unless directed otherwise.

It will transmit altitude information alternately with the code information - a Mode C transponder is directly attached to an encoding altimeter (or, more precisely, an altitude digitiser, which selects a different code to that selected in the window), but only Pressure Altitude (or FL) information based on 1013.25 (or 29.92) information is sent from the aircraft (in **100-foot increments**) - the conversion to local pressure, if required, is done inside the ATC computer. **Moving the altimeter subscale does not affect ATC's display**. In Mode C a controller's presentation gives information regarding your indicated flight level that is accurate to within ±50 ft. The tolerance is ±300 ft. The pulses are 21 microseconds apart.

MODE S (DATALINK)

S stands for *Selective*, using pulses 25 microseconds apart. It allows aircraft to have unique codes, and respond only to requests directed to them, as opposed to all requests, although broadcast transmissions of information to all Mode S aircraft can be made without needing a reply.

However, if the interrogator does not know that an aircraft has Mode S, it will not use its individual address, although there will be responses to the station's Mode A and C interrogations. The interrogator therefore sends out an occasional *all call* message, which contains an extra pulse that is a request for every Mode S equipped aircraft to respond with its address and basic information, such as the call sign, its transponder's capabilities*, and an altitude report in 25-foot intervals.

*Transponder capability is described in levels:

- **Level 1** has no data link capability but recognises an individual address - effectively a Mode C transponder with selective calling.

- **Level 2** permits standard data link communication in both directions.

- **Levels 3, 4 and 5** increase the data link capabilities beyond the standard flight information.

In a Mode S interrogation, the initial two pulses are followed by a long pulse containing a string of up to 112 bits, which are transmitted by making phase reversals in the long pulse. This string of bits forms a message, the first **24 bits** being a unique address for the aircraft allowing **nearly 17 000 000** possible codes. In this way, the problems of fruiting, garbling and over-interrogation are overcome. The transponding aircraft will reply with the information requested, in a similar phase modulated pulse. Either 112 or 56 bits may be sent, depending on what the interrogation has asked for.

The aircraft address is allocated by the registering Authority, and is transmitted in any reply except Mode S only all-call (the SI code must correspond to Box 7 in the ICAO flight plan). This reduces mistakes and allows more capacity and efficiency, because the transponder does not have to transmit so often. For example, Mode S transponders have 20-foot resolution of altitude data, while Mode C has 100-foot resolution.

Mode A/C/S all-call consists of 3 pulses P1, P3 and the long P4. A control pulse P2 is transmitted following P1 to suppress responses from aircraft in the side lobes of the interrogation antenna.

Mode A/C only all-call consists of 3 pulses P1, P3 and the short P4.

A Mode S transponder regularly delivers a *squitter*, which is a short transmission of basic data without receiving a request, simply to advertise your position for TCAA. *Extended Squitter* is additional data on the Mode S Squitter that carries position information from the GPS, so a device receiving the transmission knows the position of the transmitting aircraft without any bearing or range measurements. You can therefore have a pseudo radar service within range of a single Mode S ground station (non-rotating antenna) simply by connecting a two-wire data cable from the GPS to the transponder.

Mode S can also provide a two-way data link on 1030 and 1090 MHz, used by TCAS for manoeuvre messages, but also as a backup for VHF voice.

Mode S equipped aircraft over 5 700 kg or with a max TAS over 250 kts must use *transponder antenna diversity*.

The two main design functions of Mode S are:

- air-ground and ground-air data link

- improved ATC aircraft surveillance capability

ERRORS & ACCURACY

Modes A and C can suffer from interference, otherwise known as *fruiting* and *garbling*. FRUIT stands for *False Replies Unsynchronised to Interrogator Transmissions*. Since SSR equipment uses the same frequencies for transmitting and receiving, any interrogator can trigger any transponder within range, so any ground station can receive their replies, which appear as interference, or fruit. Defruiting uses different PRFs, and comparator circuits only pass replies at the correct home station PRF.

Garbling comes from other aircraft within line of sight range responding to the same interrogation.

Because the length of a transponder code train is about 20 microseconds, it is not always possible to decipher replies from aircraft within 2-3 miles of each other on a radial from the interrogator (you could get overlapping returns **within 1.7 nm**). The reply signals may garble and the decoder equipment can generate false targets between the aircraft or cause cancellation of all or part of either or both returns (even with altitude separation). Circuits in the decoder equipment cancel garbled replies, and controllers will often ensure that only one aircraft within a formation has a transponder operating.

Weather Radar

Although it shares the same name, this is not a good system for detecting other aircraft or ground returns because it is tuned to the average size of raindrops (when used for navigation, AWR is only a *secondary* means). In fact, the primary purpose of weather radar is to detect the

capt.gs

sort of rainfall that would indicate thunderstorms and their associated turbulence. It therefore relies on your interpretation of the screen display for best results.

STOP Weather radar is required on aircraft that can carry more than 9 passengers (i.e. 10 and above) under IFR or at night when current weather reports indicate that thunderstorms or other potentially hazardous weather conditions, regarded as detectable with AWR, may reasonably be expected along the route.

Two frequency bands are used, such as *C band* (4000-8000 MHz), and *X band* (8000-12500 MHz). C band illuminates storms beyond nearby precipitation better, but X band has more resolution, although its higher frequencies are subject to absorption, and scattering from smaller raindrops. The wavelength is about 3 cm (at **10 GHz**, or maybe 9375 MHz), to detect a 1½ cm raindrop - ½ the wavelength is the optimum object size for detection (larger droplets give good echoes and you can have a smaller antenna). Weather radar can detect volcanic ash, sandstorms and smog, but it is **unlikely to detect snow or clear air turbulence** (except with the use of Doppler).

Cumulus clouds are most readily detected with the weather beam, but the main factors that determine whether a cloud will be detected or not are the size of the water drops and wavelength/frequency used. At low altitudes, detection of turbulence may be difficult due to ground returns.

The antenna (scanner) is kept inside a *radome* in the nose of the aircraft, and there is an RT box containing the transmitter/receiver, together with a scope in the cockpit.

The antenna can be parabolic or flat, sweeping through 45-60° either side of the nose - the flat scanner reduces power demand and sidelobes. In *weather* mode, the beam is narrow, between 3-5° (pencil) and cone-shaped. For mapping, it is wide and fan-shaped (up to 50-60 nm), but for long range mapping, use weather mode anyway, because the narrow beam goes further with more power concentrated in it. The antenna is stabilised in pitch and roll, ±20° combined, using inputs from the attitude system. It is not stabilised in yaw.

Weather radar detects rainfall to *avoid* (not penetrate) severe weather, as many large raindrops in a small area are a dead giveaway for thunderstorms or, rather, their activity is - turbulence is proportional to the rate at which rainfall increases or decreases over a given distance. Whether you want to go towards the area concerned depends on the intensity of the echoes received, the spacing between them, your capabilities and those of the aircraft.

STOP A clear area on the radar screen (say between significant echoes) does not mean there is no

cloud or precipitation, as minute droplets, ice, dry snow and dry hail have low reflective levels, if at all.

In fact, a clear area is more likely to indicate large water droplets, as they will totally absorb the energy as they approach the size of the radar wave, and the screen will not be able to display the remaining thunderstorm area behind the point of complete attenuation (absence of returns produces a use for the stray side lobes mentioned above, in that the downwards one produces a **height ring** on the screen at the same range as your height above ground, so you can at least check if the equipment is working). Thus, the greatest echoes come from rain, and drop size is more important than their number.

Because of attenuation, a weak return does not mean a less violent storm - you could just be too far away from it to get decent information. As well as the nature of the target, the strength of the returning signal depends on the range of the cloud. Sensitivity Time Control (STC), or swept gain techniques are used, where the receiver gain is lowered at the instant each pulse is fired, then progressively increased so that echoes from distant ranges are amplified more than closer ones.

Operation of weather radar is quite simple, but full use on the ground should be avoided (not below 500 feet, in fact, because the radiations will affect people or equipment). Naturally, you must check the equipment before departure, but most sets have an internal procedure for this. When you do switch it on, it should be set to *Standby* for at least 3 minutes first, to allow things to warm up. When not in use, the set should always be set to SBY to keep the (roll and pitch) stabilisation gyros running - it stops them crunching together as the aircraft moves. Ground testing requires *tilting up* in weather mode.

TILT

Once airborne, the tilt capability will point the antenna up or down so you can adjust for the aircraft attitude and get more detail about approaching storm cells, but don't expect to see the tops of a storm, because the crystals won't reflect the energy in the first place, and your beam focussing will be too narrow to include it (convective thunderstorms are much less reflective above the freezing level). The tilt control is an important key to a more informative display in moderate rain, and should be used often to get a better 3D picture. Tilt down until you see ground returns, then up until they disappear, then add 2° to cover for turns. The tilt should be higher at lower altitudes and lower at higher altitudes.

To see whether a cloud return on an AWR is at or above the height of the aircraft, subtract half the beam width from the angle of tilt - the tilt angle - beam width x 100 x range in nm equals the approximate height difference of the cloud tops (in feet) from your flight level. With a 5° beam width, the tilt control should be set 2.5° up.

The tilt setting should be lower if you climb to a higher altitude.

MAPPING

In the same way, you will also get ground echoes, which are good for detecting the enemy coast ahead, but only because water will absorb the echoes and you will see a big black hole instead. In fact, it will be very hard to distinguish between the edge of the ice and the real coast in polar areas.

Buildings, etc. won't reflect properly at all - you might just see a mass of confusing colours (that's what the MAP selection is for, but that's not wonderful, either). MAP mode uses a *cosecant radiation pattern* with a *cosecant squared* antenna, so you can scan a large ground zone with echoes whose signals are practically independent of distance.

When looking at the ground for mapping purposes at fairly close range, the beam must be widened vertically as well as having its energy distribution controlled so that returns from longer range (the top of the beam) are of similar strength to those from shorter range (the bottom of the beam). The strength of the signal vertically within the beam depends upon the square of the cosecant of the angle of depression, so more energy is radiated in the upper part of the beam than the lower part.

You will have several scan ranges to choose from, possibly from 250 miles down to 5, but 80* is adequate, which is about what you would get with a modern 10 inch antenna, the usual fit in small aircraft. The smaller it is, the wider the beam and the dispersal of energy, which means that a lot of it will pass by whatever storm is around, giving you an indication much less than the true hazard. You would be safe to assume that whatever is on the screen is one or two levels more severe.

*Mapping mode is effective up to 50 or 60 nm with older radar sets, using a fan shaped beam, but the pencil shape is preferred for longer distances because more power can be concentrated in the narrow beam.

STORM PATTERNS

If you haven't got the luxury of colour and computer-controlled echo highlighting (and have to rely on steam), there are distinctive storm patterns to look out for:

- *The Hook*. These stick out from a cloud, suggesting strong wind circulations, like tornadoes, or hail, which has a wet surface and therefore reflects like a large raindrop. Both are found in thunderstorms with a marked windshear in the middle levels.

- *The Finger*. This is like a spur out from a cloud, not quite as curled as the hook, and usually in the next intense colour, such as yellow. The trick here is to look at the edges - sharp contours mean a growing storm, while fuzzy ones mean a dissipating storm.

- *The U-shape*. This is like a valley in a mountain, with strong updraughts surrounded on three sides by the sort of heavy precipitation associated with downdraughts.

- *Scalloped edges*. When round a cloud outline, particularly at the back end of a storm, they signify severe attenuation due to heavy precipitation.

Shapes can change quickly, so they need careful monitoring (hail shows up better when the gain is reduced). The heaviest precipitation, and the heaviest turbulence, will show up as black holes, or red when using colour, which is best detected in *Contour mode* (where high rainfall rates, or maximum cell activity, appears in Red).

Tip: Radar signals weaken, and might show the end of the weather falsely.

Iso-Echo (for mono screens) produces a hole in a strong echo when the returned signal is above a pre-set value. *It is used to detect areas of possible severe turbulence in cloud.* The edges of the hole that actually appears on the screen have the same rainfall rate, and is like a contour line, hence the name. When the lines are narrow, there is a strong intensity gradient, so avoid hooked echoes, especially rapidly changing ones. In fact, you should beware of thin lines of whatever colour.

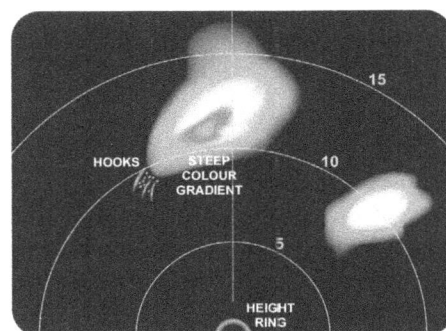

In the picture above, the line along the centre is your intended track, and the curved lines are your range markings, so there's something nasty lurking 10 nm away slightly on your port side, with a little finger (or hook) in front of you which may or may not be producing some rainfall. The colour zones closest together (or nearest the edge of the cell) indicate the greatest turbulence. Note the colour progression from green to yellow to red, and possibly magenta for maximum severity (although the most severe turbulence is shown by a steep colour *gradient*). By changing the scale to 10 nm, the returns on the radar screen should increase in area and move nearer to the top of the screen.

STOP Targets separated by a distance less than the beam diameter will merge and appear on the display as one.

Avoid the brightest returns (i.e. those that are changing rapidly, or contouring, or coloured magenta or red) by at least 20 nm. Above the freezing level, make it 5 nm and 10 nm when below. If you see anything at all between 50-70 nm, keep well away from it. The minimum height above a storm should be 1,000 feet for each 10 kts of wind speed.

Ground Radar

Those used for longer range, such as those covering airways and larger airspace, tend to have lower frequencies and longer wavelengths, lower PRFs and larger pulses to get maximum range with as little attenuation as possible. Where shorter range is good enough, say, for use near an aerodrome, short frequent pulses provide better picture definition. In addition, antenna rotation will be higher because shorter range radar will be used when things are changing quickly.

A typical long range coverage will be up to 250-300 nm, with a preferred frequency of 600 MHz and a 50 cm wavelength. Shorter range coverage is provided by.....

AIRCRAFT SURFACE MOVEMENT RADAR

Otherwise known as *Airport Surface Detection Equipment* (ASDE), this operates in the SHF* band (16 GHz), using an antenna that rotates at around 60 RPM. Its definition is such that it is sometimes possible to determine the type of aircraft from the return on the radar screen.

*EHF is absorbed and scattered by moisture in the air.

SURVEILLANCE RADAR APPROACH (SRA)

With this system, ATC can normally talk you down to within 2 nm of the threshold (on QFE unless requested otherwise), but it can get as close as half a mile. As with PAR, below, the controller will give you the headings to fly, but *there is no height information* - just ranges with heights.

As for any approach, if you are using SSR only, non-radar separation standards will be used as soon as possible.

SRE (Surveillance Radar Equipment) can be used for an SRA, which is a form of GCA (Ground Controlled Approach) given in azimuth only, where corrections are given to the centreline in numbers of degrees, but heights are given in feet at ½ mile intervals on the approach corresponding to either a 2½° or 3° approach as required. (e.g. "5 miles 1500 ft, right of centreline correcting nicely....turn right 3 degrees heading 238, 4½ miles 1350 ft, slightly right of centreline correcting slowly.....check gear down....4 miles 1200 ft, [callsign] clear to land, surface wind 240/10 knots....slightly right of centreline correcting slowly..." etc.) Since the update rate on surveillance radar is slower and the centreline is not as accurate, the SRA is a non precision approach and minimum heights are correspondingly higher.

The maximum range of surveillance radar would be in the order of 300 nm.

PRECISION APPROACH RADAR (PAR)

PAR is primarily used by the military.

It is high-definition in nature, because it uses the 9-10 GHz range and has a 3 cm wavelength, similar to weather radar, so weather clutter can be a problem (meaning you may be denied its use when you need it most!) It uses two radars (and antennas) to give horizontal and vertical guidance to aircraft on final approach up to about 9 nm within 20° of final track (azimuth) and 7° of elevation (i.e. relatively narrow beams).

It's supposed to be a landing aid, not one for sequencing or spacing aircraft. As the range is just 9 nm, PAR is limited to the final stages of approach. The display is in two parts - the lower giving altitude and distance information, and the upper azimuth and distance. Most PAR decision heights are around 200 ft agl.

The controller will give you headings to fly, plus position information with regard to the glidepath, but only if you are dangerously low will positive height information be given. In the final stages you will be told not to acknowledge the instructions as things will be happening hard and fast.

As your height is monitored, the heights to which you can descend before overshooting will be lower.

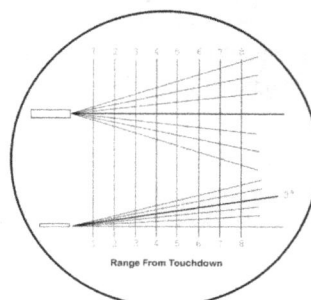

Range From Touchdown

PAR's usefulness lies in the fact that navaids are not required and neither is a compass, since the controller tells you to turn left, right, descend, etc. Also, as acknowledgments are not required, you can listen to instructions over an ADF or VOR.

While surveillance radar can be used for GCA applications if the update rate is quick enough, PAR doesn't really have the ability. There is also a PAR Azimuth Only Approach, using the PAR centreline to give a non precision approach more accurate than SRA.

DME   062 02 04

Distance Measuring Equipment is secondary radar, but in reverse. It measures the time difference between *paired pulses* sent from an aircraft being received back (on different frequencies). Then the distance is calculated.

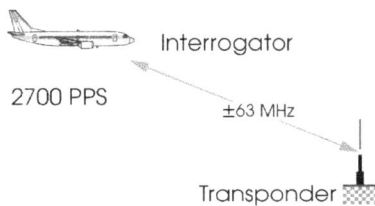

Interrogator

2700 PPS   ±63 MHz

Transponder

In other words, shaped* UHF (decimetric) double pulses are transmitted by an aircraft to a ground station and, after a typical delay of 50 microseconds**, the ground station sends them back again (with the same PRF, or jittering pattern, and pulse spacing) at a higher or lower frequency to distinguish them from ground returns. The delay reduces the chances of uncoordinated activity (echos) when the interrogating aircraft is near the station. It is subtracted during the number-crunching.

*To limit the bandwidth of the DME signal to the channel width of 1 MHz, the envelope of the pulses is shaped to take the specified rise and fall times into account.

**After a valid double pulse is received (i.e. after the 2nd pulse), the receiver ignores further interrogations for a short time after the 50 microseconds delay (dead time) to ensure that it does not trigger to its own transmissions.

DME is UHF-based, between 962 and 1213 MHz for the ground stations, so a typical frequency would be 1000 MHz. The aircraft uses 1025 MHz to 1150 MHz.

There are two DME standards, /N and /P, that mainly differ with respect to the rise time of the pulse edge. DME/P (precision DME) was defined in the 1980s for the MLS, but was overtaken by satellites.

The interrogator in the aircraft can operate in search or track mode. In search mode, the interrogator tries to set up a connection to a ground station and synchronise with it. In this mode, the pulse repetition rate can be increased up to 150 pulse pairs per second. Once synchronisation takes place, it changes to track mode, where the PRF can be up to 16 pp/s. The transmit power of an aircraft interrogator is at least 250 watts.

The auto standby (signal activated search) circuit does not allow interrogations to start unless signals are detected from the beacon, so the beacon may not reply unless it is interrogated, and the interrogator will not do so unless it receives signals. Relying on the ident feature means waiting for up to 30 seconds, so the beacon transmits **squitter** pulse pairs even without interrogations. This ensures a minimum pulse rate for synchronisation with the automatic gain control of an aircraft receiver. In addition, the most important pulse parameters of a ground station (rise and fall time, pulse width and spacing, pulse delay and pulse peak power) are continuously monitored and adjusted by Built-In Test Equipment (BITE), which only works correctly if there are enough test pulses.

Aircraft DME receivers do not lock on to transmissions reflected from the ground as they are not on the receiver frequency - that's why the interrogation and reply frequencies differ. Signal discrimination depends on *frequency separation* and *pulse spacing*.

The transponder replies constantly to whatever signals it detects, including random noise if there are no genuine signals from aircraft. These are filtered and the strongest are replied to (in theory, the closest interrogating aircraft). The transponder is able to respond to approximately 2700 pulse pairs every second.

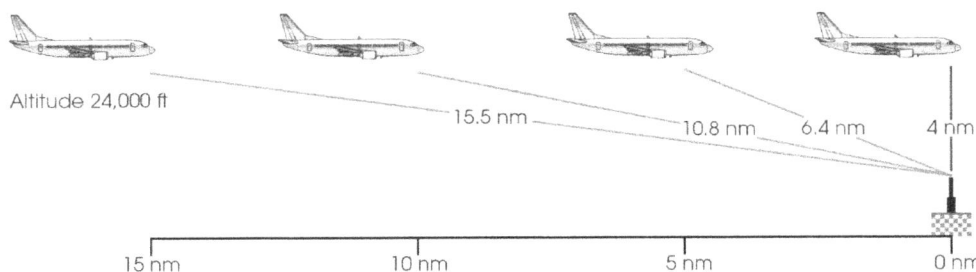

Altitude 24,000 ft

15.5 nm   10.8 nm   6.4 nm   4 nm

15 nm   10 nm   5 nm   0 nm

capt.gs

Because the transponding must be omni-directional, the DME ground aerial is a single pole antenna, cut to the ideal length for 1090 MHz. When co-located with VOR, it is placed on top of it.

The **Echo Protection Circuit** (EPC) is the generic name for a ReTriggerable Blanking Gate circuit at the ground transponder which includes the 50 microsecond delay. It prevents lock-on to signals that are reflected off other surfaces, where the echo arrives after the line-of-sight interrogation. The circuit works on amplitude, and is triggered by the line of sight signal, after which any signals with less power are ignored. Thus, the receiver is suppressed after the first pulse, so the second echo doesn't trigger a reply. In the air, only the first signal at the receiver is accepted. **The circuit detects whether the transmitter/receiver has been locked by pulse pairs.**

The DME ident is pitched higher than that of a VOR (at 1350 Hz), so you can identify it between VOR idents on the same frequency (it is transmitted only once to the VOR's four, within every 40 seconds). Instruments in the cockpit will not only show your distance to a station, but will calculate the rate of movement and display the groundspeed (just multiply the distance flown in 6 minutes by 10 if yours doesn't). The reason it's not completely accurate is because the distance is the *slant range* from the station, and not the equivalent position on the ground, just as with primary radar, although at long distances and lower altitudes, this is minimised. The groundspeed readout reduces at an increasing rate when overflying an aid, to zero at the overhead.

In practical terms, the difference is insignificant over 10 miles from the station, and the maximum error occurs overhead - at 12,000 ft, the instrument would read 2 nm, and 4 nm at 24,000 ft, and so on.

Simple Pythagoras will give you the real distance:

$$D = \sqrt{(S^2 - A^2)}$$

D is the ground distance, *S* is the readout (slant range) and *A* is your altitude in *nautical miles* (above the DME source).

The slant range itself is calculated by:

$$\text{Range} = \frac{\text{Time } (\mu s)}{12.4}$$

Don't forget to subtract a 50 m/s delay at the transponder.

Example: At FL 210, you will not receive any distance indication from a DME station approximately 220 nm away because you are below the line of sight altitude. If the time taken for an interrogation pulse to travel to the ground transponder and back is 2000 microseconds, the slant range is 158 nm (the ground transponder has a 50 microsecond delay, so total time is 1950 microseconds). The most accurate calculation of your ground speed will

come from a DME on the flight route, meaning that you will be tracking directly to or from it.

The ground station can only respond to a certain number of interrogations in a given period of time. Normally, 30 pulse pairs are transmitted per second, but going up to 150 (for searching) allows up to 100 aircraft to interrogate the system before *beacon saturation* occurs - the ground station can only cope with 2700 pps. A DME experiencing difficulty with locking on will stay in search mode, but will reduce the PRF to up to 60 PPS after 15 000 pulse pairs have been transmitted.

X/Y Channels

DME stations use channels rather than frequencies because they are normally co-located* with a VOR or ILS. The channel is paired with a frequency.

Co-located means within 30 m and frequency paired within 600 m. *Associated* means that the DME callsign ends with a Z, and that they are more than 600 m apart or within 2000 feet of each other (the maximum distance between VOR and DME/TACAN installations with the same Morse ID is 600 m if used for enroute navigation).

X channels are the most common**, with the transponded signal 63 MHz higher than the received signal. Y stations reply at 63 MHz below, and the pulse pairs are differently spaced. The information should be on the chart, but if you only see the frequency, X channels are linked with VOR frequencies ending in 0 (116.70 = 114Y) and Y channels are for those ending in 5 (116.75 - 114X). In other words, X stations use whole number decimals (114.30), and Y beacons use halved decimals (114.35). In some places, the X is not shown after the channel, but the Y is, when relevant. There are 252 DME reply and 126 interrogation frequencies in the full TACAN range.

Using X and Y Channels makes more efficient use of the bandwidth available and reduces interference.

**When the demand for VOR/DME stations increased and the frequency spacing between VORs was reduced from 0.1 MHz to 0.05 MHz, the number of DME channels naturally doubled, which is not a problem when channels and frequencies are paired but, for those people who could use DMEs separately (i.e. the military using TACAN) a workaround was required. They designated the old channels as X and the new ones as Y, reversing the 63 MHz interrogation and response frequencies.

DME is normally based with a VOR or TACAN and has a range of about 200 nm, ± 6, with an accuracy better than ½ nm or 3% of the distance, whichever is the greater (max range is determined by height). Thus, when the DME is co-located with a VOR, the two signals combined will give you a position based on a radial from the VOR and how far away on that radial you are.

Errors

Theoretically, 126 aircraft can use each station at a time, if none of them are scanning at the high rate. On average, however, we can assume that some aircraft will be attempting to lock on, so 100 aircraft is commonly accepted as the average number that can be handled at once. However, some RNAV systems alternate their DME interrogations between several stations, requiring a re-lock every minute or so, which means that they are interrogating at the high rate for much of the time. The ground stations will only reply to the 2700 strongest signals every second, so a large number of high-rate interrogations mean fewer aircraft can use each station.

If too many aircraft are interrogating it, the receiver will automatically be desensitised so it can hear and reply only to the strongest thus, busy airspace can result in shorter-than-normal DME reception range, particularly with lower-powered units. An aircraft DME in tracking mode that experiences a reduction in signal strength will switch to *memory mode* so it has something to work on until the signal gets better (display counters rotating mean that the receiver is conducting a range search).

Where the ground distance is less than or equal to 3 times the height, the inaccuracy is too much for the system. The difference is negligible for enroute navigation when the indicated distance in nm is more than the height of the aircraft above the DME in thousands of feet.

The accuracy of a position line, as required by ICAO at least 95% of the time, is ± 0.5 nm, or ± 3% of the aircraft's range if greater. As DME is the most accurate of the classic navigation aids, it is the preferred input for RNAV. Otherwise, assuming no saturation, the maximum range is limited by the line of sight formula. Most airborne equipment indicates a maximum of 200 nm, but some can reach to 300 nm, which is only really useful for Concorde (that's about 56,000 ft).

Range errors should not exceed **±0.25 nm plus 1.25% of the distance measured** so, at 100 nm, the maximum should not exceed **±1.5 nm**. The total system error for **DME-P** should not exceed 0.2 nm.

ILS   062 02 05

The Instrument Landing System is a pilot-interpreted *precision* approach aid because it includes tracking and slope guidance. It is currently the primary precision approach facility for civil aviation at all major airports, although no more will be installed in the US in favour of GPS approaches. The equipment is constantly monitored by ATC and calibration is carried out frequently by the authorities. If any limits are exceeded, transmissions will be stopped within 6 seconds The following components may be used to guide you down to a *Decision Height:*

- a **VHF transmitter** for **horizontal guidance** along the extended centreline (the *localiser*), with a 1.4° wide beam, at the far end of the runway (the upwind end), about 300m out, to stop it being an obstacle. The beam is about 700 feet wide at the threshold. If it does not go across the extended centreline within 30°, it is an *offset localiser*. The ILS frequency carrier is amplitude modulated.

- a **UHF transmitter** for **vertical guidance**, which usually produces a 3° *glideslope*, within about 120m of one side of the runway, typically about 300m from the threshold. The touchdown area is a little way in from the threshold so you have concrete to land on if you have a problem. The *Threshold Crossing Height* (TCH) is where the glideslope

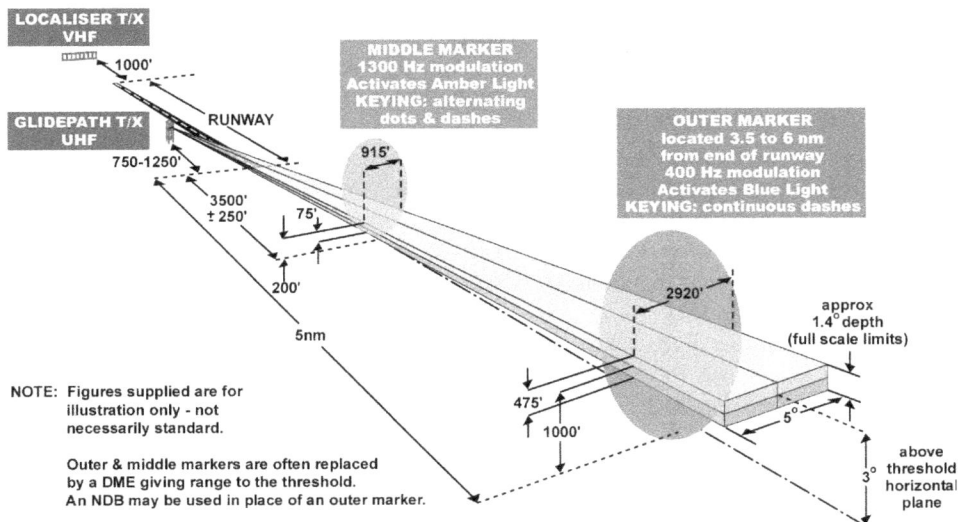

NOTE: Figures supplied are for illustration only - not necessarily standard.

Outer & middle markers are often replaced by a DME giving range to the threshold. An NDB may be used in place of an outer marker.

antenna should be to ensure that the wheels don't hit the ground if they hang too far below the cockpit, otherwise you will get a runway-assisted go-around. *Glideslope signals are only valid down to the lowest authorised DH, so if you bust minima, you need to be aware that following the needles will just take you along the runway at that height.*

- up to three 75 Mhz **marker beacons**. The Middle Marker is typically 1000 m away from the threshold, and the outer marker 4 nm.

- high intensity **approach lights** for better visual guidance in the latter stages (typically 100 feet apart, up to 3000 feet from the end of the runway).

- radar monitoring.

Types Of Approach

Approaches are classified as to equipment on the aircraft and at the airport, plus pilot training and experience.

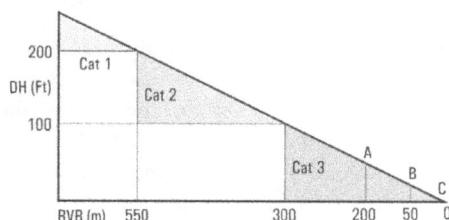

This is the ICAO standard. PART OPS allows 75m for the Cat IIIb approach.

CATEGORY I

This is the least restrictive, and the one that most people in General Aviation will use. It uses a (barometric) Decision Height* of at least **200 feet** and an RVR of 550 m, with a high chance of success. Ceiling is not a factor.

*Where the localiser intercepts the glideslope.

CATEGORY II

This takes you further down, to 100 feet DH and 300m RVR. It needs special training under an approved syllabus in the Ops Manual. Qualifications are specific to type.

For Cat II (and III - see below), the aircraft must be certificated for Decision Heights below 200 ft, or none, and equipped as per regulations. A suitable system for recording approach and automatic landing success and failure must also be established and maintained to monitor safety. There must be at least 2 pilots, with **DH determined by radalt,** and the aerodrome must also be approved. Low visibility takeoffs in less than 150 m RVR (Cat A, B and C) or 200 m (Cat D) need approval.

You also likely need the following to be up and running:

- **Lighting**: approach, threshold, touchdown zone, centreline, runway edge and end lights

- **ILS**: localiser, glidepath and middle marker

- **RVR**: two transmissometers, one at the threshold, and at the mid-point

- **Power** - airport emergency power as the primary source for essential elements, with commercial power available within one second

CATEGORY III

A Cat III ILS glidepath transmitter provides reliable guidance information down to the surface of the runway.

- **IIIa** - A DH of less than 100' with 200m RVR

- **IIIb** - Below 50' DH (or none), and 75-200m RVR

- **IIIc** - Zero-zero

Any precision more than Cat II needs a high accuracy radio altimeter, so if it fails you cannot use the procedure. The autoland facility means that you don't have a DH.

The Localiser

The localiser comes from two overlapping lobes of radio energy (notes) on VHF, the one on the left (yellow) during approach being A2 modulated at 90 Hz, and the other (blue) also A2 at 150 Hz, i.e. metric.

The principle of operation is that the *difference in depth of modulation*, or the ratio of the amplitude of the modulating waveform to that of the R/F carrier, determines the position of the needle. If the depth of modulation of both lobes appears to be the same, the receiver assumes you are on the ILS QDM in the centre, or following the *equisignal.* The greater the difference in modulation depths, the more the indicator needle is displaced. More 90 Hz than 150 Hz, for example, means fly right (and down).

Beam bends in the approach path are slight curves that can be followed by large aircraft. If the angular displacement of an aircraft doubles, so does the difference in Depth of Modulation.

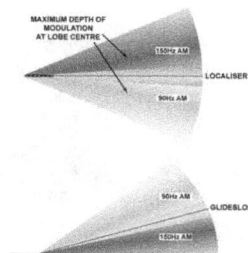

The impression given is that two narrowly focussed beams intersect to provide the guidance but the "beams" are created electronically *by the equipment in the aircraft* (that is, voltages are produced from the radio signals - they have to be at a minimum level to keep the Off flag away). This means you can get on-course or on-glidepath indications regardless of your position, as was found by an Air New Zealand 767 in July 2000, which got down to 400', *6 miles short of the runway* (check your distance and altitudes, and do *not* use equipment on test! In ILS test mode, you always get an on-glideslope indication without warning flags, irrespective of your position). The warning flags are operated by voltmeters in the indicator.

ICAO defines "established on course" as being within half full-scale deflection for an ILS or VOR/TACAN/RNAV/GPS procedure and within ±5° of the required bearing for the NDB. You are not established until you are within these limits.

Tip: When intercepting, double the track error, so if you are 4 dots off, turn by 4° until interception takes place, then turn on to the inbound track.

The frequency range for the localiser lies between 108.1-111.975 MHz (VHF), on *odd decimals* as this range is shared with the VOR, within which there will be 40 channels, so a typical frequency is 109.15 MHz. A three-letter ID is transmitted at regular intervals in Morse code (at 1020 Hz). If the localiser alignment exceeds 3° of the runway heading, the first letter will be X. If it is 3° or less, the letter is I. The normal approach is called the *front course*, and is used with the other components of the system. The course line along the extended centreline in the opposite direction is called the *backcourse*. Unless your system has reverse-sensing capability (check for the B/C button on the autopilot), you have to do the opposite of what the needle says when inbound along the back course (as you would when outbound along the front course). On an HSI, the course arrow should be set to the front beam inbound course. Aside from the reverse sensing, backcourses are not used in UK because:

- There is no glideslope (so it is non-precision).
- It is less accurate.
- There are no markers.

In any case, you can't use them unless there is a published procedure.

Disregard glideslope indications on a backcourse, unless one is shown on the chart.

ILS is 4 times more sensitive than the VOR, so full needle deflection is 2½ °, as opposed to 10° (½° per dot). One dot means you are 300 feet off course at the Outer Marker or FAF, and 100 feet off at the Middle Marker.

The system will have an **FM Immune** filter to make the localiser less susceptible to interference from commercial FM broadcasting stations (TV and radio).

Tip: When coming down the glideslope, don't forget to adjust your heading as the wind slows down and backs nearer to ground level (on an airfield near the coast, you will also be affected by sea breezes. At Southend, for example, you can suddenly get a tailwind halfway down the approach, followed by a headwind). This is particularly important for helicopters because the ILS was originally based on fixed wing characteristics. When very slow, large drift correction angles make it hard to follow a localiser.

Localiser errors are due to ground reflections. *Scalloping* means that the beam direction varies from side to side of the intended approach path.

The Glidepath

Glidepath transmissions are done in a similar way, but on UHF (between 328.6-335.4 MHz), with the frequencies paired with localiser ones (i.e. the glidepath frequency is automatically tuned when the localiser frequency is selected). The upper lobe is the 90 Hz yellow one, but ground reflections from the lower lobe produce *side-lobes* which can give false indications*. These should be above the real glidepath, but you should still be aware of them. Watch for high rates of descent, and check altitudes against distances - full deflection is only 0.7°, and one dot means 50 feet at the Outer Marker (around 8 feet at the Middle Marker).

The glidepath is set to cross the threshold at 50 feet (the ILS Reference Point).

*The 150 Hz signal can be received above the intended glideslope, occurring at twice the normal angle, i.e. 6° instead of 3°.

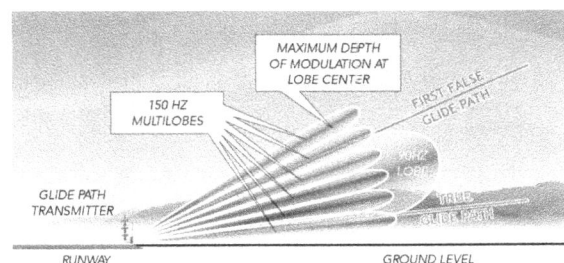

This is why the glideslope is captured from below (3-10 nm from the threshold) to avoid false readings.

The pattern is achieved through the interaction of directly radiated waves with those reflected from the ground. As the number of lobes increases with the height of an antenna above the ground, and the angle of elevation of the lowest lobe decreases with its height, two antennas, one above the other, are used to give the best effects.

The lower one radiates at 90 Hz and the upper one 150 Hz. By adjusting the amplitude of the 150 Hz carrier, the lowest lobes of the two antennas can be made to intersect at the chosen glideslope angle (usually 3°). The first false equisignal should not be lower than 10°, so there should be little risk of confusion. Because they are offset from the runway (to stop aircraft hitting them), suitable phase adjustments must be made to keep you on the glideslope. This is achieved by moving the lower antenna a few inches further away from the runway.

ILS transmitters are sensitive to vehicles, etc., around them, which is why there are *ILS Critical Areas*, in which no aircraft or vehicles are allowed to move during ILS operations. The same applies to *ILS Sensitive Areas* in low visibilities (Cat II/III). The reason why pre-takeoff holding areas are sometimes further from the active runway when ILS Category 2 and 3 landing procedures are in progress than during good weather operations is that aircraft manoeuvring near the runway may disturb the guidance signals. Look for the sign like the one left and below, and the *B Pattern* next to it on the taxiway:

The signals received in the cockpit are translated onto an instrument like the one on the left, below. The vertical needle shows whether you are left or right of the localiser and the horizontal one tells you whether you are high or low in relation to the glideslope. In the example, you are on the glideslope and *left* of the localiser, so you "chase the cross" to get back on, in this case, fly level to the right.

On the right is a picture of a *Horizontal Situation Indicator* (HSI). Glideslope indicators are on the side.

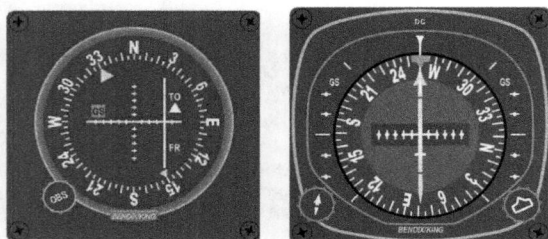

🛑 The OBS doesn't work when the VOR instrument is used for the ILS, because it is only radiating one course, but it is usually set to the inbound course for neatness.

🛑 *Glidepath* means any part of the glideslope intersecting the localiser.

Tip: When using an HSI, a smooth intercept can be obtained by keeping the top of the CDI bar next to the lubber line.

Markers & Beacons

Three beacons radiating at 75 MHz (metric) as A2A are used on the way down the glideslope to indicate that you are within the coverage of the localiser and glidepath, or to help with height, distance and equipment checks.

The Outer Marker is at about 4 miles (where you should be around 1500 feet, when the glideslope meets the minimum holding altitude), which often coincides with, or is replaced by, an NDB or DME. The Middle Marker is found at about ½ mile or 1050 m from the threshold (where you should be at around 200 feet), using a quarter of the power of the Outer Marker, and the inner marker is just before the threshold, at DH, if it is there (it's mainly for Cat II approaches). It uses a tenth of the Outer Marker power. Vertical beams are used to stop interference.

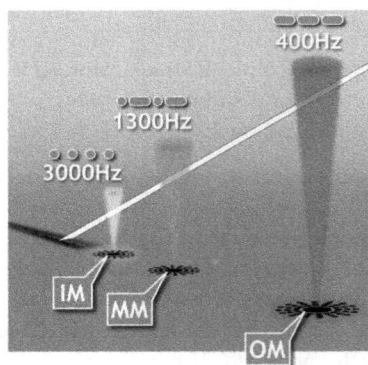

The markers don't have to be tuned, as they have their own identification.

 The outer marker produces a blue flashing light within a few degrees of the overhead. Each vertical dot is about 50 ft.

 The middle marker is amber, where each vertical dot is equal to about 8 feet.

 The inner marker is white, if used.

The markers beep as well as flash, using different tones (400, 1300 and 3000 Hz if you really want to know) in Morse. The OM uses two dashes per second, the MM dot-dash-dot-dash at two per second, and the inner marker four dots at 6 per second. Markers have a sensitivity setting. Setting the function switch to *High* enables you to pick up the signals a bit sooner, but *Low* is a bit more precise on positioning.

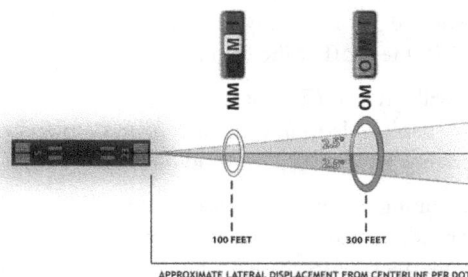

APPROXIMATE LATERAL DISPLACEMENT FROM CENTERLINE PER DOT

A DME installation at the threshold can replace the markers.

Lighting

This is meant to help with the transition from instruments to visual, although they are not actually a requirement for the system. However, if lighting is not present, the minima will be increased somewhat.

CATEGORY I

This is what you might see as you come out of the clag with a Cat I approach:

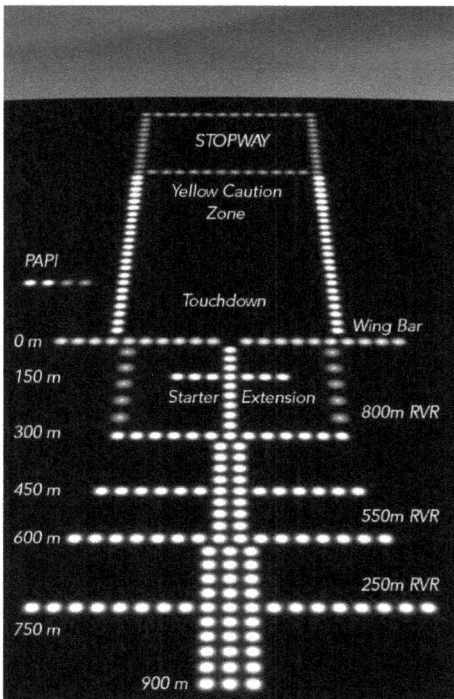

The lights begin 900 m from the threshold, with lateral bars at 150 m intervals. The figures on the right are what you might expect to see from the DH at 900 m with RVR values of 250 m, 550 m and 800 m.

Thus, an RVR of 900 m should let you (just about) see the threshold from the DH. One of 250 m would let you see just one bar of the ALS, which is hardly anything on which to base a visual glide path. In fact, it would be pretty much impossible to land safely.

If you perform a night ILS with an RVR of 550 m, you should get the minimum adequate visibility from the approach lights at the DH. However, it will be near zero outside of that, so taxying could be interesting.

Gradients, Etc

To guarantee obstacle clearance, there is usually a required climb (200 feet per nautical mile) or descent gradient (usually 320 ft/nm for a 3° glideslope) when leaving or arriving at an airfield.

The obstacle free path is based on a climb rate of 200 ft per minute after crossing the end of the runway at least 35 ft above the ground. You must also be able to climb to 400 feet above the airfield elevation before needing a turn.

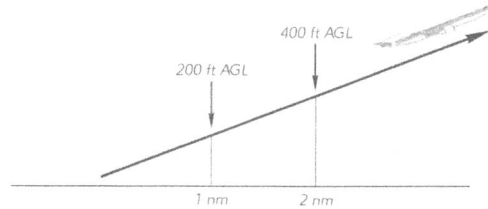

However, depending on the surrounding area, the required gradients may be different - you may well need a steeper one for a non-precision approach in the mountains.

These SIDs require a minimum climb gradient of 304' per NM (3%) up to 8000'

Gnd speed - KT	75	100	150	200	250	300
304' per NM	380	508	780	1013	1288	1510

In the normal case, to find out the minimum safe altitude at the 5 nm point after takeoff (i.e. the height required to meet the gradient), set up the $^{200}/_1$ ratio on the flight computer and you will see the answer on the outside scale opposite the 5 on the inner scale - 1000 feet.

But what vertical speed might you need? At 60 knots in the above diagram, it is 200 feet per minute. Put another way, at 60 knots, **the climb rate equals the gradient** so, if you need to maintain 304 feet per minute, that is what the climb rate should be.

The table above converts the required gradient (in ft per nm) to the climb rate (in ft per min) for specified groundspeeds, but if you set up the relevant ratio on the flight computer, you can find the corresponding rates against vertical speed yourself.

For example, $^{60}/_{304}$ means 455 feet per minute at 90 kts.

If you know your groundspeed and vertical speed you can work backwards to find your gradient so, at 120 knots at 900 feet per minute, set up $^{120}/_{900}$ and look opposite 60 on the outside scale to find 450 feet per nm.

Having found that, you can find out the altitude at a specified distance - set up $^{450}/_1$ (in this case) and the answer is on the outside scale opposite the distance.

RATE OF DESCENT

Radar will give you a distance to touchdown so you can calculate a smooth rate of descent. You don't want to be making sudden drops at the last minute to make the glideslope and risk spilling the coffee.

Glidepath gradient calculations are variations on the 1 in 60 rule - the standard 3° glidepath is an ROD of 300 ft per nm, or 100 feet per degree. 3° slopes can be calculated by multiplying your groundspeed by 5, as derived from:

$$ROD = \frac{GS \times 10}{2}$$

At 60 kts, the ROC/ROD equals the gradient.

If the speed changes on the approach, a strong headwind causes a *decrease* in groundspeed and rate of descent, and a tailwind does the opposite. Every 10 kts decrease in groundspeed on a 3° glideslope means a decrease in ROD of 50 fpm, and *vice versa*.

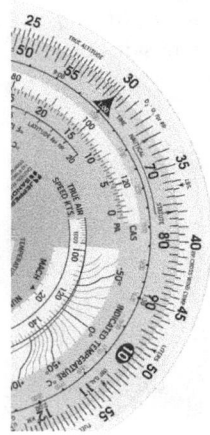

You can use the slide rule on the flight computer to solve these as a proportion problem. If you put the 60 kt index on the slide rule against 30 (3°) on the outer scale, you can read 450 fpm against 90 kts, and so on........

For a 2.5° glideslope, just put the index against 25, or 35 for a 3.5° glideslope. The rate of descent required to maintain a 3.25° glide slope at a groundspeed of 140 kts is approximately 760 ft/min.

HEIGHT ON THE GLIDESLOPE

Use the formula:

$$Height = \frac{GP\ Angle \times dist\ to\ go\ in\ ft}{60}$$

STOP The formula refers to the touchdown point. If the distance is quoted from the threshold (like with DME) add 50 feet because you will be at the screen height.

If the glideslope is published as a percentage, place the 10 index on the inner scale of the flight computer and against the percentage value on the outer scale, reading the degree value on the outer scale against the 60 index on the inner scale. In the picture above, the gradient is 5%.

EXAMPLES

1. If an ILS has a glideslope of 2.5°, what height should you be at 6 nm from the touchdown point?

At 60 nm, you would be 2.5 nm high, which is 15,200 feet. 6 nm is a tenth of that, so you should be at 1520 feet (1500 in the exam).

2. The outer marker of an ILS with a 3° glide slope is 4.6 nm from the threshold. Assuming a glideslope height of 50 ft above the threshold, what is the approximate height of an aircraft passing the outer marker?

$$\frac{Range\ (ft) \times GP\ Angle}{60} = Ht\ (ft)$$

Substituting:

$$\frac{27968 \times 3}{60} = 1398.4$$

Add the 50 ft above the threshold to get 1450 ft, in round figures. Another formula is:

$$Height = GS\ Angle \times 100 \times distance$$

where *distance* is in nautical miles.

3. With a minimum climb gradient of 200 ft/nm, at what altitude should you be 5 nm after departure to comply with the procedure?

This is simply a ratio, so:

$$\frac{200}{1} = \frac{?}{5}$$

You should be at 1000 feet. How far will you be away from the departure point when you get to 2000 feet? 10 nm. If you set this up on the flight computer, you don't even have to move the wheel for the second answer.

4. If your groundspeed is 120 kts and your vertical speed is 500 fpm, what is your gradient? Again, a proportion problem. the answer is 2.5°.

5. If your groundspeed reduces from 150 kts to 120 kts between the outer marker and the threshold on a 3° glideslope? By how much will the rate of descent reduce?

The rate of descent must be reduced to maintain the glideslope. You just need to work on the difference in speeds (30 knots) and subtract it. As every 10 kts decrease in groundspeed on a 3° ILS glidepath will need an approximate decrease in the rate of descent of 50 ft/min, the answer is 150 feet per minute.

Range & Coverage

 Outside the published range, you should not normally receive signals.

LOCALISERS

The localiser range and coverage is:

- 8° up to 10 nm
- 35° either side of the centreline up to 17 nm
- 10° either side of the centreline up to 25 nm

These may be reduced to 18 nm, 10° off the centre line if there is satisfactory alternate coverage within the intermediate approach area.

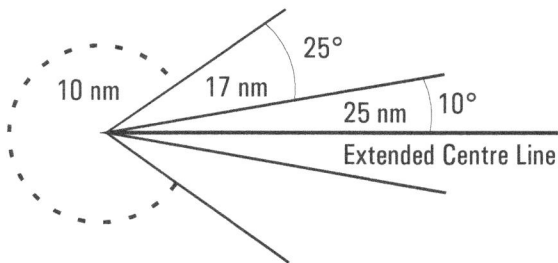

GLIDESLOPES

You should be able to receive the glideslope signal up to 10 nm. The approximate angular coverage of reliable navigation information for a 3° ILS glide path out to 10 nm is 1.35° above the horizontal to 5.25° above the horizontal and 8° each side of the localiser centreline. An aircraft tracking to intercept the localiser inbound on the approach side, outside the published ILS coverage angle may receive false course indications.

MLS

062 02 06

The *Microwave Landing System* was supposed to be a replacement for the ILS on complex approaches that require many heading and height changes, as you would get in mountains, or where ILS installations would have difficulties from surrounding buildings or interference from local radio stations. However, there is only one installation at Heathrow!

It uses a (centimetric) time-referenced scanning beam with *differential phase shift keying* to provide guidance for 3D positioning. It suffers less from interference than ILS (it is insensitive to geographical siting), and has more channels. Information can be displayed through normal or multipurpose displays. The identification is a four-letter code beginning with *M*, transmitted in Morse at least 6 times a minute. The azimuth station is broadly equivalent to the ILS localiser, but does a lot more, transmitting over 200 channels between 5031-5090 MHz on the **SHF band** (or C Band). The *elevation station* uses the same frequencies, but the signals are *multiplexed* (again, see *Computers, Etc.*)

Together with separate azimuth and elevation transmitters, the ground-based components include a **co-located** *Precision DME* to provide distance information from the runway threshold. This is so that 3-dimensional positions can be obtained.

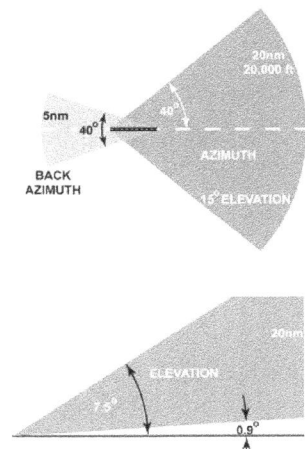

The *DME-P* is similar to the normal type, but works between 962-1105 MHz (the L Band) on a paired frequency system, and is more accurate (down to 100 feet). Without precision DME, MLS assumes the same status as an ILS.

The azimuth transmitter at the upwind end of the runway (same as the ILS) provides a fan-shaped horizontal approach zone with approach signal accuracy to ±40° either side of the centreline to at least 20 nm and 20,000 feet (15° above the horizontal in elevation). The transmitted beam sweeps back and forth between the limits of coverage, and a complete scan includes two sweeps. An aircraft on the side where the sweep starts will have a shorter interval between them than an aircraft on the far side, which is how its position is determined. The elevation transmitter is at the downwind end of the runway and works in much the same way, but elevation information is renewed three times as frequently as azimuth information.

The back azimuth at the other end of the runway, on the other hand, is ±20° to 5 nm and 5,000 feet, and is used for missed approaches, etc. However, it transmits at a lower data rate as its requirements are less.

THE FLIGHT COMPUTER

7

This chapter deals with the Jeppesen CR-3, and how useful it can be when solving many navigational problems.

THE TRIANGLE OF VELOCITIES

An aircraft in flight is affected by the wind both along its axis and from the side, or, in other words, from a head/tail or abeam component.

In flying between point A and point B, you will only get there by just pointing the nose in the right direction if there is no wind, or if there is, it is exactly on the nose or tail. This is very rarely the case, so your aircraft would *drift* off course, according to the wind's direction, if you did nothing to correct it. In other words, you would end up a certain distance left or right of the original target if the wind were blowing across your track from the relevant direction (in the early days of the North Sea, when navaids weren't around, pilots would build in a slight error to their calculations, so that they would know which side of the rig they were just in case it all went wrong).

The smart thing to do would be to make a heading correction towards the wind's direction to maintain a straight track. This, unfortunately, inclines the body of the aircraft more sideways to the track over the ground, which reduces the groundspeed, because some of the energy from the engine is used to keep it there. Thus, the speed of the aircraft through the air will not necessarily be the same as its speed over ground - if you are flying into wind, you will go slower relative to the surface, and faster if the wind is behind you:

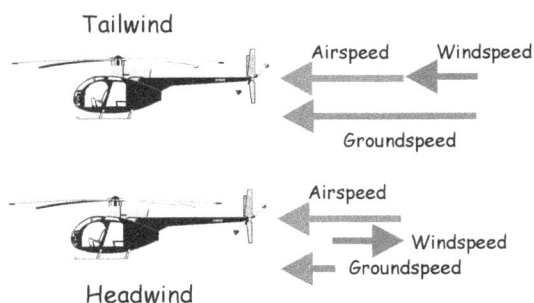

Tailwind

Headwind

You work out what the wind's effect on your trip will be by getting the forecast winds from the flight planning office, and working out a combination of three sides of a triangle, called the *triangle of velocities*, because a velocity expresses a combination of speed and direction, and we are concerned with those of your aircraft, the wind and the difference between them.

First of all, though, a few definitions:

- **Track**. Sometimes called *course*, this is the path the aircraft intends to follow over the ground, represented by the line on a map from one point to another (*Track Made Good* is the actual path - the difference between them is *Track Error*. Think of TMG as Track Made Bad, because it is where you don't want to be). Put another way, it is the angle between the direction of a meridian (True or magnetic) and the longitudinal axis of the aircraft.

- **Heading**. The direction the aircraft is pointed in, according to its compass.

- **Wind Velocity**. The speed and direction of the wind. The faster your aircraft, the less its effect. Forecast winds are given as True.

- **True Air Speed** (TAS). The speed relative to the atmosphere, not necessarily the same as that indicated on your ASI, and not necessarily the same as…..

- **Ground Speed**, or the speed of the aircraft over the ground, because of wind effects.

- **Drift**. The difference between heading and track due to wind, measured *from* heading *to* track. In sailing, this is *leeway*. The *drift angle* is the difference between the airspeed and groundspeed vectors.

- **Air Position**. The position the aircraft would have reached without wind.

- **DR Position**. The calculated position of the aircraft.

- **ETA**. Estimated Time of Arrival.

- **Fix**. Definite confirmation of position by ground observation, radio aids or astro navigation.

The velocity of an aircraft in flight (i.e. through the air) will therefore consist of its heading and airspeed.

In the diagram below, the heading is 270°(T) - the single arrow is the symbol for the heading vector, pointing the right way, of course.

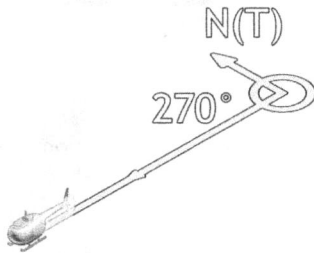

When plotting, a scale is used, so if the heading vector were 3 inches long, at 50 kts to an inch it would equal an airspeed of 150 kts, or the air position after one hour of flight. If we added the wind speed and direction to the heading vector, the resultant between them would represent track and groundspeed, also to scale.

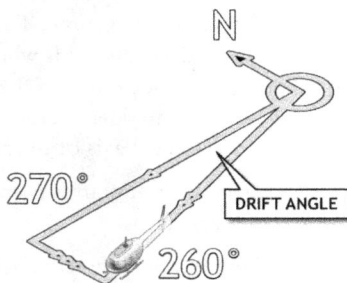

In this case, the wind vector is half an inch long, meaning 25 kts, coming from the North. Joining the ends would therefore show your ground position after one hour, and your track and groundspeed, after measurement (you will have deduced already that two arrows are used for the track and three for the wind - the track arrows always go in the opposite direction to the other two, and the wind always goes from heading to track). The *drift angle* (or track error) is measured *from* the heading *to* the track, in this case about 10°, so the track made good is 260°. It is the angle at which you will drift away from the desired track if the wind correction angle mentioned below is not applied.

The diagram above shows what would happen if you simply pointed the aircraft nose towards the West - you would drift to Port for the amount indicated. If you wanted to arrive over the intended destination, you would actually have to point the nose to the right (i.e. Starboard) enough to counteract the drift.

Just draw the wind vector on the *opposite* side of the line, and measure the length and angle of the new line joining it at the other end to find out what heading to steer (280°). The difference between heading and track is now called the *Wind Correction Angle*, or crab angle. It is the angle

through which the aircraft must be turned into wind to maintain the desired track.

Note that the drift and wind correction angles are not the same - there may be a significant difference between them if the winds are strong. The WCA is always smaller than the drift angle, but at low wind speeds we ignore it.

Don't forget to work out the variation and deviation so that the compass heading is correct.

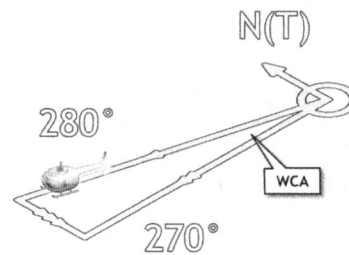

Dead Reckoning

As a navigator you need to know your present position, and how to get to another one, but the only information you have after some time in flight (if you're not looking out of the window) is your air position, based on the airspeed and heading(s) you used since you started. In theory, if you then add the wind velocity for the relevant period, you should get a ground position, which is called a *Dead Reckoning* (DR) position, because it has been deduced, or calculated, rather than being positively identified. To do this properly, you must keep an account (reckoning) of the course and distance run, and update things by using information from other sources, such as visual reference to landmarks (pilotage) or radio aids. Indeed, once the information chain has been broken, the other sources are required to re-establish your position - any errors with DR are cumulative, so the further you travel without an accurate position fix, the more the likelihood that errors will creep in.

Because you don't have room for a navigation table in your cockpit, various rules of thumb can be used in the form of *Mental Dead Reckoning*, successful use of which requires thorough flight planning and accurate flying (the 1 in 60 Rule is a good example).

DR involves the calculation of your best known position without navaids or visual fixes. In essence, it involves drawing the equivalent triangles of velocity you would create on your CR-3 on a map, although it is important to grasp that the triangle's purpose is more to do with finding directions and speeds rather than a position. With no wind, your air position would be the same as your ground position.

Dead Reckoning attempts to reconcile the two, having taken into account whatever the wind has gotten up to.

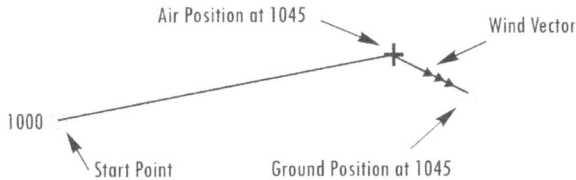

With DR, you know your TAS and the track you wish to fly, and you have a forecast wind, so you need a heading that will maintain the track, plus the ground speed so you know when you are going to get there.

Errors in DR are typically around 2-5%, usually from measurements of heading and speed. In fact any accuracy with Dead Reckoning depends on:

- The flight time since your last fix (the longer it is the less accuracy there will be)

- The accuracy of the forecast wind

- How accurately you maintain speed & heading

An air plot should be maintained constantly - every time the heading is changed, it should be recorded.

Note: There is usually a change of drift or grounsdpeed with a change of heading, which is ignored in mental DR.

FIXES

If you happen to fly over an object that can be identified from a map, you have a *position fix*, which can be used to find what the real wind is, and your actual groundspeed. On the map, simply connect a line from your air position to the fix, and measure the resulting line between them (the wind vector). The line between your start point and the fix would be the *Track Made Good*, which could be used to solve the above problem on the flight computer. The length of the wind vector is proportional to the length of time the plot has been running. Otherwise, the unit of measurement is the local nautical mile, conveniently obtained from the side of the chart in use (for most purposes, use the mean latitude. Similarly, where meridians are converging, use the mid-longitude).

When obtaining a fix, VORs are more accurate than NDBs (remember to check line-of-sight in the exam), and a 90° cut is best, always being aware of coastal effect, or coastal refraction, as described under *ADF* in *Radio Navigation*. Unfortunately, multiple position lines never meet exactly, and your position is assumed to be in the middle of the resulting *cocked hat*.

Nowadays, since fixes are readily available, the *track plot* is the favoured method, that is, the wind direction is found from the known parts of the other two sides of the triangle, using the Dalton Computer, as discussed below.

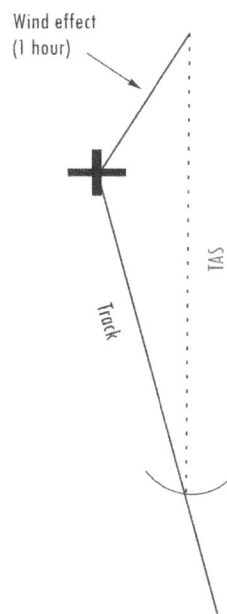

The traditional way for a navigator to do the job without a computer would be to draw the required track on the map, and an hour's worth of wind velocity from the start of that line, to scale. Then, with a pair of compasses opened out to the TAS, an arc would be described on the proposed track (the other point would be placed on the end of the W/V line). Joining the two points would produce the heading to steer to make good the track, and its length would tell you the groundspeed. The angle between heading and groundspeed is the *drift*, which could be assumed to be constant for long enough to draw a predictive series of lines for 6 minutes ahead.

As mentioned above, the lines you draw will be to scale, so one 3" long at 50 miles to the inch would represent 150 kts. When climbing and descending, take the mean TAS for the leg, and mean wind velocity.

Remember that these velocities go together:

- Heading & Airspeed

- Track & Groundspeed

- Wind Direction & Speed

The problem is that you have to find mixed pairs, such as heading and groundspeed, rather than the combinations mentioned above, because you start with a mix in the first place (you usually know the airspeed and track already). Given any four, you can figure out the others by measurement, but you can do this mechanically with the flight computer, discussed later.

PLOTTING

The above activities with triangles are part of *plotting*, which is (usually) done on a Mercator chart, because it has a latitude scale on its vertical sides, and 1° always equals 1 nm. As the latitude scale expands from the Equator, you start with that part of it nearest to your track.

- A *bearing* is the horizontal direction of one point on the Earth from another, generally expressed as an angular distance from 000° (North) clockwise through 360°. If True North is used, the bearing is a *True Bearing*. If the reference direction is the aircraft heading, it is a *relative bearing*.

- A *visual bearing* is obtained visually.

- A *radio bearing* is obtained by radio (the reciprocal of the direction of propagation of the radio wave). A *radial*, being a line of sight, is one of an infinite number of directions of radio wave propagation **from** a VOR. Radials are independent of heading.

Before being plotted, relative bearings should be converted to True bearings by adding them to the true heading of the aircraft (when the bearings were taken), and subtracting 360° when the sum exceeds this amount. Thus, TB = RB + TH.

If the bearing line is to be plotted as a straight line on a Mercator chart, you need to use a conversion angle.

LOST PROCEDURE

Assuming you have flown as accurately as possible, and the wind velocity was accurately forecast, and you made no mistakes in your flight planning, you should find yourself pretty much on track throughout the flight. However, life is not always like that, and once in a while you may find yourself unsure of your position, the technical term for being lost. The *circle of uncertainty* is a way of trying to remedy this by allowing a percentage of error and drawing a circle of appropriate size centred on your destination. In theory, you should be somewhere inside it. The diameter will very rarely be more than 10% of distance flown.

You could also find the average heading, wind velocity and TAS to estimate your ground position. Averages are based on two observed fixes.

A useful method of a pilot resolving, during a visual flight, any uncertainty in the aircraft's position is to maintain visual contact with the ground and *set heading towards a line feature such as a coastline, motorway, river or railway.*

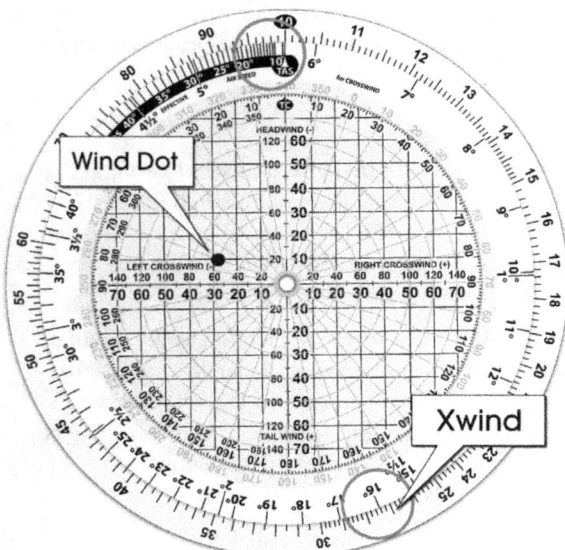

THE FLIGHT COMPUTER

The CR-3 was developed in the United States by Ray Lahr. It is a device with three rotating discs, marked with drift angles and TAS arcs, with a frosted circular screen on which you can draw the business end of the triangle of velocities.

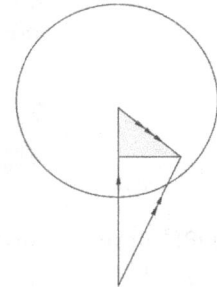

There is a dot in the centre of the screen on the vector face, around which is a compass rose that can be rotated to bring your heading or track under the lubber line at the top, labelled *TC* in the picture below. left

There are six factors to every navigation problem, namely the track and groundspeed, heading and airspeed and the wind speed and direction. If you know any four, the computer will help you find the other two.

True Heading & Groundspeed

The most common problem is to find the heading required to maintain a given track, but you still need to know the grounsdpeed so you can work out how long it will take to get to the destination. These values are not related to each other, but it's quite easy on the CR-3.

The trick with this device is to set the problem up by placing the TAS marker against the relevant value on the outer scale and the true track* on the green scale over the TC index. You should not need to move them again.

*If you are using magnetic track, set it against the variation figures either side of the TC index and the true course will be against the TC marker. See later.

Put the TAS marker against 100 kts and line up 340 with the TC marker. Place a dot at the intersection of 270° with 30 kts (the wind velocity), using the larger numbers on the low speed wind scale. You can see straight away that we are dealing with a left crosswind and a headwind.

The crosswind component is 28 kts which, read on the outer scale against the middle scale produces 16° of drift. As this is more than 10°, the TAS must be adjusted to a lower value because the nose is cocked off to the left. The result is 96 kts - as we have a headwind element of 11 kts, the groundspeed is 85 kts.

Tip: There are two degree scales on the middle disc. If the crosswind component is less than 10% of the TAS, read the crab angle on the inner scale - it will be less than 6°.

ALTERNATIVE METHOD

This method allows you to find the values required without placing a wind dot - it does, however, require the ability to gauge the wind angle off the axis of the aircraft, which some people find difficult.

For example, to find the heading & groundspeed, given:

- Airspeed: 126 kts
- Track: 040°
- W/V: 090°/20

This is the situation:

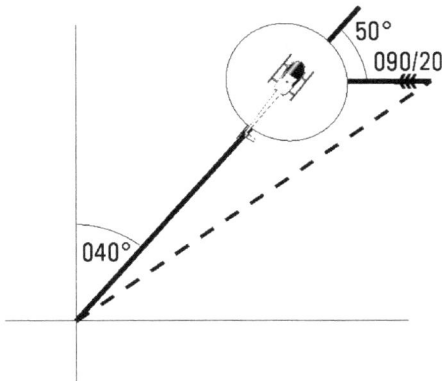

Set the relative wind angle (50°) under the TAS value on the outer scale ❶. The drift angle of 7° will be opposite the windspeed ❷.

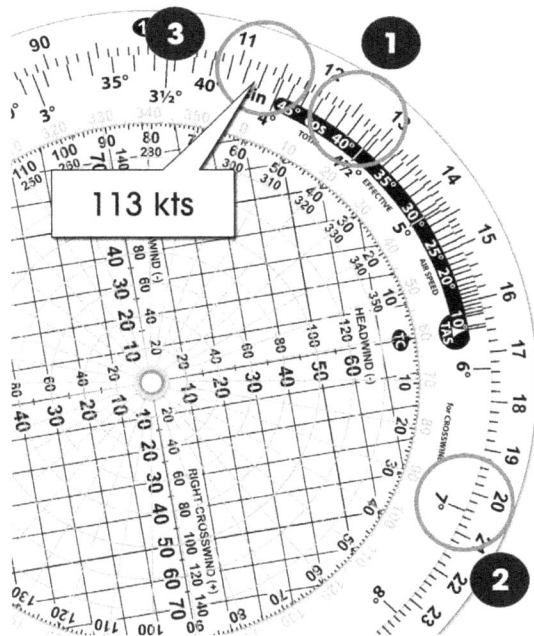

As it is a headwind, subtract the drift angle from the wind angle (50 - 7) ❸. The groundspeed (opposite 43) is 113 kts. Applying the drift angle to the track, the required heading is 047°.

The procedure is similar with a tailwind. Given:

- Airspeed: 97 kts
- Track: 352°
- W/V: 110°/15

The situation is as follows:

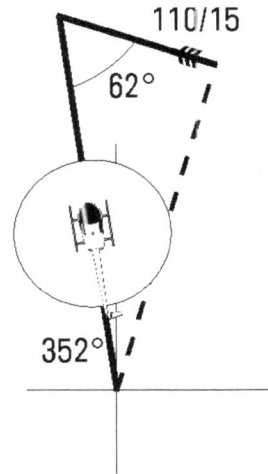

As before, set the relative wind angle (sine 62° = cos 28°) under the TAS value ❶. The drift angle of 8° will be opposite the windspeed ❷.

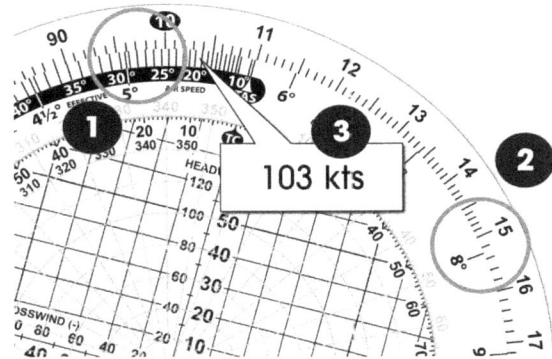

As it is a tailwind, add the drift angle to the wind angle (62 + 8) ❸. The groundspeed, opposite the result of 70, is 103 kts. Applying the drift angle to the track, the required heading is 360°.

Track and Groundspeed

If you launch off and fly in a particular direction, knowing the wind velocity and your heading (from the compass) and airspeed (from the ASI), you can find the track being made good, and your groundspeed.

The difference is that we need to place the TC index under the heading as a starting point, because it lets us at least estimate the crosswind component. Then the top disc is moved once or twice until the drift angle is the same as the difference between the heading and track.

So, having set the wind markings and placed the TAS at the appropriate speed, set the heading value under the TC index and check the estimated crosswind component and drift angle.

Rotate the top disc in the correct direction by the estimated drift angle - that is, if the crosswind is from the right, move it clockwise and vice versa. This brings the heading to the correct side of the track (use the black variation scale to help you). Check the crosswind and drift component again, and possibly again. When they don't change between movements, you have found the proper track. Now you can find the head or tail wind component.

True Heading & Airspeed

You often need to maintain a groundspeed in order to get to a reporting point or a fix at a particular time.

As the TAS is not known, we have to start with the wind, plus the true track, then use the head- or tailwind component with the groundspeed to find it.

- Set up the wind speed and direction

- Set the TC index on the track

- Determine the head- or tailwind component and apply it to the groundspeed. Place the TAS index at the TAS value

- Read the crosswind component underneath the wind dot, then find the crab angle in the usual way. If the correction angle is greater than 10°, move the TAS index again the to the *effective* TAS. Apply the correction angle as necessary.

Wind Direction & Speed

- Set up the TAS and TC indexes

- Find the difference between the heading and track and find the crosswind component opposite that value on the outer disc

- Find the corresponding value along the horizontal scale. If the drift angle is less than 10°, there is no correction for effective TAS.

- Apply the difference between airspeed and groundspeed to the vertical scale

- The wind direction and speed will be found where the two lines cross.

ALTERNATIVE METHOD
Given:

- Track: 142°

- Groundspeed: 130 kts

- Airspeed: 150 kts

- Heading: 137°

The difference between airspeeds is 20 kts and that between heading and track is 5°. We need to find a matching situation on the outer and middle scales.

Track 142, Heading 137

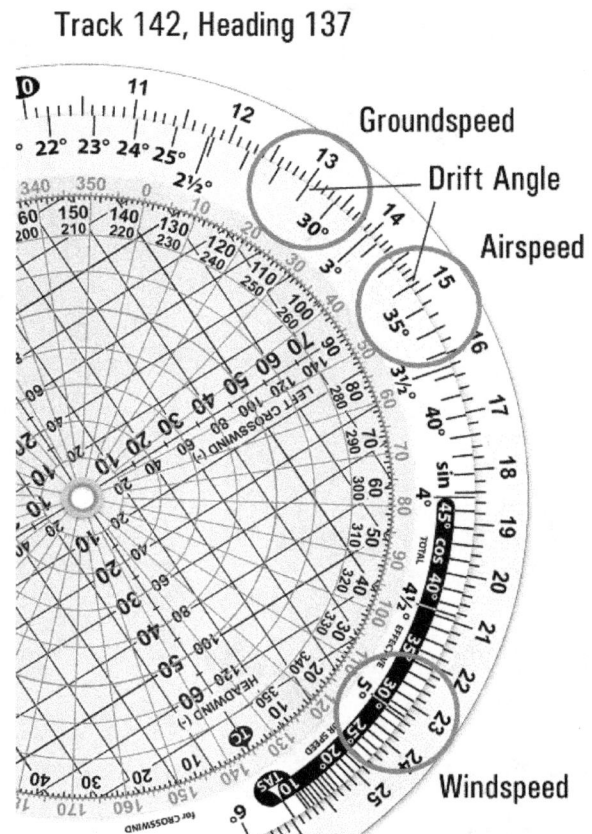

Rotate the middle scale until you find a difference in degrees that matches the difference between airspeeds.

The windspeed will be found opposite the drift angle.

As the heading is less than the track, the wind is from the left, and is 34° off the nose (based on the track). 108°.

DR Position

EXAMPLE 1

For a 4 hour flight at 180 kts on a track of 055°, find the departure and change of latitude.

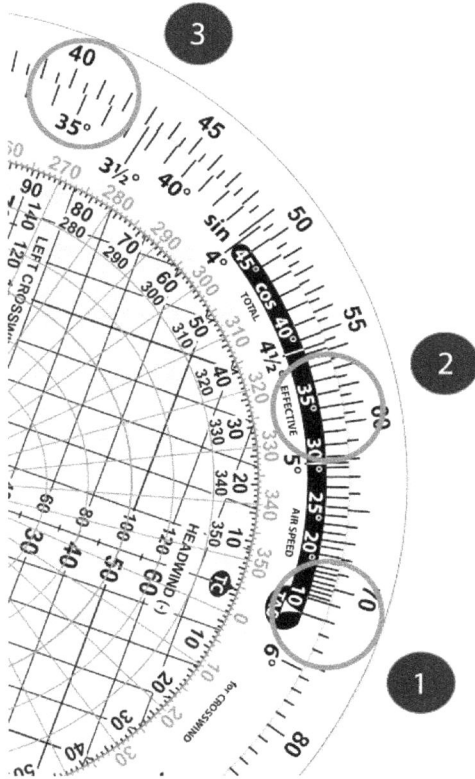

1. Place the TAS index under the distance of 72

2. Under the sine of 55° (cos 35°) read 58 nm (departure)

3. Under the cosine of 55° (sine 35°) read 41 nm (d lat)

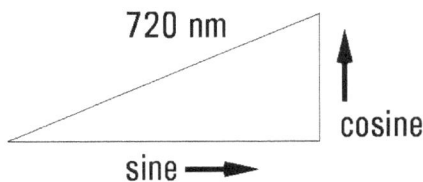

EXAMPLE 2

What is your DR position after 3 hours along a track of 242°(T) with a groundspeed of 138 kts, having started at 50° 30′N 9° 20′W?

242°(T) is too large for the scale, so take 62° off South.

1. Set the TAS index to the distance of 414.

2. Under the sine of 62° (complementary cosine 28°) find the departure of 365′ or 6° 5′.

3. Under 28° (complementary sine to the cosine of 62°) read the d lat of 194.5′ or 3° 14.5′.

4. Apply half the d lat to the start position to obtain the mid latitude of 48° 53′.

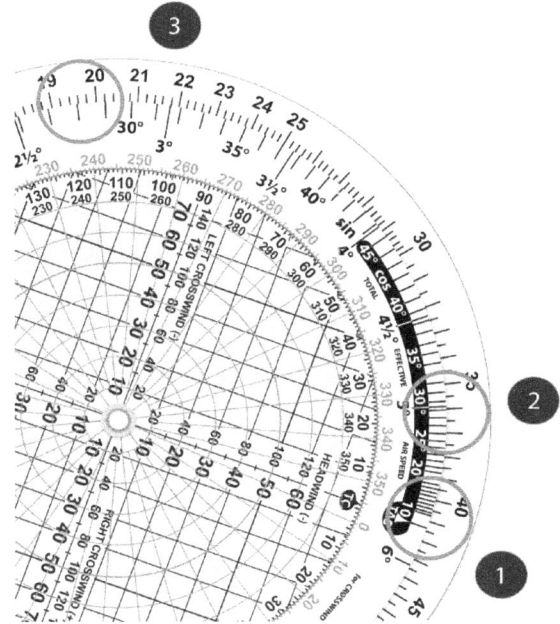

5. Under 365 (the departure), set 41° 07′ (the complement to 48° 53′).

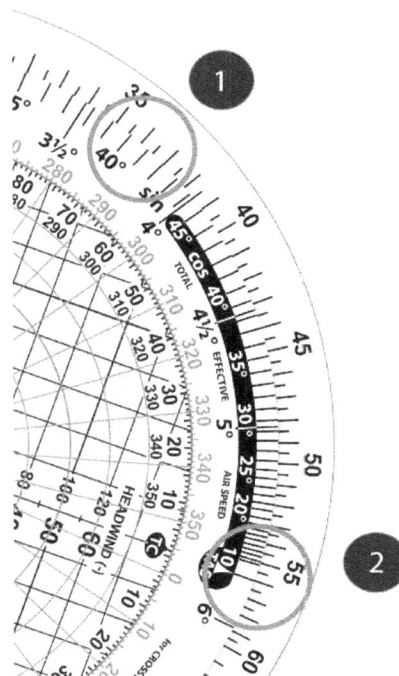

6. Read 560 (d long) or 9° 20′ under the TAS index.

The new DR position is 47° 15.5′N 18° 40′W.

Double Drift

When you're in a remote place without much weather information, it is possible to work out what the wind is by observing your drift on different headings (you might be able to find it by trying to maintain track against a navaid). If the angles are large enough (say over 60°), two readings can be enough, but three is better (see below).

If you turn away from track by 45°, then back again, also at 45°, you won't go far off track. In fact, if both legs are flown for 1 minute 20 seconds (they should both be the same), you will only lose a minute of flight time.

So, you are tracking the 200° radial inbound* to a VOR on a heading of 010°(M). Then you take the 090° radial on a heading of 080°(M). If the variation is +5° and the TAS is 240 kts, what is the wind velocity?

*A radial is from, so you will be tracking 020°.

This is how it would be plotted:

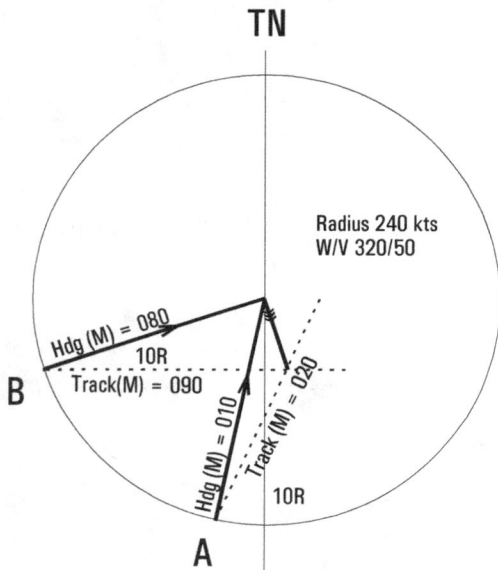

You would initially draw a radius equal to the airspeed at a suitable scale. Then draw the lines in from the edge.

On the CR-3, place the TAS marker against 240 kts. Then put 005° against the drift value of 10° (on the left because the wind is coming from the left).

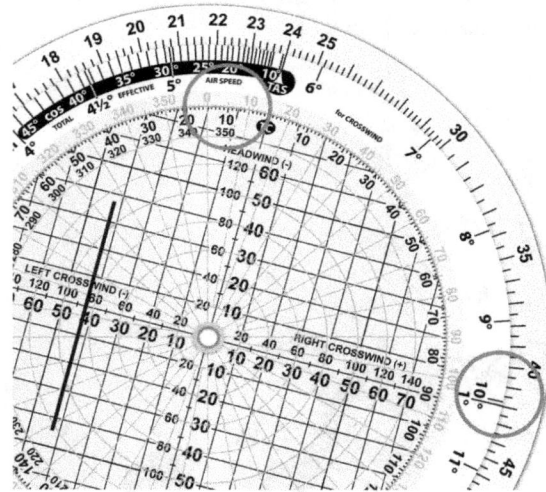

Check the crosswind component of 42 kts against the drift value on the middle ring and mark in the 42 kts line.

Next, place 075° against the same drift value:

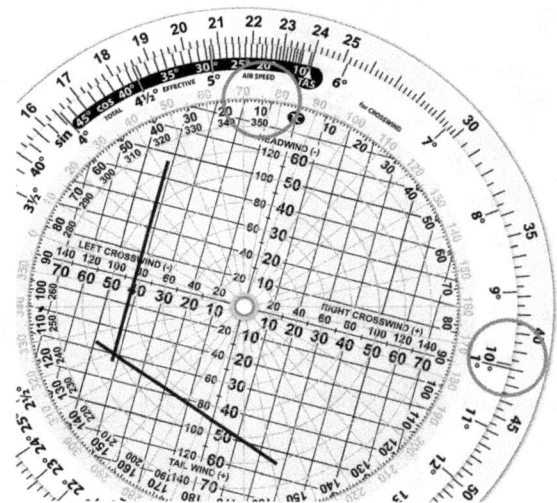

Check the crosswind component of 42 kts against the drift value on the middle ring and mark the 42 kts line again.

The wind velocity is 319/51 kts, where the lines cross.

Triple Drift

Given:

- Track (T) = 035° Drift 12°R
- Track (T) = 140° Drift 5°R
- Track (T) = 295° Drift 12°L

If the TAS is 120 kts, what is the wind velocity?

Again, this is how it would be plotted as above:

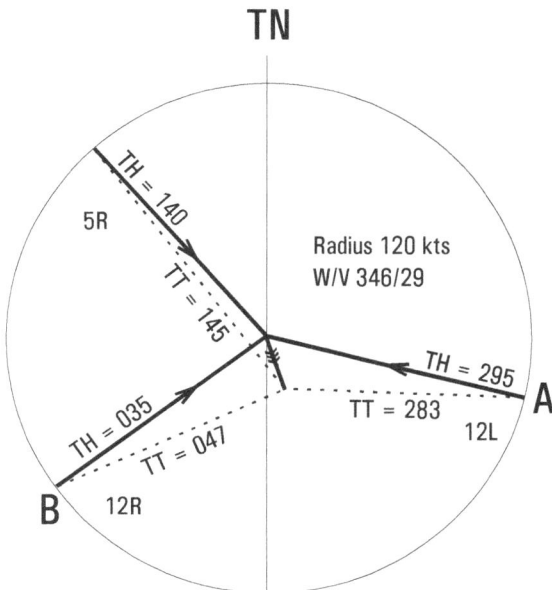

Place the TAS marker against 120 kts, then place 035° against the drift value (12°). Don't forget, the wind is coming from the left. Check the crosswind component of 25 kts against the drift value on the middle ring and mark in the 25 kts line:

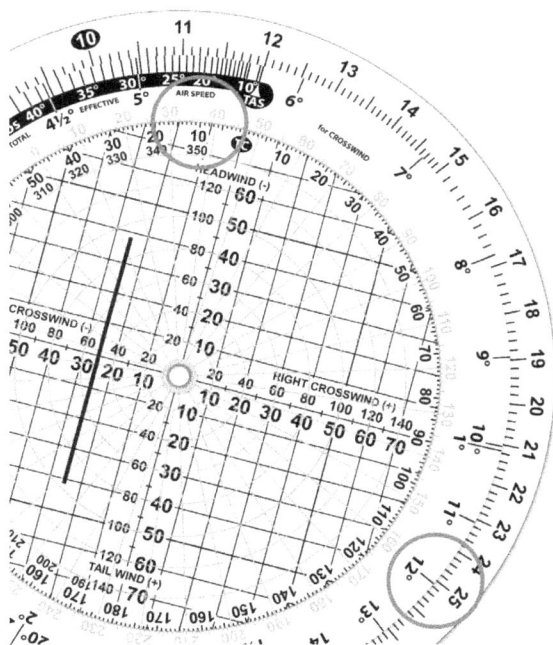

Then place 140° against the drift value (5°). Mark in the 10 kts line.

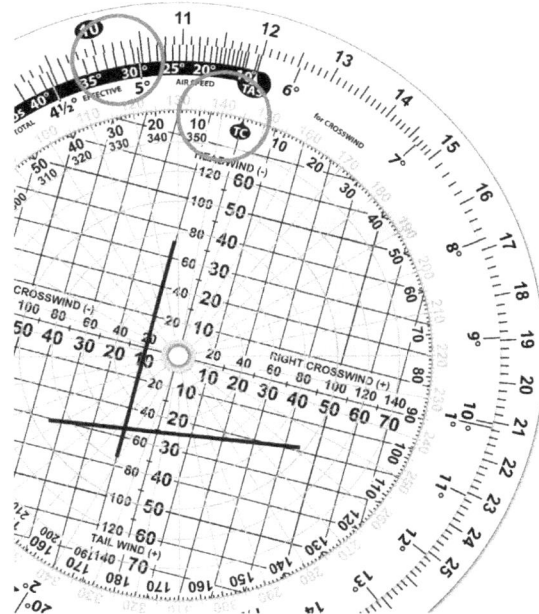

Next, place 295° against the drift value (12°L this time). Check the crosswind component of 25 kts against the drift value and mark in the 25 kts line:

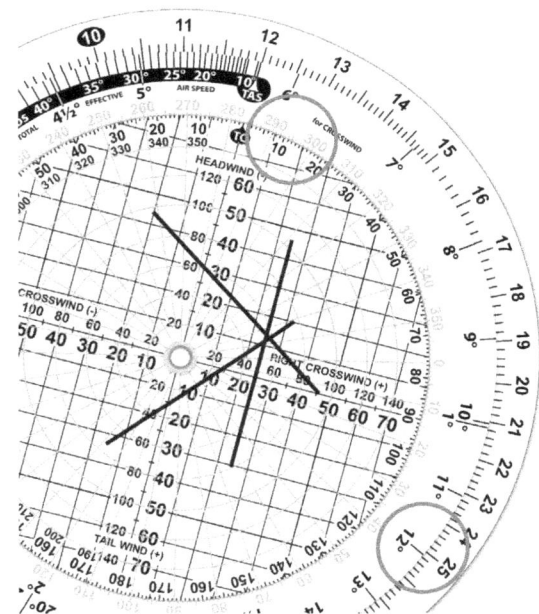

The wind velocity is 346°/29 kts.

RUNWAY CROSSWIND

Just use the CR-3 in the same way as you would for finding heading and groundspeed (see above), except that the TAS step is not required.

Variation

You can set the magnetic heading you get off a chart directly against the variation value (also from the chart) and the true heading will be against the TC index.

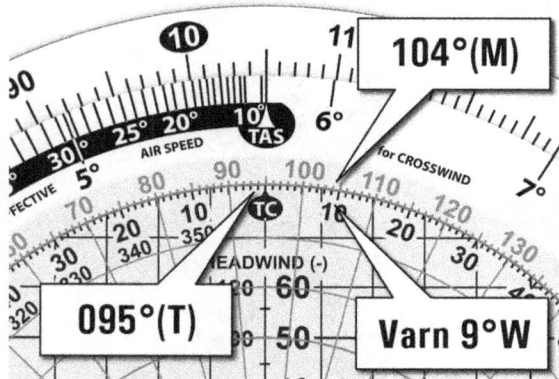

Setting 104°(M) against 9°W produces 95°(T).

Sines & Cosines

To find the sine of any angle, simply line up the TAS marker with the 10 on the outer scale and read them opposite each other:

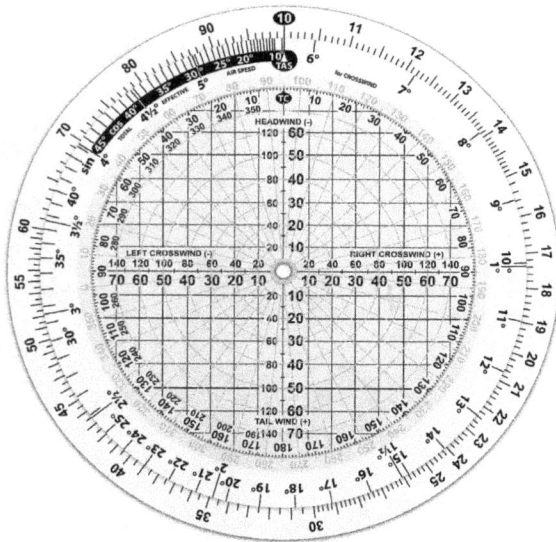

The sine scale is wrapped twice around the centre disc so you can use small angles as well as large ones. If you use the inner sine scale, you need to add .0 to the front of the digits shown. Otherwise (if the angle is larger than 5° 50´), just place the decimal point in front.

Remember that the cosine of an acute angle is equal to the sine of 90° minus the angle, so the sine of 54° has the same value as the cosine of 36°. This can be seen with the black cosine scale next to the TAS mark. The cosine of 75° is opposite the sine of 25° in the white sine scale.

The tangent is found simply by dividing the sine value by the cosine, which is done with the slide rule on the other side of the computer...........

The Slide Rule

On the reverse side of the CR-3 is a circular slide rule, with the space between the numbers (from 10 to 100) decreasing as the numbers increase.

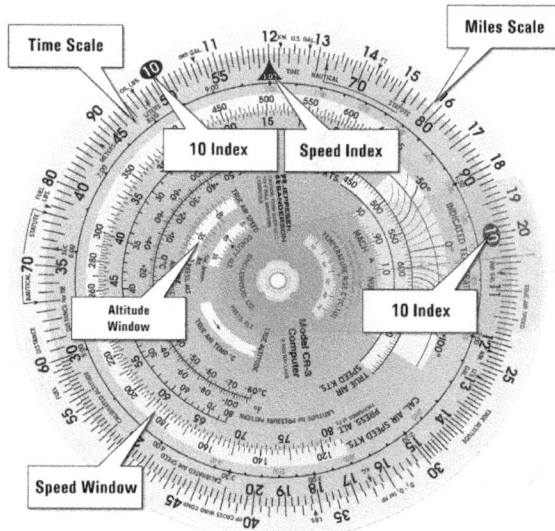

The outer, stationary, scale is called the *miles scale*, and the inner one, which rotates, is the *minute scale*, so distance and time are always opposite each other.

Only major numbers are shown on the scales - the gradations between each one are meant to be interpolated as necessary.

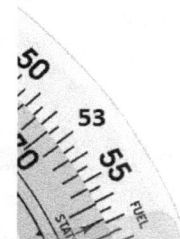

Any relationship between the numbers on each scale holds true for any other number - if you put 20 on the inner (minute) scale against the 10 on the outer (miles) scale, all the numbers on the inner scale will be double those on the outer scale.

As with any slide rule, you need the approximate answer first, as a gross error check, and to give you an idea of where to put the decimal point. For example, 1 nautical mile is just under 2 kilometres, so you would expect the number of kilometres to be larger for a given distance. It's also useful to remember that 120 knots is equal to 2 nm per minute and 180 knots is 3 miles per minute, etc.

MULTIPLICATION & DIVISION

This was the whole purpose of a slide rule in the first place, and the process is useful in solving many navigation problems, such as Critical Point, 1 in 60, etc. (if you were wondering how the slide rule works, you are adding *indices*, which is also where logarithms come from, but that is outside the scope of this book). The CR-3 is the equivalent of a 17 inch slide rule, making it 70% more sensitive that a 10 inch rule. The inside scale is the C scale and the outside scale (where the answers are traditionally read) is the D scale. This is because the cursor can be held steady against it.

Note: Do not confuse the 60 index used for solving navigation problems with the 10 index!

To multiply two numbers, place the **⑩** index on the inner scale against one of them on the outer scale. Holding the two scales so that they don't move, place the cursor over the second number (on the inside scale) and read the answer opposite on the outer scale, underneath the cursor. For successive numbers, hold the cursor where it is and move the **⑩** index on the inner scale underneath it. Then move the cursor again (holding the discs steady) to the third number to find the answer as before.

Division is even simpler - place the divisor on the inside scale underneath the number to be divided on the outside scale. The answer is on the outside scale opposite the **⑩** index on the inner scale.

RATIOS

The ratio of any two numbers is the result of dividing one by the other, which may be expressed as a fraction. In this case, the number on the outer scale is the numerator and the one on the inner scale is the denominator. This is very handy when it comes to Time, Speed and Distance problems - if you do 24 miles in 8 minutes, how long will it take you to do another 21 miles? Simply set up the problem on the scales as you would for fractions:

$$\frac{24}{8} = \frac{21}{}$$

The number opposite 21 is 7 (minutes).

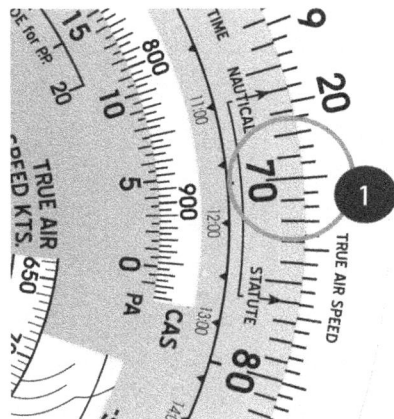

Similarly with fuel - if you use 40 gallons in 2:15 hours, and you have 25 gallons left, how much time is left? Set 135 under 40, and under 25 read 84.5 on the inner scale.

PROPORTIONS

A proportion is the expression of equality of two or more ratios - for example, 6:8 is the same as 3:4. If you set one ratio up on the computer, you can find any other easily. If asked to find what number 45 has the same ratio with as 6 does to 8, you just line up 6 on the outer scale with 8 on the inner and read off 60 on the inner scale opposite 45.

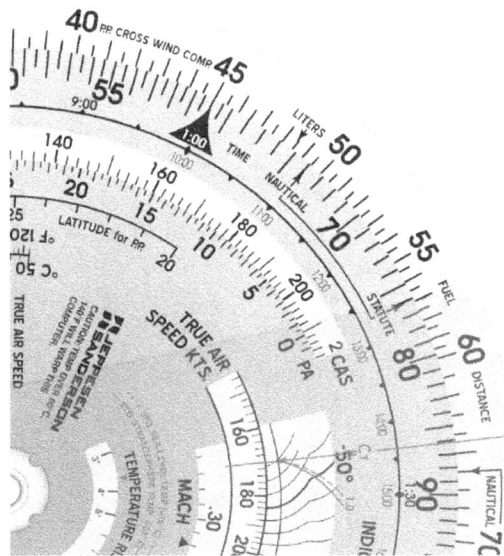

If you climb 6000 feet in 8 minutes, you will climb 4500 feet in 6.

Conversions are ratios as well.

CONVERSIONS

These are done by lining up arrows on both scales representing the commodities concerned.

DISTANCE

In the picture, the arrow labelled *statute* on the outer scale is opposite the one marked *nautical* (miles) on the inner scale. Having lined them up, all you do is read off the equivalent on each scale - here, 8 statute miles are equal to around 7 nautical miles. You can use this for mph and knots as well.

Alternatively, you can place a quantity against a mark and read the conversion against the other. The KM mark (for kilometres) is near the figure 12 (see picture below). To convert 22 km into nautical miles, set 22 against *km* mark and read off 11.9 at the *nm* mark.

VOLUMES

On each scale, there is a mark for Imperial gallons near the figure 11 and one for US gallons near 13. To convert from one to the other, simply line up the marks and read the relevant quantities on the appropriate scale.

WEIGHTS

Changing kilograms to pounds is done in a similar way to the above. The lbs mark is near 36 on the outside scale and that for kg is near 16 on the inside scale.

FUEL WEIGHTS

For fuel weights, you will need the specific gravity, which is 1 for water, and is therefore a measure of density in kg per litre. In other words, it may change with temperature. It will vary from place to place and between fuel grades, but that in the Flight Manual is the one to use.

For example, if the s.g. of Jet A1 is taken as 0.79, how much does 2000 litres weigh? Set the 1 (marked "10") on the inner scale against 2000 on the outer scale and read off the weight of 1580 on the outer scale against 79.

How many litres do you need from the fuel guy if you can carry 2600 kg and the s.g. is 8.2? Try 3170.

SPEED, & FUEL CONSUMPTION

These are the most common problems. The 60 point on the inner scale can be positioned against fuel quantity or distance on the outer scale to read time on the inner scale.

In the picture on the right, the speed triangle (60) is opposite 120 (knots or gallons) on the outer scale, which means it will take 6 minutes to go 12 nautical miles, or 6.5 to use 13 gallons, and so on. The figure 12 could mean 1.2, 12, or 120 kts/mph/kilometres per hour, depending on the problem, so you could travel 6, 60 or 600 miles in 60 minutes, respectively.

How long will you take to fly 60 nm at 90 kts? Less than hour, so place the 60 index under 90 on the outer scale, move around to 60 and read 40 mins on the inner scale.

How far will you fly in 90 minutes at 105 kts? A quick estimate suggests it will be around 150 nm - place the index against 105 on the outer scale and read off 157.5 on the outer scale against the 9 on the inner scale.

If you travel 47 nm in 24 minutes, what is your groundspeed? Place 24 on the inner scale against 47 on the outer scale and read 117.5 kts against the index.

If you used 40 US gallons over 3 hrs 20 minutes of flight, what is your fuel consumption? 12 US gals/hr.

RATE OF CLIMB

Use the outer scale for the rate of climb value or the height climbed, and the inner scale for time, then use the 10 index instead of the 60.

Place 10 against 300 (feet per minute), against the time on the inner scale (say 9 minutes), read 2970 feet climbed.

If you climb 2000 feet over 8 minutes, your rate of climb is 250 feet per minute.

1 IN 60 RULE

To use the previous example, if you are 8 miles off after 40 miles, the error angle is 12°, as indicated against the time index when you line up 40 nm under 8:

If you are 10 miles off course after 150 miles, how many degrees are required as a correction to parallel the course? Set 150 under 10, then read 4° opposite the 60 index.

EXAMPLES

Find the angles to parallel your track, the closing angle and the total, from the miles off, out and left to go:

No	Off	Out	Left	Par	CA	Tot
1	8R	100	150			
2	10R	125	175			
3	12L	60	100			
4	15L	75	50			
5	6R	96	66			

ANSWERS

No	Off	Out	Left	Par	CA	Tot
1	8R	100	150	4.8L	3.2L	8L
2	10R	125	175	4.8L	3.4L	8.2L
3	12L	60	100	12R	7.2R	19.2R
4	15L	75	50	12R	18R	30R
5	6R	96	66	3.75	5.45L	9.2L

TEMPERATURE

The temperature conversion scale (between °F and °C) is midway between the centre of the disc and the outside edge. You don't need to set anything up, just use it directly.

Note: Temperatures used for solving problems such as airspeed should be in °C.

TIME

Conversions from hours to minutes and vice versa can be done in a similar fashion to temperature, above, using a combination of the minute and hours scales.

The large numbers on the outside of the minute scale are, predictably, for minutes only. Hours are represented on an inner circle just below:

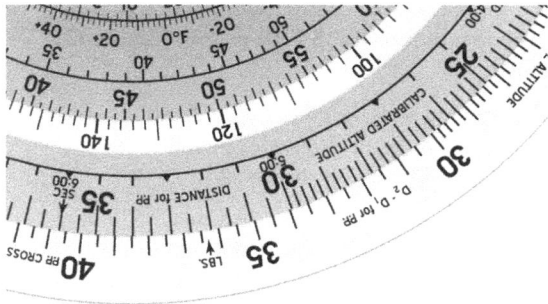

In the picture above, the small number below 30 on the inner scale is 5:00, meaning 5 hours, or 300 minutes divided by 60. It could also represent 50 hours or 3000 minutes - it just depends on the problem. Each small mark between the hour numbers represents 10 minutes. If you want to read 8 minutes, for example, just use the divisions on the larger minute scale, which are 2 minutes each, in conjunction with the cursor.

Also in the picture above, you will see a SEC mark below an arrow at 36 minutes. If you place the 60 index against a number of minutes on the outside (miles) scale, a straight conversion to seconds will be found at the SEC arrow.

Tip: Use the number 36 to solve rate, time & distance problems when you need the answer in minutes and seconds rather than hours and minutes. It is especially useful in instrument flight when you are dealing with small distances, such as between the outer marker and the threshold on a non-precision approach.

SQUARE ROOTS

These can be found easily, too (useful for VHF ranges). Find the number you want the square root of on the outer scale, then rotate the inner one until the number opposite 10 is the same as the one against your original number. For example, 400 will have 2 opposite, as well as against 10.

TRUE AIR SPEED & ALTITUDE

There are auxiliary scales in the centre for calculations concerning pressure and density altitudes.

To find TAS (using the old method for light aircraft that don't fly very fast), line up the temperature against the pressure altitude in the airspeed window, then read the TAS on the outer scale against the CAS.

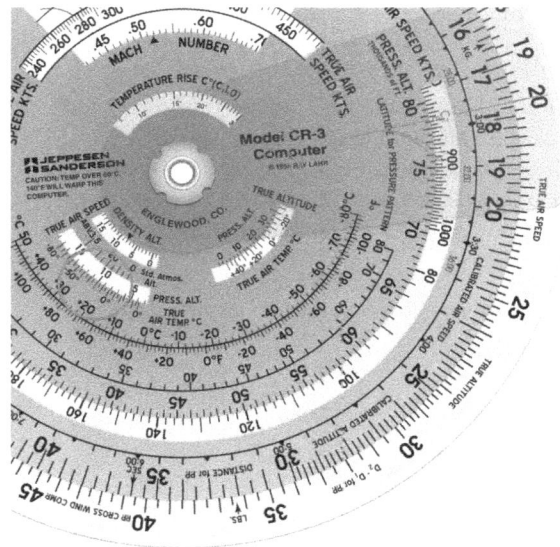

In the picture above, the temperature is -20°C at 10,000 feet. The indicated airspeed is 177 kts, and the TAS is 200. The Density Altitude is 8100 feet.

True altitude is done in the same way, but using the Altitude window to the right - lining up the same figures for PA and temperature would give you a true altitude of 18 900 ft against an indicated altitude of 20 000.

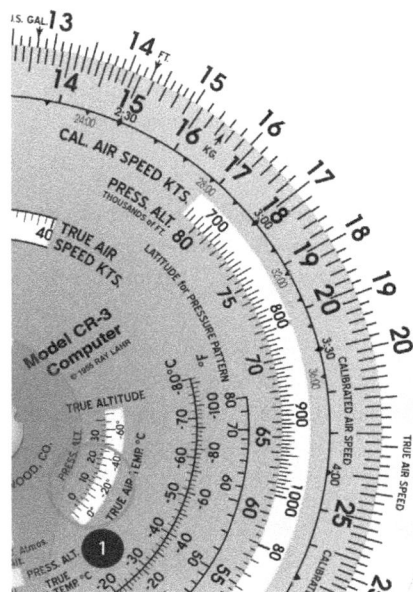

However, this assumes that the reporting station is at sea level. If you know its proper elevation, you can be a little more accurate. This is because the elevation normally allows for ISA conditions. By using the known elevation, you avoid this small error.

So, again using the values above, if the reporting station is at 4000 feet, you would work on 16,000, to get a true altitude of 15,100 feet. Putting the elevation back produces a true altitude of 19,100 feet.

MACH NUMBER

The slide rule allows you to find the speed of sound and the TAS for any Mach number (within 2 knots) in standard conditions. On the CR-3, line up the 10 index on the inner scale against approximately 650 knots on the outer scale and you will see a double headed arrow in the outer TAS window:

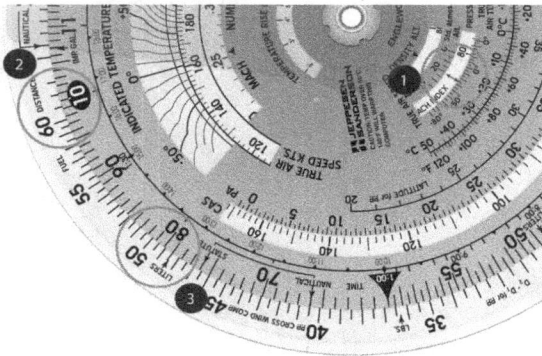

Line up one end of the arrow against the OAT (in this case -25°C), and the local speed of sound of 615 kts can be found opposite the 10 index on the inner scale, which is Mach 1. Mach 0.8 is 491 kts.

Just to add to the confusion, the OAT may be given as an ISA deviation at a certain altitude, so you must find the ISA temperature first and apply the deviation.

If the PA is placed at the top end of the Mach Index arrow, the other end will provide an estimate of it.

TRUE AIR TEMPERATURE

You can use upper air temperatures to predict your TAS, based on the fact that the speed of sound depends on the TAT, and TAS is the product of the Mach number and the speed of sound.

Line up the CAS against PA in the long CAS/PA window, the note the Mach number in the large window. Then line up the Mach Index with the TAT. Opposite the Mach number just obtained on th inner scale, read the TAS on the outer scale.

TAS (MODERN METHOD)

Finding the TAS based on the Total Air Temperature (or Indicated Temperature in Jeppesen-speak) involves using the green hairlines on the cursor, labelled C_T 0.8 and C_T 1.0, the latter being curved, and used at the stratosphere assuming a temperature of -55°C at 35,000 feet. Your aircraft will have one temperature probe or the other fitted (or something in between that needs interpolating). The dotted line is for sea level, so interpolate between there and the tropopause. **For the ATPL exams use the CT 1.0 hairline.**

Note: This method is designed to be used with knots rather than miles per hour, although it is still more accurate than the old method shown above.

To find the TAS at FL 30, flying at 360 kts CAS, with a TAT of -21°C, line up the PA against the CAS in the long CAS/PA window:

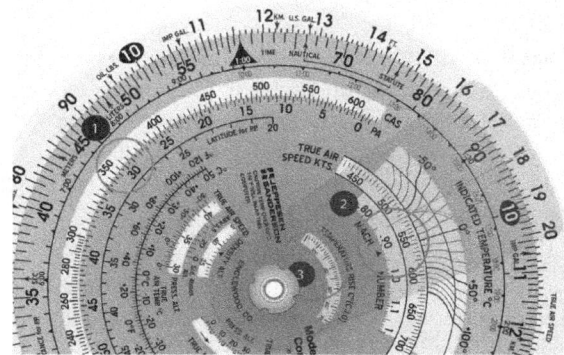

The Mach number shows up as 0.92 in the Indicated Temperature window on the opposite side. Move the cursor and place the 1.0 C_T hairline over the reference line where it cuts the -21°C line. The TAS is 524 kts.

To **find the TAS from the Mach number** and temperature, line the green cursor arrow up with the Mach number and move the cursor hairline over the temperature. The TAS will be found on the outer scale under the cursor line.

CAS FROM TAS

Sometimes you need to arrive somewhere at a specific time and may need to find a TAS that will maintain a certain groundspeed. You then need an equivalent CAS for that TAS.

In the large TAS window, line up the temperature line on the cursor with the required temperature on the top disc, then move them both until they line up with the TAS. You can read the CAS opposite the pressure altitude in the long window on the opposite side.

TEMPERATURE RISE

In the picture above, if you continue the straight line down, you will see the temperature rise of 36°C indicated against the small green arrow. The OAT is -56C.

You only need to use the values for TAS and indicated air temperature in the large window. The temperature rise is indicated as a continuation of the cursor.

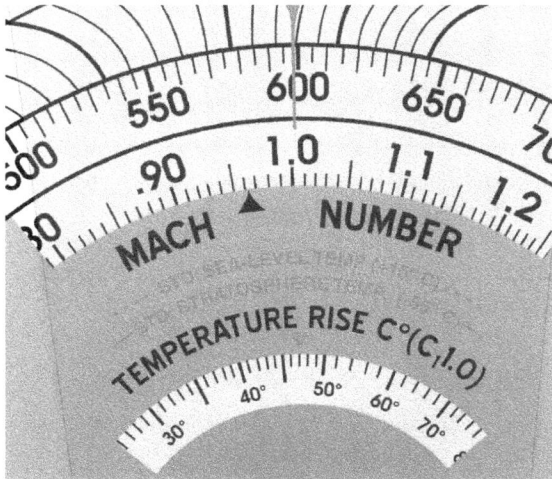

Critical Point

At some stage between the departure and destination, there is a point (on the same track) from which it will take the same time to turn back to where you came from as to carry on to where you were going, or to either of two airfields, not necessarily in front of or behind you, which is useful if you have an emergency and want to land as soon as possible. Also known as the *Point of Equal Time* (PET), or the *Equi-time Point* (ETP), this point is expressed in terms of time, assuming that the TAS, wind and fuel consumption are constant. In other words, it has nothing to do with fuel.

A lot depends on the type of emergency. If it's a medical one, for instance, or a disruptive passenger, your aircraft will have no change in performance and you won't lose any airspeed. However, if you lose an engine, it will all change drastically. Thus, there are two options to consider:

* All Engines Operating (AEO).
* One Engine Inoperative (OEI). Reduced airspeeds are used after the engine fails, of course, but full airspeed is used to calculate when you get to the CP. That is, you find the *position* (going from) with reduced speeds first, then when you will get there (going to) at full speed.

The simple formula to find the distance is:

$$\frac{D \times H}{O + H}$$

where D = total distance, H is the return groundspeed and O is the Onward. The Out and On speeds are technically different things (especially after an engine failure), but EASA do not seem to notice.

To calculate the time taken to arrive at the ~~critical point~~ PET, first find the distance, then divide by the outbound groundspeed (so in the engine failure case use the all-engines-operating airspeed) to find a time in hours.

Example: A flight is planned over a distance of 312 nm. The TAS is 162 kts and safe endurance is 2 hours 40 minutes. In still air the critical point would be half-way, 166 nm from the departure point. With a forecast tailwind of 20 knots out the groundspeeds can be calculated as 182 kts out and 142 kts home. The distance to the CP is now 137 nm. This is significantly close, because the wind will take the aircraft more quickly towards the destination.

The formula is derived from the fact that the *times* from the CP in the picture to A and B are the same, or x = y:

But time is equal to distance divided by speed, so:

$$\frac{x}{H} = \frac{y}{O}$$

where O is the groundspeed *On* and H is the groundspeed *Home* (assuming you are travelling from A to B in the first place). Take D as representing the whole distance, DO as distance On and DH as distance back.

Therefore:

```
OX  =  HY

OX  =  HD  -  HX

OX  +  HX  =  HD

X  =  D  x  H
       O  +  H
```

It can be set up to work as a proportion on the flight computer by placing the sum of the groundspeeds home and out on the inner scale against groundspeed home on the outer scale, due to shuffling the formula around:

```
CP (Distance)  =  D  x  H
                  O  +  H

CP (Distance)  =  H
     D            O  +  H
```

Example: You have a total distance of 920 nm, with a groundspeed out of 240 kts and one home of 210 kts and a flight planned time enroute of 230 minutes. Find the time and distance to the Critical Point.

First, line up the sum of the groundspeed home and out (450 kts) on the inner scale against the groundspeed home on the outer scale ❶. The corresponding times and distances will appear opposite each other, with the answers on the outer scale. The time to the CP (107.5 mins) is against the flight planned time of 230 minutes ❷ and the distance (430 nm) is against the total distance ❸. Always add the totals up (there and back) to see if they are the same. The CP will move into wind from the halfway point, where it will be in nil wind conditions.

With multiple legs (say, on an airway route), just work them out individually, add them all up and treat them as one distance.

OFF TRACK ETP

You cannot use the formula here, because you don't know the groundspeeds yet. A little diagram is best:

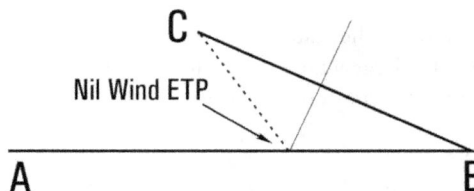

Between A to B, the point at which it will take the same time to divert to C as to carry on to B is simple to find - just bisect the line between B and C and extend it to the original track. As the result is an isosceles triangle, the distance is the same to B or C from the nil wind point. The process is the same if you have two alternates either side of the track - just bisect the line between the choices and create an isosceles triangle around them.

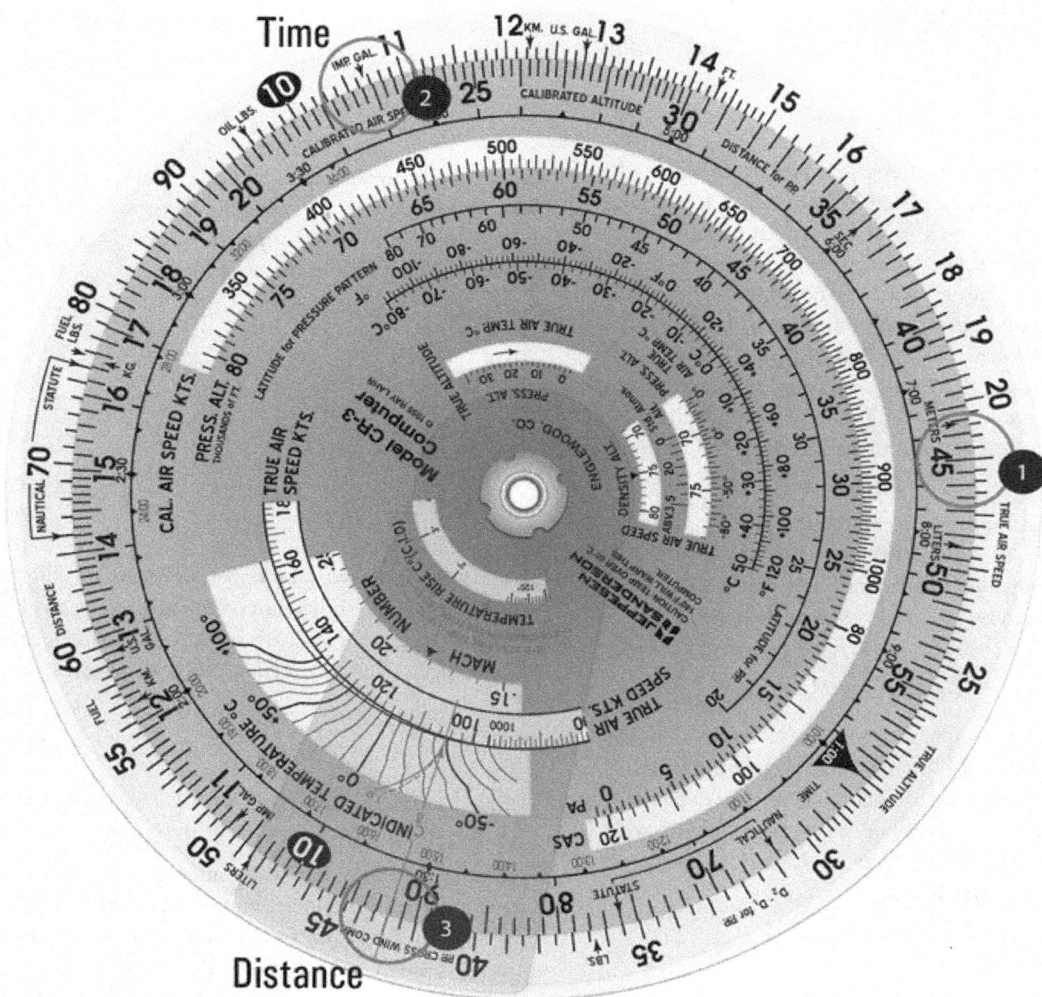

If the diagram is to scale, use the whizzie to calculate the groundspeeds, and hence the times.

If you want to draw a wind vector line, do it backward from the ETP, in the correct direction, for the right length, which you can find by dividing the diversion distance by the TAS (to obtain a ratio) and multiplying by the wind speed. Parallel the bisector through the origin of the wind vector and the adjusted ETP lies where it cuts across the original track.

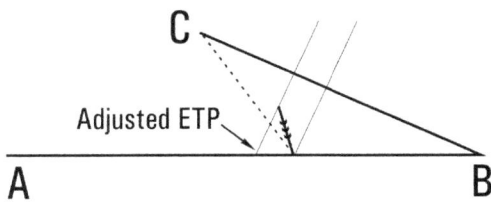

Point of Safe Return

You also need to know the point at which you cannot turn back at all, which is a calculation done every day for long offshore flights* (around 180 nm), or those over hostile terrain, or with no alternates.

*Normally, when going offshore, you need an onshore alternate, but sometimes you can nominate an oil rig.

Also known as the *Point of No Return*, this is the furthest point you can fly to and then return to a landing point behind you (usually your point of departure), based on a fixed amount of fuel, which usually, for obvious reasons, takes account of reserves. In other words, it is an on-track situation. The *Point of Safe Diversion* is for off-track problems, when alternates become involved, below.

After the Point of Safe Return, you do not have enough fuel to return home safely, hence the name. It is purely a fuel (actually, an endurance) problem, having nothing to do with distance, again assuming that the TAS, wind and fuel consumption are constant. Because you are returning to the departure point, the operating limits at the destination, including holding fuel, no longer apply, so you have more fuel to play with, which helps to compensate for the higher fuel consumption if one engine has failed. In such a situation, the speed to the PNR is calculated at full value, and the return at the lesser speed.

The principles are good for other situations, too - your destination might get socked in underneath a warm front, so you would need to know the last position enroute that would allow you to go to an alternate where the weather is better. You would check the weather at the original destination and make the decision whether to abort or not when you start to approach the calculated value. With this in mind, another definition of PSR is **the greatest distance you can go past an airfield, and return to it with required reserves intact.**

Any tailwind outbound becomes a headwind homebound and, as the detrimental effect is experienced for longer than the beneficial effect, you will spend longer beating headwinds than the benefit gained from tailwinds. If you estimate the same fuel for each leg of an out-and-back trip, and assume that the head- and tailwinds will cancel each other out, you will run out of fuel not too far from home.

As soon as a wind gets involved, you need more fuel than you would in still air.

Example: Every day, you fly from Rainbow Lake (where there is no rainbow and no lake!) in N Alberta to Shekhili compressor station, where there is no fuel. The distance is 50 nm each way and the cruise speed is 100 kts (it's a Bell 206). Fuel consumption is 29 US gals per hour. On a nil-wind day, therefore, it should be half an hour each way but, with 20-knot tailwinds outbound, you get there in only 25 minutes. The journey back, on the other hand, takes 37.5 minutes, which is 62.5 minutes in total. This may not sound much, but with 60-knot winds, you would be flying for 35 minutes longer than expected, and the figures get worse with longer stage lengths. **The distance to the PNR is greatest with zero wind**, and reduces with the wind, regardless of its direction.

Otherwise, to get the simple (normal) PNR time in minutes, we start with the observation that the distances out to the PNR and back are the same. However, distance is equal to groundspeed multiplied by time, so:

```
O x T = H x (E-T)
```

Where E is the safe endurance (i.e. allowing for reserves), H the homebound groundspeed and O the outbound.

Moving on:

```
OT = HE - HT

OT + HT = HE

T x (O + H) = HE

  E x H
  -----
  O + H
```

All it does is find the ratio of the groundspeeds and apply it into the endurance, assuming normal TAS. For example, with 3 hours' endurance, and a 90 kt groundspeed outbound, with 150 home, the equation is:

```
  180 x 150
  ---------
  90 + 150

  180 x 150
        ---
        240

  27000
  -----
   240
```

The answer is 112.5 minutes. Again, this is a proportion problem, as the sum of the groundspeeds out and back to the total time (endurance) is to the return groundspeed against the time for the outbound leg. In this case, the ratio ends up as $^5/_8$.

On the flight computer, you need to set the sum of the groundspeeds on the inner scale under the endurance (in minutes) on the outer scale, then against the return groundspeed (inner scale), read the time available for the outbound leg, before you have to turn back. To keep things consistent (because time is on the inner scale), just swap the figures around:

$$PNR\ (Time)\ =\ \frac{E\ x\ H}{O\ +\ H}$$

$$\frac{PNR\ (Time)}{E}\ =\ \frac{Home}{O\ +\ H}$$

Take an endurance of 390 minutes, with a groundspeed out of 240 kts, and back of 210 kts.

Place the combined groundspeeds on the inner scale against the groundspeed home on the outer, and read the time to PNR (182 mins) against the endurance (390 mins) on the inner scale (see picture below).

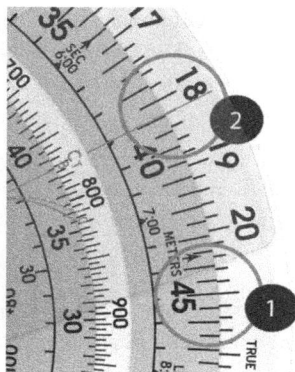

You could also place the endurance time on the inner scale under the sum of O + H speeds on the outside scale and read the time to turn on the inner scale opposite the groundspeed back on the outer scale.

As a gross error check, add the totals for the two legs together and check them against the endurance.

If an engine fails, use the full TAS to find out when you would get to the PNR, having used the reduced speed first. For radius of action (see below), mix the airspeeds (full TAS on, reduced back), so you know how long you can fly on a tank and still get back, even if an engine fails.

Just apply the groundspeed to get the distance if you want to mark it on the map, or work it out directly like this:

$$\frac{E\ x\ O\ x\ H}{O\ +\ H}$$

The endurance, however, is now in hours.

POINT OF SAFE DIVERSION

This is the maximum distance along a track from which you can divert to an off-track alternate. The calculations are essentially the same as for the normal PNR, and some of the principles are borrowed from the off-track ETP discussed above. As something to start with, to estimate the nil wind PSR, which is the longest distance you can go anyway, multiply the TAS by the safe endurance in minutes and divide by 60.

Draw a line from there to the alternate, then bisect it, as with the procedure for the ETP. The point where the original track is intersected has the same distance to the alternate or the maximum point, so it is the nil wind PSD.

Work out the times from your present position to the nil wind PSD and from there to the alternate. The result should equal or be more than your endurance, in which case an adjustment needs to be made (if they are both the same, well done!)

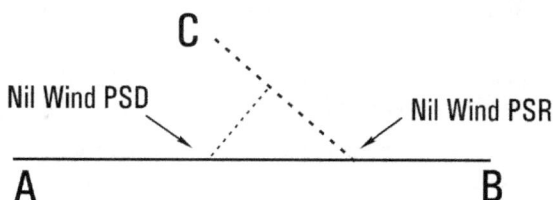

If the difference is small, you may be able to use the same groundspeeds and just change the distances, but a large difference could mean a larger track change to the alternate and recalculating them. If the alternate is still in front of you, simply carrying on may shorten the track to the alternate.

RADIUS OF ACTION

The formula above can give you a patrol range in a radius of action problem, which is the same thing (the edge of the radius is your limit to use the same fuel to fly out, perform a task and get back to base, useful in the Arctic, over water, or in similar territory). The only change is to the definition of E. Because this is now the endurance available for the journey to and from the task area, it is the total safe endurance minus task time.

EXAMPLE

Airspeed: 230 kts

Track out: 040°(T)

Wind velocity: 102/20

Endurance: 3.5 hours

The wind is 62° off the bow:

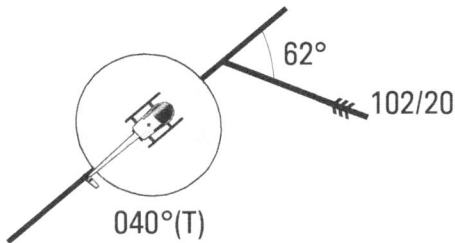

❶ Set 62° (28° cos) under 230.

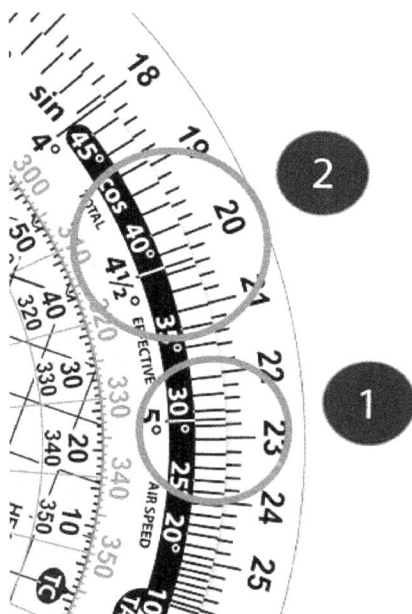

Under 20 (windspeed) find the drift of 4.5° **❷**. Under 57.5° (32.5° cos) find 220 kts groundspeed out (against the wind) and under 66.5° (23.5° cos) find 239 kts groundspeed home (with the wind).

Flipping to the slide rule, set 10 on the inner scale against 220 on the outer scale and place the cursor against 239 on the inner scale. Leaving the cursor where it is, move 459 (220 + 239) on the inner scale underneath it. Under 3.5 (endurance) on the inner scale, read the distance of 400 (actually 401) nautical miles on the outer scale.

For an alternative method using fuel flow:

$$\frac{F/F\ Out}{G/S\ Out} + \frac{F/F\ Home}{G/S\ Home}$$

PRESSURE PATTERN FLYING

In temperate latitudes (especially on long flights over water), where the winds are fairly strong, you can save about 5% of your air miles by flying a single heading rather than a single track. It's rather like the situation the early mariners were in when they were trying to get from Africa to England - it was often quicker to go with the winds and bounce off the East coast of America than to try and battle up the West coast of Europe.

In our case, if you tried to follow a straight track, you could be applying several wind correction angles over the course of a flight, and reducing your ground speed as a result. If you went with the isobars, although you might be travelling a greater distance over the ground, if you don't need to allow for drift, the total air miles travelled could be a lot less. To put it another way, a single-heading flight uses the most favourable winds, i.e. tail winds as opposed to abeam winds. As it happens, you get the same advantages if the winds are going the other way.

You calculate a single heading by working out a mean wind* to replace the variations you might encounter.

*This is not an average wind. You still use wind vectors, but you find the wind speed according to the fraction of time you intend to use them. The mean wind is weaker than the average wind, especially with many variations in wind velocity, as many of them will cancel each other out.

Note: Pressure pattern flying requires considerable preparation and knowledge of the upper air conditions. You must also maintain a constant height over 2000 feet (so you are above the friction layer), and avoid the latitudes between 20°N and 20°S for best reliability. Any errors arise from the assumption that the gradient wind is geostrophic, but they only amount to roughly 5% at any latitude above about 30°.

In the same way that the wind at right angles to the line of a front depends on the closeness of the isobars along it, the wind at right angles to the line of your flight depends on the closeness of the contours along it. The formula:

```
mean drift(kts) = 21.47 x chg ht (ft)
                    NAM x sin lat
```

uses a change of height, or the difference in height of the contours over the flight in feet. 21.47 is a constant that depends on gravity and the Coriolis effect at the latitude flown. It is found on the calculator side of the CR-3.

For example, with a TAS of 140 kts over a distance of 480 nm at 50°N, you estimate your groundspeed to be 160 kts. You plan to fly at 8 000 feet, and the height of the 750 hPa layer at the start of the flight is 8 000 feet, and 8150 at the end. The time of the flight is 3 hours at 160 knots (over 480 nm), so the air distance is 420 nm (3 hours at 140 kts). Thus the value of the wind from the side is 10 kts:

$$10 \text{ kts} = \frac{21.47 \times 150}{420 \times 0.766}$$

The side wind is 10 kts. As the height is increasing, you are from low to high pressure so the wind is from the right (Buys Ballot, etc.)

In the picture above, step ❶ is to line up the NAM under the height change, and step ❷ is to move the cursor until the green line is over 50° on the latitude scale. The mean drift will be found under the cursor on the outside scale.

To look at this in another way, you can find the wind velocity on a contour chart by taking the spacing between the contour lines (usually 200 feet), dividing it by the ground distance between them and placing the cursor over the mid latitude as above.

In Flight

If you have a radio altimeter, you can compare its readings with those of the pressure altimeter roughly every 30 minutes. The technique is to:

- Fly at a constant IAS heading and pressure altitude (on 1013).

- Subtract the PA from the radar altitude (as the pressure altimeter tends to lag, read it last). Apply the + or - signs as necessary*.

- Once you have two sets of readings, calculate the NAM flown between them (TAS x time flown).

- Find the mid-latitude, then proceed as above

*In the Northern hemisphere, if the difference is positive, the wind is from the right, and vice versa.

Crosswind Displacement

This is simply the distance you are off, rather than the degree value of the drift, which can be used to create some sort of line of position. Simply replace the distance flown in the bottom part of the formula with the TAS, assuming you have been maintaining a constant heading.

QUESTIONS

1. At 90 kts TAS heading 045° on the compass, what is the expected track if the forecast wind is 075°/12 kts? Deviation is -2 and variation is 7°E.

   (a) 046°

   (b) 058°

   (c) 044°

   (d) 041°

2. If the wind is 320° at 18 kts, what is the track and groundspeed for a heading of 205°T and TAS of 145 kts?

   (a) 212°T 151 kts

   (b) 207°T 141 kts

   (c) 197°T 149 kts

   (d) 199°T 153 kts

3. At FL 120 the wind is 290°/20 kts and an aircraft is heading 005°M with a CAS of 170 kts. If the OAT is 12°C and variation is 3°W what is its track and groundspeed?

   (a) 58°T 189 kts

   (b) 007°T 207 kts

   (c) 009°T 168 kts

   (d) 001°T 199 kts

4. At FL 350, the temperature is -48°C, at 280 kts CAS. The heading is 005°M, variation is 0° and the wind is 160° at 90 kts. What is the track and groundspeed?

   (a) 352°M 530 kts

   (b) 011°M 545 kts

   (c) 001°M 562 kts

   (d) 358°M 570 kts

5. A heading of 180°T at 230 kts TAS results in a track of 172°T and a groundspeed of 258 kts. What is the wind?

   (a) 305°/45 kts

   (b) 300°/35 kts

   (c) 320°/50 kts

   (d) 295°/40 kts

6. Tracking the 035° radial from a VOR (magnetic) with a variation of 10°W requires a heading of 041°M at a TAS of 180 kts. If the DME reads a groundspeed of 192 kts what is the wind?

   (a) 140°/25 kts

   (b) 150°/23 kts

   (c) 180°/15 kts

   (d) 165°/10 kts

7. A helicopter follows a straight power line which follows a true bearing of 334° for 4 nm. The temperature is 28°C, the pressure altitude zero and it takes 3 minutes to follow the straight section at a CAS of 90 kts. If the heading is 324°M and variation is 4°E what is the wind?

(a) 280°/12 kts

(b) 285°/22 kts

(c) 295°/15 kts

(d) 280°/17 kts

8. Desired track: 110°T

Variation: 5°E

TAS: 125 kts

Forecast wind: 040°/12 kts

What is the required magnetic heading and the expected groundspeed?

(a) 105° and 125 kts

(b) 110° and 120 kts

(c) 100° and 120 kts

(d) 095° and 125 kts

9. Track followed: 342°T

TAS: 65 kts

Wind experienced: 210° at 12 kts

What is the heading to fly, and how long will the 18 nm leg take?

(a) 339° and 17 minutes

(b) 335° and 15 minutes

(c) 347° and 14 minutes

(d) 349° and 16 minutes

10. The track from A to B is 165°T. The aircraft flies at 140 kts CAS at FL170 with a temperature of -10°C. What is the heading (M) to fly from A to B and the expected groundspeed in a wind of 200°/45 kts? Variation is 20°E.

(a) 168° and 155 kts

(b) 178° and 160 kts

(c) 175° and 150 kts

(d) 153° and 147 kts

11. Wind: 230°/70 kts

320 kts CAS

Required track 270°T

Temperature -25°

FL 220

Variation 7°W

What is the required magnetic heading and the expected groundspeed?

(a) 267° and 270 kts

(b) 264° and 405 kts

(c) 271° and 390 kts

(d) 278° and 380 kts

12. Given the following:

OAT ISA+10

FL 230

CAS

170 kts

What is the TAS?

(a) 247 kts

(b) 241 kts

(c) 255 kts

(d) 230 kts

13. Flying a TAS of 450 kts at FL310 in ISA what is the Mach number?

(a) 0.77

(b) 0.75

(c) 0.81

(d) 0.72

14. For the following:

TAS 212 kts

FL 330

ISA -10°

What is the Mach number?

(a) 0.37

(b) 0.61

(c) 0.58

(d) 0.71

15. Given a fuel quantity of 35 US gallons with a specific gravity of 0.81 what is the weight of the fuel?

  (a) 232 kg

  (b) 151 kg

  (c) 122 kg

  (d) 107 kg

16. Given the following:

  Altitude with QNH 1010 hPa set: 13,000 feet

  OAT: 12°C

What is the true altitude?

  (a) 14 200 feet

  (b) 13 200 feet

  (c) 11 900 feet

  (d) 12 400 feet

17. To fly a TAS of 120 kts what CAS must be flown at FL 70 if the OAT is +7°C?

  (a) 120 kts

  (b) 134 kts

  (c) 107 kts

  (d) 102 kts

18. At an indicated altitude of 23,000 feet at -15°C, what is the approximate true altitude?

  (a) 21 700 feet

  (b) 22 500 feet

  (c) 24 500 feet

  (d) 23 800 feet

19. If the temperature is -20°C and the PA 2 000 feet, what is the TAS of an aircraft flying at a CAS of 105 kts?

  (a) 113 kts

  (b) 105 kts

  (c) 108 kts

  (d) 102 kts

20. At FL90 what is the TAS of an aircraft flying at 85 kts if the OAT is 20° above ISA?

  (a) 95 kts

  (b) 90 kts

  (c) 80 kts

  (d) 100 kts

21. Given:

  Pressure Altitude: 40 000 feet

  OAT: -75°C

  CAS: 280 kts

What is the true airspeed?

  (a) 450 kts

  (b) 502 kts

  (c) 490 kts

  (d) 590 kts

22. Given:

  Pressure Altitude: 12 340 feet

  True Air Temperature: -4°C

What CAS should you fly at to maintain a TAS of 140 kts?

  (a) 105 kts

  (b) 115 kts

  (c) 125 kts

  (d) 107 kts

23. What is the Density Altitude when the air temperature is 86°F and the Pressure Altitude is 6344 feet?

  (a) 10 000 feet

  (b) 9926 feet

  (c) 8000 feet

  (d) 7260 feet

24. How long will it take to climb to 12 500 feet from an airport whose elevation is 6344 feet and the rate of climb is 650 feet per minute?

  (a) 6 minutes

  (b) 7 mins 40 secs

  (c) 9 mins 28 secs

  (d) 12 mins

25. How much distance will you cover climbing to 5 000 feet at 375 feet per minute and 180 kts?

  (a) 25 nm

  (b) 30 nm

  (c) 40 nm

  (d) 50 nm

26. How fast must you climb to cross a fix 6.7 nm from takeoff (elevation 6344 feet) at 8 800 feet AMSL? Groundspeed is 97 kts.

    (a) 573 fpm

    (b) 593 fpm

    (c) 613 fpm

    (d) 623 fpm

27. If the fuel flow is 15.8 gallons per hour, and fuel available is 48 gallons, how much endurance do you have?

    (a) 2 hrs 55 mins

    (b) 3 hrs 30 mins

    (c) 3 hrs 2 mins

    (d) 4 hrs 2 mins

28. How much range do you have at 123 kts over 3 hours?

    (a) 350 nm

    (b) 369 nm

    (c) 400 nm

    (d) 425 nm

29. How far have you travelled at 108 kts in 70 minutes?

    (a) 100 nm

    (b) 126 nm

    (c) 150 nm

    (d) 175 nm

30. What is your groundspeed if you take 9 mins 26 seconds to cover 17 nm?

    (a) 102 kts

    (b) 104 kts

    (c) 106 kts

    (d) 108 kts

31. How long will it take to cover 231 nm at a groundspeed of 123 kts?

    (a) 1 hr 45 mins

    (b) 1 hr 53 mins

    (c) 1 hr 57 mins

    (d) 1 hr 59 mins

32. How much fuel will you need over 1 hour 52 mins at 16 gals per hour?

    (a) 25 gals

    (b) 28 gals

    (c) 30 gals

    (d) 32 gals

Fill in the missing boxes:

No	G/S	Time	Distance
33	120 kts	1:15	
34	105 kts	0:52	
35	145 kts	1:33	
36	168 kts	1:40	
37	152 kts	0:35	
38	110 mph	1:22	
39	133 mph	2:15	
40	108 mph	2:02	
41	210 mph	0:48	
42	183 mph	1:25	
43	184 kts		62 nm
44	108 kts		268 nm
45	165 kts		100 nm
46	198 kts		202 nm
47	87 kts		127 nm
48	208 mph		104 sm
49	122 mph		583 sm
50	346 mph		213 sm
51	56 mph		298 sm
52	100 mph		250 sm
53		0:48	68 sm
54		1:48	204 sm
55		2:02	400 sm
56		1:35	108 sm
57		0:28	96 sm
58		0:13	26 nm
59		1:47	356 nm
60		2:03	457 nm
61		1:04	203 nm
62		0:58	108 nm
63	116 mph	1:04	
64	156 mph	0:53	
65	209 mph	1:56	
66	98 mph	2:54	
67	358 mph	4:59	
68	122 kts	0:47	
69	330 kts	1:13	
70	98 kts	2:56	
71	106 kts	3:26	
72	208 kts	1:37	
73	129 mph		28 sm
74	116 mph		13.5 sm

capt.gs

No	G/S	Time	Distance		No	G/S	Time	Distance
75	220 mph		66 sm		118	10		16
76	192 mph		16 sm		119	13 000		20 840
77	157 mph		21 sm		120	950		1521
78	175 kts		500 nm		121	6		9.6
79	149 kts		144 nm		122	69		111
80	118 kts		124 nm		123	62	54	
81	137 kts		183 nm		124	137	119	
82	102 kts		7.64 nm		125	356	310	
83		2:34	930 sm		126	20.3	17.6	
84		0:5.6	20 sm		127	122	106	
85		1:40	248 sm		128	115	100	
86		0:48	80 sm		129	1.36	1.18	
87		1:17	140 sm		130	57.6	50	
88		10:00	1000 nm		131	2100	1820	
89		1:23	385 nm		132	0.138	0.12	
90		0:40	125.5 nm		133		306	565
91		6:40	660 nm		134		23.7	43.8
92		0:1.1	1.56 nm		135		164	303
93	15	13			136		678	1250
94	210	182			137		13 340	24 680
95	14.5	12.6			138		16.5	30.5
96	178	154			139		115	212.5
97	57	49.5			140		239	441
98	820	710			141		3 670	6780
99	95	82.5			142		95	176
100	127	110			143	33		53
101	265	230			144	424		678
102	38	33			145	72		115
103		44.5	82		146	28.5		45.6
104		650	1202		147	38		61
105		3.9	7.2		148	3300		5280
106		800	1480		149	8.32		13.4
107		0.126	0.232		150	1.04		1.67
108		156	289		151	560		897
109		20	37		152	85		136
110		26.5	49					
111		167	308					
112		409	751					
113	36		57.6					
114	84		135					
115	9.7		15.5					
116	75		120.5					
117	115		184.5					

capt.gs

No	PA Ft	Temp C	IAS	TAS
153	10 000	0	178	
154	15 000	-20	160	
155	12 000	-25	180	
156	8 000	10	164	
157	30 000	10	192	
158	28 000	-40	190	
159	1 000	5	85	
160	4 000	-20	190	
161	5 500	15	135	
162	7 200	22	158	
163	4 000	40	89	
164	3 000	10	77	
165	12 500	-10	103	
166	9 000	-3	120	
167	18 000	-15	134	
168	23 500	-35	174	
169	8 000	5	85	
170	9 500	0	117	
171	3 000	-22	174	
172	30 000	-45	350	
173	1 500	38	122	
174	3 750	22	116	
175	22 500	-34	248	
176	17 000	-24	186	
177	13 500	-3.5	154	
178	11 000	0	122	
179	8 000	1	117	
180	16 400	-11	157	
181	10 000	10	142	
182	6 300	11	178	
183	15 500	-32		346
184	13 000	-20		136
185	10 500	-10		134
186	11 450	-2		178
187	8 000	-9		124
188	4 500	22		145
189	5 000	30		110
190	2 500	40		120
191	3 000	35		154
192	5 500	20		124
193	22 000	-33		256

No	PA Ft	Temp C	IAS	TAS
194	30 000	-45		422
195	19 000	-23		222
196	11 500	-12		203
197	10 000	0		164
198	12 000	-9		120
199	7 500	16		167
200	4 000	15		145
201	2 000	20		200
202	1 670	16		135
203	28 000	-38		278
204	16 000	-27		210
205	12 500	-14		184
206	16 000	-16		160
207	1 000	40		138
208	2 750	38		110
209	30 000	-40		456
210	13 500	-28		190
211	4 500	0		157
212	2 000	20		200

No	TH	TAS mph	TC	GS mph	W/V
213	162	132			320/16
214	36	168			135/23
215	347	128			110/34
216	122	100			035/35
217	236	137			345/26
218	122	139			119/21
219	189	214			016/11
220	122	316			256/34
221	56	114			116/46
222	108	108			180/18
223	189	146			360/21
224	356	213			101/13
225	89	103			267/26
226	112	235			116/13
227	167	126			346/24
228		153	113		222/22
229		189	214		124/17
230		239	187		046/34
231		162	102		111/11
232		347	168		137/17

capt.gs

No	TH	TAS mph	TC	GS mph	W/V
233			002	118	352/23
234			046	137	119/33
235			305	129	054/26
236			107	143	187/25
237			167	102	349/33
238			216	202	121/30
239			111	97	183/22
240			271	174	192/19
241			001	203	122/29
242			083	143	138/27
243		136	163		165/24
244		199	222		104/29
245		208	161		218/36
246		309	298		132/46
247		122	009		090/15
248		239	036		267/27
249		162	162		162/16
250		119	137		351/19
251		139	317		221/30
252		183	213		114/26
253		171	227		213/29
254		196	305		098/28
255		209	300		123/22
256		163	122		347/27
257		356	267		119/21
258	100	122	104	116	

Find the groundspeeds:

No	Dist	Time	G/S
1	90	:50	
2	75	2:00	
3	60	:40	
4	35	:16	
5	110	:120	
6	65	:30	
7	12	:10	
8	120	1:55	
9	115	:50.5	
10	90	1:40	

Find the times:

No	Dist	Time	G/S
1	80		67
2	120		60
3	150		70
4	90		130
5	95		190
6	110		220
7	170		80
8	115		90
9	300		115
10	45		83

Find the distances:

No	Dist	Time	G/S
1		:80	40
2		:30	90
3		2:00	85
4		:120	120
5		:37	146
6		2:10	123
7		1:50	175
8		:25	88
9		1:30	62
10		:07	78

Fill in the missing boxes:

No	Dist	Time	G/S
1	120	2:00	
2	156	:120	
3	104	:42	
4	75		125
5	36		120
6	42		143
7		3:00	60
8		1:10	76
9		1:37	112
10	166	1:32	
11	82		115
12		:46	111
13	81		107
14	113	:80	
15	8		117
16		:07	110

capt.gs

No	Dist	Time	G/S
17	120		72
18	80	:43	
19	125		104
20	150		137

Find the fuel consumption:

No	Fuel	Time	Gals/Hr
1	42	3:00	
2	36	3:30	
3	33	2:45	
4	6	:26	
5	30	3:15	

Find the flying time:

No	Fuel	Time	Gals/Hr
1	40		8
2	38		11
3	37		6.5
4	26		12
5	40		15

Find the fuel used:

No	Fuel	Time	Gals/Hr
1		2:00	6
2		2:20	11
3		3:45	12.5
4		1:50	7.5
5		1:18	7

Fill in the missing boxes:

No	Fuel	Time	Gals/Hr
1	39	4:00	
2	27	3:30	
3	16.5		8
4	25.3		8
5		3:00	7
6		4:10	9
7	42		14
8	37	2:18	
9	22.7		9.1
10		3:14	10
11		3:00	6.0

No	Fuel	Time	Gals/Hr
12	25		8.3
13	80	6:10	
14	11	:35	
15	58		15.5
16	70	5:15	
17		3:30	6
18		2:15	8.4
19	23.5	3:12	
20	6.2	:41	

Find the true altitude:

No	Ind Alt	Temp	True
1	20,000	-15	
2	13,000	-10	
3	30,000	-30	
4	10,000	10	
5	6,000	20	
6	14,000	5	
7	8,000	-20	
8	18,000	-5	
9	8,000	10	
10	15,000	0	

Find the temperatures:

No	Ind Alt	Temp	True
1	20,000		22,000
2	25,000		26,000
3	18,000		18,500
4	10,000		9,200
5	11,500		12,000
6	10,000		9,500

Find the indicated altitudes:

No	True	Temp	PA	Ind
1	20,000	-25	21,000	
2	10,000	-10	9,800	
3	19,000	-30	18,000	
4	25,500	10	26,000	
5	4,900	25	5,000	
6	5,500	25	6,000	

capt.gs

Find the TAS:

No	IAS	Ind Alt	Temp	TAS
1	190	10,000	-15	
2	200	20,000	-30	
3	150	5,000	-20	
4	180	12,000	-10	
5	140	3,000	5	
6	140	4,000	-5	
7	120	4,000	-30	
8	210	7,000	-15	
9	165	15,000	-20	
10	190	12,000	15	

Find the IAS:

No	IAS	Ind Alt	Temp	TAS
1		12,000	-10	150
2		20,000	5	200
3		18,000	10	165
4		6,000	-20	125
5		5,000	20	135
6		7,000	-5	107

Find the Indicated Altitude:

No	IAS	Ind Alt	Temp	TAS
1	175		-15	200
2	230		-35	225
3	180		-10	185
4	145		15	150
5	118		15	125
6	110		10	130

Fill in the empty spaces:

No	IAS	Ind Alt	Temp	TAS
1	140	5,000		156
2	178	12,000	-20	
3	235		-35	270
4		16,000	-25	260
5	116		-5	125
6	115	17,000		160
7	158	12,000	-20	
8		18,300	-18	165
9	165	18,500		210
10	190		-45	180

TRIANGLES OF VELOCITY

Find the course, groundspeed and drift:

No	W/V	Hdg	A/S	Cs	G/S	Dft
1	090/30	350	120			
2	050/20	260	140			
3	270/25	180	125			
4	300/22	360	110			
5	225/25	045	170			
6	360/30	100	135			
7	315/26	041	117			
8	180/27	090	128			
9	360/12	299	130			
10	360/11	080	90			

Find the wind speed, direction and drift:

No	W/V	Dft	Hdg	A/S	Cs	G/S
1			090	120	090	120
2			355	135	360	130
3			045	118	038	128
4			192	140	183	120
5			090	165	103	178
6			271	65	263	72
7			158	68	158	78
8			085	78	085	60
9			285	85	270	94
10			183	155	180	161

Find the heading and groundspeed:

No	W/V	Hdg	A/S	Cs	G/S
1	320/30		140	260	
2	050/20		120	230	
3	045/20		130	270	
4	090/32		110	170	
5	180/28		125	090	
6	260/15		160	180	
7	050/30		174	315	
8	050/11		110	360	
9	180/32		092	045	
10	270/32		140	180	

Fill in the missing spaces:

No	W/V	Hdg	A/S	Cs	G/S	Dft
1	270/32		115	120		
2	240/20		140	080		
3	090/22	183	135			
4	184/18	350	105			
5		270	160	270	140	
6		180	90	188	75	
7	120/20		130	170		
8	175/20	180	125			
9		255	100	265	88	
10	186/25		140	152		
11	180/25		192	270		
12	350/?	090	125			8R
13	270/?	180	150			11L
14	250/20			350	110	
15	045/20			080	157	

ANSWERS

1. A
2. D
3. B
4. D
5. A
6. B
7. C
8. C
9. B
10. D
11. C
12. A
13. A
14. A
15. D
16. A
17. C
18. C
19. D
20. D
21. B
22. B
23. A
24. C
25. C
26. B
27. C
28. B
29. B
30. D
31. B
32. C

No	G/S	Time	Distance
33	120 kts	1:15	150 nm
34	105 kts	0:52	91 nm
35	145 kts	1:33	225 nm
36	168 kts	1:40	280 nm
37	152 kts	0:35	88.5 nm
38	110 mph	1:22	150 sm
39	133 mph	2:15	300 sm
40	108 mph	2:02	220 sm
41	210 mph	0:48	168 sm
42	183 mph	1:25	259 sm
43	184 kts	0;20.3	62 nm
44	108 kts	2:29	268 nm
45	165 kts	0:36.5	100 nm
46	198 kts	1:01	202 nm
47	87 kts	1:27.5	127 nm
48	208 mph	0:30	104 sm
49	122 mph	4:47	583 sm
50	346 mph	0:37	213 sm
51	56 mph	5:19	298 sm
52	100 mph	2:30	250 sm
53	85 mph	0:48	68 sm
54	113 mph	1:48	204 sm
55	197 mph	2:02	400 sm
56	68 mph	1:35	108 sm
57	206 mph	0:28	96 sm
58	120 kt	0:13	26 nm
59	200 kts	1:47	356 nm
60	223 kts	2:03	457 nm
61	190 kt	1:04	203 nm

capt.gs

No	G/S	Time	Distance	No	G/S	Time	Distance
62	112 kts	0:58	108 nm	105	111	3.9	7.2
63	116 mph	1:04	123.5 sm	106	111	800	1480
64	156 mph	0:53	138 sm	107	111	0.126	0.232
65	209 mph	1:56	404 sm	108	111	156	289
66	98 mph	2:54	284 sm	109	111	20	37
67	358 mph	4:59	1784 sm	110	111	26.5	49
68	122 kts	0:47	96 nm	111	111	1.67	308
69	330 kts	1:13	402 nm	112	110	409	751
70	98 kts	2:56	288 nm	113	36	96	57.6
71	106 kts	3:26	364 nm	114	84	96	135
72	208 kts	1:37	336 nm	115	9.7	96	15.5
73	129 mph	0:13	28 sm	116	75	96	120.5
74	116 mph	0:07	13.5 sm	117	115	96	184.5
75	220 mph	0:18	66 sm	118	10	96	16
76	192 mph	0:05	16 sm	119	13 000	96	20 840
77	157 mph	0:08	21 sm	120	950	96	1521
78	175 kts	2:51	500 nm	121	6	96	9.6
79	149 kts	0:58	144 nm	122	69	97	111
80	118 kts	1:03	124 nm	123	62	54	55.8
81	137 kts	1:20	183 nm	124	137	119	271.7
82	102 kts	0:4.5	7.64 nm	125	356	310	1839.3
83	362 mph	2:34	930 sm	126	20.3	17.6	5.95
84	214 mph	0:5.6	20 sm	127	122	106	215.5
85	149 mph	1:40	248 sm	128	115	100	191.6
86	100 mph	0:48	80 sm	129	1.36	1.18	0.027
87	109 mph	1:17	140 sm	130	57.6	50	48
88	100 kts	10:00	1000 nm	131	2100	1820	63 700
89	278 kts	1:23	385 nm	132	0.138	0.12	0.276
90	188 kts	0:40	125.5 nm	133	111	306	565
91	99 kts	6:40	660 nm	134	111	23.7	43.8
92	85 kts	0:1.1	1.56 nm	135	111	164	303
93	15	13	3.25	136	111	678	1250
94	210	182	637	137	111	13 340	24 620
95	14.5	12.6	3.05	138	111	16.5	30.5
96	178	154	457	139	111	115	212.5
97	57	49.5	47	140	111	239	441
98	820	710	9703	141	111	3 670	6780
99	95	82.5	130.6	142	111	95	176
100	127	110	232.8	143	33	96	53
101	265	230	1015.8	144	424	96	678
102	38	33	20.9	145	72	96	115
103	111	44.5	82	146	28.5	96	45.6
104	111	650	1202	147	38	96	61

No	G/S	Time	Distance
148	3300	96	5280
149	8.32	96	13.4
150	1.04	96	1.67
151	560	96	897
152	85	96	136

No	PA Ft	Temp C	IAS	TAS
153	10 000	0	178	210
154	15 000	-20	160	200
155	12 000	-25	180	210
156	8 000	10	164	189
157	30 000	10	192	340
158	28 000	-40	190	295
159	1 000	5	85	85
160	4 000	-20	190	192
161	5 500	15	135	150
162	7 200	22	158	184
163	4 000	40	89	100
164	3 000	10	77	81
165	12 500	-10	103	125
166	9 000	-3	120	138
167	18 000	-15	134	180
168	23 500	-35	174	249
169	8 000	5	85	97
170	9 500	0	117	137
171	3 000	-22	174	172
172	30 000	-45	350	535
173	1 500	38	122	131
174	3 750	22	116	126
175	22 500	-34	248	345
176	17 000	-24	186	240
177	13 500	-3.5	154	192
178	11 000	0	122	147
179	8 000	1	117	133
180	16 400	-11	157	206
181	10 000	10	142	170
182	6 300	11	178	199
183	15 500	-32	282	346
184	13 000	-20	113	136
185	10 500	-10	115	134
186	11 450	-2	147	178

No	PA Ft	Temp C	IAS	TAS
187	8 000	-9	111	124
188	4 500	22	131.5	145
189	5 000	30	97.5	110
190	2 500	40	110	120
191	3 000	35	141	154
192	5 500	20	111	124
193	22 000	-33	184	256
194	30 000	-45	258	422
195	19 000	-23	166	222
196	11 500	-12	171	203
197	10 000	0	139	164
198	12 000	-9	99.5	120
199	7 500	16	144.5	167
200	4 000	15	134	145
201	2 000	20	190	200
202	1 670	16	131	135
203	28 000	-38	178	278
204	16 000	-27	168	210
205	12 500	-14	152	184
206	16 000	-16	124	160
207	1 000	40	130	138
208	2 750	38	100.5	110
209	30 000	-40	274	456
210	13 500	-28	159	190
211	4 500	0	148	157
212	2 000	20	190	200

No	TH	TAS	TC	GS	W/V
213	162	132 kts	160	147 kts	320/16
214	036	168 kts	029	173 kts	135/23
215	347	128 kts	336	150 kts	110/34
216	122	100 kts	142	104 kts	035/35
217	236	137 kts	227	148 kts	345/26
218	122	139 kts	122.5	118 kts	119/21
219	189	214 kts	189.5	225 kts	016/11
220	122	316 kts	118	341 kts	256/34
221	056	114 kts	033	100 kts	116/46
222	108	108 kts	099	104 kts	180/18
223	189	146 kts	188	167 kts	360/21
224	356	213 kts	353	217 kts	101/13
225	089	103 kts	089	129 kts	267/26

No	TH	TAS	TC	GS	W/V
226	112	235 kts	112	222 kts	116/13
227	167	126 kts	167	150 kts	346/24
228	162.5	123 mph	153	113 mph	222/22
229	185	221 mph	189	214 mph	124/17
230	242	154 mph	239	187 mph	046/34
231	157	109 mph	162	102 mph	111/11
232	350	153.5 mph	347	168 mph	137/17
233	000	141 mph	002	118 mph	352/23
234	058	150 mph	046	137 mph	119/33
235	316.5	123 mph	305	129 mph	54/26
236	116	149 mph	107	43 mph	187/25
237	165.5	69 mph	167	102 mph	349/33
238	207	200 mph	216	202 mph	121/30
239	122	105.5 mph	111	97 mph	183/22
240	265	179 mph	271	174 mph	192/19
241	008.5	189 mph	001	203 mph	122/29
242	091	160 mph	083	143 mph	138/27
243	163	136 mph	163	112 mph	165/24
244	215	199 mph	222	211 mph	104/29
245	169	208 mph	161	186 mph	218/36
246	296	309 mph	298	357 mph	132/46
247	016	122 mph	009	118.5 mph	090/15
248	031	239 mph	036	255 mph	267/27
249	162	162 mph	162	146 mph	162/16
250	132	119 mph	137	134 mph	351/19
251	304	139 mph	317	138 mph	221/30
252	205	183 mph	213	185 mph	114/26
253	225	171 mph	227	142.5 mph	213/29
254	309	196 mph	305	220 mph	098/28
255	299.5	209 mph	300	232 mph	123/22
256	115	163 mph	122	181 mph	347/27
257	265	356 mph	267	377 mph	119/21
258	100	122 mph	104	116 mph	049/10

Find the groundspeeds:

No	Dist	Time	G/S
1	90	:50	108
2	75	2:00	37.5
3	60	:40	90
4	35	:16	133
5	110	:120	55
6	65	:30	130
7	12	:10	72

No	Dist	Time	G/S
8	120	1:55	62.5
9	115	:50.5	137
10	90	1:40	54

Find the times:

No	Dist	Time	G/S
1	80	1:09	70
2	120	2:00	60
3	150	2:08	70
4	90	:41.5	131
5	95	:30	190
6	110	:30	220
7	170	2:07	80
8	115	1:17	90
9	300	2:37	115
10	45	:32.5	83

Find the distances:

No	Dist	Time	G/S
1	53.5	1:20	40
2	45	:30	90
3	170	2:00	85
4	240	2:00	120
5	90	:37	146
6	266	2:10	123
7	320	1:50	175
8	36.7	:25	88
9	93	1:30	62
10	9.1	:07	78

Fill in the missing boxes:

No	Dist	Time	G/S
1	120	2:00	60
2	156	:120	78
3	104	:42	149
4	75	:36	125
5	36	:18	120
6	42	:17.5	143
7	180	3:00	60
8	89	1:10	76
9	181	1:37	112
10	166	1:32	108
11	82	:43	115

No	Dist	Time	G/S
12	84.5	:46	111
13	81	:45	107
14	113	:80	85
15	8	:04.1	117
16	12.8	:07	110
17	120	1:40	72
18	80	:43	112
19	125	1:12	104
20	150	1:06	137

Find the fuel consumption:

No	Fuel	Time	Gals/Hr
1	42	3:00	14
2	36	3:30	10.3
3	33	2:45	12
4	6	:26	13.9
5	30	3:15	9.3

Find the flying time:

No	Fuel	Time	Gals/Hr
1	40	5:00	8
2	38	3:27	11
3	37	5:42	6.5
4	26	2:10	12
5	40	2:40	15

Find the fuel used:

No	Fuel	Time	Gals/Hr
1	12	2:00	6
2	25.6	2:20	11
3	47	3:46	12.5
4	13.7	1:50	7.5
5	9.1	1:18	7

Fill in the missing boxes:

No	Fuel	Time	Gals/Hr
1	39	4:00	9.8
2	27	3:30	7.7
3	16.5	2:04	8
4	25.3	3:10	8
5	21	3:00	7
6	37.5	4:10	9

No	Fuel	Time	Gals/Hr
7	42	3:00	14
8	37	2:18	16.1
9	22.7	2:30	9.1
10	32.3	3:14	10
11	18	3:00	6.0
12	25	3:01	8.3
13	80	6:10	13
14	11	:35	18.8
15	58	3:44	15.5
16	70	5:15	13.4
17	21	3:30	6
18	19	2:15	8.4
19	23.5	3:12	7.4
20	62	:41	9.1

Find the true altitude:

No	Ind Alt	Temp	True
1	20,000	-15	20,800
2	13,000	-10	13,000
3	30,000	-30	31,800
4	10,000	10	10,550
5	6,000	20	6,350
6	14,000	5	14,950
7	8,000	-20	7,450
8	18,000	-5	19,100
9	8,000	10	8,350
10	15,000	0	15,900

Find the temperatures:

No	Ind Alt	Temp	True
1	20,000	0	22,000
2	25,000	-25	26,000
3	18,000	-14	18,500
4	10,000	-26	9,200
5	11,500	3	12,000
6	10,000	-18	9,500

Find the indicated altitudes:

No	True	Temp	PA	Ind
1	20,000	-25	21,000	19,900
2	10,000	-10	9,800	10,200
3	19,000	-30	18,000	19,700
4	25,500	10	26,000	21,350

No	True	Temp	PA	Ind
5	4,900	25	5,000	4,560
6	5,500	25	6,000	5,100

No	IAS	Ind Alt	Temp	TAS
7	158	12,000	-20	186
8	123	18,300	-18	165
9	165	18,500	-41	211
10	190	3,500	-45	180

Find the TAS:

No	IAS	Ind Alt	Temp	TAS
1	190	10,000	-15	217
2	200	20,000	-30	268
3	150	5,000	-20	154
4	180	12,000	-10	216
5	140	3,000	5	146
6	140	4,000	-5	146
7	120	4,000	-30	119
8	210	7,000	-15	226
9	165	15,000	-20	206
10	190	12,000	15	238

Find the IAS:

No	IAS	Ind Alt	Temp	TAS
1	125	12,000	-10	150
2	139	20,000	5	200
3	118	18,000	10	165
4	119	6,000	-20	125
5	122	5,000	20	135
6	98	7,000	-5	107

Find the Indicated Altitude:

No	IAS	Ind Alt	Temp	TAS
1	175	10,000	-15	200
2	230	4,000	-35	225
3	180	4,000	-10	185
4	145	2,000	15	150
5	118	3,000	15	125
6	110	9,500	10	130

Fill in the empty spaces:

No	IAS	Ind Alt	Temp	TAS
1	140	5,000	25	156
2	178	12,000	-20	210
3	235	12,500	-35	270
4	207	16,000	-25	260
5	116	6,000	-5	125
6	115	17,000	19	160

TRIANGLES OF VELOCITY

Find the course, groundspeed and drift:

No	W/V	TH	TAS	TC	G/S	Dft
1	090/30	350	120	337	129	13L
2	050/20	260	140	256	158	4L
3	270/25	180	125	169	127	11L
4	300/22	360	110	011	101	11R
5	225/25	045	170	045	195	0
6	360/30	100	135	112	143	12R
7	315/26	041	117	054	118	13R
8	180/27	090	128	078	131	12L
9	360/12	299	130	294	125	5L
10	360/11	080	90	087	89	7R

Find the wind speed, direction and drift:

No	W/V	Dft	TH	TAS	TC	G/S
1	Calm	0	090	120	090	120
2	292/13	5R	355	135	360	130
3	165/18	7L	045	118	038	128
4	233/29	9L	192	140	183	120
5	350/41	13R	090	165	103	178
6	032/12	8L	271	65	263	72
7	338/10	0	158	68	158	78
8	085/18	0	085	78	085	60
9	028/25	15L	285	85	270	94
10	308/10	3L	183	155	180	161

Find the heading and groundspeed:

No	W/V	TH	TAS	TC	G/S
1	320/30	271	140	260	123
2	050/25	230	120	230	140
3	045/20	276	130	270	143
4	090/32	153	110	170	100
5	180/28	103	125	090	122
6	260/15	185	160	180	157
7	050/30	325	174	315	174
8	050/11	004	110	360	103
9	180/32	059	92	045	112

No	W/V	TH	TAS	TC	G/S
10	270/32	193	140	180	136

Fill in the missing spaces:

No	W/V	TH	TAS	TC	G/S	Dft
1	270/32	128	115	120	142	8L
2	240/20	083	140	080	159	3L
3	090/22	183	135	192	135	9R
4	184/18	350	105	352	123	2R
5	270/20	270	160	270	140	0
6	147/19	180	90	188	75	8R
7	120/20	163	130	170	115	7R
8	175/20	180	125	181	105	1R
9	206/20	255	100	265	88	10R
10	186/25	158	140	152	119	6L
11	180/25	262	192	270	190	8R
12	350/18	090	125	098	129	8R
13	270/30	180	150	170	152	11L
14	250/20	339	108	350	110	11R
15	045/20	076	174	080	157	4R

INDEX